Taming the Prince

Taming the Prince

THE AMBIVALENCE OF MODERN EXECUTIVE POWER

Harvey C. Mansfield, Jr.

THE FREE PRESS
A Division of Macmillan, Inc.
NEW YORK

Collier Macmillan Publishers
LONDON

The Free Press
A Division of Macmillan, Inc.
866 Third Avenue, New York, N.Y. 10022

Collier Macmillan Canada, Inc.

Printed in the United States of America

printing number
1 2 3 4 5 6 7 8 9 10

Library of Congress Cataloging-in-Publication Data

Mansfield, Harvey Claflin.
    Taming the prince: the ambivalence of modern executive power /
Harvey C. Mansfield, Jr.
       p.   cm.
     Bibliography: p.
     Includes index.
     ISBN 0-02-919980-8
     1. Executive power—History. 2. Presidents—United States—
History. I. Title.
JF251.M29   1989
351.003'2—dc19   89-669
                                                         CIP

The author is grateful to the following publishers for permission to publish adaptations of his earlier work:

''The Absent Executive in Aristotle's *Politics*,'' pp. 169–196 in Thomas B. Silver and Peter W. Schramm, eds. *Natural Right and Political Right*, Carolina Academic Press, Durham, N.C., 1984. Copyright © 1984 by Thomas B. Silver and Peter W. Schramm.

''The Ambivalence of Executive Power,'' pp. 314–334, reprinted with permission of Louisiana State University Press from *The Presidency in the Constitutional Order*, edited by Joseph Bessette and Jeffrey Tulis. Copyright © 1981 by Louisiana State University Press.

''Hobbes on Liberty and Executive Power,'' chapter 2, pp. 27–44, in George Feaver and Frederick Rosen, eds., *Lives, Liberties and the Public Good*, Macmillan, Basingstoke, Hampshire, England, 1987. Reprinted with permission of the publisher.

''Machiavelli and the Modern Executive,'' chapter 5, pp. 88–110, in Catherine H. Zuckert, ed., *Understanding the Political Spirit*, Yale University Press, New Haven, Conn., 1988. Reprinted with permission of the publisher.

''Republicanizing the Executive,'' pp. 168–184 in Charles R. Kesler, ed., *Saving the Revolution: The Federalist Papers and the American Founding*, The Free Press, New York, 1987. Copyright © 1987 by The Free Press, a Division of Macmillan, Inc.

To the memory of my father,
Harvey C. Mansfield,
constant advocate of a strong presidency
from Franklin Roosevelt to Ronald Reagan

If it were done, when 'tis done, then
    'twere well
        It were done quickly

—*Macbeth*

Contents

Acknowledgments

I wish to thank the following for reading and improving the manuscript: Eve Adler, Allan Bloom, David Epstein, Ernest Fortin, Richard H. Kennington, Pierre Manent, Marvin Meyers, Nathan Tarcov, Jeffrey Tulis, and Stephen H. Wirls. I am also grateful to Grant Ujifusa and Adam Bellow for ruthless editing. Elizabeth Vangel and Suzanne Watts helped with typing. The National Humanities Center and the John M. Olin Foundation provided support while I was writing. To my wife Delba I owe more than I can say.

Preface

Government that is free, yet strong enough to deter its enemies and to preserve the security of its citizens, is a recent invention, dating from eighteenth-century England and America. Today, one would have to say that the invention remains precarious, as free governments are sometimes tempted into weakness and strong governments tend to abandon or attack freedom. "Is there, in all republics, this inherent, and fatal weakness? Must a government, of necessity, be too *strong* for the liberties of its own people, or too *weak* to maintain its own existence?" Lincoln's question, posed at a moment of crisis on July 4, 1861, has lost none of its force and point today.

That the combination of freedom and strength does not arise easily or naturally is confirmed both by the general outline of modern history and by the experience of the ancients. Everywhere in the West the "modern state" was once a monarchy. Free republics came to grief, like the German cities; or faded into memories of glory, like Venice; or blossomed large and grew small fruit, like the Dutch republics; or remained locked in a mountain retreat, like the Swiss cantons. Thus circumscribed and ineffectual, republican practice seemed to partake more of medieval privilege than of modern progress. Where the republican spirit was expansive, as it was in Cromwell's commonwealth (not to mention the French republic which was to come in 1792), its tyrannical excesses left republicanism with a heavy burden of popular disgust and learned disdain. Republican principles, where they survived, became an "ideal" and took refuge in utopianism. Utopian republicans such as James Harrington (1611–1677) and Algernon Sidney (1622–1683) were lost in irrelevance when the old regime in England was transformed after 1688.

Montesquieu's famous reproach to Harrington was that he had "built Chalcedon with the shore of Byzantium before his eyes": he had built his republic in Utopia when he might have built it in England. Until America, the history of modern republics was modest, inglorious, and spotted.

But a new republicanism came forth in the American Constitution, a republicanism with the freedom of republics and the strength of monarchies. Part of the new strength came from the size of the new republic, or from the discovery that a republic need not be small to remain free. But in that republic's Constitution, the new source of strength was the executive. The executive provided the strength of monarchy without tolerating its status above the law, so that monarchy would not only be compatible with the rule of law and the supremacy of the Constitution, but would also be expected to serve both. Furthermore, the recasting of monarchy as executive power made it dependably democratic, as well as legal and constitutional.

And without depreciating the legislative and judicial powers, one can say that executive power made the principle of separation of powers workable. For executive power, always ready for emergency, ensured that the power of government was not diminished, much less stalemated, when it was separated into three branches. The energy of executive power thus gave it more importance than the strict, instrumental sense of "executive" would imply; and this informal addition of power was enough to make the executive branch equal to the two other branches. Without equality among the powers, a separation of powers could not work and could not last; but this equality was endangered by the supremacy the legislature could claim on the basis of the supremacy of law, and by the independence accorded the judiciary on the same basis. Executive power, expanding when needed, kept the rule of law from being, in effect, the rule of ambitious legislators and contrary judges.

The beauty of executive power, then, is to be both subordinate and not subordinate, both weak and strong. It can reach where law cannot, and thus supply the defect of law, yet remain subordinate to law. This ambivalence in the modern executive permits its strength to be useful to republics, without endangering them. So, to examine the nature of executive power, to see how its ambivalence was purposefully conceived and developed, is the first object of this study.

Both politicians and philosophers have always seen law to pose a problem of application. The generalities of law do not conform to the particularities of human beings, and when law is applied to them, such force may be necessary that the enforcer becomes a challenge and a danger to the law. This is a problem endemic in law, but it has several solutions, only one of which is to conceive of the enforcer as an executive. That enforcer might also be a priest or king. The Greeks, who invented political science, made little of the executive function, choosing to leave it obscure; and they made nothing of "the executive" by that name. To think about what they did instead—above all, Aristotle—is very illuminating, however, since modern political science is still most fully displayed, and to best advantage, if it is contrasted to the political science of the ancients. In any case, "the executive" did not become a theme of political science until Marsilius of Padua (1270–1342) conceived all government as executive for the sovereign; but this bold stroke, soon qualified and even retracted, did not sever Marsilius from Aristotle. It only showed the limits, set by classical political science, beyond which the modern doctrine of executive power could not develop without a fundamental challenge to that political science.

The modern doctrine of executive power was begun, or better to say founded, by Niccolò Machiavelli (1469–1527), with full consciousness of his departure from tradition, *sanza alcuno respetto*. To call it "modern" is to imply that executive power is a key element in modern republicanism. More generally, it is a key element in modern government, and thus, still more generally, in the undirected liberty over which modern government seeks to preside. Accordingly, to speak of a modern "doctrine" means that executive power was not discovered by accident in political practice, as David found a sword at the feet of Goliath. To say so is not to rule out the influence of accident and historical development on the conceivers of executive power, still less the utility to them of actual modern monarchies; but executive power was in its origin a conception and a doctrine. Some of its devices are within reach of inventive politicians, just as many persons we would now call "Machiavellian" lived before Machiavelli. But to grasp all the devices, to practice them on a regular basis, in a system of institutions, and with a clear conscience—there's the rub. To do all this is too bold and too sophisticated conceptually to have sprung to the mind of a politician looking for a weapon ready to hand. Only with the help of Machiavelli, and his principal successors in the development of this doctrine—Thomas Hobbes (1588–1679), John Locke (1632–1704), and Montesquieu (1689–1755)—could we have come to the systematic, publicly declared exercise of executive power.

To argue this difficult point—the presence of mindful choice is difficult to establish in the drift of circumstance and against the trend of contemporary historical thinking—is my second object. So my book is not a history of executives, many of whom have undoubtedly been thoughtless anticipators or beneficiaries of the doctrine of executive power. But as an analysis of executive power, the exposition here will show the thought that is necessary to the conception of executive power, and the comprehensive character of the choice it represents. As yet, the development of the thought behind executive power has not been brought to light, and its theorists have not been given their say. If I can make executive power intelligible, we shall be in a position to learn how it came into existence.

It is not hard to find the spirit of the present-day executive in the thought of Machiavelli. If a modern executive were given a copy of Machiavelli's *The Prince*, he might be impressed by the remedies or courses of action recommended: quickness of decision, dependence on oneself, manipulation of necessity, denial of responsibility, reliance on the people. Above all, there is the central notion of going behind talk to the "effectual truth" of the matter. But he would also be shocked at the criminality that Machiavelli suggests to his prince. Our contemporary executive believes, if nowadays he does not quite take for granted, that the techniques of executive decision-making can be used with a clear conscience to effect a result in which he can take pride.

The business executive's confidence in his own morality is repeated and confirmed in our politics, where the Machiavellian notion of the executive has become "executive power" and has been accepted as a regular and legitimate branch of government in the Constitution. So it is that the *constitutional* executive is an invention of liberalism, of Locke, Montesquieu, and the American founders, rather than of Machiavelli and Hobbes. Indeed, liberalism, to the extent that it requires government by constitution—with standing laws, due process, defined powers, and limited tenure—seems flatly opposed to the "effectual truth" by which you get something done by any means whatever, and without regard to constitutional, legal, or moral niceties. Accordingly, we can begin to see that in possessing executive power, the new republicanism of the American Constitution has imported not only the strength of monarchy but also some of the techniques of tyranny. It has not only republicanized English monarchy but also constitutionalized[1] the anti-constitutional Machiavellian prince, so that the impulse to get results, regardless of the Constitution, is incorporated into the Constitution itself, and the devices of Machiavelli are made available to the office first held by George Washington. Lincoln's question, quoted at the beginning of this preface, was presented to a legislature awaiting justification for his extraordinary actions as an executive. It shows too much conscience to be Machiavellian and too much awareness to exclude Machiavelli.

How did this happen? How did Machiavelli's prince, the master of the sensational execution, become the executive power of liberal constitutionalism? The answer is that the history of Machiavellism is chiefly a process of domestication, whereby Machiavelli's thought was appropriated and absorbed by liberal constitutionalism[2] so that it could be regularized and legitimated. Yet, while we might be impressed with the success of liberalism in domesticating this harsh doctrine—assuming for the moment that this was done—Machiavelli himself might remark that by adopting executive power, liberal constitutionalists have admitted that they could not do without him. Their constitutions would not work without a branch whose function could be accurately described—though you might never hear it described that way—as getting around the constitution when necessary. He might wonder, then, who was adopting whom. It would not matter to him that those who followed his advice were not usually in a position to acknowledge his influence, even if they knew of it. Machiavelli was as much aware of the need to moralize as of the need to act.

Thus, my third object in this book is to reconsider the history of Machiavellism as it affects executive power but with a reconsideration of its wider implications. As a result I find myself in disagreement with two formidable authorities on Machiavellism, J. G. A. Pocock and Quentin Skinner.[3] These scholars rightly stress Machiavelli's influence, but they do not stress it enough and they get it wrong. They believe in Machiavelli the republican, a promoter not of constitutional republicanism but of republican virtue, and they follow the line of his influence through the defenders of modern republics until those defenders bow out or lose out to liberal constitutionalism. But to study Machiavellism one must know Machiavelli. Pocock and Skinner (Skinner to a greater extent than Pocock) begin with a tame Machiavelli, and so do not see that Machiavelli had to be domesticated. They believe that Machiavelli's idea of virtue is opposed to that of self-interest, while in fact it is a recommendation of ferocious aggrandizement, sometimes camouflaged to bemuse squeamish readers. Pocock and Skinner fail to appreciate Machiavelli's boldness in breaking with the classical tradition of Plato and Aristotle. They do not see the simple difference between prizing virtue as the end of a republic, as did the ancients, and reducing virtue to the means of a republic's survival or expansion, as did Machiavelli.[4] Pocock and Skinner also fail to grasp the barely acknowledged relationship between Machiavelli and liberalism, which is accessible to us in a conception of executive power but not confined to that; for Machiavelli's slogan, "one's own arms," bears a clear resemblance to the liberal right of self-preservation. So although Pocock and Skinner make much of him, they greatly underestimate Machiavelli's influence. They treat the influence as moralistic resistance to liberalism[5] or as a building block we no longer require,[6] and therefore they do not appreciate Machiavelli's relevance today, nor do they understand either his contribution to our practices or his challenge to our beliefs.

Our contemporary liberalism—I mean the fundamental liberalism that includes today's conservatives—has an inherent difficulty which can be recognized as Machiavellian even though Machiavelli did not speak about rights. Liberalism is based on a conception of individual rights, and liberal, constitutional government is established to secure those rights. But even the most scrupulous government cannot be indifferent to the ways in which individuals exercise their rights, for what they do may endanger the rights of others or risk the security of the whole community. To respect individual rights, liberal governments must avert their gaze from the exercise of rights, since the meaning of a right is to leave its proper use to individual choice. Yet to secure rights, such governments must also do the contrary; they must keep an eye on the exercise of rights and when necessary curtail them with a view to their end. This difficulty was well known to the seventeenth-century founders of liberalism, especially John Locke, but the problem has been somewhat obscured by the appearance, since Kant, of two rival parties within liberalism, each embracing only one side of the dilemma in a frantic effort to shun the devil, or perhaps in the foolish hope of killing him.

Thus the rights-based or deontological party and the utilitarian or teleological party oppose one another in today's academic debates. Neither party has succeeded in vanquishing the other, nor will either ever succeed, because under pressure each party is compelled to admit the force of its opponent's position. The rights party, worried about how to keep rights intact, is a zealous defender of forms and procedures, and the natural friend of the judiciary and of legislatures that love to legislate. The utilitarian party, meanwhile, professes to cut through formalities and "looks to the end" (or utility) in a way Machiavelli would recognize. This party is the natural promoter of an energetic executive and compliant legislatures. While utilitarians are innocent of any intent or any desire to follow Machiavelli to his ultimate conclusions, the utilitarian reminder that rights must have a use keeps before us the Machiavellian argument that all morality must yield to physical security during an emergency. And the need for "energy in the executive"—in Alexander Hamilton's famous phrase—to act during emergencies compels us to appreciate the inherent difficulty in our liberalism, and to confront the possibility that its lineage is not quite as respectable as we now like to think.

In its attempt to expose the lineage of executive power, this book resembles a study in intellectual or conceptual history. But there are differences. I do not assume that each new stage in development is an improvement over the preceding one, or that the process is inevitable, or that it is determined by the circumstances of the time. Indeed, rather than supposing that our understanding of executive power today is at its most sophisticated and developed, I believe on the contrary that it is weak and impoverished compared to earlier insights. Therefore I try to convey as much hesitation, surprise, and dismay as I do satisfaction at the development of executive power. That history, as I have indicated, is more a concealment and restriction of the essential nature of executive power than a gradual unfolding of its early, unrecognized potentialities. But the concealment did not occur by accretion of historical accident. The changes wrought by Hobbes, Locke, and Montesquieu on Machiavelli's conception were made with a revolutionary intent of their own, and not, or not chiefly, as an accommodation to new facts. What later philosophers thought was surely affected by the consequences they saw or foresaw in the theories of their predecessors; so it makes sense to speak of a development of the doctrine of executive power with definable "stages" even though each stage when first conceived was meant to be the last.

As we shall see, the doctrine of executive power originates in Machiavelli's proclamation of the sovereignty of deeds over words. Does that sovereignty imply that new ideas arrive automatically as a result of new facts, without having to be proclaimed or thought? Machiavelli did not say so. To affirm literally that "the facts speak for themselves," one would have to believe that every set of circumstances comes fully adorned with its own explanation and justification. If this is so, all thinkers have said what they must have said—the facts left them no choice in the matter. And if all have spoken as they must, all are perfectly wise—a *reductio ad absurdum*.

In our time much is made of the need for interpretation, in the hope that each generation's or each person's need to interpret for himself will sufficiently guarantee his freedom. But if interpretation is merely self-serving, whimsical, or arbitrary, it does not escape servitude to facts. For the facts will be interpreted as each person must, and his whimsy will count as wisdom, since he could not speak otherwise. Free interpretation is not the opposite of determinism but a kind of historical necessity in which lip service is paid to ideas.

To present the development of executive power, I have chosen the thinkers I found most important. I have not attempted a complete history of the use of the word "executive." But believing, perhaps naively, that a great thinker will find the words best suited to his intention, I have fixed on the use of that word as the sign of relevance to my inquiry, rather than trying to analyze all the institutions that we would now call "executive." The point is to discover why those institutions began to be so called and so considered. I have drawn a line after the creation of the American presidency, the first executive to have been conceived and created as an executive, rather than adapted to the task like the English king. After that time—though not before—energy in the executive comes to be accepted for what Alexander Hamilton saw it to be, as a "leading character in the definition of good government."

Executive power is power exercised in the name of someone or something else—God or the people or the law. We sometimes forget this fact and cover it up when we speak of "the executive," simply, without specifying of what. And in contemporary American speech one can hear: "The Bears really executed on that play." The verb here is intransitive, and in the appreciation of perfection one loses the sense of reference to something outside the agent. Still, when we think about it, the executive remains an agent. But though formally an agent, the executive is usually much stronger than that because his job is not as easy as its harmless title promises. Yet when he encounters resistance, and needs to disarm resentment, he can say that he is merely carrying out the will of another—the Congress, the Commanding Officer, the people, the Good Book, the Board, the Company, or any other formal sovereign—even History. His formal weakness, in short, enhances his informal strength.

This seemingly simple idea is not so simple, because its essence is ambivalence. It seems simple to us because it has become so familiar; and it is familiar because it has succeeded so remarkably. How else but as amazing could one describe the acceptance of, or rather the enthusiasm for, so much one-man rule, which is what we call executive power in our modern democracies? I do not mean to say that government is always the same however it is named. But a fair look at those we call presidents, secretaries, commissioners, commissars, or executives by whatever name, in free governments as well as in the unfree, would leave one wondering why, given the power of these individuals to capture our attention and dominate our lives, we no longer speak of kings and tyrants. Someone has sold us on the idea so well that we are no longer aware of the marketing effort.

In truth, the idea of executive power has become so familiar that we have forgotten why anyone would want to rule in his own name rather than someone else's. To relearn the reasons for ruling in one's own name, I shall review the prehistory of executive power, when emergency action and individual discretion were accepted as necessary but not understood as being executive. After this reasoning is recounted—no small task since it requires a study of Aristotle's political science—we can better appreciate, if not quite experience, the shock of Machiavelli's discovery. And when that shock is appreciated, we can better understand the difficulty of absorbing it in a constitutional system. We will also have a better understanding of modern scholarship whose errors begin from overlooking the obvious.

But first we need to know better what executive power is. According to the academic tradition, which in its best sense is the Socratic tradition, the way to the nature of a thing is first through the accepted opinions of that thing. What, then, are those opinions about executive power?

1

Introduction:
The Ambivalence
of Executive Power

To understand the modern doctrine of executive power, we need to know, at least approximately, what executive power is. It might at first seem best to go directly to the thing and to ignore opinions about it. For executive power is universally agreed to be a modern necessity: why, then, should it be presented as a modern doctrine? No modern state is considered a going concern unless it is equipped with a strong executive, and every state without one is held to be courting disaster, and regarded with pity and contempt by those more fortunate.

Nor can the necessity of executive power be dismissed as an unconscious assumption which, being universal, goes unchallenged. It is challenged, but never successfully. Even though the assumption regarding the necessity of executive power is universal, there are always some and sometimes many living under free governments who grumble about strong executive actions they find distasteful. They deplore and oppose them as the practices of tyranny, calling them by one of the many contemporary equivalents for that term which our prudery requires and our experience makes very familiar. Yet the protestations subside soon enough as if in recognition of necessity, unless indeed the tune is changed and a clamor begins for strong executive actions which the formerly disapproving now find beneficial. The necessity of a strong executive has, therefore, been tested by those to whom it has not been obvious. Those who speak against it either fall silent or contradict themselves. So to present executive power as a modern doctrine, implying discovery of something previously hidden, and thus to reveal a choice among the new and the old possibilities, is to speak in the face of a need that seems obvious and compelling.

If we were at the end of our inquiry, it would be possible to argue that the early teachers of executive power intended to secure the difference between free government and tyranny by giving the former some of the power and techniques of the latter. One such technique is to make people think they are bowing to necessity when they are in fact obeying you. But here, at the beginning of our investigation, we can see an ambivalence in executive power which does not arise from ineluctable necessity, and calls for some kind of clarification—perhaps a doctrine. For although everyone agrees on the necessity of a strong executive, everyone also agrees on the use of a term, "executive," which implies in its literal meaning that somebody is not strong in his own right but is merely an agent. In other words, everyone agrees on the necessity of a strong executive, but also agrees, it appears, on the importance of concealing that necessity. Untaught necessity such as hunger speaks for itself without ambivalence or equivocation. But a necessity that needs to be concealed is more complicated, and needs to be explained. Why, in short, is it necessary to call executive power by a name that deprecates it?

The Dictionary Executive

In politics today, the word "executive" has two meanings. One is the dictionary definition, he who "carries out," as in the American Constitution the president is given the duty to "take care that the laws be faithfully executed."[1] Derived from the Latin *exsequor,* meaning "follow out," "execute" is used by both classical authors and the Roman law in the extended and particular sense of following out a law to the end: to vindicate or to punish. The Greek equivalents *lambanein telos* and *ekbibazein* are also similarly used. In this primary meaning, the American president serves merely to carry out the intention of the law, that is, the will of others—of the legislature, and ultimately of the people. But if any real president confined himself to this definition, he would be contemptuously called an "errand boy," considered nothing in himself, a mere agent whose duty is to command actions according to the law.

Going to his usual extreme, Kant has represented this meaning of the executive in the form of a syllogism, where the major premise is the legislative will, the minor premise or "the principle of subsumption" is the executive, and the conclusion is the judicial application to particulars.[2] By this syllogistic form the executive function is separated rather artificially from the judicial, but it is definitely made subordinate to the legislative.

Yet it would be unwise for any legislature that is willing to accept Kant's major premise to speak openly of its executive as an errand boy, for to hurt the executive's pride would diminish his utility. So executive pride transcends the primary dictionary definition of "executive," but is captured perhaps in the phrase "law enforcement," which suggests that carrying out the law does not come about as a matter of course. "Law enforcement" implies a recalcitrance to law in the human beings who are subject to it, making necessary a claim by the executive to some of the authority and majesty of the law itself. To execute the law it is sometimes not enough for a policeman to ask politely; eschewing the role of an errand boy, he does something impressive to make himself respected. And if a policeman must be more than an errand boy, so too must a president.

Perhaps the authority of law is better connoted in the term "law enforcement" than is its majesty. The end of law as stated or implied in the law (the final cause) is a noble thought which we respect, to which we are dedicated, and for which government would execute the law in the primary, instrumental sense. But the idea of execution as law enforcement puts us in fear and reminds us of the reason why laws are made (the efficient cause): to dispel fear and provide security. The latter makes use of legalized lawlessness, that is, of retaliatory or anticipatory actions which would be illegal if they were not performed by the police. These are punitive actions, sometimes done so impressively as to suggest that the purpose of law is mainly to punish. Such action also permits or even requires the executive to gather in his person the power that enabled the first lawgiver to awe his unsettled subjects, and to exude the fearsomeness of a being who makes and executes his own law, as if he were an angry god. One would not suggest too much in saying that executive pride smacks of tyr-

3

anny, so radically does it enlarge upon the instrumental executive.

It is all very well to speak sententiously of a government of laws, not of men, but to an executive that may be so much unsupported assertion of legislative pride. Legislators may fervently believe that to change behavior it is enough to pass a law. But laws that are mere demonstrations to the intellect are like prayers to the deaf. Because the government of laws rules over recalcitrant men, the laws are nothing in fact unless they are executed, and to get them executed, the executive must be given some or most or all of the legislative pride. By this view, a government of laws addressed to men is reducible to a government of men.

Thus, recognizing executive pride, we find in the American Constitution that taking care to execute the laws faithfully is only one of the duties imposed on the president, for the performance of which he is given several powers. Among them are powers that are neither executive in nature (the veto of legislation) nor subordinate (commander-in-chief of the army and navy). Moreover, he is vested with "the executive power," which according to Hamilton's famous argument,[3] has a nature of its own, bounded only by necessity, that is not exhausted by the enumerated powers; and he takes an oath to faithfully execute not the laws but his *office*.[4] But, for Kant, not only is the executive represented as a minor premise, but he is also described—with the covert, corrective realism that is as usual with Kant as his theoretical extremism—as a moral person of coordinate power with the other two powers.[5] We see that the real, practical, informal executive is, if not a tyrant, far more powerful than the supposed, theoretical, formal executive.

He is also quicker and more masterful. In today's political science the term "decision-making" is sometimes applied indiscriminately to all governmental actions or to all actions whatever, conveying a sense that all decisions are similar and none of them particularly "executive." It is admitted, however, that decisions sometimes follow one another in a series, and so one hears of "the legislative process," "the judicial process," and "the administrative process." But one does not hear of "the executive process."[6] In actual usage, as distinguished from intent, executive decision-making retains a decisive aura and seems distinct from the general, workaday, reassuring process of ordinary "decision-making."

Two Schools of Interpreting the Executive

In the academic literature on the American presidency, the ambivalence of the executive is clearly apparent. Of the two works that have helped to define the field, Richard E. Neustadt's *Presidential Power* represents the real, informal presidency, and Edward S. Corwin's *The President: Offices and Powers* the limited, formal presidency. Neustadt defines two conceptions of the office as clerkship and leadership, and clearly prefers the latter—a president who creates strength of position from his own initiatives, using the formal powers of his office to transform himself from clerk to leader. Corwin, for his part, does not deny the reality of a president's personal power, but he deplores it. So rather than analyzing examples of executive power, as Neustadt does, he divides it into powers or functions or roles, thereby defining and delimiting it.[7] Corwin is not ashamed to present the "literary theory"[8] of the presidency as found in part, he says, in the intention of the Framers of the Constitution, and at length in cases of constitutional law. His understanding is legal and prescriptive rather than realistic, and if Corwin does not reduce the president to a clerk, he asks us to recall John Dunning's resolution in the British Parliament on the influence of the Crown in the eighteenth century and revise it thus: "the power of the President has increased, is increasing, and ought to be diminished."[9]

Corwin's view, of course, was very much in the minority during the administrations of Franklin Roosevelt and Harry Truman, was almost forgotten in the lauding of the presidency that accompanied John F. Kennedy's accession, and then gained favor while Richard Nixon and Ronald Reagan served.[10] Putting partisan feeling aside, we should observe that the realistic school of interpretation, even with the advantage of long periods of dominance, has never succeeded in destroying the formal school, just as the formal school has never quite succeeded in defining the reality of executive power. One school serves justice, the other serves necessity; and both serve political partisans as they claim justice when in opposition and necessity when in power.

When examined, moreover, each of the schools reveals something of the other in itself. Corwin admits that the Constitution, though a formal document, reflects an informal struggle between two conceptions of executive power that may be identified with the two points of view: a weak executive resulting from the no-

5

tion that the people are *represented* in the legislature, a strong executive from the notion that they are *embodied* in the executive.[11] Though Corwin would seem to prefer the former conception, he never questions the need for both. And it is hard to see why the people should be embodied in one man if not to secure the unity of executive powers, despite their separate definitions, through the unity of one human body. Corwin proposes to control presidential power, to make it more regular and less personal, and to establish a cabinet council including legislative leaders, but not to remove executive power from one man. As the reality of that one man is quite personal, so must be the reality of the power formally conferred on him.

Or does the reality of the president's power depend on the form? Neustadt's main argument is that the president must acquire and use personal power in order to secure the formal power promised, but not guaranteed, by the "literary theory," the constitutional forms, and the developed expectations of the office. Neustadt holds that the president is formally a strong executive, and in reality either weak or strong according to his personal strength. But with this view one takes for granted the opportunity for strength afforded by the Constitution, since it is the Constitution (as we shall see in Chapter 10) that gives the president "his unique place in our political system" and enables or requires him to "sit where he sits"[12]—a favorite phrase of Neustadt's borrowed from Harry Truman to denote a base of operations rather than formal occupancy of an office. Neustadt makes a distinction between formal power and "effective influence," thus making it clear that for him formal power is ineffectual. Formal power is the power to compel, and Neustadt's book is devoted to the proposition that the power to compel is worthless by itself. And that power becomes positively harmful if a president believes that he can rely on it; formal power, for Neustadt, is useful only if it is understood as a subordinate factor in the work of persuasion, or as "incidents in a persuasive process."[13]

But is it not more reasonable and realistic to suppose, on the contrary, that persuasion is incidental or instrumental to compulsion? Although the power to compel must often or even always be supplemented by persuasion, a president's power to persuade would be greatly weakened without his coercive power. The rational appeal to interest is much diluted without a capacity to engender fear. Moreover, to the extent that he must persuade (which is admittedly considerable), is this not by command of the Constitution? Persuasion (or bargaining) is made a regular necessity for the president, and generally in American politics, by the peculiar separation and sharing of powers ordained by the Constitution. As Neustadt says, "the limits on command suggest the structure of our government"; and he traces that structure to the Constitution. Who are the persons necessary in the end to be persuaded? Are they not those with the constitutional power to compel? It would seem that "effective influence" is thereby grounded in formal power. But Neustadt does not acknowledge the magnitude of his concession, for he concludes shortly thereafter that "the probabilities of power do not derive from the literary theory" of the Constitution.[14] Neustadt, accordingly, takes for granted the potential strength of the presidential office, which might become active in the most self-effacing personality with or even without the tutelage of Neustadt's own "literary theory."[15] A latent teaching exists in the constitutional powers themselves that is discernible or at least presentable to politicians.

Besides taking for granted the formal strength of the executive, Neustadt overlooks its formal weakness and thus its ambivalence. "The limits on command" that pertain to the structure of our government also suggest that formal restraints impose real restraints, compelling presidents to bargain rather than command. Moreover, although convinced of the need for a strong executive, Neustadt pays no heed to the dictionary definition of executive and takes no account of the modest pretense to be executing the will of someone else—a pretense required especially of the strongest presidents. He identifies the formal executive with the constitutional presidency, but as we have seen, the latter includes powers that go beyond the merely formal executive power. It is perhaps by constitutional design that the president must achieve his leadership, and that the alternative of clerkship is open to him either as a refuge from responsibility or as a cloak for his aggrandizement.

Neustadt rightly emphasizes the truth that persuading others means persuading them that something is in their interest. But to succeed in such persuasion, it is useful to have the instrumental conception of the office whereby it can appear that the president himself is nothing, a mere representative of stronger forces that are more important, more sovereign than he. Thus he need not demand obedience to his will but need only implore his petitioner

7

to take pity on him for what he must do. The very notion of "interest" in political science disguises assertiveness, as it proposes something abstract and objective to be followed, distinct from will or caprice. What I must do in my own interest is, as it were, imposed on me. Too bad for you, but surely you understand?

As for the president's personal power, one can sometimes get more out of a broker's commission than from a direct payment. Neustadt knows this and says that "persuasion becomes bargaining,"[16] but he does not say that the president's formal weakness is suited to the character of his personal power. One is left wondering what the president's personal power is. Neustadt is ambiguous as to whether it is the power of the office, with which the president identifies himself, or the pursuit of his private interest, to which his official power is merely an instrument. Given the ambiguity between constitutional role and Machiavellian self-aggrandizement, the president's "unique place in our political system" cannot guarantee that his only concern is for the whole of our polity. He may serve the whole only so far as the whole affects him. So then is the rule of law necessarily reduced to executive pride served by executive connivance? If so, the executive would be more than the leader-as-clerk; he is more like a tyrant with the conception of clerk serving as a mask.

If one were to carry Neustadt's theory to an extreme, the president's personal power could be described only in the style of each president, as biography.[17] Thus Neustadt's book, while formally a study of presidential power, could be understood in fact as a critical biography of President Eisenhower: Neustadt accepts the critique of President Eisenhower by his predecessor, Truman, who thought the general a bumbling innocent in politics.[18] A more recent book, Fred I. Greenstein's *The Hidden-Hand Presidency* (1982), does not examine the sinister potential of personal leadership directly, perhaps because Greenstein, despite his partisan inclination, was persuaded by the evidence to admire President Eisenhower's personal skill.[19]

Unlike Neustadt, Greenstein argues that leadership can sometimes be more effective if it does not appear to be leadership: having a reputation for cleverness is not the same as being clever. Eisenhower, according to Greenstein, was eminently skilled at getting what he wanted without seeming to have had a hand in the result. Where he was in fact evasive, he seemed guileless; and while always calculating, he appeared merely lucky. To achieve the effect, Eisenhower used the formalities of his office to make himself look non-partisan. Or should one say that since the general content of Eisenhower's partisanship could not remain hidden, he used the informalities of his office to achieve what formally it is supposed to be? The public smile covered the hidden hand, but the hidden hand created the conditions for the public smile.

Greenstein, in short, introduces us to the complexity of the relationship between formal and real power, something not as simple as formal theory *versus* real deeds. The president's formal, non-partisan office as chief of state can serve partisan ends by concealing the use of partisan means, so that formal power can become real power; but the hidden partisan means must be used to serve ends that do not have to be concealed, ends that can be announced or proclaimed to produce Eisenhower's electoral successes. So understood, real power is identical with formal power.

Another recent book, Richard M. Pious's *The American Presidency*, has the merit of being hard to place on either side of the formal-realistic dichotomy. On the formal side, Pious wants stricter standards for the exercise of prerogative powers in emergencies, but more as a grant of power than as a diminution of it. He believes that emergencies arise oftener than they should because the president is too weak in both formal and informal power.[20] More formal power for the president will reduce the need for his informal power. Yet, as a realist, Pious strongly feels that the Constitution is the source of the president's informal power. The Constitution, Pious asserts, speaks plainly on some matters and remains silent on others. What it says to establish the three branches of government enables them to fill the silences that were left by the Framers of the Constitution. The president, with his expansive office, is particularly adept at filling the void: "The president claims the silences of the Constitution."[21] Thus, the reality of his power is not described in the Constitution, but it depends on what is described there. One cannot make the distinction, as Neustadt does, between formal power and effective influence. To describe the "effective influence" of the president precisely, one must take account of the "literary theory" of the Constitution.[22] Pious takes note, moreover, that the formal offices of the Constitution have not only been used to serve partisans, but they also have created partisans—"presidentialists" and

9

"congressionalists"—who, by Montesquieu's prediction, defend their favorite offices to some extent apart from other partisan considerations.[23]

How deliberately the Framers may have left silences in the Constitution to complement its express statements is not made clear in Pious's book. He writes: "While the Framers were brilliant politicians, they were cautious draftsmen."[24] Pious does not venture to say: *Because* the Framers were brilliant politicians, they were cautious draftsmen. So we are kept wondering whether the ambivalence of executive power was the product of constitutional design; nonetheless by Pious's own "theory of presidential power"[25] we are shown some part of how that ambivalence could have been consciously planned.

Another more psychological theory of the informal executive has lately emerged, purporting to lay bare the personality of the president. Here the individual personality is assumed to be critical, rather than the president's political situation or the demands of his constitutional office. One might expect, therefore, that the fearsome aspect of the executive, which is the more personal, would be emphasized, and its lawful character played down. This expectation is neither entirely frustrated nor happily fulfilled. In the theory, personality is divided into personalities, which are defined as types or roles with much of the formalism used by constitution-makers to define offices. James D. Barber, in his influential book, *The Presidential Character*,[26] identifies the "active-positive" personality which makes for the preferred type of president—someone who goes about his work free of the compulsive drive for power for its own sake. Such a personality is very fortunately composed: he is, by definition, active, and so escapes the mean compliance of what Barber calls the "passive-positive" executive as well as the dutiful propriety of the "passive-negative" type; but since he is also positive, he escapes those temptations to violence to which the active-negative executive yields, given his silly heroism and braggart masculinity. Finally, the active-positive executive is permitted and even encouraged by Barber to indulge his love of fun and his belief that politics is play.[27]

The sunny democratic optimism of this character and his scholarly creator is quite remarkable. Barber apparently assumes, contrary to his premise that personality is more important than institutions, that the modern executive cannot be either passive or weak. Accordingly, he implies that the weak executive is in thrall to compulsive legislators, meekly executing the laws they pass, and thus becomes strong by servility to strength. For Barber, the modern executive must be strong somehow. In any case, Franklin D. Roosevelt cannot be described as weak, and he clearly loved politics. But did he love making the stern, hard decisions that strength makes possible, among them ordering his country to war? And did he love to deceive, as he sometimes did, using his political skill?[28] Was not Lincoln's melancholy irony, though negative, something Barber could applaud?

If a strong executive is necessary, his strength is not needed to lead the nation at play, unless the game played is understood as a competition. In which case, it is too much to believe that a politician's desire to win will rouse him from passivity without carrying him into a dangerous desire for mastery. So the active-positive character is simply a wish, a political hope displaced upon psychological theory. Such a character could not check his own desire for mastery without possessing the diffident "civic virtue" of the passive-negative character. Moreover, if he were checked by others with institutional restraints in the spirit of *Federalist* 51's maxim, "Ambition must be made to counteract ambition," such a president would become one active-negative character among others.

Barber's work has prospered because psycho-history is currently fashionable, and also because Barber can claim to have called the turn on active-negative Richard Nixon. But Barber's proximate intellectual antecedent is Harold Lasswell, whose *Power and Personality* (1948) also reflects—and more sharply—the problem of a not-so-playful desire for mastery.[29] Lasswell was never loath to grasp the far-off and far-out consequences of his fashionable ideas, and his chief merit is the unfashionable zeal with which he promotes them. He shows them for what they are and may yet, perhaps, unwittingly sound an alarm with the piercing shriek of his trumpet of progress. When he describes the traits of the power-seeker, he does not avoid the ineluctable conclusion that the power-seeker is completely satisfied only by ruling the world.[30] And Lasswell is not embarrassed to say that the aim of his policy science, long-term, is to "get rid of power,"[31] to get rid of politics, because politics includes—or rather centers on—what he clinically calls "severe deprivations."[32]

In the short run, however, Lasswell wants to curb and chasten power by promoting the democratic personality, which is free of social anxiety and accompanying unhealthy negativism. In government, Lasswell would generally favor the "agitator" type—responsive to change, flexible in crisis, and tolerant of diversity—over the "bureaucrat," whose compulsive desire for uniformity masks a desire to avoid responsibility.[33] Agitators, like Barber's active-passive presidents, are intended to be strong executives, though not too strong. But again, the notion of executing another's will, which is essential to the institution of executive, awkwardly and noticeably limits the psychological construct that has been arbitrarily designed to replace that notion—as if nature had undertaken to provide souls suitable for democratic leaders.[34]

Leaving aside consideration of the American presidency for a moment, we find two notable works by M. J. C. Vile and W. B. Gwyn on the history of the doctrine of the separation of powers. Here again we encounter the ambivalence of executive power. Both authors insist that the doctrine of separation of powers must be understood as connected with—or, as they say, confused with—the notion of the mixed or balanced constitution.[35] The cause of this confusion, it would seem, is the problem of executive power. Because the separation of powers, according to them, is based on an analysis of functions, and because the executive function is considered subordinate to the legislative, the result is a weak executive. Yet the powers do not remain separate operationally unless they are strong enough to defend themselves against each other, and thus are independent. In such circumstances a strong executive is required. Obviously because no formal dictionary or functional definition of "executive" power can produce equality with legislative power, a supplementary and informal reality must be found and justified by the doctrine of the mixed or balanced constitution. This in itself requires only an informal mix or balance of functions and not a formal demarcation of them. To secure an actual separation of powers, therefore, the doctrine of separation of powers must reach outside its formal justification for that separation and necessarily grasp some notion of expansive, informal, executive power. A recognition, more or less understood, of this necessity has produced the supposed confusion of the separation of powers and the mixed constitution. Accordingly, the history of the doctrine of separation of powers needs to be considered with special emphasis on executive power.

Form and Reality in the Executive

If the weak and strong executives are admitted to be both persist-
ent and pervasive, and if today one is never found without the
other, we can say that they depend on one another.[36] For executive power is typical of modern government, where form and reality are to be found at a certain distance from each other. How
so? Modern government claims to represent the people as a
whole, but in reality some people are better represented than others; it claims to be democratic, but is actually oligarchic or elitist;
it claims to be constitutional, but extra-constitutional institutions,
such as parties, actually run it; it claims to be merely instrumental
to the "pursuit of happiness," but in reality fosters a certain notion of happiness; it claims to be universal, but actually works
only under certain conditions; its peoples claim to be citizens, but
are in fact no more than voters, if that; and its leaders claim to be
executives, but are actually rulers.

The pattern is sufficiently distinct so that today we tend to think
that the form is necessarily separate from the reality. But I shall
argue that this feature of modern government, both liberal and
illiberal, was *deliberately contrived.* Its origin is to be found in liberal
constitutionalism, where the forms of the constitution are held
out in public view and the Machiavellian practices needed to
make them work are concealed.

I have suggested that the weak, formal executive is an aid to
the strong, informal executive. When explaining the policy laid
down by the emperor Augustus, Gibbon says on the first page
of his history that "the Roman Senate appeared to possess the
sovereign authority, and devolved on the emperors all the executive powers of government."[37] He meant that the real government (the emperor) was apparently acting on behalf of the supposed government (the Senate). So from early on, the notion of
the executive seems to have connoted not weakness but the sem-
blance of weakness, a presumed drawing of its own strength
from the strength of another: the retiring disguise, combined
with the efficient activity, of the *éminence grise.* For it adds to one's
power to conceal it or deprecate it, and the regular pretense of
"executing" another's wishes, however easily penetrated, is not
at all distasteful to anyone who thinks he himself cannot be
fooled. In time, he comes to value the courtesies of his "execu-

tives" just as he would enjoy the exercise of his own power. Indeed, modern citizens in liberal democracies take a perverse pleasure in figuring out the tricks by which they are not deceived, to be sure, but merely governed. And our modern political science, conveying neither surprise nor anything more than routine indignation, offers its findings to support the curiosity of citizens. Even our most forceful contemporary politicians claim only to be stewards of the people, and find it useful as well as necessary not to claim more.[38]

Yet it is also necessary to consider the strong executive as an aid to the weak, and to make another obvious observation. For if the weak executive is bashful and retiring, the strong executive is bold and impressive. Instead of a cloak to wear, the strong executive has an image to create and to cultivate, an image of masculine energy impressively controlled because it is just barely so. The regularity of his performance is interrupted by unpredictable shifts of policy which can later be interpreted by the sophisticated courtiers of modern democracies: journalists, commentators, and political scientists. A strong executive may well be regarded as having a disconcerting taste for the sensational, so eagerly does he seize upon an accident of politics to magnify it for his own use. He may even create accidents; he is a master of what Neustadt calls "initiatives," which are motions toward something new—designs for him, surprises to others.[39] He surely does not shrink from raising alarms, or from forcefully reminding others of what is what and who is who. His indulgences are sweetened by his punishments, and the effect of his active-positive smile is enhanced by the occasional appearance of his active-negative frown. The purpose of all this, however, is not merely to boost the ego of the weak executive (a comic character), but also to make lawful executions easier and less oppressive. A snarl or a bite every once in a while, if it is carefully chosen, will quiet the brave and satisfy the multitude by venting pent-up humors and releasing a wholesome, wondering fear.

The result is more useful to free governments than to tyrannies, because the necessary exactions of any government bring more danger and dishonor to free governments than to tyrannies. Every dissipation of the hatreds that a free people inevitably begins to feel toward government reduces its resistance to the necessary exactions that must be made upon it. And then too, a single, quick stroke is always impressive and nearly painless. When such thoughts have been elaborated to explain "the economy of violence"[40]—which one might counter by asserting the humanity of violence—the strong executive can be seen to make possible the weak. The strong executive's very energy makes it possible to move government away from "ruling" in the classical sense to something more limited in scope and ambition—"representation" in the modern sense, that leaves government the servant of the people.[41] Or one could say "the steward of the people," for a strong executive of the people's will is, in principle and intent, a weak ruler over the people.

The ambivalence of the executive, therefore, must be understood less as embodying two rival, contrary conceptions than as the same thing in two phases or aspects.[42] One must look beyond the differences between strong and weak presidents—such as Theodore Roosevelt and William Howard Taft—to a conception of the executive that unites them, reflected in the simple and obvious fact that both have held the same office. What is the nature of an office that can survive, and satisfy, both men? So Barber's psychological theory fails to recognize the fact that the matrix of personalities proudly set forth is not a discovery but a creation of the office itself. For the psychological realists have construed their reality out of another's creation. If an executive can be described as active or passive, positive or negative, this is because the office itself encompasses the behavior. So it is only by the design of the creators of the office that such descriptions seem to correspond to what we observe in the character of the president.

The unity of the office implies the possibility, though a remote one, of an ideal executive. Such a person would combine in himself the ambivalence inherent in the office, ducking out of sight and leaping into view when necessary and appropriate. And his knowledge, part of which is understanding how to tolerate the ignorance of others—for executives usually excel in being either weak or strong, not both—would encompass the doctrine of executive power, uniting its two aspects while justifying their separation. When separated, the two aspects demonstrate the gulf between weak formal power and strong informal power. But when together in hypothetical perfection, the formal ambivalence in the office would cause a real ambivalence in the executive's behavior. This presumed result suggests a puzzle about the relationship between formal and real power that has not been solved, or even understood, in the literature we have surveyed. We have seen a formal executive and an informal executive, and we have had a glimpse of the complexity of their relationship. But no scholar has made this relationship his theme or answered the following simple question: Is the formal executive power merely a cloak for the real executive, or is it also the cause of real power?

Recalcitrance and the Executive

A doctrine is needed to combine the two aspects of executive power not only for the constitutional executive but for the party executive as well. Confining ourselves to the free and civilized world, we can discern two basic kinds of chief executive: a constitutional executive like the American president, who draws his powers from a formal document, and a party executive like the British prime minister, who derives power from an informal source, a political party. The American executive, having powers formally stated in the Constitution, does not rely on strict party discipline in the legislature when he exercises his authority. But he does need, it would seem, the help of some general understanding favoring strong executive power to resist legislative usurpation and its partner, overbearing bureaucracy. He needs a doctrine, a "literary theory," to protect himself against the partisan application by the legislature of the dictionary definition of executive, which would reduce him to its instrument.

In such a case, necessity might recommend an executive capable of strong action, but necessity teaches only those compelled to recognize it, and recognition often comes too late. Moreover, necessity cannot teach successfully if the required actions leave a bad conscience in the strong executive and rebellion in those who acquiesced. Even the constitution would not be enough to defend the executive if no public argument existed to inform the citizenry why the executive should have access to extraordinary powers that are not strictly executive in the instrumental sense. The American president, for one, is not sufficiently fortified by his constitutional powers, because in practice they might be denied to him. The ambivalence of executive power compels every president to defend himself by claiming the powers that are formally his. For this the president must have something convincing to say. He needs a doctrine, a justification, such as Hamilton's argument in *The Federalist* 70–77, to show why a strong executive is compatible with republican government. The institutions of the constitution must be filled out and backed up by constitutional speech. And the party executive, the beneficiary more of party discipline than of formal constitutional powers, needs the same protection from party dictation that the constitutional executive needs from legislative usurpation. Here even the legislature is sustained against party dictation by the reasoning that justifies the strong executive. For while legislative independence is greatly restricted by party discipline, it can be sustained by the responsibility to call the strong executive to account, a responsibility that cuts across party lines; parties functioning as such cannot by themselves curb the executive as effectively.

If a doctrine is needed to explain and support the ambivalence of executive power, what might it be? What advantages are expected from an office that expands and contracts, that alternately reveals and hides itself? A general hypothesis may now be suggested. From the superficial observation with which we began, that everyone agrees on the necessity of a strong executive, it seems evident that the executive cannot merely "execute" in the dictionary sense. Yet if he must therefore acquire and exercise a "personal power,"[43] the danger of tyranny becomes equally obvious. Why the executive cannot merely "execute" in the formal sense should now be clearly stated, so that the necessary risk of tyranny may be fairly estimated.

An executive could execute the law dutifully and faithfully, without an insubordinate exercise of his own power, if the law were reasonable; that is, if it could make all necessary distinctions among individual cases, and if its provisions did not omit anything that might make its intention impossible. For a reasonable law must first be exact, and then self-sufficient or perfect. But in fact a law can be neither. It cannot be exact because it is addressed to human beings, who are recalcitrant to reason. And their recalcitrance, though by no means simply deplorable, takes the form of a stubborn insistence that no matter how reasonable the law or how wise the lawgiver, I want to be able to say "no." The right to say "no" is exercised often enough to prevent anyone from believing that the very human insistence on it is abstract or whimsical, no matter how abstract or whimsical any particular "no" may be. This insistence is responsible for the need to punish those who offend against the law. Both the need to say "no" and the need to punish compel the legislator to forfeit exactness in making the law. In seeking consent for the law he must make it conform to what most men like, which is to some extent different from what is good for them; and in punishing offenders, he must make the punishments seem reasonable to most men, which is to some extent different from what is reasonable. For consent, he must define privileges according to what men like; and for punishment, he must define offenses according to what men will accept. Both needs, therefore, compel the legislator to move from exactness toward generality, with either a welcome to the undeserving claimant or a denial to the deserving exception. Even the best law is always too general to be reasonable because it must in some way or another defer to the human naysayer.

Naysaying stems from the brute fact that every human being has a separate body that constitutes his unshareable self-interest. Someone else may be wiser than you, but since he cannot care for your body to the extent you can, and also must look out for his own, the suspicion always arises that his wisdom is not applicable to your good, and hence your insistence on a right to veto him. The naysayer regards the generality of law as usually offering more useful protection than does the exactness of wisdom, and the legislator accepts the naysayer's suspicion as prudence, or rather he transforms it into prudence.

The separateness of human bodies, which makes the law inexact, also shows us the law's imperfection. For it would not matter that human bodies are separate if they were not mortal. Only the imminent return to ashes and dust makes us aware that we are not only surrounded by alien matter but actually encased in it. This material fact causes us to fear, and to regard the law's provisions for us—which to our vision extend only from cradle to grave—as quite inadequate. For the law to lay claim on our obedience because it takes care of us may seem nothing but human boasting,[44] and so we are disposed to disobey when it seems necessary.

That the law cannot control nature is the fundamental cause of its injustice and of its inability to remove fear. Because of its generality, law becomes injustice when measured against exactness, and is received as justice only if measured against outright favoritism. Since injustice and fear necessarily accompany law, law can be executed only by means of injustice and fear—the injustice that institutes executive pride and majesty, and the fear that overcomes our recalcitrance. It must be said, then, that since some taint of tyranny necessarily accompanies law, law can only be executed tyrannically: for injustice and fear are the bases of tyranny.

We can either recoil in shock from this extreme conclusion, or respond with amusement, contemplating, for instance, the necessary tyranny of William Howard Taft. For the American executive and some others, the power to punish (originally regarded as an executive power even in the weak sense) has been removed and given over in good part to an independent judiciary. There the tyranny of punishment is effectually concealed as "judgment not will" by judges who are checked by a jury, so that punishment seems to come from one's peers.[45] And though it might be urged that naysaying to reasonable law is not reasonable, it is not unreasonable to respond that men cannot help being unreasonable. The same is true for the generality of the law and the fearsomeness of the executive. But this argument does not impugn the conclusion. It only gives us reason's reason for coming to terms with unreason, whose human name is tyranny.

It is important to recognize that reason must come to terms with tyranny because there is more than one way to do it. Two ways have been found by which political science, being unable to escape tyranny, attempts to tame and use it. The first is the Aristotelian way, in which the political scientist takes the place of the tyrant and, to the extent that he can, transforms the tyrant from the destroyer of law into a king, the guardian of law. The Aristotelian performs the task as unobtrusively as he can, without making a public office of his responsibility and without openly proclaiming the inadequacy of the law. The second remedy was first proposed by Machiavelli, though it was substantially modified by the time the American founders made use of the discovery. This is to recognize openly the necessity of tyranny in the character of the prince, who initiates and innovates, even while he seeks democratic sanction for his actions so that he may seem merely to execute the people's will. Later, chiefly by the thinking of John Locke, the Machiavellian prince was regularized as an office, called the executive, and juxtaposed to the legislative power in a constitutional framework, in the ambivalent form we recognize: now subordinate, now independent. In the deliberate design of this ambivalence may be found the modern doctrine of executive power.

The scholars we have examined look either to the weak or to the strong executive as the essential executive. They do not perceive the ambivalence of executive power because they do not see it as a piece, and they fail to do so because executive power appears to them as a given necessity, not as a choice. Living with executive power and seeing it everywhere, they take it for granted and vainly attempt either to formalize it or to personalize it when both are required. They do not see executive power as a remedy for human recalcitrance, chosen to replace another remedy, because its success has completely obscured the problem, and with it the possibility of choice.

Some who witnessed the Watergate scandal in America think "cover-up" when they hear "executive power." And they are not wrong to think so because cover-up is indeed in the nature of executive power. In operation, executive power covers up because the successful executive does his best to represent his choices as necessities unwillingly imposed on him. He did not *choose* to get in your way, and therefore he is not responsible for harming or offending you. But if we are fully to understand executive power, we must see it as a whole; and to do that we must try to imagine how government would be if there were no executive power. Thus we can begin to see executive power as a choice, embodied in a doctrine. Fortunately, our task does not require any hypothesis contrary to fact. And imagining government without executive power is made easier by the existence of Aristotle's *Politics,* from which the executive is almost absent.

I

The Prehistory
of Executive Power

2

Aristotle: The Executive
as Kingship

The prehistory of executive power begins with Aristotle, and after Chapter 5 we shall see, I hope, that with him that phase was essentially completed. But what does it mean to say that executive power has a prehistory? After all, if executive power was invented, it was not an invention like the compass which represented an unequivocal advance over far less adequate instruments. Political thought prior to the invention of executive power does not manifest a primitive or unreflective understanding, and later opinion does not show a clear advance because, as we know, executive power obscures or covers up the problem it addresses. That problem is the human resistance to law and reason, the human insistence on choosing one's own way without reference to superior instruments like the compass.

Executive power has a prehistory consisting of a different mode of addressing that problem. But the problem itself was seen just as clearly or more clearly before the startling innovative appearance of executive power. To look at the prehistory of executive power, therefore, is much more instructive than studying the ignorant self-satisfaction or the half-conscious groping that may precede the engineering of a technical breakthrough.

Nothing about executive power should surprise us more than the fact that Aristotle has little or nothing to say on the subject. All modern governments keep or try to keep a strong executive, and all modern experts agree that a strong executive is more or less necessary, disagreeing only on the more or less. One could not make the point more forcefully than did Alexander Hamilton, at a time when it was still necessary to insist that "Energy in the executive is a leading character in the definition of good government'' (*Federalist* 70). In this and other Federalist Papers devoted to the proposed American presidency, Hamilton did not stop to explain why this was so, but applied himself instead to proving that an energetic executive was consistent with the genius of republican government.

But in Aristotle's *Politics* the reader is not asked to endorse a particular constitution and is presumed to have both the leisure and the inclination to investigate conventional assumptions. Comprehensive in character, the *Politics* aims at no less than the ''definition of good government.'' No general defect in the author's attentiveness has been found, and no specific defect, such as Aristotle's supposed blindness to the evil of slavery, can be alleged here. Yet nowhere in the book does Aristotle even suggest that energy in the executive is a leading characteristic of good government. In fact, his book contains only one passage that directly addresses executive power.

In Book IV of the *Politics* Aristotle gives his famous treatment of the mixed regime and the parts of regimes. The latter discussion is rightly taken to be his contribution to the modern doctrine of separation of powers. But of the three parts of regimes, the one corresponding to the modern executive—the ''offices''—does not refer to an executive office (*Politics* 1297b–1301a15). The executive is mentioned only in a second, less conspicuous discussion of offices in Book VI, where Aristotle adds the powers he had omitted earlier and distinguishes between necessary and noble offices. Among the necessary offices, almost the most necessary and most difficult, he says, is the one that carries out punishments and guards prisoners. It is difficult because it brings odium rather than respect, but it is necessary because judgments are useless if they are not carried out (1321b2–1323a11). Aristotle's only advice is to divide up the job so that no one person takes all the discredit.

That is all Aristotle says about executive power. Although I shall interpret this passage in due course for what it may imply, one's dominant impression remains that executive power in the modern, expanded sense is missing from Aristotle's *Politics*. He seems to have in mind strong-armed functionaries of the lowest rank—not energetic executives eagerly promoting their initiatives, but toughs fit and ready for subduing resisting criminals. One thinks of bailiffs, fine collectors, prison guards, and executioners. And to confirm that impression of an absent executive, Aristotle's advice to spread the odium of executing (so basely understood) goes directly contrary to the modern imperative, first proclaimed by Machiavelli, that all executive power be gathered in one person.

If we let ourselves be surprised at Aristotle's neglect, and do not try to suppress it with a sophisticated excuse, we shall be led to look for the reasons why Aristotle chose not to speak to executive power. When these reasons have been found to involve the fundamentals of Aristotelian political science, we shall be ready to appreciate the first appearance of executive power, and our surprise at Aristotle's neglect will have prepared us to be properly shocked at Machiavelli's ingenious but devilish invention.

The whole story of executive power depends on understanding why it is absent in Aristotle. The history of executive power depends on its prehistory, and we must consult Aristotle at length, paradoxically because he devotes so little space to it. Such elaborate courtesy will not be extended to other thinkers who make little of executive power, on the supposition that they were influenced by Aristotle's reasons, or discovered them on their own. We turn to Aristotle in order to dispel the sense of inevitability about the modern executive and its attendant charisma. This inevitability may have been anticipated, for it is an important feature of the doctrine of executive power that the questions Aristotle raises be resolved, contained, or, as we have seen, covered up with an institution. But to understand the institution one must take it apart and reopen these old questions, to see not only how but why the institution was made.

All modern political science is reactive to Aristotle's, but in such fashion as to direct attention away from Aristotle. Machiavelli, Hobbes, Locke, and Montesquieu all oppose Aristotle without directly arguing with him. The result—not unintended, of course— is that although they were aware of Aristotle's presence and relevance, we, as the heirs of the great modern thinkers, have forgotten Aristotle. The political scientist today no longer has much more than a glimmering, if that, of the traditional alternative to modern political science in its various forms. For this inquiry especially today's political scientist lacks acquaintance with the essential Aristotelian conception of rule, which makes so perfect a contrast with "execution." I shall try to supply the defect, but the remedy cannot be quick or easy.

25

One could also look to Plato's *Laws* for the necessary background, since that dialogue raises questions found in Aristotle, and likewise avoids creating an executive.[1] Rather than seizing upon the criminality of mankind to justify a terrifying or at least impressive magistrate, the Athenian Stranger (the dialogue's principal interlocutor) begins his treatment of punitive legislation by deploring the shameful necessity for it.[2] And when he comes to the inevitable inexactness of law, it is not to recommend an executive to prescribe where law cannot. Rather, he invokes the unlikely possibility of some human being born so wise by nature and divine grace as not to need laws to rule over him, since knowledge is stronger than law and creates its own order. But in the absence of such wisdom, he concludes that we must settle for second best, namely, law and order, without suggesting an executive as a more likely, more effectual, and more legal remedy than the rule of wisdom.[3] In Plato's *Republic*, Socrates is shown developing the first, unlikely possibility of rule by an extraordinarily gifted human being, rather than conceiving government by an executive.

Another useful preliminary to our study is Xenophon's *Cyropaideia*, the first in the genre of Mirrors of Princes, which instruct by holding up to princes for comparison a picture of the best prince. *Cyropaideia's* most distinguished rival is Machiavelli's *The Prince*; Machiavelli seems to make Xenophon his favorite classical author in that work (*The Prince* 14, 16, 17). Xenophon presents Cyrus as nothing less than the man who has solved *the* political problem—the one we have discussed—of ruling human beings with their willing obedience (*Cyropaideia* I.1.1–6) Proving his capacity, Cyrus ruled not just one small community of his like, but many men, cities, and nations. And to acquire this remarkable empire, he used some Machiavellian tricks that we would recognize among the tools of executive power.[4] But at the end of his conquests he made himself king rather than executive, explaining to his friends upon that occasion that as king he could no longer be as close to them as he had been when a general (VII.5.46). A king necessarily pretends to be above other humans, and needs to have some of the inaccessibility of a god. As with Aristotle, Xenophon's political science culminates in the kingship of a man who is a god among men, and does not attempt to establish the contrary pretension permeating the modern executive of being "your humble Servant."

26

Yet with no disrespect to Plato and Xenophon, and to avoid unnecessary complication, we turn to Aristotle's *Politics*, a book that covers perhaps all of the terrain in both the *Republic* and the *Laws*. The *Politics* is the foundation as well as the most imposing edifice of pre-modern political science. If it has been obscured because early modern thinkers chose to dismiss it rather than to argue with it, another later cause peculiar to us makes the *Politics* difficult to recover. This is the historicist tendency to regard the test as fixed in its own time, incapable of instructing us. Accompanying this tendency is a disbelief in the possibility that an author might intend to instruct those beyond his time as well as his contemporaries. Since, it is believed, his text has nothing to teach us, it is treated with disrespect and impatience. Aristotle's hesitations are misunderstood as inconsistency, his obscurities as ignorance, his repetitions as forgetfulness. His text, under such treatment, loses both surface and depth. The reader is not required to pay sufficient attention to surface detail, and thereby ignores superficial problems that would lead him to deeper ones. Indeed, the reader never sees that he is being led, that the text has movement and a rhetoric designed to teach him in stages. What Aristotle says on behalf of democracy in the middle of Book III of the *Politics* is no longer appropriate when he speaks for kingship at the end of Book III, or for the mixed regime in Book IV. To understand Aristotle's political science one must follow its presentation. One must read the *Politics* as a book—as a resource of learning—and not as a source of Greek opinion, most of which Aristotle disagreed with.

Our purpose here is to find out why executive power does not appear in Aristotle's political science. But even where his political science seems lacking, it deserves respect. There may be good reason for the lack, as opposed to the mere excuse that Aristotle could not have anticipated our problems. Perhaps he had a better idea. Let us suppose that he did. (All other presuppositions, especially the historicist one, take the opposite point of view, relying on the arbitrary assumption that Aristotle simply could not have known better.)

A weaker version of our hypothesis that Aristotle knew better is that he had a coherent viewpoint necessary to consider. Perhaps this less demanding presupposition will suffice at the start. At any rate, the two passages most relevant to the executive, in Books IV and VI of the *Politics,* will bear a greater weight of detailed analysis and concentrated speculation than most scholars today would suppose, and more than is consistent with the widespread belief that Aristotle's *Politics* is a hodge-podge of obscurities, repetitions, and inconsistencies.[5] The reader must suspend this belief and consider the text afresh with the hopeful hypothesis (which one must never fail to test) that the obstacles placed in his way are puzzles arranged for his instruction. I shall follow Aristotle's text because I do not know how to present his political science better than he. I do hope to have provided the reader a compelling motive to join the search for what Aristotle has to impart.

These two passages must be considered from a point of view wider than that of a political institution only. Having already spoken of human nature in its resistance to law (which makes the strong executive necessary), we shall find it necessary to speak of non-human nature. For a different attitude toward nature in Aristotle and Machiavelli is what separates the prehistory from the history of executive power. But let me introduce this necessity by returning to the problem of executive power as it appears in the scholarly literature, that is, the problem of the formal and the real. Why are the form and the reality of executive power at odds with each other? To answer the question, we need a better understanding of the formal—one might say, of the *reality* of the formal—than we get from our contemporary political science. Aristotle explains the importance of the formal in Book III of the *Politics*. His explanation leads to a defense of kingship at the end of that book, which in turn determines the course of his argument in Books IV and VI and the undeveloped state of the executive in the *Politics* specifically and in the tradition of Aristotelian political science generally.

The Status of the Formal in Politics

We have seen that our political science tries to understand executive power either as formal or as real. The formalists try to define it using impersonal roles or functions, the result being to show what executive power ought to be. The realists argue that a formalized picture of the office does not capture the actual personal essence of executive power, which cannot be divided into, or delimited by, functions defined from outside by persons not wielding such power. Despite the concessions each side makes to the other, executive power for the respective parties is essentially formal *or* real, not both. If it were both, they would have to question whether formal power is essentially opposed to real power. Aristotle argues that it is not.

Aristotle might even suggest that our contemporary political scientists rush too quickly to define directly the *nature* of executive power. They try to say too soon what it is, by which they mean how it operates, not how it is regarded. It would be better to tarry awhile with the common discourse on the subject instead of dismissing such talk as unscientific. What do people say about executive power? The first thing they say is that it is "executive." What does the word mean? Not a single political scientist whose work I know reflects upon the meaning of the word "executive." It is as if the idea were simply a given, with no interest in why it is called what it is. But as we have remarked, "executive" power is power wielded in someone else's name, not in one's own. The literal or dictionary meaning of "executive" is a subordinate or dependent power. Is this not a fact of some interest? Why do the elite in our society, in and out of government, refuse to rule in their own names? Why does no one say, "We are not merely executives, we rule"? We say, "The people rule." But the people do not say, "We rule." They elect a government that represents them or rules in their name, containing a legislature that does not rule because it merely passes laws, a judiciary that merely enforces laws, and an executive that merely carries them out.

The reason for not ruling in one's own name is that all exercise of power is thought to be unjust. Rule, when it is perceived to be rule, is perceived to be unjust; so no one wants to claim responsibility for it. This resistance to ruling and being ruled is more than the resistance to law and reason discussed earlier. Whereas that resistance lies in human nature, this resistance springs from a convention of modern politics whose origin we shall find in Machiavelli. The common use of "executive" today has its origin in bygone political science. But resistance to rule and resistance to law and reason have an identical consequence: the necessity of a strong executive to get around the problem. It is precisely the resistance to rule that makes necessary the strong exercise of rule.

The less legitimate it is, the more it must operate and manipulate to compensate for its lack. People then find that a strong executive gives them all the government they need or want; so they have no reason to reduce their hostility to rule and to revise their opinion that it is unjust. As the weak, formal executive maintains the strong, real one, so the latter maintains the former. Thus we have derived the mutual dependence of the formal and real executive—the ambivalence of the executive—merely from listening to what is said to name it.

The difficulty that emerged in our initial discussion remains, however: if executive power has to hide behind the claim that it is executing the will of someone else, why is it in fact so strong? It would seem that the strongest power in any society is the power that does not have to conceal itself behind the claim that it is merely executive. The strongest power is the one that can *say* it is the strongest and not be contradicted. This is the *formal* power, the power that can afford to appear as the strongest and most confident in public speeches, documents, and constitutions. Informal powers do exist, of course, but as long as they do not control the public forms of a society, it is because they are too weak to challenge the powers that do. What is said in private may often be more interesting, but what can and cannot be said in public is more important: the latter is the best indicator of who rules in a society. Public speech in its various forms and formalities expresses the claim to rule of those who are ruling.

But in modern democracies, as we have seen, no one claims to rule: not the people, not their government, not the executive. The claim to rule of those ruling in our democracies is precisely what is "covered up" by the modern doctrine of executive power, which is a claim *not* to rule—in fact, a disclaimer. This disclaimer is reflected in the very strength of the ruling term "executive": why do we not say "king"? By studying the nature of executive power directly, without consulting the public speech on the topic, we cannot explain the strength, or the continuing necessity of the formality by which we call a king an "executive." The definition of executive must include how it is *regarded* with how it *is*, the "ought" and the "is" together, the literary theory inseparable from the personal reality, the formal identical (or almost identical) to the real. Having followed this Aristotelian analysis of executive power, we are now ready to look at why Aristotle did not himself conceive a doctrine of executive power.

Aristotle discusses the formal in politics in Book III of his *Politics*,[6] not earlier, even though the status of the formal is the key to his understanding of politics. Earlier, in Books I and II, he attempts to explain politics without reference to the formal by talking about what is natural in politics, or by assuming that politics begins from what is natural (*Politics*, 1252a25, 1260b37). Both efforts resemble those of the political scientists today who try to understand the nature of executive power directly without considering opinion about it;[7] Aristotle's efforts can be described as constructive failures. The subject of Book I is who owns what, and the question is whether nature secures or preserves what human beings regard as their own; the answer appears to be that we do not know whether we are nature's property or nature is ours.[8] In Book II, the question is what things human beings hold in common; but by consulting nature we are unable to identify what is common to us as humans as opposed to what is common between us and non-human nature (1260b40, 1267b28). Thus the "teleological" understanding of nature, alleged to be Aristotle's by commentators who want to make things easy for themselves, leads in different directions or nowhere in particular, as we might suppose from the absence of "natural law" in the discussion. Instead of trying to unearth the natural substratum of politics, one must begin from the superficial fact that one *hears*, for in defining man as by nature a political animal, Aristotle cited as evidence our human power of speech (*logos*) (1253a2–19).

In politics one hears citizens defining the city (*polis*) by defining themselves in a regime (*politeia*). They themselves say what politics is when they establish their politics, for politics is always someone's or some group's particular politics. Accordingly, to attempt to understand politics directly from nature fails to grasp the element of choice and freedom by which we assert what we want or think fitting. This *what* of political speech is the *what* of politics, since it defines the citizen (*politēs*), who emerges only in politics, unlike the individual or family that may exist before or outside politics. One could never define the what of politics—what it is as a whole and what distinguishes it from other things—without the initiative of citizens who define it for themselves. In short, politics has a human beginning, and citizens are made, not born. They define their rule as producing or promoting the common benefit. The word "rule" (*archē*) also means "beginning," or together—a beginning, ruling "principle" directed toward an end.[9] But the end is made visible to the public in a certain order that Aristotle calls its form (*eidos,* 1276b2). We see politics in visible differences of institutions as they are publicly interpreted (for example, a Fourth of July parade on Main Street by contrast to the commemoration of the Bolshevik Revolution in Red Square). We see politics in the contentions where our principle of rule is asserted against another, and one whole made distinct against its adversary.

Much more could be said; and Aristotle says it in his characteristic manner, which makes it difficult to judge whether he is reporting, commenting, or speaking his own mind. But the crucial question, assuming politics is defined by the assertions of citizens, is how well these assertions stand up. Aristotle says that the city is defined ''above all''—that is, chiefly but not entirely—by its regime (1276b11). Its form is almost identical to its reality, because the form is the regime established by the rulers, and hence (if established successfully) unchallengeable in public.

Americans, for example, frequently reproach themselves for not living up to their professed ruling principle that all men are created equal. But they do live by that principle in the sense that no one can challenge it in public, and that they do not reproach themselves for failing to admit that some men are created unequal. The question, then, is whether it is possible to live by the Declaration of Independence, and whether it does indeed assert self-evident truths. Only if the formal regime states a truth, indeed the whole truth, can it capture the reality of politics. If it is false, or more likely, only partly true, then political behavior will always tend to escape from the imposition of political principle. For if it is not true that all men are created equal, how can we live by that principle? How indeed is it reasonable to try—except after comparing our principle with partially true principles of other regimes, and then accepting it with due scepticism?

When he says that the form of politics is ''above all'' the reality, Aristotle implies that political assertions are more than mere wants or wishes set forth with no regard to truth or reality: They are arguments about what politics requires, setting forth claims to be worthy of ruling or sharing in rule for good reason (1279a1–10, 1283a16–42). No one can be a ruler merely because he wants or need to rule. Rather his need must arise from some alleged competence, some positive contribution offered to the whole. His claim to speak the truth about politics must be assessed, since in that truth there will be, accidentally as it were, a place for his contribution and his rule. And to withstand the scrutiny of being assessed, such a claim to truth must address the *nature* of politics, which stands apart from assertions and preserves us from a mere relativism of regimes, each claiming a truth that cannot be established. It might seem that law is a refuge from relativism and a guarantor of impartiality, but law, as we shall see, is relative to the regime and thus reflects the relativism of regimes.

It if is not possible to establish the claim of a regime, then its rule would be tyranny—it would be a regime or non-regime that rules for the private benefit of the ruler and not for the common benefit. If no claim whatever can be established, then all politics is tyranny—and justifiably so, because inevitably so. For the claimed form of every regime would be in conflict with its reality. This, we have seen, is precisely the presumption behind executive power, that all rule being unjust, all rulers must seek to avoid the appearance and evade the responsibility of ruling. If there is no best regime according to nature, if no one is inclined toward it, then politics will always be an imposition and fraud: the weak executive will be necessary to conceal the rulers and the strong executive necessary to make the ruled obey. So, after two failed beginnings from nature in Books I and II and a new beginning from human speech in Book III, Aristotle brings his discourse back to nature and to the political philosophy—as distinguished from political claims—that is needed to discern nature and to judge by it (1275b26–30, 1282b23, 1287b38–40). To begin directly with nature leaves human freedom and choice out of account; but to fail to return to nature would leave freedom an arbitrary quirk and without a guide.

Does nature provide the support for political claims that lifts them above mere assertions? The political science of executive power, we shall see, states that no such support is possible or knowable. Hence it concludes that there will always be a conflict in principle between the assertions and the truth of politics, between the form and reality. Aristotle's conclusion on this fundamental point is not made easy to discern, but at the least it is obvious that he attempts to judge whether a best regime exists by nature, and then to assess the claims that regimes advance in politics against it. This attempt is contained in Aristotle's argument about kingship, the prearranged substitute designed to forestall executive power.

Kingship

The argument leading to kingship begins with the rival claims made by democrats and oligarchs, who both assert that their particular regime makes the city a whole. The contest between the many and the few appears to be the most obvious comprehensive choice in politics. Indeed, it is so comprehensive that men do not ordinarily have the opportunity to make the choice. Yet within cities they form parties dedicated to one or the other and live their lives, as it were, poised to make a decision should the opportunity arise. The democrats characteristically argue that the city is a whole. They say that the city must include all human beings, which it does most surely by allowing them to share in government. Furthermore, to include all human beings, one must define them by what each has in common with others, and this common denominator would seem to be the possession of a body. Democracy, in short, is the regime which does not leave any *body* out. But when the city has been defined visibly and altogether obviously as a whole of bodies, no boundary is left between human bodies and all bodies or indeed all body.[10] On the democratic principle that having body defines sharing in rule, not only everybody but *everything* is a ruler; and the city is a whole only if understood (in the manner of Spinoza) as a homogeneous part of the whole of nature. Such is the reach of the democratic claim.

When examined, however, these bygone democrats prove not to mean quite everybody. They wish to exclude aliens, slaves, children, and females, and do not know how in reason to reach the results dictated by convention. Democrats of our day, though appalled at the exclusion of slaves and females, would undoubtedly wish to exclude aliens and children, and would have the same difficulty in justifying themselves. The democratic discomfort is seized upon by the oligarchs and made the beginning of their argument.[11] Any exclusion from the governing "all" implies a distinction, and therefore a principle with which to make it: some notion of superiority or excellence, however bland and widespread. The oligarch, with his partisanship for the few and opposition to the many, is characteristically more receptive to the notion of excellence than the democrat, although he usually misunderstands excellence vulgarly as wealth. Some oligarchs at least may be taught to take excellence seriously, and to seek or at least appreciate the rarest and the best type or types of excellence; for to take excellence most seriously is to be prepared to make the most uncompromising and intolerant distinctions on its behalf.

Such reconstructed oligarchs would demand that the city not leave out any human excellence; indeed, they would demand that it devote itself to such excellence to the exclusion or depreciation of anybody not so gifted or accomplished. Oligarchy would be the regime of choice in which those who are most choiceworthy rule over the despised and the rejected. But again, the political principle reflects an understanding of nature. The excellence that distinguishes men from other men would also distinguish men from the rest of nature, if only in the power to choose and the opportunity for excellence. Thus an oligarchical view of politics implies an oligarchical view of nature in which the human good is distinct from and superior to the rest of nature, while democracy in politics implies that nature is also a democracy in which men are nothing special.

The oligarchs might point out that the democrats cannot explain themselves. Their view fails to take into account the very passion with which they enforce their opinion, for it is not merely a theoretical understanding but also a decree imposed sometimes with a tyrant's anger, in which nature is used to suppress the human excellence it cannot recognize, as if they were whisking off aristocratic heads (1281a17, 1284a26–38). Is not the tyrant's passion the most heated expression of democratic partisanship?— of a partisanship rooted in the recalcitrance that makes men say "no" in order to assert their individuality and support their freedom? The democratic principle of "having body" confronts the democratic fact that all have bodies, and confronts also the passionate defense of self which separateness inspires: the latter culminates in an insistence on the right to choose for oneself. So the deeds of democrats seem to belie their "natural" principle and to proclaim the special freedom of human beings from nature as they understand that freedom.

Yet the oligarchs have problems too. Arguing from the specialness of human beings, they are so preoccupied with distinction and division that they do not take sufficient thought for the whole—either of the city or of nature. This means the oligarchs do not sufficiently consider whether or how much the best men depend on the less-than-best, the few on the many, and human choice on natural necessity. They tend to assume that an assertion of choice is enough, and forget to measure their power and to determine whether they are supported or opposed by outside forces. Becoming arrogant and imperious, they set themselves up to be brought down. Just as the democrats cannot explain the freedom they claim for themselves, so the reconstructed oligarchs cannot explain their claimed excellence or virtue. They would have excellence as choice, so that they can take pride and honor in being few against the many. But the oligarchs forget the need for a standard for determining choice-worthiness. That standard is not chosen. So whatever they choose is not entirely their choice. It is their honor to compare themselves to whatever this principle might be honoring—in short, to something better than themselves—and submitting themselves to its rule. Failing to account for forces outside themselves, the men of choice neglect not only their baser but also their more honorable dependency. They need to understand the whole in which they are something special to be sure, but are not on top of things—rather, in the middle.

The whole is then the reconciliation of nature and man—of democracy, the principle of nature; and of oligarchy, the principle of humanity. In the wider implications of "democracy" and "oligarchy" we see that the city is a whole that reflects nature as a whole. We have seen that, Aristotle says, a city must be said to be the same above all with regard to its regime (1276b11–12), which he has likened to its "form," leaving the "race" (*genos*) analogous to matter. That is, a city is chiefly not the race or nation or matter out of which it has been formed, the democratic principle of body, but rather the chosen form, the oligarchical principle. Yet the regime is not above matter entirely, as the uncognizant oligarchs would presume to be, with their inhuman indifference or arrogance to the many beneath them. It is *in* the matter that it forms, shaping it to the extent that it can. Every regime has something of oligarchy and something of democracy in it, since the oligarchical and democratic principles cannot stand by themselves; but every regime, according to Aristotle—who joins in the promotion of human excellence—is a bit more of an oligarchy than a democracy. Even a democracy, when it is a chosen form, paradoxically owes more to the oligarchical principle than to the democratic.

Aristotle presents two difficulties in his notion of regime which further refine the controversy between democracy and oligarchy, and lead him to add a "kingship" to them as a necessary element to make the city a whole. First, from the standpoint of oligarchy he questions whether the virtue of the good man and the serious citizen is the same (1276b16–1277b33). If the good man is perfect, he would apparently be perfectly independent above or apart from the regime—apart from politics. He, or the knowledge he has, might then serve as the standard by which to judge the various regimes. But how can someone or something whose goodness is *above* politics serve as a judge *within* politics? Elevation might be achieved at the price of relevance—in particular, relevance to the freedom human beings insist on. Our recalcitrant naysaying to what nature prescribes for us, as if for nature's good, shows the specialness of human beings within nature and our doubt that nature's good is the same as the human good. The good man can learn to doubt in this very way from the serious citizen, who can show him the knowledge required for and derived from ruling free men. The serious citizen can show this to the good man when telling him that what he thinks is good may not be thought to be so by others (1277a15–16, 1277b8–9).

Yet the freedom men display as citizens cannot be taken for granted. Just as an "oligarchical" difficulty exists in the relation between natural goodness and human goodness, so there is a "democratic" difficulty in setting off free men from those whose menial tasks make them resemble slaves; or put another way, it is difficult to distinguish freedom from necessity. Are the "banausics" (menial laborers), who do not share in rule, to be counted as citizens (1277b33–1278b5)? If they are made citizens, they are citizens without having the virtue of citizens; if they are not, they are not granted the freedom and honor of a human being. Aristotle seizes the opportunity here to make the point that freedom exists for the sake of virtue; yet one cannot promote virtue among human beings without slighting the freedom of human beings within nature: the oligarchical specialness competes with, and in the end must take precedence over, the democratic specialness. Democrats may wonder about this,[12] and they may be right to object if the virtue preferred over freedom is the ordinary honor-loving of political men, well below the virtue of the good man.[13]

In practice, then, it might seem that democracy should be favored. It is the regime of the free, and freedom accrues to the common benefit of mankind.[14] Aristotle now calls the city self-sufficient, and says that the virtuous can contribute to it as can the wealthy (1280b35, 1281a1–9). So the regime of the many poor can become a multitude of free men, with those not poor contributing to make the city self-sufficient (1279a38, 1271b20–1280a7). This multitude might best be made sovereign in the city, since the respectable are few and too many others would be dishonored if only the respectable ruled (1281a29–35). After giving us reason to trust in a certain multitude, and perhaps reason to hope for an approximation of that multitude, Aristotle concludes that the multitude is justly sovereign in greater matters (1281b21, 1282a39). On second thought, however, he says that the laws when correctly laid down ought to be sovereign, while the ruler, whether one or more, should be sovereign where the laws cannot speak precisely because of the difficulty of making clear the whole for all things (1282b6).

We are thus suddenly confronted with a ruler that looks like an executive of laws that are said to be imprecise. But Aristotle does not here, in a context full of promise, develop a version of executive power. He insists, rather, that the laws are made by the ruler and hence relative to the regime. How, then, may we ask, could the laws be sovereign? Since some human multitudes are no better than multitudes of beasts (1281a37–8, 1281b18–22, 1282b8–14), how could the laws made by a bestial multitude restrain it? It appears that either the laws are too far removed from human passions to satisfy human choice and freedom, or the laws themselves are captives of the passions and reduce men to the level of multitudes of beasts.[15] In either alternative the specialness of men is not respected. Making the laws more precise is a task that requires making clear the whole in regard to all things, that is, the reconciliation between humanity and nature (1286a17–20). To execute a law that is a decree of nature or one that is a whim of human beastliness does not make the law more precise, but on the contrary makes it a sweeping edict that cannot discern human excellence. Using such obtuse imprecision, a meek surrender to nature and a mere assertion against nature become one and the same. Aristotle would therefore have objected to both the weak and the strong executive, and for the same reason. The weak executive publishing laws that enslave men is no weaker than the strong executive proclaiming decrees by which men degrade and enslave themselves; moreover, the strong executive is no less just outside such laws than the weak executive is within them. Thus, at this critical point when Aristotle might have developed a version of executive power, he embarks on the defense of kingship in order to make the laws speak precisely. His defense invokes the aid of political philosophy, the science or art which reconciles human goodness with nature's ends in the "benefit in common" (1282b14–23).

The political philosopher, whom we have seen before as the "serious citizen," investigates the claims men make that they themselves rule and that all others be ruled by them.[16] With the claim to rule other men, men must also claim to rule all other things, for we now recognize that even the democrats make a claim to rule nature when they assert their freedom and the specialness of human beings. But the political philosopher soon concludes that all the standards by which men claim to rule are incorrect, as each can be pressed to a subversive extreme (1283b27). The rule of the wealthy can be narrowed to that of the wealthiest one, for if wealth is the principle of rule, why should not the wealthiest one among them rule? Similarly, the rule of the free can be narrowed to that of the one best born, the rule of the virtuous men coming down to that of the most virtuous man. Even in a democracy, is there not good reason for all to admire the one best democrat among them—a Thomas Jefferson, or more likely, an Archie Bunker? Such is the dazzling paradox showing monarchy at the base of all politics. Accordingly, Aristotle adds, if the multitude should be sovereign because it is better than the few, and if one or several are better than the many, they rather than the multitude should be sovereign (1283b15–27). Thus Aristotle is led to say, that if one or more so exceed the rest in virtue, he or they cannot be counted a part of the city. Such a one would be like a god among human beings; and a law could not apply to such, for they themselves are a law (1284a3–14; cf. 1253a25–30).

This virtuous "one" is usually not specified as a man or a human being. He or it would be literally "monarchy," a single ruler or ruling principle which so exceeds the rest that it becomes a law. Such a monarchy is above the other regimes, or in a way above all regimes, because it carries the human claims to rule to non-human extremes. Aristotle confirms the inference by discussing next the practice of ostracism by which democrats rid themselves of outstanding men they hold dangerous; and he says that similar practices can be found in all regimes, including the correct ones, and in foreign policy as well as domestic (1284a18–

b18). We have remarked that the human resistance to being ruled is democratic in origin, but it extends to being ruled by *any* outstanding one, even including the outstanding representative of one's own claim to rule. Since the *archē* of the resistance of one's own body is body, one can restate the difficulty of making the city a whole as that of bringing together the two ruling principles or monarchies—body or nature, and human choice or virtue.

That Aristotle emphasizes "one or more" is a hint of his solution: the "one" becomes a law for men by being repeatable in the multitude of human beings. He develops his solution in a description of five kingships, which are then reduced to two, the Spartan kingship of a generalship for life and kingship over all (*pambasileia*). The former had been described as autocratic powers vested in a general, including in ancient times the power to kill when in the field. Aristotle said Homer attests to this power when he has Agamemnon enduring reproach in assemblies but threatening death to cowards on the battlefields.[17] Agamemnon's threats remind us of the ambivalent executive of imprecise law that we have imagined, executing nature's decree that cowards must die. Or, since cowards do not die automatically as people die of starvation, is he a strong executive enforcing a man-made distinction to which nature is indifferent?

Aristotle remarks now that such a generalship can exist in all regimes, again as if it could be developed into an executive, and he seems to promise later treatment (perhaps the passage in Book VI that we shall examine); but he dismisses it for the present as having the aspect of the laws rather than the regime (1286a3, 1287a3–9). The laws can be made a whole only through the regime of "kingship over all," in which the regime above regimes is made a regime, and Aristotle launches an inquiry into whether it is better to be ruled by the best man or by the best laws.

To those who hold that being under kingship (not "kingship over all") is advantageous, it seems that the laws articulate only the whole and cannot address particular events that may occur. They liken laws to the written rules of an art which an artisan might publish; but his art would be superior to them and the artisan himself might well disobey them.[18] Against this, it might be said that those ruling ought to possess "the speech of the whole," for in departing from what is written they may be influenced by their passions. What does not have the passionate element (*to pathetikon*) is better on the whole than something to which it is naturally bound; and while the law lacks this element, every human soul necessarily has it.[19]

It now becomes clear that in discussing kingship, Aristotle is talking about the soul. Laws issue from the rational part of the soul, and they are opposed by the passionate part or by anger. Clearly there ought to be laws, but where the law cannot judge either on the whole or well, should the best one rule or should all rule? Aristotle offers "the multitude" as a corrective for the individual's angry misjudging, but again the multitude is specified as that of the free, or rather that of good men and good citizens. The latter will be as "serious" in soul as the superior (virtuous) one. This multitude, unlike the one previously discussed which Aristotle said was justly sovereign, is joined through the soul.[20] The soul is the regime in which the city becomes a whole.

Then three practical objections to kingship are offered: kingship is obsolete now that large democracies have come into existence; kingship suffers from the problem of succession; and kingship needs a dangerous degree of power to sustain the law. This last might have been an executive power, but Aristotle prescribes that it be the king's, and that it be less than the power of the multitude (1286b27–41). The king must be reconciled to the multitude in some way other than by serving as its executive. That is why Aristotle now says that the argument has arrived at the king who does all things according to his will, the so-called "kingship over all." For this is the kingship "according to which the king rules all things according to his own will."[21] Aristotle says that he rules "all things," not "all men" or "all citizens," because he wishes to maintain that kingship is according to nature and is therefore the reconciliation of nature and humanity we have been seeking.[22]

Now it seems to some that Aristotle's reconciliation is contrary to nature, since he makes one man sovereign over all citizens when the city consists of similar men. Similar men are equal because they are similar in claiming honors; they are similar not so much in appetite (*epithumia*), which makes some men behave like beasts, as in spirit (*thumos*), the resistant naysaying of self-defense which distorts the rule of even the best men. Aristotle makes three statements about law here which qualify his earlier statement that the law does not possess the passionate element. He says that for equals to govern and to be governed in turn is law, for order is law (1287a17–19); that is, the order law effects is the form and body of the spirit of self-defense in the soul. Law does not possess this part of the passionate element but it does reflect it. And after saying that *thumos* distorts the rule of even the best men, Aristotle concludes that law is intelligence without desire (*orexis*).[23] Men believe they are unable to judge truly in their own cases, and in seeking justice they seek the middle ground, which law is.

Thus, despite being intelligence without desire, law is not the best but the middle. Law abstracts from the desire of the best man in order to protect men from the distortion caused by his *thumos*, let alone that of others. But in this very abstraction it reflects the distortion it combats: to prevent the partiality of one, the law adopts the general, ostracizing envy of the many, and creates impartiality out of inferior vanities. Law so conceived and directed against the best reminds us of the modern law originating in Hobbes, a law fundamentally democratic because it is established to preserve each person's self, and all equally. Aristotle does not share Hobbes's unconcern for the best man, yet he does not balk at this seeming injustice to him. His argument shows that the best man would himself adopt the law as it is, desiring or willing its stolid mediocrity for the sake of self-protection in common with all other men.

Moreover, in adopting the law for himself despite the apparent claim that his superior nature would seem to give him, the best man adopts it on nature's behalf, as it were. He accepts nature's gift of *thumos* to all men, and he also accepts its consequences; he wills human willfulness. This willing and intelligent adoption of nature's ends is the meaning of Aristotle's rather grandiose title, "kingship over all." The best man does all things according to his will because he wills the "according to which" by which he rules all things; that is, he wills nature's kingship as his own. Thus his will is neither arbitrary nor unfree. Neither his kingship nor the restriction of his kingship is contrary to nature, even though the kingship is over similar and equal men and the restriction is of the best. One can neither simply reject the claim of the best man, nor simply accede to it.

Aristotle obviously does not deny the possibility of tyranny, but he denies that the tyrant's skill is according to nature (1287b40). When the tyrant chooses tyranny, he does so on his own responsibility and cannot claim to be acting in accordance with nature; for tyranny is contrary to our *thumos*, our natural resistance to tyranny. Still less can he claim to be executing nature's decree, like a weak executive who adds nothing of his own, or like a strong one who needs to impose his will on nature. Those who resist tyranny, however, cannot justify their resistance without reference to that resistance in the best man. His *thumos*, hence that of all other men, is ennobled by its connection to the best in men, and at the same time that best is humanized by its connection to what is common to the human soul. The best man, then, chooses according to nature as if nature were his own will. He also chooses as if human choice, especially past human choices bound up in custom, were nature's (1287b5–8). This assumption of nature, law, and custom, which is part deference, part presumption, is what it means for men to *rule:* they make themselves the beginning principle (*archē*) of themselves and of things. This is the very opposite of the notion of executive power, in which the ruler presents himself as an agent of some other power (human or not), or as one who is forced into action by brute necessity. We see the distinction in the very words used: in Greek to rule means to begin; but to execute, from the Latin *exsequor,* means to "follow out" what has been begun by someone else.

My account would not be complete, even as a schematic summary, if we did not take note of the "as if's" which Aristotle's argument and his hesitant expressions seem to require.[24] Near the end of Book III he says it is almost the same education and habits that make one a serious man and one skilled as a citizen and king (1288b1). The man who is serious about his humanity and the responsible (and therefore kingly!) citizen cannot be equated, even if they could be reconciled in the single virtue of the good man which "we assert" to be complete. His virtue must be asserted as complete because it is neither clear nor proven that nature can be adopted by the citizen-king without harm to the specialness of humanity. The job of the serious man is to find out whether it can be. While trying to determine whether men's assertions about their humanity are true, the serious man does not rule so much as he judges (1287b24). The difference between judging and ruling (of which more later) suggests diverse education and habits which might be developed into the distinction between intellectual and moral virtue that Aristotle makes in another work, the *Nicomachean Ethics* (1103a14–18). And however this may be, we should take note that Aristotle does not speak of a philosopher king. With Plato, Aristotle thinks that the best regime is the kingship of the best men and that political science is essentially the study of this regime, but Aristotle proceeds differently. Rather than founding a best regime on paper, as it were, and awaiting the coincidence of philosopher and king (*Republic* 473d), Aristotle, like the serious man, adopts the material given him for examination. He turns to a discussion of actual regimes and of how they may be improved without being ruled directly by a philosopher.

3

Aristotle:
The Absent Executive
in the Mixed Regime

How to improve an actual regime is Aristotle's working political science. What we have examined in Book III of the *Politics*
might be called his critical political science, because the "kingship
over all" he presents there is not intended as a practical proposal.
That kingship is developed out of actual regimes by refining the
claims such regimes set forth to justify themselves. Aristotle, the
political philosopher, descends into politics himself to argue with
political actors. He points out to them that their justifications imply the possibility of one man who would have in the highest
degree all the qualities the regime claims to promote. Why should
he not be king? But if he is, how can the regime survive? Obviously, the rule of the most oligarchical or the most democratic
man would be fatal to oligarchy or democracy.

It is apparent, then, that the politics of actual regimes generates
claims that cannot be satisfied. Or if there is satisfaction, it is in
understanding rather than participating in politics. Although Aristotle defines man as a political animal by nature, he does not
promise him fulfillment of his nature. Other animals, non-political because they lack the power of speech, can live contentedly
and accomplish their natural ends; but man talks himself into
problems, especially the problem of the whole. Man wants to ab-
solutize his particular concerns and to live by a principle or a rule
(*archē*): this is what it means to be a political animal. But the principle, when it is developed into kingship over all, becomes self-
critical. Aristotle's entry into politics demonstrates to rulers and

45

citizens that they cannot have what they want from politics. For to live by the principle they advance, they would have to make him king.

Nonetheless, the king is not content to mock the impossible desires of his fellow human beings. Aristotle has something constructive to say in Books IV–VI of the *Politics*, not only out of philanthropy but also for the sake of his own understanding. While improving actual regimes, the political philosopher learns about human resistance to reform and how to overcome it. After the critique of all actual regimes against the utopian standard of kingship, he discovers an encouragement to virtue in the practical construction of a mixed regime. By thinking to the extreme of kingship, political men learn not to attempt too much; and by practicing compromise, they find out that they should not despise what is practicable.

Aristotle's working political science in Books IV–VI is preceded by his remark at the end of Book III that we must now attempt to speak of the best regime, how it naturally comes into being and how it subsists, and that it is necessary to make the appropriate inquiry about the best regime. These last words are repeated at the beginning of Book VII, which (with Book VIII) is expressly concerned with the best regime, while Books IV–VI do not consider the issue expressly. Commentators have thus been led to conclude that Books IV–VI are an interpolation not intended by Aristotle. But it is safer to assume that he means what he says, and so to suppose that Books IV–VI tell how the best regime naturally comes into being, as Books VII and VIII tell how it subsists.

The Coming-into-Being of the Best Regime

The best regime naturally comes into being through the material that nature provides, which is human bodies ordered in actual regimes. It is fitting, then, that Aristotle should compare the political scientist with the gymnastic coach at the beginning of Book IV (1288b18). The coach works with men's bodies as they are, and he improves them by training, not by ruling. The training of men by a coach of political science to correct existing regimes is no less difficult a task than founding a regime from the beginning, just as (Aristotle goes on to say), relearning is no less difficult than learning from the beginning (1289a3–5). The practical task of improving politics to be undertaken in Books IV–VI is equivalent to the theoretical examination left implicit from Book III, whether nature allows men to rule in kingship. It must now be shown that the "whole race" of men is capable of kingship (1288a16, 35), an examination and a task in which the improving of men as they are is carried on together with the discovery of what they can be. Aristotle does not claim that what is practicable here and now is the best: that is the mistake of the ordinary political partisan. But he also seems to avoid the philosopher's mistake of despising what is practicable, because that mistake arises from or leads to irresponsibility in both citizenship and science. So while not confusing the practicable and the best, he studies them together in the realm of the practicable (1288b22–40), correcting the partisan's mistake more openly than the philosopher's.

Aristotle's discussion of actual regimes in Book IV concludes with an analysis of the three parts to be found in all regimes which the serious legislator must observe. Aristotle indicates that the three parts must be considered separately as well as in common, and since his three parts, the deliberative body, the magistracies, and the judiciary, resemble the modern legislative, executive, and judicial branches, his analysis has been reasonably taken for an early, if not founding, statement in the history of the doctrine of separation of powers.[1] Yet two things in it must strike us as peculiar. The magistracies are discussed in the plural without reference to the need for unity in one man that modern theories of the executive assert, or to the monarch out of which the modern executive developed historically. It might be thought, to excuse Aristotle's neglect of monarchy, that his imagination was bounded by the Greek city-state, which had no monarch. But then he has just discussed in Book III a particularly aggravated kingship, and he was quite familiar with barbarian monarchies, speaking of them often elsewhere.

We also need to explain the strange formality of his analysis which concentrates on the manner of composing the three parts, especially whether by choice or by lot, and on the order of forms and modes to be followed. Indeed, Aristotle seems to be carried here by theoretical enthusiasm away from his task of examining actual regimes, not so much to the best regime, as to all possible regimes. In any case, the extreme democratic procedure of composing bodies of government by lot seems unduly prominent, even given Greek or Athenian experience. Aristotle is more interested in the formal ordering of the parts than in their actual powers, and he puts off discussing the powers of the magistracies to Book VI, for reasons we must seek to understand. The magistracies as they appear in Book IV only correspond to our executive, and are not identical with it, because they are not said to have the power or duty of executing the law even though the deliberative body seems to be concerned chiefly with legislation.

Both peculiarities can be seen to arise from the attention paid to the human body in Book IV, which is forecast in the earlier comparison of the political scientist with the gymnastic trainer. In the middle of the book is a very brief consideration of tyranny in which Aristotle mentions three forms of tyranny, the third form thought to be especially tyrannical and the "counterpart" of the kingship over all discussed in Book III. It is the counterpart because the third form shows us the resistance to that kingship or indeed to any intimation of it. No free man, Aristotle says, willingly tolerates a monarchy that rules, without being held to account, over similars and betters for its own benefit, not for that of the ruled (1295a18–22). These two criteria—irresponsible rule and rule not to the benefit of the ruled—do not necessarily coincide. We can see this difference if we consider *inferiors* rather than similars and betters. What is irresponsible rule over inferiors for *their* benefit? The answer implied is that for free men, this also is tyranny because they will not tolerate irresponsible rule however beneficial.[2] Free men will insist that their rulers rule accountably as well as for the benefit of the ruled, and when these two criteria diverge, free men will demand accountable rule even against their own interest.

The same human recalcitrance in self-defense which we have seen in the generation of executive power, and in the argument between oligarchy and democracy, necessarily understands itself as freedom and the contrary as tyranny. Thereby it admits that tyranny can be to one's benefit. Tyranny would then be the counterpart to kingship over all, with the difference that the king, unlike the tyrant, willingly adopts the freedom of his subjects. But can he do so, if free men reject kingship for their benefit as tyranny? The rejection of rule by one's betters for one's own benefit is a claim to rule oneself regardless of benefit, hence a claim to rule others, including one's betters. For in capacity to will, one's betters are one's equals, and no claim to rule oneself can resist extension to others like oneself. The free man's claim to reject as he wills amount to the tyrant's claim to rule as he wills. Hence all regimes share in tyranny when they take account of willingness without regard to benefit—as actual regimes must, precisely when they attempt to take account of freedom.

The "certain share" of tyranny in regimes (which Aristotle remarks upon casually)[3] may thus be traced to the need to consult men's willingness when governing them,[4] to their recalcitrant insistence on being consulted, to their resistant nature, and ultimately to the resistance of nature itself. Nature is more ornery than the most ornery of men. As mere resistance, the human desire for freedom from nature leads back to the very tyranny of non-human nature which it resists, a connection which reminds us of the kinship in politics of democracy and tyranny (1292a18). Only human excellence can rescue human freedom from the willfulness which disguises the submission of freedom to lower nature, but this excellence seems especially to be tyrannical (1295a19). Excellence looks like willfulness to willful men, as they attribute the principle of their own conduct to the government of nature. They run from the appearance of tyranny to the reality. Tyranny in the brief discussion of Book IV recalls the Spartan King of Book III,[5] the general for life who could exist in all regimes (1286a4) as the element of resistance we have been considering. It would be the strength of this "kingship" that calls into question the kingship over all to which the third tyranny is here said to correspond. If kingship over all requires a willing adoption of nature, as we supposed, it must be recognized that adopting bodily nature is adopting that which resists and rejects adoption.

The Mixed Regime

Aristotle's solution to the difficulty is the mixed regime, which he makes the theme of Book IV. The mixed regime consists of democracy and oligarchy, or of natural necessity and human choice (1291a7–10, 24–28), or, as we shall see, of lot and choice. For the democratic principle of lot stands for what is given, or rather imposed, by purposeless nature. What comes to us by lot appears to take no account of what we would choose; so the opposition of choice to lot is the view of nature looking at things from the battlefront of human recalcitrance. Through the notion of the mixed regime Aristotle teaches uninstructed recalcitrants that some things are outside our choice and must be accepted, indeed that there is some advantage in accepting them.[6] Here he does not attempt to argue directly that nature gives us more than our lot or fate or (as we would say) our environment; he does not now speak of nature's ruling principle or of its end. He avoids the question of the whole (1296a5–6). Aristotle keeps his discussion at the level of democracy and oligarchy and does not introduce kingship, for kingship, even or especially of the best, looks like tyranny to men who regard excellence as an unfair portion of the lot distributed by purposeless, willful nature.[7]

The mix of democracy and oligarchy and of choice and lot is shown, then, in a visible order—an order of bodies or of parts of the city or of governmental "organs" and "bodies"—rather than in an invisible whole that must be conceived in thought. This visible order reveals the character of the mix—how much of each—in its form, enabling democrats and oligarchs to see and appreciate what is their own and what must be conceded to the other party (1294b13–18; 35–37). Thereby they receive an intimation of the reason why the mixed regime is beneficial, and are given a gentle push in the direction that reasoning would take them.

Aristotle uses the formality of order to represent its intelligibility. When he likens the parts of the city to the parts of an animal near the beginning of Book IV (1290b25), he implies that nature's forms indicate its intelligibility too, and that human purposefulness in the making and mixing of forms is supported by nature's intelligibility. Since formality is the visible outer appearance of rationality, we are not surprised to see that the formality of mixing culminates in the discussion of the three parts of regimes at the end of Book IV. For the three parts of regimes are also three functions of the rational soul: deliberating, ruling,[8] and judging. From the analogy between city and animal, which implies many distinct cities with unmixable regimes (you never see the smile of a fox on the face of an ox), there is a movement in Aristotle's argument to the presentation of interchangeable parts at the end of Book IV, some of them mixed to create fantastic regimes.

By the ordering of bodies we are introduced to soul, an acquaintance not merely for philosophers, because it is only through soul that can we understand how reform in politics is possible. There must be something in men that enables them to change their way of life and overcome the lot which, in the case of other animals, decrees their fate. As Aristotle shows that bodily forms imply the existence of the rational soul, the soul so revealed is nonetheless the bodily part of the soul. It is the part Plato called *thumos* (as distinct from appetite or eros), which is occupied with the spirited defense of one's body rather than being devoted to something outside oneself. But, as we have seen in the consideration of tyranny, human recalcitrance can be so ornery that it acts against a man's own interest merely for the sake of preserving his willfulness. But his very willfulness, then, illustrates his freedom from self-interest. Even at their most irrational, human beings show the capacity for detachment that is required for rationality and, in politics, for reform. From Aristotle's presentation it would seem that the very basis of reform is to be found in human stubbornness.

Again we watch Aristotle passing up an opportunity to develop executive power. He does not enlarge upon the tyrant's share of regimes to establish a fund of arbitrariness with which to govern willful men. Nor does Aristotle construct a disguise of legality under which the executive would innocently transmit nature's arbitrary decrees to foolish men. He holds to his statement in Book III that the tyrannical skill is not according to nature but he gives effect to his judgment otherwise than through a kingship ruling over all. We have seen the political scientist appearing as a gym coach training human bodies; and later, when explaining the middle class between the rich and the poor, Aristotle speaks of a trusted arbitrator who mixes and as it were replaces the middle class, whose best virtue is mediocrity (1296a6–7). This arbitrator, we soon see, practices ''sophisms'' in order to make his mixes. He is not so truthful as the gym coach perhaps because he cannot speak so candidly of the charge's unsuitable desires (1288b17–19; 1297a15, 35). But even with his sophisms he mixes democracy and oligarchy, and thus reasons to the factions he arbitrates, as much as he can, through the significance to be found in the ordering of regimes.

The Parts of Regimes

We come now to a closer look at the passage at the end of Book IV on the parts of regimes.[9] Speaking of these, Aristotle makes the parts correspond to whole regimes. The first part is ''the de-

◆

liberative about common things,'' and since deliberation leads to choice and choice is selective, the deliberative part has the tendency of oligarchy. The third part is what does the judging (*to dikazon*), for which Aristotle used the verb for the judging of democratic assemblies; and as this judging is a calling to account before the many, it is democratic. It also recalls the necessity of confronting human choice with bodily nature. The second part is ''that regarding the offices,'' not deliberating or judging, or any other activity; and the offices or ''rules'' (*archai*) are plural. We have noted that monarchy does not appear as a part and these *archai* may be referred to the ''polity'' that Aristotle has set forth in Book IV as the mixed regime. The oligarchic and democratic functions are separated by the offices rather than united by the single office of a monarch as in Book III, for in ''polity,'' the particular regime whose name stands for the class of regimes, one can move or reform in any direction toward any of the other regimes, especially toward either democracy or oligarchy, not just toward monarchy. Polity is the regime of the ''hoplites,'' heavily-armed infantrymen (1297b23–25). When such a class rules, they may constitute a regime or they may be willing to defend any regime; similarly, ''polity'' is conceivable not only as a particular regime but also as that which enables all regimes to rule and thus to be regimes.

When the two typical regimes (oligarchy and democracy) and the generic regime (polity) are seen as parts of all regimes, one can recognize that the three parts together form the soul of all regimes. They are found in common or together in each regime and separately in the governing bodies of each regime as well as in the dominant tendency of each regime; and each regime may be reformed by separating and recombining its parts.[10] The parts of the regimes are in fact the rational and ruling functions of an individual human soul, deliberating and judging, and they are also the offices or ruling principles of that soul, though Aristotle does not point this out. For he is anxious now to protect human choice from the tyranny of excellence as it is exercised through the soul.[11] His presentation of every regime's regime reminds us of understanding the human soul as Plato does in his dialogues, through understanding the typically various human souls. But Aristotle must be mindful of the danger posed to human freedom by the most excellent soul. He therefore suggests that understanding the soul is possible, and political reform practicable, through the generic soul rather than the best soul, at least up to a point (as we shall see). Every regime has something of oligarchy and something of democracy, but also something of polity, which mixes oligarchy and democracy and yet remains separate from them, with open potential for change.[12] This analysis of the parts of all regimes shows how each regime can exist by showing "the serious legislator" what is beneficial for each.[13]

By contrast, the three parts of the modern schema, legislative, executive, and judicial, do not describe rational functions of the soul. They center on the law which is to be made, enforced, or adjudged, but the law is understood as a product of the mind, abstracted from the activity necessary to produce it. The modern schema is indifferent to how the law is made and in its most intransigent formulation it especially avoids saying that legislating is deliberating: according to Thomas Hobbes's doctrine of sovereignty, legislating may be deliberating or it may be whimsically resolving or surrendering to necessity. Perhaps something of the last is indicated: legislating does not have to be deliberated because it must respond to paramount necessities. Aristotle says that when the parts of the regime are noble (*kalos*), the regime must necessarily be noble; and he has previously emphasized the difference between the necessary parts of the city that minister to bodily needs, and the noble parts—such as deliberating and judging—that pertain to the soul (1291a18–27). But the modern schema is designed for limited government in the realm of bodily need or comfort, and it cannot afford to insist on the nobility of human choice in the activity of legislating. It forgoes insistence on deliberation while encouraging wary calculation instead.

The Deliberative Part

Aristotle not only insists upon deliberation but calls it "sovereign." His judgment sounds foreign to us because it too is contrary to the modern schema; we believe that legislative power is sovereign, whether it decides after deliberating or not. For the sake of determinacy, we identify an *office* or an *institution*, not an *activity*, as sovereign. In our view it is better to know for certain who or what is sovereign than to have to pass uncertain judgment on whether it deserves to be sovereign because it has deliberated well.

It turns out, however, that the modern sovereign is not as determinate as we might think. In the ambivalence of the modern executive, there remains an ambiguity between the formal and the real sovereign. If the legislative power is sovereign, the executive is formally subordinate; but if execution requires something more than legislating, the executive becomes sovereign in fact. However carefully we try to specify a sovereign office, we cannot deny the sovereignty of the activity that the office defines more or less imperfectly; but in order to keep our distance from the soul, we call this activity "behavior." This is the root of the difference in today's political science between the institutional and the behavioral approaches. The drive toward scientific determinacy produces a characteristic indeterminacy between two determinacies—the one that tries to specify the institution, regardless of what it does (called "institutional political science"), and the other that tries to specify the behavior, regardless of where it is done (called "behavioralism"). Each determinacy is a vain attempt to supply what is missed by the other.

Aristotle's discussion of deliberation does not vainly attempt to impose scientific precision. But neither does it rest on the "unrealistic" assumptions, rejected by modern political science, that we always think before we act and that we think most about the most important decisions. When Aristotle calls deliberation sovereign, he is indeed examining the limits of human sovereignty. Deliberation in his account, unlike modern scientific reason, does not make its way solely on the basis of its own premises to create its own sovereignty. For Aristotle, deliberation must deal with things beyond human power and somehow bring them within human power. While facing the difficult, perhaps indeterminate, question of what is beyond and within human power, Aristotle does at least avoid the necessity embraced by the modern schema of claiming that we are sovereign even when we give no thought to the matter at hand.

Aristotle has said that the first part of regimes is what deliberates about common things. Deliberation is not defined here, but in the *Ethics* he says that we do not deliberate about things we cannot affect or attain; we do not deliberate about eternal things or about things determined by necessity, nature or chance. We do not even deliberate about all human things; for example the Spartans do not deliberate about the best regime for the Scythians. We do not deliberate about ends but about means, and we deliberate to find the best means, and then the means of those means until we reach the first cause, which is the last to be found. This cause—last in the analysis, first in the genesis—is ourselves, and whatever is dominant in us that chooses (*Nic. Ethics* 1112a18–1113a14). Deliberating is thus primarily for one's own good, but Aristotle emphasizes its social character (he speaks of ''us'' and mentions deliberating with friends and in politics) because a man sharing reason with other men can do more with them than alone.[14] His most valuable tool is held in common with other men, and so his own reason, which might be feeble or ill-informed by itself, gains access to the power of human reason generally.

The subjects of deliberation, meanwhile, are similarly broadened from individual concerns to the common concerns of men, concerns that are also reasonable. To neglect the best regime in the Scythians, therefore, may have been a fault in the Spartans, whose regime did not permit, much less attempt, such apparently aimless philosophizing. For it means that they did not deliberate about the best regime for themselves. Not being satisfied with Spartan oligarchic complacency, Aristotle in this section of Book IV of the *Politics*, raises the question of the extent of the common things in our power about which we deliberate. He does it in a suitably muted way, because there is after all something sound in the Spartan contempt for the vagaries of far-off barbarians.

The deliberative part of regimes is said to be sovereign about three sets of things: first, war and peace, and alliances and dissolutions; second, the laws; third, death, exile, and confiscation, and the audits. While in the modern schema laws are paramount, for Aristotle they are only one concern of the deliberative part. They are the central concern, as one can see from the order of this seemingly miscellaneous list;[15] but they are surrounded by subjects of deliberation that reveal the limited power of human legislation to fend off war, to choose one's partners, to prevent disobedience, and to change what is past. In deliberating on foreign affairs, men deliberate about other men on what men consider in regard to nature as a whole: whether man's relation to nature is war or peace, alliance or dissolution. And in deliberating on punishments, men intend the effects that may be inflicted by fortune or the gods, and that one may do no more than wish or pray to escape. When Aristotle says that the deliberative part is sovereign, he finds it necessary at the same time to concede that

55

the integrity of the human good on which men deliberate is questionable. Rather, he shows that men make this concession themselves in the very subjects of their deliberation.

Earlier in Book IV Aristotle had defined deliberating as "the work of political joining," without explaining further; from the context we may suppose he means that when deliberating in politics, men join the human good that they choose with the nonhuman necessities or goods they must accept.[16] Here the deliberations are unexpectedly called "judgments" (*kriseis*), which for Aristotle are discriminations of one thing from another, judging between them; in Greek "to judge" has the meaning also of separating.[17] It appears that the work of joining requires separating, that deliberating requires judging; that to learn what we may deliberate about, we must be abstracted from our own concerns that are the reference point of all deliberation. In particular, men must be separated from their habitual prejudice in favor of either democracy or oligarchy so that they may deliberate by joining.

For all judgments to be made by all is "demotic," Aristotle says, since this is what the demos seeks. But there are several "modes" (*tropoi*) of deliberating all on all: all may serve in turn rather than at once; all may assemble for certain purposes, with magistrates for the remaining purposes; all may meet to deliberate about all things, with magistrates to prepare the agenda. These modes are then called "democratic." They were at first called "demotic," what the demos seeks; but the demos must rule according to the necessities it finds, and "demotic" becomes "democratic" because nowhere, not even in the last mode of modern democracy, do all actually deliberate on all things (1298a10, 34). No democracy is perfectly "demotic."[18] When we say, for example, that one democracy is more democratic than another, we imply that all the regimes are contained in each and that every regime is a mixed regime.

Similarly, there are different modes of oligarchies, and the most aristocratic of them is not perfectly aristocratic. As we have seen, all men will want to defend themselves and to insist on auditing their rulers, however superior (1295a20). The actual aristocratic regime, therefore, allows all to make some decisions while reserving some decisions to some. The regime could even be said to resemble the last democracy because it intimates that the most an aristocracy can do is to "prejudge" or predispose human deliberations. Every order or (as we say in our modern Greek) "system" of deliberation, even the best, is a lottery because one cannot guarantee that the best men will be placed in office. This is true especially of the last democracy, in which the demagogue may be either Pericles or Cleon, but it is also true of aristocracy which is here fittingly provided with the unaristocratic, but "political" institution of lot.[19]

Having shown that the best regime has a democratic element, Aristotle is ready to advise democracies and oligarchies how to improve their deliberation by mixing their deliberative parts. He openly advises the modern democracy to adopt oligarchical practices in courts and assemblies to insure that the demos deliberates in common with the notables (1298b21), and he counsels oligarchies to allow the demos a share in deliberation—not to vote decrees as in present regimes, but to reject them. Aristotle's counsel to both sides should induce his readers to think about the sovereignty of deliberation, a question which for us is connected to the necessity of executive power. The democrats forget that choosing loses its dignity when it descends to whimsical decreeing; it is no longer properly choice nor distinctively human. We might also put the proposition here to modern political science, which has redefined deliberation as "decision-making." To protect the distinctiveness of choosing, moreover, the demos must deliberate with distinctive men or "notables" (*gnorimoi*), because the exercise of choice implies respect for the differences men find choiceworthy, especially in wealth but also in birth and in virtue (1289b34–1290a5). How can democrats condemn the notables to a dishonoring equality when they themselves would choose the things for which the notables are noted? In our day, is it reasonable to be jealous of the "celebrities" we ourselves celebrate?

Oligarchs, who are too confident of the power of choice, should allow the demos to reject decrees and thus confine their own claim to the duties of preliminary councillors (*probouloi*) or lawguardians (*nomophulakes*) which already exist in some regimes, indeed in democratic regimes. In advising that the power of rejecting be conceded to the demos, Aristotle recognizes the naysaying *thumos* of human beings; and also, without making a point of it, he admits the necessity of decrees despite the sovereignty of deliberation. To allow the demos the power of rejecting is to concede the right of human stubbornness against the dignity of deliberate choice. More than this, it is to concede the power of nature to decree limits to human choice, because for deliberation, a decree of nature is no more intelligible than a demotic whim. What the people reject and what the philosopher or scientist says nature will not permit converge in the political necessity of decrees. Aristotle, ceasing to distinguish democracies from oligarchies, proposes to reverse the practice of the many proposing and the few rejecting (1298b35–1299a1). This reform sounds sweeping but is in fact modest. It implies that all actual regimes are ruled by chance and necessity rather than choice, because they employ democrats for deliberating and oligarchs for rejecting; but for the sovereignty of deliberation, the reform suggests that oligarchs— that is, human beings in their capacity of choosing—must rest content with having the first word. Nature and human nature— that is, the democrats—have a veto power.

In modern states this veto power is given to the executive to exercise in the name of the people. And if the executive is also granted the power of direction, and direction is thereby understood as a function somehow executive, then we conceive the sovereignty of deliberation[20] yet more modestly than Aristotle. In relinquishing the power of having the first word and in always choosing what we believe to be necessary, we almost replace the sovereignty of deliberation with the sovereignty of decree.

The Offices

"Connected" to these things, Aristotle says, is "the distinction" regarding offices (*archai*, 1299a3), which are the second or central part of the regime. He does not say precisely what the distinction is, but we may suppose it to be that which keeps offices plural and prevents them from being subordinated under one office that would be a monarchy over all. This is the part of the regimes in Aristotle's schema corresponding to the modern executive power, but his offices lack the unity at the top embodied in the single modern executive. Their being plural is the outstanding fact about them, for Aristotle as well as for us. Aristotle thinks plurality necessary to maintain the sovereignty of deliberation, to which the offices are "connected."

At the beginning of his discussion, Aristotle raises the strange possibility that offices might be eternal or ancient (1299a9) as well as of shorter term. The eternal is of course too long for human tenure, but we can make sense of it as a reference to the other meaning of *archē*, the beginning or ruling principle. Aristotle wishes to ensure—as the special task of Book IV of the *Politics*—that human government is free, and therefore no mere conduit of natural necessity or divine anger to individual men. Men are not under the rule of nature or god such that their own rule merely reflects a grander principle ruling them. Thus, as we have seen, neither democracy, nor oligarchy, nor monarchy, nor any one regime by itself is the natural or the divine regime. All of them have support in nature, and so our freedom to choose among them is preserved. The "distinction" he has spoken of here is that between *archē* in the grand sense of ruling principle and the human *archai* he must keep plural to protect human choice from the *archē.*

Accordingly he raises a question which might have been unexpected about what sort of office should be *called* an office, since the political community requires many chiefs not assumed to be officers (that is, rulers).[21] It matters whom we call rulers, since our opinion reflects our capacity for freedom and self-rule. Aristotle says that those especially to be spoken of as offices are the ones assigned deliberation about certain things, judging, and ordering, especially the last as this is "more ruling."[22] Ordering is "more ruling," it seems, because of the lack of correspondence between these offices and first principles, which must here be kept at a distance from human government. Still again we perceive the possibility of an executive power that orders or commands, but, consistent with his defense of bodily freedom, Aristotle does not mention any law to be executed and he indicates that the rulers order or command themselves (that is, not as executives of something or someone alien to them) while ordering others.

All offices are oligarchic in the sense that they institute a choice. Aristotle remarks that some offices are peculiar to certain regimes, such as the preliminary councillors (*probouloi*), who are undemocratic as opposed to the council (*boulē*) which is demotic. Yet there must be some such office to do the prior deliberating for the demos, he says; and preliminary councillors are necessarily few, hence oligarchical. He points out to the democrats that as free human beings they are few among the demos of all things, and that to protect their humanity they must "predeliberate" or assume those principles which distinguish them from the rest of (unfree) nature. Such principles (*archai*) must be given recogni-

59

tion in political offices if they are to be effective, for as he says, the power even of the demotic council (*boulē*) is dissolved in democracies where the demos deals with all things (1299b38). In our terms, a democratic legislative assembly is not deliberative unless it provides for offices composed of a few, such as committees, in which men use their leisure to deliberate. In our offices we presuppose our human distinctiveness, and we give effect to it even when our primary intention is to be democratic and not to insist on human superiorities.[23]

In regard to the modes of appointment to offices, Aristotle says that one should attempt to discuss the establishment of offices "from the beginning" (*ex archēs*), which can also mean "from the beginning principle." The beginning principle that is being "attempted" (Aristotle does not say it can be accomplished) in Book IV is that of human choice. Human choice finds itself confronted with what is not chosen, which from its standpoint appears to be merely given by chance or lot. Aristotle teaches us from actual political practices that the dichotomy between choice and lot, though initially impressive and "first for us," is not conclusive. For in practice we do not choose to be governed only by choice: we choose to be governed, sometimes and in different ways, by lot. Any established office, as was remarked, is a kind of lottery because in establishing the office we do not know who will fill it. We do, however, have some idea of the character or nature of who will fill it—the "qualifications" for the office—and this suggests that what first appears as chance may be, in some reliable degree, intelligible nature. Like the king over all, but more modestly, we can choose in the sense that we intend this intelligibility. If intelligently contrived, an office may be a wise choice and a good bet on what cannot be chosen; for example, the American founders could not choose American presidents but could expect certain characters to be called forth by the nature of the office.[24] Thus Aristotle may preserve the difference between choice and lot while suggesting how they may be combined under one principle.

In the discussion of establishing offices that follows, Aristotle excels himself in terseness. The mathematical, combinatory character of his treatment is meant to train the "serious legislator" in looking for possibilities that are not actual or prevalent, and to correct the two sorts of complacency one still finds among liberals and conservatives today: that of supposing we can choose anything we like, and that of making do with what chance supplies. Aristotle mentions three ways in which offices can be either democratic (all appoint, from all, by lot) or oligarchic (some appoint, from some, by choice). But given these three ways, democracy and oligarchy have been removed from actual regimes where one or the other is established as sovereign, and are presented in an abstract regime as if on a platter to a statesman with perfect freedom of choice. At the same time, it is clear that the abstract regime, if it exists, must be a democracy with freedom for both democratic and oligarchic choices.[25] For though oligarchy is in need of democratic elements, it is exclusive and therefore not potentially democratic in the way democracy is potentially oligarchical. One must have "some" *in* "all" rather than *opposed to* "all" in order to make all the possibilities manifest. Instead of opposing the few to the many in the oligarchical manner one must survey the diversity of "somes" in the human race.

Thus, if the human race is divided into some men of property and some men of virtue, all appointment by lot will reflect this distribution: these kinds of men will show up in the offices. Ordering in the nature of the "all" from which men choose supports and even guides human choice, since one can expect certain offices to appeal to certain human types. Yet ordering in the appointers and the mode of appointment prevents nature from determining human choice. For the various "somes" can be scattered or fixed in a political-social hierarchy contrived to restrain them, and kept from dominating political deliberation. Human, that is, political ordering in offices (*archai*) prevents the beginning principle (*archē*) of nature from being distributed to each individual human being—prevented, that is, from ruling. In offices, men free themselves from such determination from above by ordering themselves and thus regarding themselves, not as nature or god, but as the beginning principle. For freedom, perhaps our most urgent need is to escape the rule of one, when that "one" is our enslavement by bodily nature; and this need forces us to distinguish and also to mix choice and lot. Choice and lot are the plural *archai* which we can neither identify with each other nor hold separate and unmixed. We equate them at the peril of our freedom and fail to mix them at the risk of our security.

Aristotle says, more precisely, that the differences must be "coupled" to retain both elements rather than "mixed" so that each element loses its identity.[26] The "joining" of deliberation must be arranged in the "coupling" of offices. Aristotle speaks of "couplings" by which offices may be ordered, as some appointing to some and all to some, and so forth. This possibility reveals the dual character of each ordering as a coupling of choice and lot, the deliberated and the given, the human and the natural. When men articulate their ordering, they couple their choices to nature's givens so that they can take advantage of nature's articulation of "all" into "somes" without surrendering to it.

Aristotle seems to advise us that the fundamental issue between democracy and oligarchy, when both are moderated, is whether a group claiming to rule takes its turn or seeks to perpetuate itself in office as an exclusive "some." This statement of the case once again seems to favor democracy as the more moderate alternative. Oligarchy is oligarchy because if the "some" from which offices are filled is exclusive, it matters less that all appoint, or that appointment is by lot—the same sort will get in. But democracy (properly understood) is a coupling of oligarchy with democracy, as demonstrated in the democratic practice of ruling in turn, wherein at all times only some rule. Nonetheless, neither democracy nor oligarchy makes the other unnecessary, since democracy secures only rule in turn, not permanent rule, for the most choiceworthy regime, and that regime cannot perpetuate itself except with concessions to "lot." Thus the coupling of democracy and oligarchy in the ordering of offices points to the superiority of artistocracy where the most choiceworthy regime is coupled with the natural principle (*archē*) which ensures that it will be chosen.[27] Such an aristocracy is the best result, the perfect coupling of oligarchy and democracy, of choice and lot. But does it anywhere occur? Aristotle merely leaves it as the boundary beyond which only monarchy remains with no offices to be ordered. Accordingly, this best result need not be actual, yet it can still guide the ordering of actual regimes.

At the end of the section on offices, Aristotle makes it clear that he has not discussed the *powers* of offices, which he will do in Book VI. Here he has abstracted the ordering of offices in actual regimes to place them in an abstract regime, combining modes as if they were numbers. This abstract regime is not equipped with a law to be executed, which would have to be human law generally or natural law; and so Aristotle is not called upon to produce an abstract or generalized executive power in the manner of John Locke. We may suppose that in Aristotle's view a single natural law would make men heedless of the need to mix lot and choice. They would either accept the natural law God gave them to execute, or rise up and take the executive power in their own hands. Or can they manage to do both by means of the ambivalence of executive power?

Judging

The "remaining" part of regimes is the judicial or *dikastikon* (the word, we have noted, for judging in a democratic assembly). Aristotle does not say it is "next" or "connected" as he said about offices to the deliberative part. He will consider the modes "under the same assumption," he says. That assumption is that he must treat the existing in order to bring the best into existence, in particular (in Book IV) the human body and the spirited part of the soul that speaks for the body in the soul. We therefore find no law stated by which men judge, and no standard or *archē*, as in Book III, of "that according to which the king rules all things according to his own will" (1287a10, 35). For such a law would seem to spirited men to support their angry judgments, and they would misinterpret the law in partisan fashion in order to indulge both sweeping democratic indiscrimination and arrogant, oligarchic assertiveness. Since Aristotle means to reform such men, he must remove that prop from their judgment temporarily until they learn to use it as a guide to moderation. This momentary separation of judging from the standard of judgment was also necessary, as we saw, to protect the right of human initiative in deliberation; but it is now needed all the more for the complementary purpose of enabling men to criticize what they do on their own.

In Aristotle's discussion of courts we note that by comparison with the offices, the question of whom men judge has replaced the question of who does the appointing. Courts are distinct from other offices (or from offices) in that the appointers are less important than the judged, the end more important than the beginning. We are not surprised to see in them that the first of the eight forms of courts is the court of audit or calling to account, the claim on one's betters that men insist on making. The first five forms of courts are made to form a group of political courts, to suggest perhaps that men should call their rulers (or betters) to account on behalf of the regime rather than merely to express outrage. Although regimes differ, these courts defend a non-partisan regime. Aristotle can discuss the powers of courts and still maintain the formality of his analysis because courts, when compared with other offices, are less relative to any particular regime. The kinds of crimes that at first glance do not appear very distinct demand the formation of different forms of courts, dividing among themselves the jurisdiction of a single court which otherwise might be too closely identified with the regime. They scatter judgments that might otherwise come too readily to a focus on the safety of the regime, and they encourage moderation by requiring the judges to attend to the kind of case. There is no court for cases of impiety because Aristotle does not want divine anger executed on humans.[28]

Besides these five courts are three that are non-political. As for the last of these, the least political, the word for judgment that Aristotle uses is now *krisis*, implying discrimination, or separation. To judge and to call others to account one must have a standard outside of oneself and beyond the threat to one's own preservation. Here Aristotle's doctrine differs from that of Locke, who accorded every man a natural executive power of the law of nature to exercise whenever he felt threatened and had no appeal to government. For Aristotle, such an allowance does not take sufficient account of the fact that "most [people] are bad judges of their own interests" (1280a16).[29] If they judge by the standard of what is good for the regime, men achieve a certain distance from their own interest and a wider perspective. Yet as the regime is nothing but an elaboration of their own interest, they must be required further to judge by what is necessary for any regime, if not by the best regime. To judge by the common necessities of all regimes, however, they must have a notion of what is political and how it is related to what is non-political. For example, in judging homicide they must have a notion of the dignity of man and his place in nature; and in judging foreigners, they must have a notion of what makes men foreign to each other and therefore of what is foreign to man.

In all this, Aristotle has said nothing explicit about what judging is (though elsewhere he has),[30] but he has left something to be inferred. Judging seems to be discriminating on the basis of a standard, and that standard, if it is not merely to replicate the things being judged, if it is to allow a critical distance, must be non-political and non-human; it must be an intelligible nature that does not depend on human artifice for its intelligibility.

One can now interpret the four modes of courts Aristotle lists (1301a11–15). Demotic courts would be those in which all things are judged from the standpoint of all nature; oligarchic, those in which all things are judged from a human standpoint; aristocratic and political, those in which some things are judged from the standpoint of nature, and some from a human standpoint.

At the end of Book IV of the *Politics* Aristotle leaves us with the inevitability of the mixed regime, understood fundamentally as a mixture of choice and lot, or of deliberating and judging. Whereas deliberating is a social act of human initiative connected to offices, in which rulers "begin" the rule they choose for themselves, judging is a private act requiring that one separate himself from what he has begun, to achieve a critical detachment. When judging, one does not merely accept what one is given; one may reject one's "lot." But to reject it, one must rely on and accept some standard of judgment; so judging is accepting with the possibility of rejecting, an activity of thought that gives human recalcitrance its say but accepts the sovereignty of what is outside oneself, of nature. As deliberating implies a soul that can begin the motion of a man's body, judging implies a soul that can separate a man from his body, that can call him to account, and make him self-critical. But while showing us that the mixed regime is inevitable, Aristotle does not say how it might be just or noble.

Powers and Offices

When we come to the reconsideration of offices at the end of Book VI, including Aristotle's only explicit discussion of the executive, we find the discussion of "powers" promised in Book IV (1300b8). The offices are now divided according to their powers into two main groups, the necessary offices and the noble ones. From this division we learn something more of the noble mixed regime than could be seen in the abstract modes discussed in Book IV. It appears that a noble regime must retain the distinction between the necessary and the noble. The reason, we can surmise, is that noble men distinguish themselves as noble from the ignoble, and their consciousness of the distinction is necessary to the definition of nobility. Nobility is visible because it must be visible to those defining themselves against the ignoble, and in Greek, conveniently, the word for "noble" (*kalos*) also means "beautiful."[31] But when the noble regime makes this concession to the (perhaps questionable) perception of noble men, it encounters the difficulty that the ignoble offices may be necessary because they are just. For justice can sometimes be ignoble, especially in execution of penalties.

To retain the distinction between necessary and noble offices in the mixed regime, Aristotle must retain the distinction between choice and lot and must align the two distinctions. He must present choice as something noble, not merely deliberate, and keep it distinguished from lot in order to promote the nobility of not accepting one's lot. Thus the vulgar democratic spiritedness of naysaying about what is good for you is transformed, or almost transformed, into a striving for the noble. In making his mixed regime noble, Aristotle allies himself with human dissatisfaction or indeed with human indignation. After the abstract regime at the end of Book IV, he takes up the regime in motion or revolution in Book V, which we must look at briefly.

Regimes are put in motion or suffer revolution for cause, and there are two kinds of cause, clearly but not explicitly marked out by Aristotle, corresponding to the difference between justice and nobility (1301a25–1301b5 and 1302a16–1303b17). The first kind is the single cause of all revolutions, which is the injustice of all existing regimes (1301a36). The imperfection of regimes would have an unfailing cause in the imperfection of human beings; and if this imperfection were viewed from a sufficient philosophic distance, one might conclude that revolutions cannot remedy human injustice and do not matter. Aristotle remarks that men superior in virtue, who would become revolutionaries with the most justification, are least inclined to revolt, while those superior in birth (*genos*), who make a claim to be unequal, are more inclined to revolution, justified or not (1301a39–1301b5; 1304b5–6).

The second kind of cause describes the things that move most (non-philosophic) men to revolution, especially noble honor-lovers.[32] In their indignation at the injustice or slights they receive, the possibility of significant improvement or even perfection is preferred, for it makes no sense to become angry at imperfections that cannot be corrected. This kind of cause is plural because it is occasioned by accidents (1303b17; see 1301a38;

Book V abounds with fascinating examples) which are important to men. The philosophic view, in which revolutions merely exchange one system of injustice for another, must be combined with the perspective of political men striving to be noble and seeking honor, to whom changes of regime are all-important. With the philosophic view Aristotle can avoid inflating the expectations of political men, but the political view encourages reform and keeps its makers occupied in wholesome or at least more constructive activity.

In Book VI the lovers of honor are presented with the noble opportunity of founding. But the regimes they are to found are democracy and oligarchy, nothing better, and democracy, which would surely be the last regime an honor-loving founder would choose, receives first consideration and more ample discussion by far.[33] Aristotle does not bring up the mixed regime. Instead, he says that since democracies and other regimes happen to exist, one must determine what is appropriate and beneficial for each (1316b39). As in Book V, where he advised how to preserve each regime (1304b20, 1307b27), so now he accepts that each regime will have what is appropriate to it (oikeion) and will not be required to sacrifice this to a mixed regime. The concession follows from Aristotle's acceptance of the legitimacy of revolutionary indignation in Book V, for political indignation is partisan rather than neutral and detached.

But in Book VI, the honor-lovers who are to bring the noble regime into existence are required, as founders, to combine the beneficial for each regime with the appropriate, even if it is uncongenial to them as partisans. When the partisan takes on the responsibility of founder, he must swallow the bitter with the sweet, but he should be the more ready to do that, because founding is more noble than partisanship and indeed because bitter tastes sweeter to the noble. They are confronted with the imaginary task of founding a democracy, and thus made to pretend that democracy is agreeable to them to the end that they may appreciate how it is beneficial to them as anti-democrats. The "greatest work" of the legislator is not only to construct a regime, but to make it last, as it is not difficult to make a regime hold up for a few days.[34] Making a regime last, it turns out, especially requires finding resources and occupation or activity for the poor (1320a33–1320b16; 1267a10). In this subtle way the nobles are induced to exercise their nobility in ignoble necessities they would

67

rather ignore. When they are at last given the opportunity of founding an oligarchy, they are merely told that oligarchy is the opposite of democracy; and in the congenial task of ordering for war, they are reminded of the political consequences of relying on heavy or light infantry, cavalry, or the navy; so that they do not forget to conform the order of war to the occupations of peace. As their last preparation for reconsidering the offices that were taken up in Book IV, Aristotle appeals to their sense of honor over their desire for gain, and he recommends to them the noble but expensive virtue of magnificence.[35]

The offices are given their powers, which they were not in Book IV, now that the powers (*dunameis*) are understood as potentialities for noble men. The offices do not govern men as if they were external powers or laws from nature guaranteeing the regularity if not the perfection of human behavior. Rather, men must assume the offices and make the potentialities actual with their own virtuous activity. In their self-government, to repeat, they do not merely execute a rule or law that has its origin outside themselves. They must act virtuously or nobly on their own; their freedom and their ruling are compatible only through their nobility. Noble men will be attracted by the difference between potentiality and actuality in the offices, providing what we call a "challenge." Thus they may be attracted even to the necessary offices without which it is impossible for the city to exist, as well as to those offices providing good order and ornament without which it cannot be nobly managed.[36] Of the seventeen offices Aristotle lists, twelve are called necessary, but the first two, offices for the market and for common and private properties in the city, have as an object besides the necessary cares the maintenance of good order (*eukosmia*). These offices, though necessary, may be ennobled or beautified to attract those who are attracted by the noble. With the executive, however, the difficulty is more severe.

On the list of necessary offices, the sixth, "almost the most necessary and the most difficult of the offices," is one "regarding deeds against the condemned and defaulters according to the lists and regarding the keeping of prisoners."[37] Here is the slighting treatment of the executive from which we began. The office is difficult because it involves much odium; so no one undertakes it willingly except for great profit, and those who do undertake it are unwilling to act in accordance with the laws. But it is a necessary office because there is no use in judgments of justice if they are not "exacted to their end" (*lambanein telos*).[38] This may be taken as Aristotle's expression for "execution." He accepts the office and says that it is necessary,[39] but since it cannot be beautified, he minimizes it. He does not expand the office into the awesome modern executive by taking advantage of its odium to make it more powerful and more efficient. On the contrary, he counsels that it be not "one same office" but different offices from different courts, that one try to divide up offices concerning public notice of those written down as defaulters,[40] that judgments of outgoing magistrates be carried out by new ones, and that the doer (the executive) be other than the condemner. For, Aristotle says, the less odium there is for the doers, the more the deeds will be brought to their conclusion. When those who condemn and those who carry out are the same, there is twofold odium, and for the same ones to carry out all such judgments makes them enemies of all. But would they not be feared and respected by all?

It is difficult to dismiss the larger implications of the office which Aristotle admits could possibly be "one same office." If one person held this "one same office" of condemning and executing, and of executing all judgments, and did so not until he is replaced but for all time in perpetuity, he would be a god, the chief god. Any human being who took this office with the necessary human limitations would be the imitator or executive of this god and his government a punitive theocracy. In Book III Aristotle said that ostracizing a man of outstanding virtue would be like claiming to rule over Zeus and partitioning his offices.[41] In Books IV and VI Aristotle himself does precisely this: he ostracizes the monarch in order to rule over Zeus by partitioning offices. Aristotle's partitioning is his "separation of powers." With it he seeks to awaken virtue rather than stimulate fear and desire for gain, as Machiavelli was to do. But to awaken virtue, two phases are necessary. First, Aristotle must make an uncompromising argument for virtue in his notion of kingship. Then he must prevent his kingship, in the person of an angry god, from cowing respectable people and empowering potential tyrants. Only with such a procedure will virtue not become its own worst enemy.

The difficulty in the office of executive is not merely that it is unattractive to the noble or the "respectable" because of the odium attached to it, but more that precisely because of the odium it is attractive to the "base." Speaking of one duty of the executive, the guarding of prisoners, Aristotle says that the work must be kept separate from executing. He goes on to say that although the respectable especially avoid the duty, yet it is not safe to make the base "sovereign," for rather than being capable of guarding others they themselves need a guard.[42] How could the base be made "sovereign" by being entrusted with the duties of jailers, duties which might seem particularly suited to give honest employment to disreputable characters? When Aristotle spoke of "the guards of prisoners" he said literally "the guards of bodies" (1322a2): is it not imaginable that, in keeping with the concern of Books IV to VI for the political importance of human bodies, all human government could be comprehended in the office of jailer? Here is a hint, but no more than a hint, of the outsized modern executive.

Aristotle has combatted the notion that to guard men one need only guard their bodies, and thus guard them as prisoners, but (as we have seen) there is some truth in it; and so to minimize the danger from base men—not the modest vulgar in the people, but the seekers of tyranny misled by false nobility—he minimizes the opportunities of the office. To do that he has supplied in a treatise on *Politics* an understanding of nature intended to reassure men and to moderate their angry desire to punish. Nature understood as unfriendly to men gives human justice no support and compels human government to imitate angry gods, to rely on fear as the motive for obedience, and to loose hatred against its enemies. This was Machiavelli's way but not Aristotle's.

Aristotle asserted or discovered an understanding of nature, contained in his notion of kingship, that was favorable to human ends and the human good. His purpose was to preserve the practical feasibility of behaving nobly, to enlighten the ambition of those who seek to act nobly, and thus to avoid making the Machiavellian princes sovereign. Aristotle's kingship is the end of all politics, since every regime makes a claim that is best represented in its one best citizen (even a democracy, as we have seen, culminates in its own most democratic citizen); and at the same time it is beyond all politics, since there will be many who do not conform to the rule of the one best, who indeed have a legitimate claim against it. Because kingship is in one sense beyond all politics, it remains a theoretical best regime against which to measure actual regimes. Aristotle's practical preference is for the mixed regime and the rule of law its impartiality makes possible. In the

best circumstances, he would not have approved the modern executive in whom one-man rule becomes actual and the rule of law
comes to seem theoretical.

From the ambivalence of kingship, we see why the forms that
define politics have two contrary functions: they reveal the ends
toward which politics aims and also control the movement
toward those ends. The first function is the primary one for Aristotle, and is set forth in his discussion of the regime as a form in
Book III of the *Politics*. There we learn that the end of democracy
is best revealed in the forms of democracy. The second is shown
in the forms of institutions or "offices" (in the plural, I emphasize
once again) considered in Books IV–VI. These forms have the virtue of reminding the established regime of the other regimes, and
of the mixed regime; and they serve as barriers against hasty action and admonitions against singleminded devotion to the main
end of the regime.[43] Forms in this sense were adopted in modern
constitutionalism, whereas forms in the first sense were regarded
with suspicion, as we shall see, because of the religious issue. We
have thus come today to understand "constitutionalism" primarily as checks or restraints upon government, which is the lesser
aspect of Aristotle's understanding. It is doubtful whether, with
such a reversal, we are faithful to the capabilities of the American
Constitution, for the forms of that Constitution show what free
government aspires to as much as they check its ambition. But to
the extent that we are mainly concerned to be "realistic," we are
compelled to set the forms of politics against its realities. In no
part of modern politics is this discrepancy more marked than in
the idea of executive power.

Theoretical best : Kingship - embodies the best.

Practical best : Mixed regime.

4

Proto-Executives

Aristotle had opportunities to discover and develop the notion of executive power in his political science; but, either ignoring or minimizing them, he passed them over. In the centuries following Aristotle and preceding the discovery of executive power, several proto-executives appeared and a proto-theory of executive power was even conceived. The consuls and dictators of the Roman republic were what we would call strong executives in a republican setting. In this chapter I shall consider the Roman consuls as presented by Polybius, and the Roman dictator as described in several sources, to see whether they were really executives. The medieval ruler—whether king or emperor—was regarded in some sense as an executive of a higher power, the will of God. But was this the modern executive? To answer, I shall show in Chapter 5 how Aristotle's kingship was applied and adapted to the medieval ruler by Thomas Aquinas, Dante, and Marsilius of Padua. In the great *Defender of the Peace* of Marsilius of Padua we see the idea of "executive," indeed the word itself, become a theme of political science.

Other possible executives might be sought and found elsewhere in both theory and practice, for as I have said, some of the devices of executive power, like the tricks of Machiavellians, are always within the reach of inventive politicians. And who could prescribe limits to the powers of imaginative thinkers? But it would not serve our purpose to fill a book with ghostly anticipations of executive power, because, as we shall see, these practical executives were not understood as executives. The theoretical executive was put in view and then retracted—in sum, the proto-executives were pseudo-executives. It would overstate the case to say, as did Hobbes, that before his own writing Aristotle controlled the university. By this, Hobbes meant that Aristotle controlled the political world. But we shall find that when Aristotle's specific formulations are abandoned (or, in the case of Marsilius, explicitly corrected), the fundamental considerations that kept Aristotle from uncovering executive power remained in force for others in the tradition of classical political philosophy, and proto-executives were held under the constraint.

With Rome, there arose a new distinction among regimes that was to rule Western political science and political consciousness until the nineteenth century. No longer was the outstanding dispute held to be that between democracy and oligarchy; henceforth it was between republic and monarchy. The Greeks were aware of barbarian monarchies, but popular belief regarded them as primitive regimes not suitable for Greeks in their prime. Greek political philosophy was not so disdainful: Xenophon made Cyrus his model statesman; Plato imagined a philosopher-king; and Aristotle developed the invisible kingship we have studied. But these were presented as models for imagination and understanding, not goals for action.

In the Greek cities, the two competing parties, and the two dominant regimes, were democratic and oligarchic (but open, as in Periclean Athens, to temporary domination by one man). That is why Aristotle was able to begin his discussion of regimes in Book III of the *Politics* with the partisan dispute between democrats and oligarchs. His guidance of that dispute toward kingship was not intended to introduce kingship as a practical possibility, or to establish a new frame of political dispute between republic and monarchy or empire.[1] Instead, Aristotle turned to the mixed regime, which was in fact a mixed republic. In Rome, the overthrow of the Tarquin kings and the simultaneous founding of the republic did change the parties of political dispute. After this event, the republic became so powerful that when it fell centuries later, the empire had to be introduced under republican forms, not under its own name.

The idea of empire, however, has a certain natural appeal as well as a latent presence in classical political philosophy. If one man really is best, what besides prejudice and convention will prevent the extension of his rule to the limit of the known world? This possibility is adumbrated in Book VII of Aristotle's *Politics* (1325a34–39) and developed, as we shall see, in Dante's *Monarchy*. It is neutral because it appeals to the universality of human nature and demands that this universality find political expression in the rule of the best human being. When emperors and monarchs became dominant after the fall of the Roman republic, they could begin to dispense with republican forms; and they could denounce the turbulence and sedition of that republic and the vices of republics in general. As the virtues of empire were defined against the vices of republics, political argument was transformed from dispute between democracy and oligarchy to that between republic and empire. In this way the Roman republic had a long afterlife of ill repute under the empire, longer even than that of the Tarquin kings during the republic. But perhaps the politics of Rome would not have been sufficient by itself to establish a new framework of political dispute without a natural basis for it. Just as Aristotle found that democracy and oligarchy reflect competing claims about human and non-human nature, so also one might find (with Aristotle's help) that the dispute between republic and empire is, so to speak, a natural argument. Whereas the idea of empire appeals to the universality of human nature, however distant men may be from one another, the idea of republic expresses all that men can do together and hold in common.[2]

One might have thought the new Roman polemical framework favorable to the development of executive power. However one might reconcile the universal and the common in human nature, if indeed that is possible, a kind of mixed regime composed of republic and empire might seem available in the idea of the executive. Monarchies easily discover the virtues of one-man rule, while republics must learn to conceal them if they want to preserve them: all that was necessary, it would seem, was to combine these two insights. But in fact, executive power no more emerged from the politics of Rome than from the political philosophy of Greece. Executive power had to be invented.

Consuls in Polybius's Roman Republic

Polybius, the Greek historian of Rome, provides an analysis of the Roman regime in which the consuls appear as promising proto-executives. Looking back on Rome's success in conquering "nearly the whole world" (220–168 B.C.), Polybius attributes this triumph to the regime that enabled the Romans to withstand the reverses of fortune, above all to recover from the defeat by Hannibal at Cannae (*Histories* I.2.7; VI.12). The principle of this regime is not a harmony of functions such as we have seen in Aristotle, but rather tension and fear between opposing elements. It works by checks and balances in a way that reminds us of a modern regime of separated powers counteracting each other.[3] The power to punish, prominently featured, is shared by all three elements (consuls, Senate, and people). But the almost uncontrolled power of the consuls when on military campaign might seem to give them an advantage tending toward the modern outsized executive (VI.12).

The image of one regime in tension is enhanced by a view of the purported cycle of regimes which turns by means of their unnoticed degeneration and the opposition awakened by it. The cycle begins with the discovery of the just and the noble, so that these notions appear to be humanly created rather than natural, in a manner consistent with the need for humanly managed fear to enforce them. And to complete the resemblance to a realistic modern analysis relying on institutionalized fear rather than education in virtue, Polybius calls his enterprise "pragmatic history."[4] Modern writers such as Machiavelli and Montesquieu bear witness to this resemblance: Machiavelli, by appropriating Polybius's account of the cycle and using it at the beginning of his *Discourses on Livy*; Montesquieu, with many references to the man he calls the "judicious Polybius."[5]

When we examine the apparent resemblance, however, it begins to fade. First, Polybius looks on Rome's success as a spectacle; his "pragmatic history" is not merely utilitarian.[6] When he seems to confess that he is a popularizer of Plato and other philosophers,[7] he should not be taken for a popularizer in the modern sense. Polybius was a thinker subtle enough for us, and many modern commentators underestimate him.

Introducing his idea of a cycle of regimes, Polybius indicates two opinions regarding regimes that he wants to oppose: They are that the three regimes of Greek political science (kingship, aristocracy, and democracy) are the only ones, or that they are even ("by Zeus," he swears) the best (VI.3.5–7). The first mistake is that of nonpartisan, conventionalist philosophers who conclude wearily that no substantial difference exists between the three good regimes and their bad counterparts. The second, worse mistake (as indicated by the oath) is made by partisans who are attached to their own regimes and are unwilling to mix them with the others. Countering both, Polybius says he relies on "nature." Nature will show that partisan choice is limited so that we cannot live just as we would like but must accept a mixed regime. And nature will also show, addressing the contrary errors, that the differences in regimes which men believe to be important are so in truth, and are not merely accidental and artificial.

Unlike Aristotle, Polybius does not begin from partisan dispute, even though he had before him the great dispute of the Roman republic between the plebs and the Senate. Instead he begins theoretically from nature, from the natural cycle of regimes in which he shows how both government and partisan, political opinion are generated. The cycle, as Scipio would say in Cicero's *Republic*, is the "head of civil prudence."[8] But since only a small segment of the cycle could be part of any statesman's experience, to rely on it as Polybius (and Cicero) does is to promote the discerning philosopher to a more visible position as teacher than Aristotle was willing to allow. At the same time, despite Polybius's acknowledged dependence on Plato, this more visible position is not used to demote actual politics as in the case of Plato's imagined philosopher-king; on the contrary, the position is made to serve responsible statesmen such as his friend Scipio. Polybius, as he tells us, had to confront Rome's success in conquest, which might seem to have put an end to argument over the best regime. Thus, whereas Plato wished to transcend this argument and Aristotle wished to exploit it, Polybius had to revive it in the face of Rome's tremendous and daunting success.

The cycle of regimes takes a long view—much longer than Rome's existence or its advance. It begins with a primitive monarchy that emerges after a natural cataclysm has destroyed human civilization, when the survivors out of weakness band together under one who is stronger and bolder. Then the "first notions" of the just and the noble arise because of their utility—justice when parents become disgusted with ungrateful children, and nobility when one man who defends others in danger is honored. But unlike modern realists and ancient conventionalists, Polybius does not say that these "first notions" are all there is to morality. The notions make use of the distinctively human power of reason, and as they develop, primitive monarchy becomes a reasonable kingship over willing subjects. Next, however, the kings become hereditary, and since they are no longer chosen for their excellent qualities, they are free to indulge luxurious and erotic license and their kingship becomes tyranny. But their behavior is intolerable to the most high-minded men, who form a conspiracy, overthrow the tyrant, and with the consent of the people establish an aristocracy. After this experience the nobles and the people conceive a dislike for every kind of one-man rule, and the nobles, having power in their hands, choose not to relinquish it: this is how partisan opinion favorable to one of the regimes is generated. And so the process continues through aristocracy decaying into oligarchy, democracy into ochlocracy, the people degenerating at the end into beasts who find a "master and monarch" that begins the cycle again (VI.5–9).

There are several puzzles in the account, but what is to be learned from it? As I have said, Polybius stresses the naturalness of the cycle. Both the unnoticed degenerations of regimes and their conscious corrections are natural; thus the regular motions of nature include both human weakness and human virtue.[9] So when the cycle is presented to prudent statesmen, they will neither be complacent nor despair; rather, they will embrace a mixed regime, as did Lycurgus in his foresight and the Romans in the midst of struggles without foresight.[10] The cycle also teaches partisans that their favorite regime may, indeed must, degenerate, and that other regimes exist which have preceded and shall follow theirs. Their exclusive devotion to one above all is made to look ridiculously short-sighted or "uncyclical," as we today might condemn a parochial outlook as "unhistorical." But we say "unhistorical" in order to narrow a choice (which history forecloses), while Polybius uses the cycle to expand the outlook of partisans and the range of partisan choice. Furthermore, the cycle teaches those who are inclined to despise morality and politics as being beneath consideration or beyond correction, that although men begin naked and weak, they have nature's help in self-improvement; and if degeneration is natural when we are inattentive, justice and nobility are also possible and available.

Yet if the cycle of regimes is natural, what is the basis for the mixed regime that contains all three of the good regimes?[11] Why is it that according to Polybius a statesman who understands the cycle is liberated from it by his very understanding, and enabled to found a long-lasting mixed regime as did Lycurgus? History can neither be halted nor transcended, and so every reference to a statesman's "historical context" describes his constraints. But for Polybius, the cycle can apparently be stopped, at least for a time. The basis for this claim must be the view that nature is a *whole*,[12] and not just a term of distinction. In one sense "nature" is distinct from human reason and chance, because it operates with independent regularity. But in another sense, of course, nature includes reason and chance, so that the chance that some statesman may be able to achieve a limited stability by the exercise of reason is as natural as the degeneration of regimes in the absence of such a reasoning statesman.[13]

To understand nature as a whole is to be elevated above natural processes in the first sense, and the elevation is a *distinction* because it depends on the *whole*. Understanding the cycle as a whole is what distinguishes the statesman Lycurgus, and the political philosopher who interprets him, from the political partisans who are fated to remain within the cycle (VI.10). We may well doubt that Lycurgus, who could not have read about the cycle in Plato, had the understanding Polybius imputes to him. Then we see how close Polybius has brought political philosophy to actual politics and how boldly he corrects its natural tendencies—not on its own premises, like Aristotle, but with a new consideration opposed to those tendencies.

Polybius does say that Rome achieved a mixed regime without the help of either a Lycurgus or a political philosopher. Yet it was in order to explain the Roman regime that he proposed the cycle of regimes, for that regime, he said, had from the beginning (*archē*) its composition and growth according to nature (VI.4.13, 9.12–14). But the principle of the Roman regime, we have seen, is mutual fear among the three parts, not the principle of foresight or reason as in Lycurgus' Sparta. In the cycle, however, the mark of the three good regimes, and in particular the distinction between kingship and tyranny, is the overcoming of fear in voluntary and reasoning accord among the few and the many (VI.4.2, 6.11–12, 8.1, 9.1). Polybius asserts that the Romans have achieved just what Lycurgus did by "always choosing the better" in time of conflict (VI.10.14); so in building their regime they did not merely react without thinking. Yet their regime is not a whole; it is a mixture of three parts or portions in which each form, conceding nothing to the others, appears to be a whole when one looks at it alone (VI.11.12). In other words, it is a mixture because three parties claim it as their own and one does not know what else to call it.

Partisanship for the three forms remains intact because no modification of partisan souls through education has been attained.[14] The form (*eidos*) that gives the consuls separate powers does modify their behavior. Though consuls were (usually) men of senatorial rank who left the Senate to become consuls and returned to it at the end of their consulates, they were separated from the Senate by virtue of this form (their office). That is why Polybius, following the argument for the importance of forms that we have seen in Aristotle, differs from modern historians who believe that the social origins of the consuls override their formal advantages in office. Polybius therefore calls them a monarchical element distinct from the aristocratic as well as the democratic.

Since the three parties of the Roman regime are at loggerheads, they cannot make a whole, like the three functions of Aristotle's regime or of a modern constitutional government. None of them can act unchecked. When one party tries to become dominant, the other two combine against it. How this regime came into being Polybius does not say; the various powers appear to have been dealt out by an even-handed but fuzzy-minded judge.[15] Cicero provides an account of the formation of the Roman regime in which he attributes incredible constitutional foresight to men scrambling for advantage at different times—as if Rome were planned not by one but by a series of founders.[16] Some scholars have attributed a similar "archeology" to Polybius (so that it can serve as a source for Cicero!), but perhaps, having supplied an account of the cycle, he was not obliged to give an account of accidents in Rome that would merely illustrate it.[17] He does say that the three elements are brought to act together by menace from outside; when that happens, they stop checking one another and begin competing to see who can best meet the emergency (VI.18). Rome excels in meeting danger, in answering the test of bad fortune such as the defeat by Hannibal at Cannae. Its entire regime, not merely an executive branch of it, seems to be directed to this end. When we see that Rome's regime becomes a whole only in meeting outside emergencies, we recognize the cause of its great success in war and conquest. Recounting this success Polybius in effect provides the "archeology" of the regime, and we are not surprised that he next describes the organization of the Roman army at considerable length.[18]

How does Polybius value a regime that he shows to be organized for empire? Some believe that he was dazzled by it,[19] but there is reason to think that on the contrary, he was deeply critical of it. He says that the Romans, by "choosing the better" in time of conflict, have reached the same end as Lycurgus, "the best system of the regimes in our time" (VI.10.14, 18.1). Here he seems to put Rome and Sparta on a par, each the best in its time; but as he goes on, he avoids a direct comparison.[20] Despite his promise that the cycle will show Rome's acme and decline, he immediately predicts only its decline (VI.9.12–14), as if Rome would have no acme. Before speaking of the Roman regime, he warns of deliberate omissions (VI.11.8); and in his account we note that he says nothing of private life and education in Rome, though in praising Lycurgus he asserts that concord among citizens as well as bravery against enemies preserves governments (VI.46.7). But the principle of the Roman regime is the same as that of tyranny: not concord but fear. Most notably, Polybius says nothing of the ability of the Roman regime to withstand *good* fortune, despite having emphasized that the test of a man or a regime is to be able to bear good as well as bad fortune (VI.2.5–7). Will Rome, like Athens, be ruined by success in war and descend into mob rule (VI.44)?

The lesson of the cycle appears to be that regimes degenerate from internal causes that cannot be allayed by external adventurism.[21] Unlike Machiavelli, Polybius avoids making a clear judgment between Sparta's stay-at-home regime and Roman imperialism. But in keeping with the parallel between regimes and individuals, he leaves it to individual choice whether to seek the glory and power for which the Roman regime was framed (VI.50.3). His own pupil and friend Scipio was his model of a perfect man, and he quotes Scipio's everlasting epitome of the classical spirit in politics, while contemplating the ruin of Carthage: "A fine thing, Polybius, but I fear and foresee the same fate some day for my own country" (XXXVIII.21; cf. XXIX.21).

In fact, the Romans make both mistakes that Polybius opposed at the beginning of his analysis of their regime. They assume, like all partisans, that their regime—or really, regimes—are immortal, hence that there is no need to mix them. And they doubt that any natural basis exists for the good regimes; hence they rely on fear, superstition, and imperialism. Polybius' "naturalism," far from reflecting Roman power, is intended to be a gentle but firm corrective against it (Polybius, as a prisoner-of-war of the Romans, was in no position to denounce them). His naturalism, unlike the modern version, counsels acceptance of and reliance on nature. It does not reduce nature to blind necessity or chance, nor does it regard politics as human weakness driven by fear and love of glory. So Polybius's naturalism does not propose the conquest of nature or the overcoming of chance. His natural cycle of regimes is not, therefore, the state of nature in which modern political science placed men, and from which it would remove them by means of the rational manipulation of fear. This science would give the powers or functions of government new definition, in a context where the fear Polybius thought characteristic merely of Rome's regime has been projected as the nature of the human situation. For Polybius, the executive is still kingship, still responsible for producing virtue, not yet a power loosed from natural restraint. To the extent that the Roman consuls as he presents them are Machiavellian princes, he deplores the resemblance.

The Roman Dictator

In modern times the dictator of early and classical republican Rome (c. 501–217 B.C.) has enjoyed an afterlife of great success in theory, and of singular infamy in practice. The fascist dictators and the communist dictatorship of the proletariat that we have experienced in our time account for the infamy, but their bold exploitation of a republican device follows its adoption by such thinkers as Rousseau and Marx.[22] In the dictators of our day we see the culmination of the outsized modern executive, in which the executive rejects constitutional limitations and seizes power for itself, though still in the name of the people or historical forces. But if the dictator becomes a central character in the later history of executive power, he also has a supporting role in the story I have chosen to tell of the development of the constitutional executive.

When presenting the necessity of "energy in the executive" in the American presidency, Alexander Hamilton refers to the "formidable title of dictator" as evidence that the Romans had recognized the same necessity (*Federalist* 70). His opponents, the Anti-Federalists, also admitted the force of the example, but they were likely to refer to the abuse of the office by Sulla and Caesar which led to the destruction of the republic.[23] How frequent were appeals to the Roman dictatorship in early modern political science can be learned from Carl Schmitt's *Die Diktatur*, where its executive character is also remarked. But Schmitt characterizes this interest in the Roman dictator as distinctly modern, and tied to the formation of the modern state. In modern writers, according to Schmitt, such discussion was a way of bringing the question of sovereignty to the fore—of demanding that even a republic have a method of resolving disputes by referring them to "one alone."[24] That demand, we shall see, was first voiced by Machiavelli, the founder of the modern executive.

But was the Roman dictator therefore a genuine modern executive? I think not. The modern afterlife of the dictator is more exciting by far than its ancient history, and does more to conceal than reveal the meaning ancient writers give it. Even while moderns legitimize, expand, and exploit the Roman dictator, the ancients minimized and deplored it.[25] The moderation of their judgment is not so easy to appreciate now, amidst the din of recent events. And modern writers such as Machiavelli and Jean Bodin disguised the extent of their innovation by invoking the misleading Roman precedent. One beautiful instance of this magnification can be found in Jean Bodin's *Six Books of the Republic* (1576). Bodin cites the dictator to prove that even republican Romans admitted the necessity of sovereignty and the advantages of monarchy; then he clinches the point by quoting Tacitus: "Tacitus saith, that for the execution of great exploits the power of commanding must be restrained to one alone."[26] This remark rudely distorts Tacitus but is faithful to Machiavelli,[27] and with this textbook case of *Tacitismo* (the sixteenth-century fashion for putting Machiavellisms in the mouth of Tacitus) Bodin attributes Machiavelli's great interest in the dictator to the Romans.

Ancient writers on dictatorship did otherwise, playing down the need for a dictator. The clearest instance of this ancient tact is in Book VI of Polybius's *Histories*, the study of the Roman regime analyzed earlier. Polybius simply fails to mention the dictator, much less discuss him, anywhere in that Book, most notably in the place where he speaks vaguely of the union of the three parts of the regime in emergencies (VI.18).[28] Earlier Polybius had dwelt on the naming of Fabius Maximus as dictator after a disastrous Roman defeat, when the people and Senate had abandoned their elected rulers (III.86–87). Here he says nothing of resorting to the desperate expedient, but merely gives the credit for united action in emergencies to the character of the regime (VI.18.4).

Perhaps the omission is an aspect of the careful criticism of Rome's regime that Polybius carries on amidst his praise for it. Dionysius of Halicarnassus, writing at a time when there was little or nothing left of the republic to be saved, is much franker in his account of the dictator. His elevation was, Dionysius says, a deceit of the Senate against the poor, and was devised to suspend the law providing for an appeal to the people. The dictatorship was thus a voluntary or elective tyranny called by a nicer name for use when the laws could not provide justice, as in the case of military emergencies, or in domestic seditions when the magistrates could not uphold the laws (V.70–74). In sum, the occasional resort to a dictator constitutes an admission, contrary to Polybius's assurances, that the Roman regime did not hold together in times of bad fortune.

The truth blurted out by Dionysius is covered up by Livy and Cicero, both Romans who lived when it was possible, or necessary, to feel a sense of responsibility for the republic. But this concealment took two different forms. Livy concedes that the dictator was resorted to on "fearful occasions" (*in trepidis rebus*), both domestic and foreign, when the state of the regime was disturbed, and that it went beyond "accustomed remedies" (*consuetis remediis*) because the creation of the dictator did not provide for appeal to the people or other orderly procedure. Thus, there was no time for deliberation.[29] But Livy insists, and maintains that the Romans insisted, on the legality of the procedure by which dictators were named. He tells a story of how the Romans took great pains to consult the Senate before naming Camillus dictator, by sending a youth to float down the Tiber past the threatening Veii into Rome and back to the army with the Senate's full authorization (V.46). Then again, when Fabius was made dictator by the people rather than by the consul and the Senate, Livy contends that he was not truly dictator but *pro dictatore*, "in place of the dictator" (XXII.31).

Instead of trying manfully to keep the dictator within the rule of law, Cicero does his best to assimilate him to the virtue of kingship: rule of law and kingship are the two alternative remedies for tyranny that we have seen in Aristotle (*Politics* 1286a8–

10). Cicero says, through his spokesman Scipio, that the dictator was seen as a new kind of power "near to the image of a king" (*Republic* II.32), and not as a tyranny. Dictatorship is like the familiar consulship in this regard. Explaining to the Stoic Laelius, Scipio says that in grave crises one seeks the help of an expert, a pilot or a doctor for example. The Roman people, he adds, have sought such help in their more serious wars, when they obey a dictator as they would a king (I.40)—implying (unlike Dionysius and Livy) that the dictatorship was willingly and reasonably consented to, rather than imposed.

Earlier Scipio had argued that every regime, if it is to be permanent, must be ruled by some sort of deliberation (*consilium*, I.26). And in explaining why, of the three simple regimes, he preferred kingship, he had introduced the analogy of kingship to the minds of men, where the best part, deliberation, must rule as one (I.38).[30] This one is a part that brings unity to a larger whole; it is not the *uno solo* who is Machiavelli's executive, the one who is a whole by himself. Cicero maintains the fiction, for it must be at least in part fiction, that the dictator continues, even embodies, the rule of reason under the principle of kingship and the examples of experts. True, he mentions two experts, as if to cast doubt on his own contention; for one could wonder during an emergency whether to obey a pilot presumably taking you to your destination or a doctor presumably keeping you alive. And is the one who is most expert necessarily most just (I.41)? So the kingly concept of the dictator seems as difficult to accept as the legal one; and in fact Cicero himself gives a legal statement of the dictator's office comparable to Livy's insistent description in his own more legalistic dialogue (*Laws* III.3.9).

Maintaining the legal formalities of the dictator and elevating him to kingship were two ways of serving the same end of reducing the scope of his power. In their own interpretation of the office, ancient writers recoiled from the opportunity to conceive—even when the fact was there to be exploited—a robust executive power exempt from the law and unbounded by the need to deliberate or consult.

The Theologico-Political Executive

With the advent of Christianity, the theologico-political question that we have seen in the background of Aristotle's kingship comes to the fore. Aristotle took pains to prevent his argument for kingship from being useful to those who might understand it as personal divinity. In Book III of the *Politics* he introduces the political philosopher who is to resolve all issues without resort to the gods; in Book IV he divides monarchy into the elements of the mixed regime; and throughout, he keeps a close guard on the pretensions of poets and priests. But the precautions against the excesses of the sacral city were carefully muted, as if Aristotle feared the fate of Socrates and wanted mainly to let sleeping dogs lie while alerting to the problem only those readers he had already awakened. Aristotle does not hold a distinguished rank in the history of anticlericalism, and for the most part he leaves it to be inferred from the self-sufficiency of the city that citizens or rulers do not and should not have to regard themselves as executives of the gods.

In the most conspicuous statement on politics in the New Testament, however, St. Paul says of the ruler: "For he is the minister of God to thee for good. But if thou do that which is evil, be afraid; for he beareth not the word in vain: for he is the minister of God, a revenger to *execute* wrath upon him that doeth evil."[31] The actual political meaning of this passage is unclear, especially since the New Testament is mostly nonpolitical and counsels peace. Christianity, unlike Islam, did not spread by waging Holy Wars of actual conquest.

Christianity's way was conversion or subversion by the work of a Church that was not, especially in the West, an instrument of the secular authorities. Generally speaking, in continuing disputes in the West between the Church and the medieval Empire or monarchy, one side could argue that since rulers are subjects of God, kings should be subject to the pope, the chief minister of God, while the other side asserted that since rulers are *ministers* of God, kings have an undoubted divine right of their own. In fact, the title *vicarius Christi*, which was at first shared between the pope and the emperor, was gradually assumed exclusively by the pope.[32]

Over centuries the papacy continued to set forth the pretensions it had first asserted in the fifth century, especially in the doctrine of Gelasius I (492–96), that conceived secular rulers as executives of the pope. When in 800 the pope crowned Charlemagne "Emperor of the Romans," he actually created on the basis of papal doctrine an office, later called the Holy Roman Emperor, that seems at least proto-executive and perhaps more.[33] In the East the Roman emperor was not crowned by the pope or anyone else in a way to make him appear to be minister to the Church. The Eastern emperor claimed to be the vicegerent of God and styled himself *autocrator*. He was his own mediator with God and kept the Eastern Church subordinate, with a patriarch of Constantinople as its head. Under Constantine the Great Eusebius formulated a doctrine using the claims of absolutism made on behalf of the Hellenistic Kings and transforming them with a Christian appointment. Since there was one God and one law in Heaven, the same was true on earth; and though the emperor was not divine himself, like the Hellenistic king, he was God's sole vicegerent. This argument was restated and improved in the sixth century by the emperor Justinian, whose codification of Roman law opposed the papal pretensions and justified his Christian monarchy in terms historians now call "Caesaropapism."[34]

In the West, the theologico-political landscape was quite different. After the barbarian invasions, the popes saw an opportunity to create an Emperor of the Romans from a king of the peoples that had defeated the Romans. Since there was no Constantine in the West with a legitimate claim of succession to the Roman Empire, the popes would create an emperor of their own who would, therefore, not be an *autocrator*. He would be their executive, ruling by grace of God as validated and interpreted by them. Empire by grace would replace claims of right based on merit and contribution in the Aristotelian manner, and all politics would be suffused with the spirit of this example of papal coronation at the top. This plan was thought up, set in motion, and pursued for centuries by the popes with varying results but with set purpose.[35] They never succeeded in actually making the emperors their ministers, but they did achieve considerable independence for themselves and a power, never uncontested but never suppressed, to intervene in political disputes when and where it pleased them. They proceeded by stages marked by the efforts of the great popes to gain new points and additional advantages. One such attempt was the forged Donation of Constantine in the eighth century, purporting to be a grant by Constantine, made in the fervor of his conversion to Christianity, of all his empire, West and East, to the pope.[36] The pope could then dispose of the empire as he wished, temporarily; for though Constantine's donation was for good, as to the successor of St. Peter, the pope's was to an individual and could be revoked if the pope pleased. This situation was to be expressed in the ceremony of coronation in which the pope created the emperor. If the document was forged, it was done out of charity to the Christian intent of Constantine and all other Christian rulers to follow him.

Is the Holy Roman Emperor, then, an instance of executive power? If so, it would be all the more impressive for being conceived in theory and sustained for so long despite the realities of power that generally favored the emperor over the pope, and the territorial princes and kings over the emperor. The basis of the papal theory was the principle of Pope Zosimus in 420 that the pope "may not be judged."[37] Machiavelli, commenting on Charlemagne's coronation, said that "Charlemagne judged that the pope as vicar of God could not be judged by men."[38] With this repetition of the word *judging* he meant to indicate both the inevitability of human judgment and the human desire to mask one's judgment. In this case the judgment to abide by the pope was masked by the pope's claim to enjoy the grace of God. In Christian doctrine, the claim to grace takes precedence over any claim of right. With a claim to grace, a ruler does not take responsibility either for his selection or for his deeds as ruler; he neither becomes ruler because of his merits nor rules well because of them. He cannot assume responsibility for the gifts and limitations of nature in the Aristotelian manner because, even in a Christianity modified by philosophy, grace is superior to nature and no human can presume upon grace. In the papal theory, the emperor is the pope's executive, but the pope is an executive too, the vicar of Christ or of God. That is why the pope cannot be judged. But the Western emperor could and did answer in kind to the pope, in a manner similar to the pretension of the Eastern emperor, who claimed to be God's vicegerent.

The claim to grace, it appears, is as disputable as the claim of right: You're my executive! No, you're mine. No way exists to resolve this dispute except, perhaps, by understanding it as a dispute over right: the right of the pope deriving from his function, compared to the relative ranking deserved by the emperor because of his function. But then the nature of the dispute has been changed, and besides, as we have seen in Aristotle, any resolution of the dispute in terms of right leads toward kingship or the mixed regime, not toward executive power. Executive power is power that is visibly and decisively executed, as opposed to the papal *plenitudo potestatis*, which was always, necessarily, more pretense than reality and never produced clear-cut decisions carried out by the emperor for the pope. This lack of execution is reflected in the paradox Machiavelli seized on: that Christianity in its political consequences is both too soft and too cruel. It is too soft when divine commands get in the way of political necessities ("Thou shalt not kill"), and too cruel when they exceed political necessities ("Thou shalt have no other God"). Machiavelli's solution to disputes over both grace and right, we shall see, is to introduce the principle of human necessity. What is necessary to us is both providential and just; and though my necessity may conflict with yours, under the principle of necessity we shall dispute no more than is strictly necessary. Machiavelli's introduction of necessity into political dispute pushes aside the question of responsibility, since no one is responsible for his necessities.

Yet if necessity is inevitable, there is nothing inevitable about the *principle* of necessity that Machiavelli presents as his solution to disputes over divine grace and human right. The pope did not in fact attempt to make the emperor his executive out of respect for the sovereignty of human necessity, nor did the emperor defend himself with that argument. The Holy Roman Emperor was not a modern executive, whose effectual actions are designed to end all dispute, but a theologico-political executive, whose claim to grace is essentially contestable. If we call the emperor an executive, it is because he is executive for the pope: or is it vice versa? But whatever the modern executive says, he is in truth his own man, not another's.

Thus, despite the unpolitical character of Christianity, the resulting uncertainty over the status of politics, and disputes in Christendom between Church and State, an obvious danger was that men would give their worldly conflicts a divine interpretation and understand their own wrath as God's. Instead of diminishing conflicts, the disputants would magnify them, and instead of tempering human anger they would inflate it, not by imitating fiercer religions, but merely by being tempted to abuse the human inclination to call on divine aid.

The Christian Church, therefore, could not be ignored as Aristotle ignored the city's priests, nor the Bible dismissed as he both dismissed and used poetic theology. For political scientists, the new circumstances would make it impossible to adopt his strategy of covering up the theologico-political question, to use Spinoza's term for what is perhaps *the* permanent question of politics. Political science had to confront the issue, and then to present an understanding of human politics that produced a safe alternative to one that was open to abuse by political men who could approach human politics as the vengeful execution of divine rule.

5

The Theologico-Political
Executive

How can men, who are ruled by God, rule themselves? The theologico-political question was the constitutive issue of medieval politics, setting bishops against kings in particular realms and culminating in the dramatic struggle between the pope and his hoped-for executive, the emperor. We could, therefore, examine the issue in many, many places both in history and in thought. But because we are concerned with the interpretation given to events and have remarked the absence of the executive interpretation in Aristotle, I have chosen three prominent Aristotelians—Thomas Aquinas, Dante Alighieri, and Marsilius of Padua—to determine what additions and adjustments they made to the Aristotelian schema in order to deal with the threat of the theologico-political executive. All three were well known to Machiavelli, who faced the same threat. But none of them would have advised him to leave Aristotle behind. Against the idea that human government executes divine will, they attempted to restore and adjust the Aristotelian argument for ruling, in which men take responsibility for governing themselves. None conceived Machiavelli's idea of evading that responsibility by appropriating the pope's executive role for the use of secular princes, governing on the basis of human necessities.

Aquinas on Kingship

Thomas Aquinas is the classic standard of Christian Aristotelianism. He was the best, the most comprehensive, and nearly the first of Aristotle's Christian interpreters. Confronting the dubious status of politics in Christian teaching, Aquinas gave politics an integrity of its own while denying its independence from God. Thus politics could be understood as *guided* by God's commands but not merely *executing* them. To accomplish the task, Aquinas seized on Aristotle's conception of nature which had been made available by the rediscovery of Aristotle's *Physics* in the thirteenth century.[1] But he brought the conception to bear on politics with a degree of emphasis not to be found in Aristotle himself.

For Aristotle, nature acts for an end; the inanimate and animate beings in nature have an internal motion to a specific end for which their form or constitution suits them. The nature of a thing is what it is *intrinsically*. Combining this Aristotelian conception with the Christian doctrine of the createdness of nature, Aquinas concluded that God was the author of nature. Thus all natures and the intelligent nature in human beings were considered intrinsic, or natures in their own right, in addition to being created; and their having been created did not make them instruments or puppets of the gods, because God created them as natures within nature for ends of their own, and nature's own, as well as for His end. Aquinas applies this intrinsic character of nature to politics in two different ways that we shall consider in turn—natural law (in the *Summa Theologica* especially) and natural sociability in his *On Kingship.*

Aquinas's celebrated discussion of natural law in the *Summa Theologica* was much elaborated by others who succeeded him, but it is only one of 514 Questions in his work. The discussion occurs within the context of a general consideration of law, which, with grace, is an exterior principle of human action coming from God, as contrasted to the virtues, which are interior or intrinsic or voluntary. Because law is exterior to human actions, Aquinas's discussion of natural law (Ia IIae 90–108) is isolated from his treatment of the virtue of justice (IIa IIae 80, 122).[2] The isolation results in a certain legalism that puts a distance between natural law and politics. Beginning with the "nature of law," Aquinas remarks that law is an ordering to the common good performed either by the "whole multitude" or by "some viceregent" of it, the "public person" who has its coercive force. The viceregent is not an executive, for he is later defined in Aristotelian fashion, within the context of human law (Ia IIae 95.4), as the ruler (*gubernans*) or regime (*regimen*). But if he is not an executive of the people, no more is he an executive of God. And the function of Aquinas's conception of natural law seems to be precisely to counter this possibility.

Natural law is part of God's eternal law, the part in which humans share through their faculty of reason. It is also distinct from divine law as revealed in the Bible, which is not available to unassisted human reason. Hence natural law is neither simply independent of God's law nor merely executive of it. Insofar as it is *law*, it is exterior to man; insofar as it is *natural*, it is intrinsic or interior. Allowing for human freedom, yet limiting it, natural law transforms our freedom from a rebellion against God into pious accordance with both His law and our will. Natural law for Aquinas is not at all the denial of freedom that it might appear to be today, or as it perhaps became in the elaborate codifications of sixteenth- and seventeenth-century jurists. To assess the meaning of natural law, which is partly intrinsic to men, one must compare it to divine grace, which is purely extrinsic (though it presupposes something in the soul to receive it, Ia IIae 110.1). Aquinas says that although grace "is more efficacious than nature, yet nature is more essential to man, and therefore more permanent" (Ia IIae 94.6).

Nor does natural law determine human law in any way that makes the latter executive of it. Natural law consists only of the most common principles of human action. Rather than determining human law, natural law must be determined (in the sense of *specified*) by human law, and these determinations are made by prudence, not by the fixed rules or methods of an art (Ia IIae 57.4, IIa IIae 47.4, 15). The determinations by human law are *derived* from natural law, but they are not part of natural law and do not carry the authority of its universality. The law of nations, to be sure, is derived from natural law as conclusions follow from principles, but civil laws are derived from natural law "by the mode of particular determination according to which each city determines for itself what is fitting" (Ia IIae 95.4). In explaining the relationship between human and divine (or revealed) law, Aquinas does not consider why, given divine law, human law is necessary. To the contrary, he shows why divine law is necessary (Ia IIae 91.4). The reasons he gives—the human inclination to eternal happiness, the uncertainty of human judgment, the hidden character of motives, the impossibility of punishing all wrong-doing—sum up the necessary imperfection or human law. But in so doing they liberate human law from the demand that it imitate, approximate, or execute, divine law.

Accordingly, Aquinas treats punishment and vengeance in a manner to prevent their being misused in attempts to execute God's wrath, while leaving scope for human anger to express itself. Anyone can reward, he says, but punishment belongs only to the minister of the law (Ia IIae 92.2). This promising remark does not introduce an expanded executive who exploits the minister's power to punish, however. Similarly, in the question devoted to vengeance, Aquinas allows that it is not in itself evil and harmful. On the contrary, vengeance is natural because it is an "inclination of nature" to get rid of what is harmful: indeed, it is even a virtue. And he cites St. Paul's warning (*Romans* 13:4, KJV, quoted in Chapter 4 above) to justify vengeance within the limits of "divinely instituted order" (IIa IIae 108.1). Thus vengeance is neither denied to men nor imposed on them. Aquinas's conception of nature protects the execution of human law from the twin dangers of being suppressed and being appropriated in the service of an interest extrinsic to humanity.

In his *On Kingship*, an incomplete work dedicated to the King of Cyprus,[3] Aquinas does not speak of natural law and relies instead on the sociable nature of man. This nature requires not any kind of society, however, but a free one that exists for its own sake, not a society of slaves that exists for another. The distinction leads Aquinas to praise the virtues of the Roman republic, which depended on a republican spirit hostile to kings. He also insists on a difference between kingship and tyranny: one cannot simply rest satisfied with the Biblical analogy of king to shepherd (*On Kingship* I.1.12–13; 4.35; 6.51).

In Book III of the *Politics*, Aristotle develops the notion of the common good out of arguments advanced by democrats, then finds that argument supported by nature in the kingship of the best man. But Aquinas is in a different historical situation in which kingships abound and Christian opinion hesitates to make this-worldly political claims. He begins immediately from human nature itself in order to improve kingship, using the notion of the common good to correct Christian indifference to the spirit of free politics. His argument culminates by understanding the king as founder, who by establishing a kingdom makes a kind of new beginning for men.[4] The founder is less than a creator; he must accept and make use of things that already exist in nature—he must accept nature as it is and will God's creation as it has been created (II.2). Thinking of the king as a founder reminds us that we rely on God, yet do not submit to His law as slaves. Humanity is a "multitude of free men" (I.1.10) whose freedom is secured by its nature, that is, precisely by its special kind of unfreedom.

Whether everything that reason finds and supports in human nature is consistent with all that Christian doctrine requires is a difficult question that comes to a focus in politics as much as in metaphysics. How does one treat human recalcitrance? Is it a crude sense of freedom to be ennobled, as does Aristotle; or is it pride that needs to be humbled, as in the Bible? Aquinas makes a friendly compromise between the two treatments, each of which is equally far from the political science that Machiavelli conceived in order to develop his idea of the executive.

Dante's Monarchy

For Thomas Aquinas, the ecclesiastical hierarchy and the authority of the pope are not in question. In *On Kingship* he advises the king to accept the Church and the pope willingly. The king must accept the superiority of the supernatural to the natural, or the spiritual to the temporal, and Aquinas announces that kings must be subject to priests, and especially to the chief priest, the pope (II.3). Perhaps the subjection might be justified on natural grounds, necessary to secure the difference between kingship and tyranny and providing surer rewards and punishments from God than men on their own can know or provide (I.7–11). Thus, to keep himself a king and not a tyrant, the king should willingly accept the limits to his own power that come from the powers of the church insofar as the Church constitutes a temporal establishment of the spiritual power. But Aquinas is not very explicit here, and in any case the practical import of such subjection to the pope was not clear.[5]

With the publication of the Papal Bull *Unam Sanctam* in 1302, the import was clarified in an explicit and extreme manner by Pope Boniface VIII, in his own favor. Here we find the doctrine of two swords, based on Luke 22:38, where Christ tells his disciples that swords will be needed, but that two are enough.[6] These are interpreted as the spiritual and the temporal sword, both to be in the power of the Church. The temporal sword is in the hands of kings and soldiers, but it is to be exercised, according to the bull, "at the command and sufferance of the priest" (*ad nutum et patientiam sacerdotis*), and in this expanded sense "temporal authority must be subject to spiritual powers." The statement seems, at least in its claim if not in its practical intent, to go beyond occasional interference from the Church in temporal affairs for the purposes of self-defense or in a spirit of tolerant superintendence. It seems indeed to raise the possibility of a downright theocracy of one sword—in which case secular political authority, confined to punishing and soldiering, would be executive for the Church, and would exercise both instrumental functions on command of a spiritual authority that as such cannot wield an actual sword or "coactive force" (*vis coactiva*).

Against the claim of Boniface,[7] Dante argued that the secular prince, the emperor, has his authority directly from God and not from the Church. The emperor's end is the securing of happiness in this life as instructed by philosophy; the Church's end is happiness in eternal life, from spiritual instruction. Neither is subordinate to the other, nor are they equals in the same sphere. Both are superiors, but of different kinds: the pope has a relationship of paternity over men and the emperor has one of lordship (*dominatio, Monarchy* III.11).[8] Let us see from *Monarchy* (*ca.* 1312), Dante's chief political work, how he dealt with the danger, as he reckoned it, of a secular government subservient to the pope. (Much politics will also be found in the cantos of the *Divine Comedy*, but I cannot take up the difficult question of the relationship between these two works.[9] Whereas in the *Divine Comedy* Dante attacks the pope and says little on monarchy, in *Monarchy* he is deferential toward the pope and makes monarchy his theme.)[10]

In *Monarchy* Dante does not immediately set out to argue that the emperor has his authority directly from God and not from another, namely God's minister or vicar, the pope. That is his third proposition, in Book III, after showing, in Book I, what temporal monarchy is, and, in Book II, whether the Roman people rightly lays claim to this monarchy—namely, the monarchy of the Holy Roman Empire. The reason for not coming more directly to the point, we may suppose, is that Dante did not want to free the emperor from papal authority so that he could endorse the emperor's own claim to execute God's laws as he desires: Dante, in short, did not attack the pope in order to create a modern sovereign. Instead he offers eleven arguments in Book I to prove that temporal monarchy, "a single principality over all men in time," is "necessary for the good of the world" (I.2). He does not mention Aristotle's *pambasileia*,[11] the kingship over all men and all things, but together the proofs constitute an interpretation of Aristotle's kingship—a very strange interpretation, though Dante does not say so. For he supposes, unlike Aristotle himself, that Aristotle's kingship can be actualized, that one prince might be made ruler of the whole world. Thomas Aquinas in *On Kingship* had supposed no such thing; he takes for granted that the king and the kingdom he addresses are one among the many. But Dante points to the emperor Augustus as a temporal monarch actually ruling the world (before the popes, something he did not need to say, I.16), and in Dante's own time he had the much reduced and embattled Holy Roman Emperor to serve as the beneficiary, if not as an example, of his arguments.

The consequences of making Aristotle's super-kingship actual are, apparently, to depart from Aristotle and to distort him.[12] Whereas Aristotle begins his more directly political argument in Book III of the *Politics* from the *form* of a city, Dante begins his only argument from its *end*, as if there were no need to discuss form.[13] Moreover, because Aristotle regards kingship as above regimes, his actualization of the best regime in Books IV to VI of the *Politics* proceeds through the several regimes, preeminently the mixed regime. But Dante assumes that when God, the author of nature, established the end of humanity, He made it achievable through the one form of government, monarchy, that can unite men. Aristotle, in keeping with the plurality of regimes, makes a point of the difference between the good man and the serious citizen even in the best regime (*Politics* 1276b36–1277a25). But Dante, quoting him, asserts that they are identical under the best regime (I.12).[14] Finally, Aristotle's tone is sober and responsible, and his arguments proceed from political speech and stay within the realm of the political. But Dante appeals to the character of nature as a whole in proofs that seem more physical or metaphysical than political. Although he distinguishes theoretical from practical sciences, he allows the practical to appear as mere extensions of the theoretical,[15] perhaps replying in kind to Boniface's *Unam Sanctam* (I.3, 4). Altogether, he seems utopian; but in a medieval setting, with man in his place in nature and under God, Dante's *Monarchy* is easily distinguishable from the triumphant, humanistic idealism of Kant's essay, *On Perpetual Peace*.

Instead of beginning from political dispute, Dante begins from the principle (*principium*) that is the final end of all nature, including human beings. And Dante equates the principle with temporal monarchy. But, just as in Aristotle's discussion of the single *archē* in "kingship over all," an essential equivocation underlies the equation of the rule or principle of nature and of human beings: does man serve the end of nature or does nature serve the end of man? Dante expresses the equivocation in the notion of "possible intellect" that derives from Averroes (1126–1198), the Arabic philosopher and non-Christian Aristotelian. Since nature gives everything an end and makes nothing in vain, men must have a specific end not shared with others: this is the possible intellect. The specific human work is to actualize the possible intellect, a task that Dante understands as political.

Dante's politicizing of the possible intellect, though he proceeds in a manner unlike that of Averroes[16] and Aristotle, does serve Aristotle's purpose of raising doubt about nature's teleology. The same equivocation that we saw in Aristotle reappears: when the possible intellect is actualized, do men serve nature's end or do they make nature serve theirs? If men merely serve nature's end, they must be nature's slaves; if they serve their own end, they possess no limitations on their freedom. Dante's argument in Book I of *Monarchy*, like Aristotle's in Book III of the *Politics*, moves between and weaves together unacceptable extremes.[17] Dante keeps a balance between the good of the world, which is nature's good, and the necessity of a world, which is man's good. The result is that nature permits human perfection and suggests what it is, but does not guarantee it—indeed nature leaves its actualization to us. Thus, nature neither compels man to accept the weak executive of a higher law that will make him perfect, nor does she require him, using the manners and modes of a strong executive, to seek his own good unprotected from necessity and unprompted by healthy inclinations. Dante's politics can be found in the free space between the two extremes that constitute the ambivalence of the modern executive. Dante's monarch is to be regarded, not as an executive, but rather as *minister omnium* (I.12), the minister of all things including all men. As he serves all things, he keeps men to a standard of perfection; as he serves all men, he advances their claim to self-rule.[18]

In Book II of *Monarchy*, Dante admits that nature (or God through nature) does not guarantee the rule of a monarch. Such rule must be achieved as the Roman people acquired their empire. The question Dante examines here is whether the Roman people acquired their empire, and with it the office of temporal monarch, by right or justly (*de iure*). But this rather narrow question actually continues the broader inquiry of Book I into the possibility of human justice. Is human justice the execution of divine decree or natural law, or can men maintain the distinctions of justice important and relevant to them in consonance with nature, though not in simple obedience? Augustine had argued the first point; Cicero the second; Machiavelli was to give a third answer in refutation of them both and of Dante as well.

For Augustine (*The City of God*, Book V) the long life of the Roman empire shows, despite the virtue of its heroes, the insufficiency of human virtue and the need for divine reward, both in this life and the next. For Cicero, the history of the Roman republic (*Republic*, Book II) shows, after considerable embellishment, that a people can acquire and exercise its rule justly, hence that human justice (or natural right) is attainable without descending to criminal actions. Dante's treatment of the same evidence seems closer to Cicero than to Augustine (though he could not have read Cicero's *Republic*, as yet undiscovered). Abandoning the necessity of universal peace postulated in Book I (I.4, 14), he settles for the success of justified force—and then bestows justice on successful force through the justice of duels that sanctions taking the fruits of combat (II.7–9). Instead of subordinating human justice to divine providence like Augustine, he brings divine providence to the aid of human justice—even if justice means no more than that, in a dispute between two princes, we humans need a winner (the argument, one recalls, of I.10). But Dante does not go so far as to abandon justice and to proclaim a new virtue without justice, as did Machiavelli, for whom the history of Rome shows the power of human virtue rather than the necessity of divine providence, and the impotence rather than the attainability of human justice.

Dante avoids these Machiavellian conclusions. In Book III of *Monarchy* he maintains that the emperor has his authority directly from God, not by way of the pope. His crucial argument (III.8) is directed at the text in Matthew (16:19) that gives Peter the power of binding and loosing "in all things"—especially, said the pope's advocates, in all human laws and decrees. Dante rebuffs this claim with the explanation that "all things" are divided into natural classes that must be treated with respect for their differences; in particular, he reminds the popes, human beings form a class of willful animals who cling to their own and resist penitence. They need a government suited to their willfulness, one neither overbearing nor subservient.[19] Here is the same human recalcitrance that was featured in Aristotle and Aquinas as the boundary between man and nature, or man and God.

Dante, like Aristotle, identifies the emperor with the philosopher (III.12, 16). But Dante is not led to reject the pope's authority, as one might have expected. A concluding passage has been interpreted in contrary ways: Either as an expression of his ineradicable Christianity, or as an ironic, superficial concession,[20] Dante says that Caesar owes to Peter the reverence that a first-born son owes to his father (III.15). If that is Dante's concession to the ruling authority of his time, perhaps it is not a superficial one, but a profound recognition of the need for a conventional—that is, paternal—authority[21] to keep men mindful that the ruling authority must come from above. To safeguard human liberty, better that this authority be twofold, spiritual as well as temporal (III.16).[22] But human liberty cannot in any way be ensured by reducing both to one earthly authority in man alone. The need for unity between nature and man set forth in Book I of *Monarchy* could have been answered with a forcible assertion of human sovereignty over nature, but this would have foreclosed the possibility of justice that Dante advances in Book II, and denied the meaning of authority that is his theme in Book III. Looking back at Dante from the secularism later established by Machiavelli, we see limits to Dante's anticlericalism created by his own intrepid moderation rather than by a halfhearted refusal to be, in Machiavelli's phrase, "altogether bad."[23]

Marsilius and the Executive Ruler

With Marsilius of Padua's great work, *Defender of the Peace* (1324), we come almost to the point of departure for the modern doctrine of executive power. For the first time "execution" and the "executive" become a theme in political science. Marsilius is one of the greatest of political philosophers, and I propose to treat him as such—which means, as a political scientist. Usually he is treated historically, either for his many tantalizing anticipations of modern ideas or for his influence on Church reformers, including later Protestants. His thought on the executive is surely one of the anticipations. But it can be properly appreciated only if it is examined for its value as political science. Unexamined, such an anticipation may appear to be no more than a lucky, unwitting stroke of invention, fundamentally uninteresting and likely to flatter us in the belief that our predecessors were children. The interest rises, however, when a great thinker, like Marsilius, gives us pause by his very failure to carry through his anticipations. We are impressed by the hesitations, or rather rejections, that confine the anticipations. In that case we learn something about what is essential to our modern idea, and concurrently, about the historical age in which other ideas prevailed. In current terms, one could say that the text leads us to the context. Why, then, did Marsilius *almost* come to the modern executive?

It appears that Marsilius conceives the ruler or the entire government as executive for the sovereign people; and he makes the task of executing law central to the success of government. Philosophers who help by opposing wrong doctrines and advancing new truths will not only defend the peace of their commonwealths but perhaps also find the wisdom they seek as philosophers. Marsilius brings us very far from the studied dismissal of the executive by Aristotle, and yet, with a carefully measured limit to his prudent and respectful departure, he returns to Aristotle's principles, within which the executive must have a subordinate place.

Marsilius seems to break the pattern we have seen in the Christian Aristotelians of relying on nature to meet the threat of the theologico-political executive. He speaks of natural law only twice, and then as a quasi-natural law (*Defender of the Peace* I.3.4; 19.13; cf. I.1.4). In one place only does he speak of natural right, and there he declares it "natural" only metaphorically (*transumptive*; II.12.7). The examples he gives of natural right refer only to the minimal actions necessary to maintain society, far from the perfection of human life in the best society that we saw in the natural right of Aquinas and Dante. Marsilius rejects the higher view, which identifies natural right with right reason, because what is reasonable is not universally agreed to, and what is universally agreed upon is not reasonable (II.12.8). Natural right must be enacted into civil law, whereupon it loses its rationality whether in the minimal or the perfect sense. Should an individual wish to intervene where law does not exist or is imperfect, he obeys a quasi-natural law that lacks the assurance of both reason and law. Although Marsilius sets forth the Aristotelian distinction between living and living well (I.4.1), he never cites, among many Aristotelian quotations, Aristotle's definition that man is by nature a political animal.[24] What man is by nature, it seems, does not tell us enough about his politics. In sum, Marsilius—unlike Aquinas and Dante—seems to make little use of nature either to guide or ground politics.

The difference does not imply that Marsilius was satisfied with the conduct or the pretensions of the papacy. No more determined enemy of popes has perhaps ever lived—not Dante, not even Machiavelli. Dante was willing to compromise with the pope and Machiavelli accepted a commission (to write his *Florentine Histories*) from a cardinal who became a pope. But Marsilius did not hesitate to say in his book that popes who foment civil disunion should be visited with capital punishment (II.28.29). Their interference in temporal politics, justified by their claim to hold full power (*plenitudo potestatis*) over earthly sovereigns, constitutes a "singular cause" of revolution not listed among the causes of revolution in Book V of Aristotle's *Politics* because it could not have been known to him. After recognizing the new circumstance and judging what to do, Marsilius found more help in prudence than in natural law. He also wanted to prompt certain men to act positively rather than rely passively on nature to make things right: the emperor, citizens, philosophers, and even priests (for priests are given as his addressees, II.1.2). And rather than moderating the execution of divine law through natural law, he wanted to accomplish that task by promoting the status of human law.

If human law cannot rely on a natural inclination to sociability or politics to inspire obedience, and if lawmakers do not want to make human law subordinate to divine law for the same purpose, then human law must generate its own power of enforcement. Rather than look to the right reason of philosophers or to the sanction of the Church, Marsilius turns to popular consent as the source of "coactive power" or enforcement. The people do not exercise such power, but by their consent they establish it in government. Marsilius calls the government an "executive" for them in an expanded sense.

Executio was used in classical and medieval Latin in the two senses we have today of "to carry out" and "punish." Thomas Aquinas spoke generally of *executio iustitiae* to designate the function of punishment. Justice, for him, was divisible into an architectonic virtue and a *virtus executiva et ministrans*.[25] He also used *executivum* to expand an Aristotelian distinction between the legislative and the political arts, explaining that politics means executing the legislator's universal reason on particulars.[26] His use of "executive" was for something instrumental and subordinate, more pertinent to subjects than to kings.

Brian Tierney has found a papalist contemporary of Marsilius, Hervaeus Natalis, for whom *executio* is the work of secular regimes on behalf of the pope—just the sort of "execution" Marsilius feared.[27] Alan Gewirth, in his notable work on Marsilius, found a similar use by the papalists Giles of Rome, James of Viterbo, Augustine Triumphus, and Alvarus Pelagius, who held that temporal rulers have their power *secundum executionem* for the pope but not *secundum auctoritatem* on their own.[28] Marsilius himself considered—and attacked—the distinction because it derives from a mistaken discussion of St. Bernard's on the two swords doctrine (II.28.24). But when the papalists came to consider the temporal ruler's executive power on behalf of the pope, they made no further distinction within it between legislative and executive. Dante, arguing against the notion that temporal rulers execute for the pope, kept the roles of *legis lator* and *legis executor* together within the power of the monarch (*Monarchy* I.13). Marsilius is the first to conceive the ruler entirely as an executive for the people. He does not go so far as Hobbes, who said that it ought to be their representative, but Marsilius comes very close to it (*Defender of the Peace* I.15.4).

With the expansion of the idea of the executive come other novelties. Marsilius strongly implies that since his teaching has to make its way against the "habit of listening to and believing falsehoods" (II.1.1), his teaching is altogether novel. Accordingly, though Aristotle's political science was defective only on a single point, Marsilius had to revise it entirely. Namely, to prevent the pope from ruling, he had to redefine ruling as executing by distinguishing ruling from legislating, the function of the people. The efficient cause of government, by which the people establish the ruler, gains prominence over the final and especially the formal cause. The reason why human beings first need government—to supply punishment for crimes—takes over the end of government, so that political science is confined to the needs of the body, broadly considered. As the ground or the guarantor of these needs, the human will with its "executive or motive power" (II.12.16) makes a claim to freedom as the end of government and seems to push aside the higher claims of the soul.

Marsilius does not appear to allow for, and he does not discuss, the possibility of natural slaves, as does Aristotle (II.12.13, 14.23; cf. I.9.4, 12.4, II.26.13). Since government is an executive for the citizenry, or its "weightier part" (Marsilius's famous equivocation, I.12.3), the form of government does not announce the kind of rule; for the weightier part can shift toward either democracy or oligarchy,[29] and a monarchy by popular election might be more popular than monarchical in spirit (I.9.5). Thus a discrepancy opens up between the form and the reality of government, seemingly favorable to the modern executive. All this is an intimation, even an adumbration, of the essentials of modern political science, for which Marsilius has been too eagerly given and too grudgingly denied credit by scholars.[30]

Marsilius could have begun the "new modes and orders" that Machiavelli was to undertake, but he did not have Machiavelli's intent. Marsilius presents himself as an Aristotelian. His revision of Aristotle is excused by the appearance of a "singular cause" that Aristotle could not have known, Marsilius says; and the many strange distortions and misinterpretations of Aristotle, not avowed by Marsilius, can be seen to have been intended in Aristotle's interest. Marsilius's proto-executive is in the end still Aristotle's kingship.

Because of the actions and pretensions of the pope, Marsilius faced a task that Aristotle did not—the making of a sect. With characteristic boldness Marsilius remarks that philosophers used to lay down a divine law that prescribed rewards and punishments after death for those virtues and vices that human legislators cannot ascertain through legal methods of proof. The sects thus created are necessary to civil happiness, and the priests-poets-philosophers (Marsilius blurs the difference, I.5.11) who think them up form a part of the city, Marsilius says contrary to Aristotle.[31] Aristotle could use or refine the sects that had been founded by Hesiod and Pythagoras (since he was aware of the phenomenon of sect, I.10.3), but Marsilius in his time had to formulate a new doctrine of ecclesiastical polity.

It is unclear whether the new doctrine is an act of prudence required only in this situation or a part of political philosophy essential in any time or place, which Aristotle was able to take for granted in his own singular situation.[32] Borrowing from the Arabic philosophers, Marsilius presents a doctrine of sect that is almost thoroughly neutral on the distinction between true and false sects (see I.10.7); only once, in his eleventh use of the term, does he use it pejoratively—to refer to Christians.[33] Machiavelli would appropriate Marsilius's neutral doctrine of sect, which in its indifference is effectively hostile to the Christian claim to be the true religion. In Marsilius's time the Christian sect is being brought into disrepute as Christian priests, and especially the pope, show by their ambition how little they believe in Christian contempt for worldly honor.[34] Thus, in resolving the problem on behalf of the Christian sect, Marsilius becomes a defender of the (Christian) divine law or theology before the bar of unassisted human reason or philosophy. This tended to produce public respectability for philosophy at the cost of being associated and confused with theology. Marsilius follows Averroes in justifying philosophy as an activity essential to political life, but one that should be pursued within the limits and under the conditions of political life. Dante had done the same in *Monarchy*, but took the high road. He showed that philosophy was necessary to express the fullest and highest claims of political life, so as to prevent the pope from claiming the highest ground, and therewith all remaining ground whenever he liked, for himself alone. But Dante's strategy does not surely deny the pope's claim to interfere, and it leaves the scandal of Christian clergy ruling and claiming to rule.

Marsilius, who does not refer to Dante by name in *Defender of the Peace*, took the low road; he found philosophy necessary to the first and lowest necessities in political life.[35] Like Dante, he did not claim public status for philosophy; his sect-making in *Defender of the Peace* might be compared with Dante's poetry in the *Divine Comedy*. Marsilius's political action consisted in prompting others to act. Though philosophy is necessary to political life, it does not claim in its own name to guide political life. In this it serves as an exemplar of the "voluntary poverty" that is the essential and original Christian teaching (II.12–14), and thus as a reproach to the Church in its present corrupt state.

It we examine Marsilius's political philosophy more closely, we can find a two-fold conception of executive, both weak and strong, that resembles the modern ambivalence explained earlier.

What prevents Marsilius's executive from being Machiavelli's is that Marsilius keeps it within the orbit of law, or—when that is not possible, thanks to the defects of law—under the control of virtue. His executive is ambivalent in legality and popularity rather than in power, and he remains a ruler rather than a subordinate, an interloper, or a manager. But the resemblance here to the modern executive must be pursued to see what precisely were the inhibitions (to speak as Machiavelli would) that had to be overcome. Although Machiavelli wrote two centuries after Marsilius, when modern monarchies were being constructed, and the two made different choices and devised diverse arrangements, the general political condition in which the two lived was the same. This condition had been identified by Marsilius as the ''singular cause of revolution'' posed by the pretensions of the popes, or more generally, by the religious or theologico-political issue we have been discussing. Like Marsilius's executive, the modern Machiavellian executive came into being as a response to the religious issue.

Marsilius's famous argument for popular sovereignty yields a weak executive, a rule that executes the popular will. It begins from a view of the origin of the city or government that stresses the need for punishment. On the same topic Aristotle had spoken of slavery and acquisition in Book I of the *Politics*, questions that suggest man's dependence on nature and the difficulties of his struggle to free himself from it. But Marsilius avoids those questions[36] and finds the origin of politics in the need to enforce justice, as when, for example, the village elder intervenes in a family crime by using some reasonable ordinance or quasi-natural law (I.3.4). Marsilius makes it clear that men in an imperfect original condition claimed the power to punish for themselves; it was not granted as a remedy for sin after the Fall from a perfect condition (I.3.2; 6.5–6). By concentrating on punishment, he takes human freedom for granted,[37] and leaves its relation to nature and human nature unspoken. He does not go to the extent of proclaiming, like Hobbes and Locke, that men originally exist in a state of nature in which they are perfectly free.[38]

Marsilius comes back to the question of human freedom and nature, but does not attempt to resolve it, as we do, by proclamation. Though at first men were simple and rude, with the development of the arts they became more sophisticated and practiced excesses that required more complicated punishment. No longer transparent simpletons, they acquired knowledge and desires distinguishable as either immanent—desires which do not lead to action or affect others—or transient, i.e., desires which *do* affect others. These excesses compel the formation of a ruling part of the city, and, in addition, a warrior part that both defends the city's freedom from external oppressors and executes its judgments with "coactive power" (I.5.7–8). By introducing warriors, Marsilius promotes the executive function above the low necessity it seemed to Aristotle (in Book VI of the *Politics*), and makes it something honorable. For in the context of the Biblical account of punishment as executing God's will, merely to punish low crimes as a human necessity can be a defense of human freedom.

Then, still speaking of punishment but now in an honorable sense, Marsilius describes the priestly part of the city and makes priests serve the cause of human freedom. He introduces his discussion of the sects made by philosophers (*philosophantes*), whom he apparently equates with myth-making poets, and considers both as teachers within the priestly part. They teach the rewards and especially the punishments in the next life insofar as they affect civil happiness in this one, thereby apparently connecting, and subordinating, immanent knowledge and desires to transient ones. Through their salutary teachings, philosophers take a subordinate place and become executives of the executive government. They are not teachers of founders, for founders do not have any place in Marsilius's account of the origin of the city— again contrary to Aristotle.[39]

Instead of founders or founder-legislators, Marsilius sets down the people or the multitude as the *human* legislator determining the regime and the politics of a city. For Aristotle the regime is the fundamental fact of politics, the source of laws beyond which one cannot go, but Marsilius finds an underlying cause of the regime, an agent that creates the ruling part (I.9). This agent is the efficient cause of the city, the cause that makes it capable of creating the final cause, which, we have seen, is enforcement (in an expanded sense) of justice. Rather than being its own efficient cause, as in Aristotle, the regime or government is caused, not by God (I.9.2), but by the election or consent of human beings.

Marsilius then distinguishes temperate and diseased regimes according to whether they have been elected.[40] He concentrates on the issue of elected or hereditary monarchy because he is less interested in evaluating, much less promoting, democracy than in securing human choice; and human choice, in its bare principle, needs to be protected from being determined and interfered with by divine law. Marsilius immediately inserts an unannounced discussion of law (I.10; see I.9.3) to make it clear that human choice must be lawful. And in the following chapter, relying on Aristotle (I.11), he argues that since the law must be impartial, and the many are more impartial than one or few, the law should be made by many. In fact, he selects Aristotle's discussion of the claim of one regime—democracy—to rule, and makes that the standard or basis of a choice that is prior to rule.

It is as if the democratic claim to impartiality were simply true, so that one could ignore its democratic origin and character, that is, its partisanship. It is as if the human claim to rule could be stated without specifying what kind of rule. Marsilius, as is his wont, transforms Aristotle's dialectical argument—which advances, criticizes, and refines the claim of a regime—into a demonstrative argument that attempts to supersede that claim. The point to be demonstrated is that the law, having been made by the human legislator, the impartial many, has no force behind it other than human will, getting no help for its enforcement from either God or nature. And where is human will favorable to enforcement to be found? The universal citizenry (*universitas civium*), Marsilius continues, will best observe a law that each citizen seems to have imposed on himself (I.12.6–8). So much for the impartiality of law! It is composed of the partiality of citizens. Speaking without Aristotle's reserve on this point, Marsilius has anticipated, if not equalled, Hobbes.

Those citizens, or their weightier part, have the actual power (*potestas*) who have the potential coactive power (*potencia coactiva*) over transgressors:[41] the legal power, that is, goes to the physical power. The best laws are the ones best observed, and to support this un-Aristotelian conclusion, Marsilius quotes the passage in Aristotle that we have studied on the necessity of "taking a law to its end" (*Politics*, Book VI, 1322a5). But is human will sufficient to secure the enforcement of law? Marsilius cites an example from Aristotle that is a necessary qualification of the argument he misappropriates. A certain very prudent king, called Theopompus, gave up some of his power by establishing the democratic office of ephors. When his wife asked whether he was not ashamed to leave his children a smaller kingdom than he had received, he replied: "Not at all, because it is more lasting" (I.11.8). The necessity of law, for Marsilius, arises from the necessity of denying oneself a "plenitude of power" as did Theopompus—that is, the scope of divine rule the pope was claiming.[42] The self-denial is an accommodation to the will of the many; it allows them the assertion of a will that one prudently denies to onself. And the same self-denial suggests the possibility of a king who royally condescends to be elected. Such kingly prudence reminds us of Aristotle's kingship in the very midst of an argument that seems to deny Aristotle's.

Marsilius's very prudent elevation of will over prudence results in a distinction (foreign to Aristotelian political science, but familiar to Lockean) between the sovereign legislator and the executive ruler or regime. The form of the city is therefore in the law, and not in the ordering of the regime. Instead of the form's being determined by the kind of order in a city, the form is strangely disjoined from order. The result, if we compare Marsilius to what we have seen in Aristotle, is to separate the city from the soul— Marsilius's purpose being to prevent the ordering of the soul from determining the ordering of the offices.

In Aristotle's argument at the end of Book IV of the *Politics*, the parts of the regime (deliberative, ruling, judging) turn out to be parts of the soul; as such, they reflect the human needs to resist nature and to submit to it, as well as the further need to bring the two contrary needs together. But Marsilius distinguishes between offices of the city and habits of the body or soul (I.6.9). For example, he says, as habit of the soul, the final cause of shipbuilding is the ship; but as office of the city, the final cause of housebuilding is not the house but protection of the body. In fact, all the offices of the city, including the priestly office, are directed to the perfection of human actions and passions, hence in a general sense to the protection of the body.[43]

Later, Marsilius worries that he may have contradicted himself in arguing that the human legislator is the cause of all offices while admitting that the priesthood was established by Christ (II.15.1–2). Then he reminds himself of the distinction he had made between offices of the city and habits of the soul: Christ appointed the priesthood only in the soul, not in the city. But who appointed Christ? Since He was a human priest (II.15.2), He must have been appointed by a human legislator who considered His teachings useful to the city. Marsilius tries to isolate the soul or the submissive part of the soul from politics because he fears it gives a handle to contentious, usurping priests. He does not try to deny that the submissive part of our nature exists, as do modern writers who say that men are by nature "perfectly free." But politics stands in need of the higher part, and Marsilius admits, or rather asserts, that priests are a necessary part of the city. The political difficulty consists in using the priests—or the higher natures of men in general whom Marsilius lumps together with priests—without being used by them for their rule.

In practice, it appears, the difficulty can be resolved only through the restraint and self-abnegation of these higher natures, as in the example of King Theopompus. He (like Christ in Marsilius's interpretation) was willing to submit to the necessity of accommodating the desire for freedom in his fellow men; they, in turn, must submit to the necessity of recognizing the value of prudent men. Thus only at first consideration but not in the end is it possible for Marsilius to distinguish between habit of the soul and office in the city. At first the distinction saves him from justifying tyrants and usurpers, but in the end it would keep him from resorting to the prudence necessary to defeat them.

Having seen that Marsilius's elevation of will over prudence makes the ruler a weak executive, we are now in a position to appreciate the reversal by which he elevates prudence to create a strong executive. Marsilius had spoken of the class of men "apt for prudence" that nature supplies as the material cause of offices in the city (I.7).[44] As little as he thinks men naturally free does he deem them naturally equal. But, as with Aristotle, does the form of the regime take advantage of this natural class of men by promoting them to office? Marsilius, given his ambiguous notion of the "weightier part" of the multitude, leaves it uncertain whether number or quality will prevail. His disparagement of nature (as helpful to the legislator) is the counterpart of his disregard for political form (in which the legislator takes advantage of nature's help). One could say that his conclusion expresses only a fond wish (I.14.4): if only the better were stronger! if only the stronger were better!

After establishing the sovereignty of the multitude as legislator, Marsilius says that prudence in execution is required (I.14.3).[45] His first example of an executive is "Cicero the consul" who, when defeating the conspiracy of Catiline, had the conspirators executed in prison without due process of law, because to have proceeded correctly would have opened a civil war. This is prudence against the law, to uphold the law. It cost Cicero much popular hatred, since the prison, Marsilius notes, was thereafter called "Tullian."

What of prudence altogether opposed to the law? For it might be prudent in some situation, if not in Catiline's, to begin a civil war. As John Gibbons has pointed out, it is precisely in circumstances of grave responsibility that the full range of qualities of the "perfect ruler" (the subject of I.14) would be revealed. But Marsilius, like Cicero, wants to uphold the law; to do this he must keep the law paramount and thus suppress the cunning and violence that prudence needs to have at its command precisely in the service of the best cause.[46] Marsilius's executive ruler is strong: he compares it to the heart (I.15.5), which is a "nobler and more perfect part" of an animal, not executive of the rest. And he proceeds to advocate at considerable length (in I.16) not representative democracy but elective monarchy, using eleven undemocratic arguments that do not accord with his argument for the sovereignty of the people. But Marsilius's executive does not display, or achieve, his strength by sensational demonstrations of illegality, like the Machiavellian executive. Marsilius's policy is to respect the law, the *human* law. And if that policy proceeds from an extralegal consideration of the singular cause of unquiet that he faced, so that Marsilius, like Cicero, is no mere law-abiding conservative, yet it conforms with what the law reasonably commands—namely, that not even the most prudent should have full power. The trouble is that what the law reasonably commands is not simply reasonable; so law needs support from outside itself.

The extralegal consideration that supports law is natural right. If an illegal executive is not necessary (and it is, according to Machiavelli), then legality must have some advantage over illegality in politics, some assistance from nature. It must not be the case that men are compelled to create their own executive unassisted, which is what we are led to believe from Marsilius's depreciation of nature, his emphasis on punishment of entirely human origin, as well as on human arts in Discourse I of the *Defender of the Peace*. In Discourse II, Marsilius undertakes the discussion of natural right that had been omitted from his earlier presentation. This he does in the midst of an argument directed to Christians and especially to priests on the true foundation of authority in the Church. For having established in Discourse I that only the human legislator (not the pope) has coercive rule in any community, he needs to show in Discourse II that the arrangement is also the consequence of divine law. In the earlier presentation (I.11–13) Marsilius had already made it difficult to tell whether he was talking about human law or divine law, since he had defined law in one sense as "sect" (see II.8.5 and cf. I.10.3 and I.12.1). In Discourse II Marsilius proposes a new doctrine of authority for the Christian sect, denying all ecclesiastical hierarchy by divine law, which comes out in his advocacy of a general council for the Church—in the "conciliarism" for which he is noted (II.6, 21). While arguing his case, he speaks at length (II.12–14) about the example of the evangelical or "voluntary" poverty of Christ and his disciples, and here refers to natural right (II.12.7–8).

Thus Marsilius's reliance on natural right occurs in the context of his own reform of the Christian sect to revive and sustain its original meaning. To propose reform is an act of intervention by Marsilius according to what he calls a quasi-natural law governing the duty of friendship and human society (I.19.13). The intervention is not strictly an executive act like Cicero's in the conspiracy of Catiline, which presupposes an existing law and a regular office of execution, but Marsilius introduces his proposal with a quotation from Cicero, which says that it is as much an injustice not to repel injury as it is to inflict injury.

Cicero is Marsilius's model of a philosopher who assumes political responsibility in a crisis, but Marsilius takes up the mantle differently. Cicero the consul, as Marsilius calls him, had a regular office and therefore could not escape the odium of an unpopular act of execution, however just and necessary it might be. But Marsilius joins the sovereign multitude (whom he himself has so to speak appointed sovereign), and from the multitude itself offers his legislation asking for the consent of the multitude and for action to be taken by its representative, perhaps his friend and protector Emperor Ludwig (I.1.6). Marsilius knows he will be hated (II.1.1), but hatred for him personally will not attach to the free government whose authority he wants to promote.

In his refusal of official responsibility Marsilius behaves like Aristotle's invisible king without coactive power who merely advises, except that the sect-making character of his advice makes him conspicuous even as adviser. He quotes Cicero favorably in *Defender of the Peace* except in one instance where he stands against him, using the authority of Aristotle. Cicero's remark against the ambition to be found in the greatest spirits and in

112

splendid talents might seem to justify a hereditary monarchy that would hold the force in check, but Aristotle's reminder that the magnanimous man desires great honors with reason shows that such a man would have reasonable grounds for sedition if no provision were made for his ambition, which an elective monarchy permits. Cicero understood political responsibility but not the forebearance on one's own behalf (the example of Theopompus) and the indulgence of the ambition of others necessary to carry it out.[47]

Marsilius the philosopher will not imitate Cicero the consul. His task is to bring out the hidden cause of disquiet and to unmask the sophism of his opponents. The cause is not visible, or apparent to politicians, and it is Marsilius's task, as it was Dante's, to bring it out into the open. Politicians see the conflict of Church and State, but they do not see its hidden cause in the nature of the Christian sect, not knowing how to deal with the worldly claims of a religion that claims to despise the world. Marsilius will show them how to respect Christianity without yielding to its claims to rule; this is the effect of his doctrine that all authority comes from the human legislator. With the same stroke he will save the Christian sect from its ridiculous contradiction—that of simultaneously prizing and despising worldly honor. Its pretension to rule is a "sophism" because it recalls the ancient sophists who believed that one could rule by speech alone or by "wisdom" without holding coactive power. Between the incomprehension of secular rulers and the delusion of the Church stands Marsilius with a proposal for harmony by which Church and State—but not the current Church hierarchy—can live in mutual respect.

Marsilius presents his doctrine of voluntary poverty and natural right with a marvelous intricacy that is necessarily obscured by any summary. But by concentrating on the question of execution, we remain faithful to his theme and his intent. Evangelical poverty was the way of life of Christ, His apostles, and His earliest followers. But Marsilius gives us a general definition of "voluntary poverty" that is not specifically Christian. It is a free way of life because the renunciation of whatever exceeds poverty is voluntary. But Marsilius suggests that poverty may not be a condition of weakness. Perhaps the excess to be renounced is merely the sacrifice of an overabundance of riches, so that to be "poor" means to have sufficient wealth (I.12.26–31; 13.17). In any case, one cannot renounce everything; one cannot renounce one's voluntary will, the natural "executive and motive power" that constitutes freedom (II.12.16; 13.9). The natural freedom of Marsilius is to be contrasted with the natural necessity that looms behind the Machiavellian executive and also with the natural freedom in a necessitous state of nature with which the Lockean executive operates. Marsilius's natural freedom reminds one more of the Aristotelian moral virtue of liberality than of Christian charity, because it is practiced more for one's own sake than for others (II.13.13, 17, 21; 14.12, 16).[48]

Since voluntary poverty does not require renouncing everything, or even sufficient things, such poverty is not inconsistent with ownership or lordship (*dominium*), which can be exercised over persons as well as things (II.12.12, 16, 23; 14.23). But priests are required by Christian divine law to renounce rule over others. They are judges; but there are two distinct kinds of judges: knowers, and rulers or executives of the law (II.2.8; 5.2),[49] and priests are merely knowers. Marsilius quotes the critical passage in Romans 13 that judges are ministers of God and avengers to execute His wrath. But while agreeing that vengeance is necessary and is allowed by Scripture, he denies that priests are judges in this sense (II.8.6). As knowers they renounce rule over others: since rule requires executive force, which can come only from the consent of the legislator, knowledge does not entitle one to rule.

And yet Marsilius cannot, and does not, leave it at this. In one sense of *dominium*, ownership (or lordship) belongs to the one who knows how to use a thing or rule over a person (II.12.13, 21), for what else would justify the intervention of Marsilius himself in the crisis of rule? He knows what needs to be done and how to do it; from that knowledge comes an implicit responsibility and claim to rule. Marsilius is aware of the Aristotelian kingship of the best man, whose outstanding virtue or knowledge makes him *dominus* over all (I.9.4).[50] Such a person might be said to renounce any rule that comes from force or consent rather than reason and virtue. But by renouncing the support of convention, he relies on the support of God or nature, or on the intelligibility of things that makes knowing possible. Such a person has "supreme poverty" because he has the "perfect use of reason" (II.13.27); he has no desire for glory or political office. But his very renunciation of rule on conventional grounds implies a claim to rule on natural grounds. The priests, philosophers, and poets who make up the doctrinal or sect-making part of the city, according to Marsilius, would by the nature of their contribution to the whole be justified in a claim to rule over the whole. The Platonic reasoning here, fully present in Aristotle's kingship, is also present in Marsilius.

The flaw in Aristotle's kingship, for Marsilius, is that it can be and has been claimed by the pope. Aristotle had foreseen the flaw in general, of course (*Politics* 1302b15–21), and had attempted to bring the best regime (of *Politics* III) into politics by working through the mixed regime (of *Politics* IV). But Aristotle's solution was not open to Marsilius, who had to face in actual politics the claim of "plenitude of power" that Aristotle could only imagine. Through the claim to hold a "universal care for souls" the pope would make himself universal king and all other humans his slaves (II.23.5–7; 26.13, 19). His Christian renunciation of worldly rule is false; it only masks his design of tyranny and reflects the desire to rule that it professes to renounce (II.12.32).

And Marsilius does not have in mind merely the danger to his native Italy. The menace is most visible in Italy, but the contagion has infected every state (I.1.3; II.26.19). It cannot be resisted by philosophy alone, or by giving philosophic wisdom public status in the manner of Thomas Aquinas, because public status can so easily be converted to the worldly advantage of priests and popes. In his discussion of voluntary poverty, Marsilius translates the Christian sense of the phrase into its philosophic sense, so that philosophers like himself can exercise dominion over priests. But the translation merely reflects the disastrous reverse possibility of interpreting Aristotle's kingship as plenitude of power.

Marsilius therefore sought an accommodation between philosophy and human freedom; and he found it in natural right. Aristotle sought and found the same—but Marsilius had to do it differently. For both, the difficulty is that political men are in need of philosophy; but if they use philosophy, they are in danger of surrendering to it. The need for philosophy is most acute under the reign of the Christian sect, where political men are bewildered and beset by the claim to rule of those who claim not to rule. But when political men have recourse to philosophy, must they not submit to those who claim to rule because they know? How can philosophy respect the claim to rule of the ignorant? How can it justify the freedom of self-rule that Marsilius describes as a natural executive power in men?

One can answer that men will resist slavery to their betters willy-nilly, by the naysaying self-defense natural to them, and that the business of philosophy is not merely to defer to such resistance but to endorse and applaud it. Such is the doctrine of modern political philosophy from Machiavelli on. But resolution by abnegation leaves no accommodation between knowing and freedom, between the realm of necessity and that of choice. And since the relation between knowing and ruling cannot be denied—to which Marsilius's retraction of his argument for democratic consent gives ample testimony—the modern resolution leaves no accommodation between ruling and freedom. It instead gives the impression or even teaches the lesson that politics is necessarily oppressive, that men cannot find freedom in self-rule.

Natural right, for Marsilius, is an accommodation, not a full reconciliation, between the knowledge philosophers might achieve and the agreements political men might reach among themselves. Men agree, he says, that God should be worshipped, parents honored, children reared, injuries prevented and lawfully repulsed, and the like (II.12.7). All these things depend on human legislation, yet are called "natural" metaphorically because they are agreed upon everywhere. We note that all the items except the first are based on the notion of reciprocal duties, but God, of course, has no obligation to men in return for being worshipped. Human freedom, represented in the necessity of human legislation even in matters on which all human beings agree, resides in the space left by the lack of divine obligation. Human laws, then, are not merely executive of the divine law.

Out of respect for the conventional character of human legislation, Marsilius also refuses to identify natural right as right reason, in contrast to Aquinas and Dante (II.12.8). In their resistance to being told what is good for them, political men do not agree to what philosophers might prescribe for "rational actors" (to borrow a term from our time). Marsilius's examples, we have noted, constitute only a minimal natural right. But these agreements are an approach to the lower reaches, if not the full heights, of right reason; they are not mere collective irrationalities with no relation to human needs and desires. Being an approach to reason, they make freedom intelligible: what free men reasonably choose in their laws. And since agreement on such laws can be expected, the measure of force necessary to execute them is reduced. The fact that men execute their own laws does not mean that their enforcement must be manufactured to any arbitrary end. It is easier—it requires less energy—to enforce laws that require that parents be honored and children reared than their contraries: a simple, fundamental fact. Marsilius's discussion of voluntary poverty contains his remarks on natural right because the possibility of voluntary poverty signifies a reliance on nature. We can afford voluntary poverty because nature does not leave us poor. But a great part of our natural endowment is our freedom, so that nature's goodness does not leave us with nothing to do on our own. So, at the end of his book, Marsilius says that he has taught rulers and subjects what must be done to preserve their own peace and freedom (III.3).

We have seen enough to conclude that Marsilius's executive is Aristotle's kingship in a different guise. Like Aristotle's, the executive is a divided kingship, but with greater emphasis on the consent of the people, which leads Marsilius to challenge and then to accept the Aristotelian doctrine of regime. For the kingdom (*regnum*) in one sense is distributed to all moderate regimes (I.2.2). Marsilius does not combine all executive force in the person of one man alone, as Machiavelli was to do for his prince. The unity Marsilius insists on (so as to keep Church a part of State) was a unity of office, not person (I.17.2). His unwillingness to concentrate human force comes from his reliance on nature, despite first appearances. He says that his power (*potestas*) to discern "has been given to me from above" (I.19.13), and this is not a conventional acknowledgment. He is not a rebel against God or nature; he does not complain of his malignant fortune, as did Machiavelli; he is not seeking to rise in the world but, to the contrary, offers a supreme instance of the meritorious poverty he praises. And because he is neither king nor prince but a divided part of kingship, his political science does not generalize. He begins from a singular cause—the threat of the pope's sophistic claim to power—and however far he legislates, he never forgets this beginning in the singular.

Accordingly, the current interpretation by Quentin Skinner of Marsilius as civic humanist is as wrong as the older view of the philosopher as imperial publicist, because both believe him to be propounding a generalized institutional solution and neither takes him seriously as political philosopher.[51] To take him seriously one must keep in mind his singularity as well as the singularity of his time. Rather than generalizing or universalizing the singular—which is the essence of modern political science—the singular and the universal must be combined so that both are retained. This means that when circumstances change, a new Marsilius will be needed. Marsilius does not submerge himself and his like in the legislation he proposes. Although his doctrine is novel, he does not put forth ''new modes and orders''—in our day, called institutions or constitutions—that are to be a permanent solution to the problems of politics. To begin such an attempt was the conceit of Machiavelli.

II

The Discovery
of Executive Power

6

Machiavelli and the Modern Executive

The modern executive, whether in politics or business, feels a vague but uneasy kinship with Machiavelli that he rarely seeks to define or escape by reading the works of Machiavelli. Perhaps the executive simply delegates the task to the appropriate scholars. But most scholars assume that Machiavelli, despite his reputation as the philosopher of scheming evil, was neither a deep thinker nor a teacher of anything to make us uneasy. In fact, whether out of complacency, pride, or fastidiousness, scholars have refused the commission and have not explored the instinctive feeling of kinship between Machiavelli and the modern executive. If they had they might have found a kinship so definite as to compel them to wonder whether Machiavelli might have actually authored the modern executive. For not only do these two share an attitude and certain methods; Machiavelli also was the first writer on politics to use the word "execute" frequently and thematically in its modern sense.

What is that modern sense? An answer might begin with Machiavelli's attack on the Christian religion and his new understanding of nature. Machiavelli's attack could hardly have been bolder in his time, when criticism of religion was deemed dangerous to a regime, and was therefore undoubtedly dangerous to the critic. But the depth of his attack and its new grounding are not obvious, because Machiavelli does not appear to be a philosopher. His principal works (probably written in the period 1513–19) are *The Prince* and the *Discourses on Livy*. The former belongs to an established literary genre of Mirror of Princes dating back to Xenophon's *Cyropaideia*, which also does not appear to be a work of

121

philosophy. The *Discourses on Livy* is a relaxed commentary on the Roman historian in which Machiavelli appears to write unconnected essays on Roman and modern politics, as if inspired irregularly by Livy's text.

These two books are his principal works because in the prefaces Machiavelli says they contain everything he knows. Just how much this is, however, was not made clear to the general reader until the publication of Leo Strauss's *Thoughts on Machiavelli* in 1958. Before that event, scholars could see that Machiavelli was read by all modern philosophers, but they did not infer that Machiavelli belonged in the company of the modern philosophers, indeed at their head. Strauss showed that he did. Strauss took his start from Machiavelli's reputation as the enemy of morality and religion and went on to consider the reasons he might have had for teaching men to do evil. Strauss's discovery was an affront to previous scholars who had overlooked so much in Machiavelli, and he was hardly greeted with the welcome he deserved. But the recent contention by Pocock and Skinner that Machiavelli was the source of modern republicanism owes something to Strauss's demonstration of Machiavelli's seriousness as a philosopher.[1]

Like Aristotle, Aquinas, Dante, Marsilius (not to mention other philosophers we have not studied), Machiavelli used "nature" as a source of intelligibility independent of divine revelation. Because men have direct access to the various natures of things and perhaps to nature as a whole, they do not depend on God alone for all they need to know. But Machiavelli conceived of nature differently than did Aristotle and the Aristotelians. The latter had supposed that nature indicates to human beings what is good for them; and if Christian revelation did not precisely accord with what our natural reason discerned, at least reason and revelation shared the end of showing men their good. Thus compromise was possible between the philosophers' nature and the Christian God. But Machiavelli conceived of nature in a way that necessarily set philosophy against Christian teaching, not merely in the role of a thoughtful critic from the outside, but as a more or less openly declared enemy. After Machiavelli's fundamental stance on Christianity and nature has been set forth, I shall connect it to Machiavelli's uses of "execute" and develop his conception of *esecuzioni* and the executive.

Christian Weakness and Christian Cruelty

Despite the passage of two centuries and the occurrence of many changes that have since induced historians to fix the origin of modern history in Machiavelli's lifetime, Machiavelli starts just where Marsilius did. Both faced the theologico-political question of whether, and how, God rules men. But Machiavelli does not present himself as an Aristotelian. He does not begin within Aristotelian political science, as Marsilius does when he excuses Aristotle for not knowing in advance that popes would prove to be a singular cause of strife. At the outset of his *Discourses on Livy,* Machiavelli proposes "new modes and orders" that display a novelty and enterprise comparable to that of the New World explorers, and show that he is not out merely to reinterpret or rearrange the traditional Aristotelian regime. Nor is he satisfied with overturning the church hierarchy, like Marsilius, and reducing the power of priests to that of teachers in a neo-Aristotelian order. It is precisely Christian teaching that Machiavelli inveighs against, and he writes with a boldness and force that can still provoke a jaded modern reader.

Machiavelli borrows the notion of a religiously neutral sect from Marsilius (who had taken it from Arabic political philosophers), and he appears to share Marsilius's desire, as philosopher, to remedy the defects of the sect called Christianity.[2] But instead of seeking a place for Christian teaching in the Aristotelian regime by interpreting Christian evangelical poverty in terms of Aristotelian kingship and natural right—that is, instead of seeking compromise—Machiavelli appropriates the Christian teaching in order to show people as well as princes how to get ahead in this world. For Machiavelli was not content to complain about certain untoward consequences of "the present religion" (*D* I. proemium), as he referred to Christianity, impudently implying his doubt of its eternity and truth. Nor was he satisfied, as an anti-Christian, to compromise with a religion which might have virtues together with its faults and which, once undermined or destroyed, might easily be replaced by another religion with worse faults. Nor yet, for all his praise of the ancient Roman religion, did he propose or even desire a return to it. Machiavelli was not a "pagan," as he is sometimes called by those who tremble to use the word "atheist." Least of all did he desire a reform of

Christianity in the interest of Christianity, like the Protestants. All of these possibilities were half-measures, and Machiavelli insistently repeated his counsel against adopting half-measures.

The only way to oppose Christianity wholly is, paradoxically, to appropriate it. Whereas Marsilius, for all his emphasis on human necessities, keeps his eye on the good life as the ground where Christianity and philosophy might meet, Machiavelli turns Christianity against itself and perverts it altogether. Machiavelli fastens on the twin evils resulting from Christian doctrine—weakness and cruelty. The two evils were far from unknown to Christian thinkers. In fact, Christian weakness was the main theme of Augustine's *City of God*,[3] and Christian cruelty, as we have seen, was the concern of the Christian Aristotelians. But in his analysis, Machiavelli shows how Christian weakness and Christian cruelty can be turned to political advantage, especially to the advantage of men who know how to be executives.

Machiavelli observed that the central event in Christian revelation is an act of execution: Christ's sacrifice celebrates human suffering rather than human triumph and glory. Our religion, Machiavelli says, makes men esteem less the "honor of the world." Instead, it causes men to contemplate rather than act, and to regard the highest good as humility, abjectness and contempt for human things. Men are strong to endure but not to resist; so the "present religion" has made the world weak and delivered it to wicked men who take advantage of Christian forbearance. Meanwhile, those who would otherwise be engaged in virtuous enterprises suffer a kind of constraint and discouragement that Machiavelli calls "ambitious leisure" (*D* I. pr., II.2).

In his famous attack on Christianity, we note that Machiavelli himself esteems worldly honor less than human strength and even ferocity, a quality shared with wild beasts that does men no particular honor. Comparing the ancients to the moderns, he praises the ancients for greatness of spirit rather than greatness of soul. Machiavelli wants to inspire the men of his time and times to come, but without subjecting them to any requirement that they lead perfect lives. Such a demand would come from the soul, but Machiavelli loves his native country more than his soul. In *The Prince* and the *Discourses on Livy*, he does not mention the soul. His political science unlike Aristotle's is soulless. It does not refer to human nobility but rather appeals to the restlessness that honor-seekers experience under Christianity. Machiavelli favors

124

a Renaissance of "ancient virtue," not of ancient learning or phi-losophy, hence not of ancient virtue as understood by the ancient philosophers, in which virtue is above all virtue of the soul (*P* 15; *D* I.pr., II. pr.; *Florentine Histories* V.1). His will be a new, ferocious virtue—the virtue of the lion and the fox (*P* 18).

Yet Machiavelli's new virtue will also be humane, again unlike Christian virtue. For the other quality of the Christian sacrifice, the counterpart to its weakness, is its cruelty. Machiavelli under-scores the cruelty of a father's sacrifice of his son in a thinly dis-guised parallel to the crucifixion when he lauds the useful sever-ity in Junius Brutus' sacrifice of his sons at the founding of the Roman republic (*D* III.1–3).[4] Thus Machiavelli introduces the cen-tral event of Christian Rome into the politics of ancient, republi-can Rome. By reinterpreting ancient Rome, he contrives to ex-plain Christian cruelty in thisworldly terms as a useful political trick. Apart from this ingenious anticipation of Christian politics, Christian piety in modern times not only leaves the weak at the mercy of the wicked but also creates a new kind of wickedness that Machiavelli calls "pious cruelty" (*P* 21). He applies the term to Ferdinand of Aragon's expulsion of the Marranos (forcibly con-verted Jews and Muslims) from Spain in 1501–2. Machiavelli, inci-dentally, was perhaps the only Christian writer of his time to con-demn Ferdinand's action.

One could also find pious cruelty, though Machiavelli does not use the term, in his descriptions of the Crusades and of the "countless men" killed by Moses for standing in his way (*FH* I.17; *D* III.30). Moses was hardly a Christian, of course, but since he was a "mere executor of things that had been ordered for him by God" (*P* 6), his actions may serve to demonstrate, at little risk to Machiavelli, how Christian piety operates. Machiavelli says, incredibly, that Moses was *forced* to kill countless men who op-posed him out of nothing but envy.[5] But as a pious man Moses was compelled to the execution, because no wholesome or rea-sonable motive exists for opposing the design of God. To dis-agree, or merely to stand in the way, is not at all innocent, since all human motives are tainted with pride and thus with envy of those with pure motives who execute God's design. An idea or even a doctrine of holy war can develop out of faith in the God of Love and can propel the imperial interests and instincts of secular princes such as Ferdinand. *Bellum justum est justitiae executio:* just war is the execution of justice.[6] A notion of aggressive justice can arise in which one's duty becomes to seek out and rectify injustice instead of waiting passively for it to strike, and to take offense at those who do not share such zeal, rather than allowing the more patient to mind their own business. Under this influence the magnanimity and preoccupation with self characteristic of the Aristotelian gentleman give way to the demanding code of the chivalric knight. The model of the knight in *Don Quixote* has been interpreted recently as part caricature, part acceptance of the need for the just to strike first.[7]

The aggressive tendency among Christians was opposed by such figures as Augustine and Thomas Aquinas. In the sixteenth century, it was similarly opposed by schools of Dominicans and Jesuits who revived Thomist natural law. An early leader was Francisco de Vitoria, who in about 1532 (the year that Machiavelli's major works were published posthumously) addressed in lectures questions of justice arising from the Spanish conquest of the Indies. In *De Indis* Vitoria rejects the idea that the Indians' not being Christian justifies war against them. But to support the conclusion he concedes to zealous Christians that an offensive war to avenge and punish wrongs can be just according to natural law.[8] Natural law is a standard that ascribes punitive rights of execution to a community or republic constituted out of a natural inclination, not an unlimited piety. The result is to eliminate the elements of heathen envy against Christians and of offense to God inherent in the doctrine of holy war, which could justify the plunder and enslavement of heathens by Christians. Since heathens have rights according to natural law, the pious cruelty of the crusading executive against them is moderated by the proportion of revenge that a natural executive might exact. God's vengeance is left to God, and the unlimited punishment that an offense to God might seem to deserve is denied to men. Although Vitoria criticizes Spanish crimes against American Indians, he is far from proclaiming a modern right of self-determination for them. But when the Spanish go to war against the Indians, they must do so for the Indians' welfare and not for their own profit.

Unlike his disapproval of the expulsion of the Marranos, Machiavelli feels no qualms over the subjugation of the Indians and seems rather to endorse the spirit of the enterprise. And when it comes to "pious cruelty," he does not oppose the cruelty so much as the piety that hugely expands cruelty beyond the point where it is useful. Machiavelli is notorious for recommending cruelties well used and even "inhuman cruelty" (*P* 8, 17). Although he clearly makes the recommendation, like Vitoria, to attenuate the cruelty of the world of pious cruelty, the ambition of his real intent encompasses something much greater than that. As we have seen, he does not want to cleanse or reform or otherwise temporize with Christianity. He does not even want to destroy Christianity, since something like it might return in its stead. Machiavelli's undertaking (*impresa*) is much more radical: like Christianity itself, it is intended to effect a permanent improvement in human affairs. Moreover, the change will come by boldly appropriating the Christian doctrine of holy war and adapting it to the acquisition of worldly empire. The subversive means by which Christianity conquered the world without overturning governments will be turned against Christianity. And *the* means, above all others, is the central Christian act of execution. The worldly executive, with the ambivalence of his weakness and his cruelty, now secularized and politicized, will be the first among Machiavelli's new modes and orders. And in place of God's commands, he will execute the decrees of natural necessity.

Just how radical Machiavelli's undertaking is becomes evident in his new understanding of nature, one that overturns natural law and natural right in the Aristotelian tradition. To see why a new understanding is required and what it means, one must recall the problem for which the modern notion of executive power is a solution. This problem is that law cannot attain what it attempts. Law is too universal to be rational, and needs assistance from outside to specify what is reasonable in each case—assistance that may be against the spirit as well as the letter of the law. Moreover, even if law were rational, it would need help in demonstrating its rationality against the stubborn insistence of human beings on having things their own way. When law encounters human stubbornness, it resorts to universality and asserts: you are treated no differently from everyone else. Thus the second difficulty feeds the first: the more unwelcome a law, the more undiscriminating it needs to be. Law leaves a problem it cannot resolve on its own.

Executive power is only one solution, however. The other general solution in political science is Aristotle's kingship. The kingship of the good man, or the best man, is above the law because of his extraordinary virtue. Although it may be impossible or impracticable, Aristotle's kingship reminds us that although law never attains virtue, it aims at inspiring virtue. If it could be shown—and Aristotle doubts that it can—that virtue is man's perfection and that man's perfection makes a necessary contribution to nature as a whole, then the kingship of the good man would be according to nature. One could then assert that departure from the law in the direction of kingship is not tyrannical but accords with natural right, that the problem of law can be resolved, or at least treated, by appealing to the virtue that our nature permits us.

With Machiavelli, this assertion is not merely doubted; it is denied. Of his many and various statements by indirection, he says the most by remaining resoundingly silent on natural right or natural law, neither of which he ever mentions in any of his works. Here is his most evident difference from the classical tradition. Indeed, neither the political science of his time nor of his tradition gave precedent or excuse for this omission, which cannot possibly be inadvertent.[9] With it, the real Machiavelli is called forth from the "context" into which he is often squeezed today, a context that makes his thought appear derivative and harmless. In fact, the real Machiavelli proposes something extraordinary and profoundly unsettling. Though he agrees with Aristotle that law is not enough, he denies that any departure from it can be justified by natural right. And without a trace of squeamishness, indeed with evident relish, he concludes that tyranny is necessary to good government. Since law cannot demonstrate its reasonableness, it needs force; since nature does not supply or does not justify such force, men must find or generate their own. They must exercise force beyond the law in order to compel obedience to law, in repeated, sensational acts of execution—*esecuzioni*, Machiavelli calls them—which have, so to speak, nothing to do with either law or justice. In Aristotle what is beyond law is above it, while in Machiavelli what is beyond law is below it. And where Aristotle always respects the law and requires that even the kingship of the best man adopt it, Machiavelli openly mocks the law; and while not denying the need for good laws, (see *D* I.33), he openly asserts that "good arms" are enough to ensure good laws (*P* 12). Good souls are not needed for this purpose; perhaps, indeed, they get in the way. So it is not surprising that Machiavelli's soulless political science is also unlawful. An unlawful political science needs good laws to deter and restrain the errant, but at the same time it urges disrespect for law in order to encourage the enterprising.

Even though he never refers to natural right, Machiavelli does mention "nature" and, as everyone knows, he speaks frequently of "virtue."[10] But his nature and his virtue are not those of Aristotle or the tradition of classical political science. For Machiavelli, nature is understood as, or replaced by, the necessity that forces us to seek nutriment, safety, and glory;[11] and virtue becomes the habit or faculty or quality of anticipating that threefold necessity. Aristotle had shown, in Book I of the *Politics*, that man can be regarded as nature's property and nature as man's property: man is both within nature and distinctively above it. But the two possibilities are connected, because man can be above nature, hence acquisitive, only through the use of natural faculties that also show him to be nature's property. For Machiavelli, however, any such reference to human distinctiveness restricts human acquisitiveness too much. Men must be free, in their acquisitions, to imitate beasts and act ferociously. Nature, he thinks, cannot be a standard to guide human behavior, because we cannot afford to regard it as beyond our control. The Aristotelian philosophers who appeal to nature have left us in subjection to God, the author of nature—which means that they have in effect turned us over to those who claim to know God: the priests. Since men cannot afford to regard nature as beyond their control, they attempt to govern it through religion. Machiavelli merely wants to make "religion," which represents nature as human necessity, available to acquisitive princes instead of lazy priests. To make the change, he must deprive men of their distinctiveness, pushing them down to the level of beasts, and nonetheless teach them how to master the nature to which they have been reduced. Aristotle's ambivalent teleology, in which man both belongs to and stands above nature, will become Machiavelli's ambivalent necessity, exciting man's fear and inspiring his glory.

So nature, the necessity first shown to be man's master, must then be mastered by human virtue. The transformation of virtue required for its new function, in which it is no longer either an end in itself or devoted to human perfection, is indicated by the reluctance of Machiavelli's translators to render his word *virtù* as simply virtue. They call it "ingenuity" or "valor" or "vigor," and thereby reveal that something new is intended while ignoring the fact that Machiavelli calls it by an old name, *virtue.*

In its anticipation of necessity, Machiavellian virtue has a twofold character that seems to account for the peculiar ambivalence of the modern executive, who is strong, but always claims to be acting on behalf of a will or force that is stronger. Virtue overcomes necessity, and in this sense is understood as opposed to nature (unlike Aristotelian "natural right"). But to overcome necessity, virtue makes use of necessity, and is so understood in obedience to nature (also unlike Aristotle's natural right, which permits human choice). Thus, to anticipate necessity, you must get ahead of the other fellow; but when you have "secured yourself" (*assicurarsi*), you have defeated the other fellow but not the necessity of defeating him—and others after him. Your virtue is both strong and weak: strong because you have chosen to do what you would eventually have been forced to do, weak because you had no other choice.

Accordingly, Machiavelli speaks of "executors" with ambivalence. At one point, as we have seen (*P* 6), he describes Moses as a "mere executor of the things that had been ordered for him by God," but later (*P* 26) he praises "the virtue of Moses" in taking advantage of an opportunity afforded him, and elsewhere he says that Moses was forced to kill countless men who out of envy were opposed to "his designs" (*D* III.30), implying that the designs were really his, not God's. And as if to balance the single mention in his writings of a "mere executor," in *The Prince* (6), he refers once, in the *Discourses* (III.1), to the need for "a determined executor" (*uno ostinato esecutore*).

So much describes the grounding and the rough form of the Machiavellian executive. He is more usually known as the Machiavellian prince, and of course more commonly called that by Machiavelli. But we shall find that the ways of this prince are essential elements of the modern executive; so Machiavelli's frequent use of "execute" was far from incidental to his main conceptions. Scholars can learn much about Machiavelli by studying what he says on *esecuzione.* But for the modern executive, his thought is truly fundamental.

Seven elements of the modern executive can be found in Machiavelli: the political use of punishment, which demands an outsized executive; the primacy of war and foreign affairs over peace and domestic affairs, which greatly increases the occasions for emergency powers; the advantages of indirect government, when ruling is perceived to be "executing" on behalf of someone other than the ruler; the erosion of differences among regimes as wholes, through the discovery or development of techniques of governing which may apply to all regimes; the need for decisiveness, arising from the fact that the action of government is best done suddenly; the value of secrecy in order to gain surprise; and the necessity of the single executive, "one alone," to take on himself the glory and the blame. Each of these elements can be contrasted to Aristotle's political science to see how Machiavelli's executive was revolutionary, and all will be illustrated with his usage of the term[12] "execute."

Political Punishment

Among the many sensational statements Machiavelli delights in making, few are more shocking than his pronouncement (in *D* III.1) that "mixed bodies" such as sects, republics, and kingdoms need periodic "executions"—this to return them toward their beginnings and thereby rid them of corruption. Certainly this is the most prominent of his remarks on executive power; the rest dwell in the shadows of other eyecatching statements and have not attracted attention or study. The "executions" in question are both killings and punishments of lawbreakers—executions in both primary meanings of the word, coinciding in capital punishments. The executions punish criminals, but they are praised more for their "good effects" than for their accuracy in retribution.

For Machiavelli, in other words, it does not seem important that a formal law has been broken, still less that procedural regularity has been preserved. If a law has not been transgressed, then "orders" may need to be revived which are corrupt when used merely for self-advancement or when they prevent self-advancement. Indeed, it is human ambition and insolence that need to be restrained and managed rather than actual violations punished. Machiavelli even promises that had Rome been able to schedule important executions every ten years, "it would follow of necessity that she would never have become corrupt" (*D* III.1; see III.22). He entertains no doubts from the scrupulous as to whether criminals would always appear to suit his schedule.

What matters is that the executions be "excessive and notable." Machiavelli then drops any explicit reference to laws and says: "after a change of state, either from republic to tyranny or from tyranny to republic, a memorable execution against the enemies of the present conditions is necessary" (D III.3). The execution may be legal or tyrannical, as long as it is memorable. Its "good effect" is to revive "that terror and that fear" (D III.1) that men knew at the beginnings of the sect, republic, or kingdom in question, but that has gradually faded from memory. Thus criminal justice is used—why not say perverted?—for political effect. The effect is not marginal, as if we would lose nothing significant by foregoing it for the sake of legality; memorable executions are crucial to the salvation of the regime.

Aristotle would disagree completely. In the *Nicomachean Ethics* he distinguishes criminal from distributive justice, and connects only the latter, not the former, to politics and "political justice." Criminal justice, hardly discussed, is categorized with the justice of contracts as a kind of transaction (NE 1131a2), and is regarded as neutral to or consequential upon the politics of a city. In the *Politics* little is said of punishment and nothing made of the offices of punishment because Aristotle wants to remove politics from subservience to punitive gods. The true beneficiaries of an enlarged executive power would be, in his view, mainly priests; and these he wanted to keep in subordination to the offices of a regime in which human choice and deliberation could prevail.[13] The sacral cities he saw around him were not to be encouraged in their desire for revenge and punishment. The anticlericalism in Aristotle has to be discerned through the delicate conciseness of his rhetoric and the moderation induced by atheist philosophers whom he also opposed. In the very different circumstances that Marsilius faced, with the popes a "singular cause" of disunion, Aristotle's implicit dislike became more evident.

Machiavelli easily surpassed both Aristotle and Marsilius in anticlericalism, and he surely wished to hold priests under political control;[14] but he also thought it necessary to express or purge the spirit of revenge and then restrain it through fear rather than justice.[15] The fear generated by a return to the inhuman chaos of beginnings replaces fear of God, which Machiavelli remarks (D III.1) is used by priests but not felt by them: "they do the worst they can, because they do not fear the punishment they do not see and do not believe in." Memorable executions not only restrain the ambition and insolence of men active in politics but also purge the people of the ill humors they feel against a prominent citizen. The accusations that Machiavelli says are necessary to keep republics free (*D* I.7) definitively conclude with an "execution" that must be made without recourse to "private" or "foreign" forces—forces that priests, especially, have at their call.

Similarly, Machiavelli explains that the Florentine people, through too much mercy, once allowed disorders to spread that could have been quelled with a very few examples of cruelty; for disorders harm a whole people, but "the executions that come from a prince hurt one particular individual" (*P* 17). Machiavelli's lesson here is that too much love leads to cruelty; but the economy of single executions should not be mistaken for justice. Nor does Machiavelli hang back when it comes to punishing a multitude. He praises the greatness of the Roman republic and "the power of its executions" among which the decimation of a multitude was "terrible" (*D* III.49). For when a whole multitude deserves punishment, and only some chosen few receive it because all are too many to punish, one does wrong to those punished and inspires the unpunished to err on another occasion. But when a tenth selected by chance are killed, and all deserve it, the punished lament their bad luck and the unpunished are afraid to misbehave the next time.

The discussion here could easily be interpreted (or misinterpreted, if one insists on preserving Machiavelli's innocence) as a political appropriation of the Christian doctrine of original sin, just as the memorable execution can be seen as a suggested political use for the Christian doctrine of redemption.[16] Machiavelli, it would appear, was not above reviving states through a notion of punishment taken from the very institution which he accused of having "rendered the world weak and given it in prey to wicked men" (*D* II.2; see I. pr.). In other words, the modern doctrine of executive power had its beginning in Machiavelli's appropriation, for worldly advantage and human use, of the power that men had been said to exercise in executing God's will.

At the end of Machiavelli's little-known dialogue on *The Art of War*, the principal interlocutor, Fabrizio, laments that nature either should not have given him the knowledge of how to revive and expand states or else should have given him the faculty of "executing" it (*AW* VII, p. 367b).[17] Since nature gives men knowledge without power, men must execute on their own, using (in

Machiavelli's famous phrase) their own arms: they must not wait for help from God or nature. But they do have at their disposal, from nature, the knowledge of their own nature, including certain truths discerned and misapplied by Christian doctrine, now to be interpreted "according to virtue" (D II.2) by Machiavelli. Machiavelli attempted to make "the world," that is, mankind, strong again, but did so precisely by showing it how to submit to its own nature.

Because neither God nor nature can be relied on to help execute human laws, there being no natural law or natural right behind those laws, the power of execution must be expanded. Execution must escape the close subordination to law which it retains in Aristotle and Marsilius. Only once in Machiavelli's major writings, I believe, does "execute" occur with "law" so that clearly a law is being executed (FH VIII.3). In other cases, the following are said to be executed: "authority" (FH I.16), "undertaking" (FH VI.29, VIII.4), "office" (FH VI.21), "thought" (FH VII.34), "conspiracy" (FH VIII.4, 5; D III.6—of which more later), "desire" (FH VIII.26), "public decisions" (FH VIII.29; D I.33), "important thing" (D I.49), "everything" (D II.2), "these things" (AW V, p. 331b), "preparations" (AW I, p. 274b), "policy" (AW VII, p. 362b), "evil" (P 19), "command" (AW VI, p. 348a), and "commission" (FH IV.10; D III.6). Only the last two might be called a "weak" use of "execute."[18] In many cases, what is executed is left unstated—clearly a "strong" use (see especially D III.27; FH II.12, 25, 26, 34; III.14, 19; VII.6, 21, 32, 34; VIII.36). Nor must we forget the notable executions already discussed, where law is conspicuously absent (D III.1, 3; see also FH II.34; III.19, 21; IV.30).

In sum, these uses of "execute"[19] imply an outsized executive who, because the function of punishment must be understood politically, is not confined to carrying out the law. Executions do indeed cause laws to be obeyed, so that in a general sense they are subordinate to law. But *legal* executions do not suffice for political purposes, and law must accept the help of illegality to secure its enforcement. That is why Machiavelli does not attempt the independence of the judicial function upon which we, following Montesquieu, insist. To keep judges separate from politicians as in our current modern practice would, for Machiavelli, inhibit the prudence of both; judges could not see where their judgments were leading, and politicians could not manage their policies all the way to their outcome.

The Primacy of War and Foreign Affairs

Once execution is liberated from its clear subordination to law and to justice, the technique becomes available as a remedy for emergencies generally, not merely for the exigencies of law enforcement. Such emergencies may as easily arise from sudden dangers in foreign affairs as from obstreperous ambition at home, and to be met they require a large delegation of power. One of Aristotle's five kinds of kingship was the general with powers delegated for war; but he was a regular official who, Aristotle said, ruled in accordance with law (*Politics* 1285a4, 1286a3). By contrast, Machiavelli praises the Roman practice of creating a dictator in emergencies, "when an inconvenience has grown in a state or against a state" (*D* I.33, title). This was "to give power to one man who could decide without any consultation and could execute his decisions without any appeal."[20] Machiavelli denies that dictatorial authority was harmful or that it was the cause that brought tyranny to Rome, as had been alleged. The dictator was very useful not only when the Roman republic was threatened from without but also—Machiavelli now reverses the moral ground—"in the increase of its empire." It is Machiavelli, as I have said, who promotes the Roman dictatorship, opposing its depreciation by ancient writers; he first conceived its modern afterlife.[21]

Thus, just as with punishment Machiavelli steps past the difficulties of law enforcement to embrace the necessity of injustice, so with foreign affairs he turns from dealing with emergencies that may arise for any state minding its own business to those that a state with imperial ambition necessarily seeks out or creates to serve as pretexts (see *D* III.16). While Plato's *Republic* and Aristotle's *Politics* deal summarily with foreign affairs, Machiavelli's *Discourses on Livy*, according to its announced plan, is half devoted to foreign affairs, and *The Prince* at least as much. Polybius deals at length with foreign affairs, and he appears to favor the imperial Roman republic. But comparing Roman imperialism and Spartan moderation, Polybius is open, and implies that those who adopt imperialism do so as a choice and not in response to necessity (VI.50.3). Machiavelli makes the same comparison in a context where he has been borrowing from Polybius (D I.2, 6), and he concludes definitively that the choice is foreclosed in favor of imperialism by necessity.

When fear replaces justice as the ground for politics, acquisition is loosed from restraint; political science then assumes the task of explaining to princes how they must acquire and keep their states, and to republics how they must overcome corruption and expand. Governments must be taught to treat their own peoples as they would treat subject foreign peoples—not necessarily badly, but not with trust or justice.[22] The notable executions that perpetuate states, along with the dictator's power to execute his own decisions to expand his state, indicate Machiavelli's new emphasis on survival in politics. Classical political science, assuming that all regimes moved through a cycle and were fated to die, judged regimes by how they behaved, not by how long they survived—precisely the point of Polybius's discussion. Machiavelli dismisses the notion of a cycle, holding to the pragmatic view that states would surely become subject to better-ordered neighbors instead of suffering through their own ills in isolation (D I.2). His new domestic policy justifies (or is justified by) the primacy of foreign policy, and both are supported by an expanded executive power.

Execution as Universal Technique

The best regime, whose definition is the theme of classical political science, does not exist, according to Machiavelli. The knowledge of natural right that would be needed to elaborate the best regime, even if only in speech, does not exist, he claims. Hence, politics cannot be guided by any notion of the best regime. Machiavelli shows disdain for such "imaginary republics and principalities" (P 15), and elsewhere goes on to say that in all human affairs one inconvenience can never be cancelled without giving rise to another (D I.6). He asserts that he wants to understand actual regimes, and their deeds, not the speeches in which they claim to be best, to be wholes, and to be capable of advancing the common good. Such claims give any regime its distinctive character; they had been seized on by classical political science as opinions capable of being refined to measures of judgment.[23]

Machiavelli, who rarely speaks of regimes (there are two instances in *FH* II.11, 32), abandons the ancient classification of six regimes (see *D* I.2) and adopts from Roman tradition the distinction between republics and principalities (*P* 1). But while using the distinction, he does not preserve the characteristic opposition between republics and principalities in the contempt they express for each other. He makes light both of the typical republican hatred for the "name of the prince" and the "name of king" and of princely disdain for the fickleness of popular government (*D* I.58, II.2). He also erodes the traditional distinction with such phrases as "princes in the republic" and "civil principality," which imply both that republics need princes and that principalities can be regarded as republics. Republics and principalities converge because both are to be judged, not by their contrasting claims of virtue and justice, but by a single standard, the "effectual truth" of those claims—their ability to acquire glory and maintain security. By that standard the boastful claims of regimes are reduced to their capacity to produce palpable and beneficial effects, rather than being taken seriously as containing possible elements of the best regime. And the benefits conferred by republics and principalities do not include the honor of living in a republic rather than living under a prince, or the reverse. In short, for Machiavelli, the form of government is not in any sense an end of government.

Accordingly, though Machiavelli speaks of "virtue" or "goodness" in republics, he does not speak of "republican virtue," in which devotion to republicanism as a form or regime is identifiable apart from the benefits of republics.[24] He does express a preference for republics over principalities, but it is carefully qualified: the common good "is not observed if not in republics" (*D* II.2). But the common good of a republic does not extend to its neighbors, since to be conquered by a republic is the hardest form of slavery, though not really common, since it consists of oppression of the few by the many. Machiavelli says that in republics everything "is executed to its purpose," while what helps a prince most often harms the city (*D* II.2). But that observation must be balanced against his statement praising the "more merciful" prince Cesare Borgia because he knew how to confine his executions to a "very few examples" unlike the well-meaning republican Florentines, whose misguided leniency harmed the whole people of Pistoia (*P* 17). More important than regimes are the two diverse "humors" or "natures" of princes and peoples lying behind regimes which are to be found in both republics and principalities: the prince's desire to command, and the people's desire not to be commanded (*P* let. ded., 9; *D* 1.5; *FH* III.1). Success in governing requires prudent management of the two humors, and this can be effected in the form of a principality as well as a republic.

Or should one say that the advantage tips to republics, since Machiavelli asserts that "a republic has greater life and good fortune for a longer time than a principality" (*D* III.9)? Again, nothing is said about the greater lawfulness of a republic, nor indeed (by contrast to *D* II.2) about the common good. And why do republics live longer? Republics can accommodate themselves to a greater diversity of circumstances because they have at their disposal a diversity of citizens instead of just one prince. But their institutions (or "orders") would not permit them to make use of this diversity, given their notorious slowness to decide (*D* I.34, 59), if their institutions did not include the office of dictator, or something like it, enabling them to delegate executive responsibility to one person possessing the qualities most needed at the moment. The dictatorship both is and is not an "order." Machiavelli says at first that the executions of accusations (which require a dictator or someone like him) are useful because they occur "ordinarily" without resort to private or foreign forces (*D* I.7). Later he praises the Roman republic for instituting dictators for immediate executions in an "important thing," when the ordinary course would cause delay (*D* I.49), or when one man is needed to decide by himself without appeal (*D* I.33). Between these passages Machiavelli has shown that the "orders" of a republic become corrupt, and its authority goes stale, if ordinary "modes" are not periodically revived with "extraordinary modes." So far from ruining republics (*D* 1.7, 34), extraordinary modes are necessary to them (*D* I.18, II.16), culminating in the aforementioned "notable and excessive" (*D* III.1) and "memorable" executions (*D* III.3). These require taking up an "extraordinary authority" (*D* III.3), to be assumed "without depending on any law that stimulates you to any execution" (*D* III.1). Thus, the ordinary course of "orders" depends on the occasional resort to extraordinary "modes" for the renewal that gives a republic long life, indeed promises it perpetuity (*D* III.22).

In this way, the distinction between lawful and unlawful, in which republics might have taken pride by contrast to the willfulness of princely rule, is transformed into a continuum from ordinary to extraordinary, which allows or requires republics to exchange lawfulness for longevity. For that, they must themselves incorporate the principality; the Roman republic was a succession of "countless most virtuous princes" (*D* I.20). Its long life, according to Machiavelli, was due to the Roman combination of a republic with the princely state that secured the advantages of quick execution. But one could as easily say that a principality might combine itself with a republic in order to have, when necessary, a quick change of prince.

Thanks to the need for executions, the inner working of politics is not determined by its outward face. The contending forms by which regimes distinguish themselves from one another, holding the loyalty of their own citizens while directing contempt at their enemies, no longer constitute the true political divisions. Whatever his final estimate of republics and principalities may be, Machiavelli does not make an *issue* of republicanism or absolutism. He analyzes the political disputes he finds, and does not judge them as claims to define the best regime. He assumes, even before he begins the analysis, that men in politics do not know what they are talking about. Their publicly expressed concerns are inflated in their rhetoric, which he dismisses as our political scientists often do today. The Aristotelian regime has been replaced by Machiavelli's informal "new modes and orders" (*D* I. pr.).

Indirect Government

When a government, like Moses, claims to be merely executive, the insiders pretend to take direction from the outward authority. But as execution proves to require a "determined executor" (*D* III.1), the inner working moves by its own initiative without such direction, and produces memorable and surprising executions when it finds them necessary. Machiavelli's executive government is not ordinarily visible, unlike the Aristotelian regime where the form of politics shows the character of politics, and political appearance in general corresponds to political reality.

But the executive is not simply invisible, either, because government cannot work without making an impression, and thus cannot always hide itself behind some other authority. The inner working of government must reveal itself on extraordinary occasions, when it is impressive because the action is not expected—in executions that jolt men into recalling both why they need government and what government can do to them if disobeyed. Only on such occasions does political reality correspond to appearance. But precisely during an execution when primal fear is shown to be the first mover of politics, as well as when running its ordinary course, government appears to be necessity personified, reminding men of their beginnings. Even at its strongest and most impressive, government acts *for* men in an executive role. Men do not govern responsibly according to principles they choose and profess, as they are reputed to do in the classical regime. Rather, they are governed by a prince who periodically reminds them that necessity is stronger than principle. Hence good effects are politically more useful than respect for forms. The indirectness of government lies in the fact that this necessity must be brought home to each of us (see *AW* VI, p. 348a), since we are ordinarily filled with complacent partisan notions of how things should be run. Government is neither a choice by the rulers, nor an imposition on the ruled, but a revelation to each—and not from on high—of what is most powerful, not best, in him. "Good effects," have the double sense of effects that effect good, and effects that make an effect. To produce them, government must have the ambivalent quality of acting on its own, although ultimately it acts on behalf of the people.

The popular humor *per se* is not the desire to rule but the desire not to be ruled; nonetheless, the people must be ruled. This difficulty defines the political problem: how to rule the people without their developing the intolerable sensation that they are being ruled. To accomplish this—and Machiavelli does not doubt he has a "remedy" for it and for every other difficulty he uncovers—he adopts as his fundamental strategy a comical maxim of human perception: "Wounds and every other ill that man causes to himself spontaneously and through choice, hurt much less than those which are done to you by someone else" (*D* I.34). Why should

140

kicking oneself hurt less than being kicked? And yet self-imposed taxes will be consented to more willingly than taxes imposed from above. Government should contrive, then, to let its exactions and especially its punishments seem to come from the people being mulcted and punished, at their behest or with their consent. Thus, although the people can never rule on their own without princes to serve as their "heads," and democracy strictly speaking is impossible, all government, whether republican or princely, must appeal to the people. This was the virtue of the Roman mode of accusation that makes the people responsible for the attribution of guilt and for execution (*D* I.7). Not only republics but also principalities are counselled by Machiavelli to adopt a generally democratic policy and to rely on the people rather than—or as opposed to—the few (*D* I.49, 55, 58; *P* 20). Apparent here is the contrast to Aristotle's generally aristocratic policy and his appeal to the kingship of the best man.

An appeal to the people is not aimed at their good nature or impartiality. It is rather the means of involving them in the necessities of government they would much rather ignore. Speaking of the Swiss army, Machiavelli praises its method of punishing soldiers "popularly by the other soldiers" (*AW* VI, p. 345a), for if you want someone not to defend or sympathize with a criminal, get him to do the punishing, because he will look on the punishment differently if he is the "executor" of it than if the execution comes from someone else. Another example of executions in an army makes it clear that law and justice are not relevant to the political problem. A contingent of rebels from the Carthaginian army was incited by its leaders to kill emissaries from that army, along with prisoners they held, so that this "execution" would make them "cruel and determined" against the Carthaginians (*D* III.32). Thus, common involvement in a "crime" works as well as common involvement in the punishment of a crime. Both are "wounds" that the army inflicts upon itself, which hurt much less than if the executions were committed by, or in the name of, a prince. As we have seen (in *D* III.49), Machiavelli generalizes from the decimations by which Roman armies were punished to the proper way to punish "a multitude": to make those who are guilty but unpunished see the future. Though unpunished, indeed through relief at being unpunished, they nearly govern themselves.

It is a mistake to give the power of executing punishment to a foreigner, in the vain hope of finding an impartial judge, says Machiavelli (*D* I.7; 49; *FH* II.25). That foreigner will simply use executions to gain power for himself. Nor should one give it to the few, for "the few have always been the ministers of the few" (*D* I.49). Rather, as we have also seen, executions should be used against the few to hold down their insolence and to dispel envy (*D* III.1, 30; *FH* II.22). The few may be deterred, and the many will be impressed. To repeat, executions are never the un-prompted act of the people, who would prefer to forget such ne-cessities; to act, the people must be led or given a "head" (*D* I.57). But the people have a love of the sensational that causes them to be easily impressed by bold actions (*D* I.53), and the com-mission of great crimes is no bar to their favor (*P* 8, 9). In every regime they are natural allies of the strong executive who rules them indirectly in their name.[25]

Suddenness

To make a strong impression, execution must be sudden. In prais-ing Giovanni and Lorenzo de' Medici, Machiavelli remarked that they were quick (*presto*) to execute (*FH* VII.6; VIII.36). We today praise executives as "decisive" and "energetic" in their "initia-tives," terms that bear witness to the effect of suddenness as it seizes our attention by bringing regular (or "ordinary") proce-dure to an abrupt halt. One of Machiavelli's favorite phrases de-scribes this event: "at a stroke" (*ad uno tratto*). At a stroke the forceful executive can change the whole situation so that all eyes turn to the one who has disturbed and reordered it. People learn that they cannot rely on the familiar (recall that the terrible Ro-man "mode" of decimation was a chance operation, *D* III.49), and that they must therefore look to the prince.

By an impressive stroke the prince renews his authority and makes himself new, for a renewed authority is a new prince. His personal power, instead of disappearing into the regularity of his laws and his ordinary ways, becomes visible again; his actions, if sufficiently ambitious, may achieve "the greatness in them-selves" that silences criticism (*FH* I. pr.). In dealing with parties in Pistoia, for example, the weak Florentines did not know how to follow the first and safest method of simply killing the leaders:

"such executions have greatness and generosity" (*D* III.27). The generosity lies in not killing everyone (*P* 16).

In a paraphrase of Livy, which, Machiavelli notes, should be chewed on by every prince and every republic, he says that when there is ambiguity and uncertainty over what others want to do, one cannot find words; but once one's mind is made up, and one has decided what is to be "executed," it is easy to find the words for the action (*D* II.15). One must accommodate words to deeds, not deeds to words, which one does by acting first, confronting others with a new situation. The Roman dictatorship in time of necessity offered the advantage of immediate executions (*D* I.49). But here Machiavelli goes beyond responding to necessity; he actually advises that one create necessity for others. Slow deliberations are always harmful, he says in the same place (*D* II.15), especially when it comes to conspiracies, where threats are more dangerous than executions (*D* III.6, p. 200b). Dangers in executing conspiracies arise in part from men who lose heart (*FH* VII.34), but can be avoided by stepping up the pace of the execution so that the faint-hearted have no time to suffer an attack of conscience (*FH* II.32, *D* III.6, p. 208a). Indeed Machiavelli gives two examples of conspiracies that were executed first on fellow-conspirators before they were executed on the objects of the conspiracy. The conspirators were told they must join a conspiracy against a tyrant or be reported to him for treason! (*D* III.6, p. 204a) In short, if possible, the executor makes use of "the necessity that does not allow time" (*D* III.6, p. 206a), that is, time to reflect or repent.

In no respect does Machiavelli's executive differ more obviously from Aristotle's regime than in the attribute of suddenness. For Aristotle, the sovereign part of the regime was the deliberative, and though deliberate is not the same as slow, deliberate in the sense of slow is the first part of deliberate in the sense of prudent. The deliberative part, therefore, was chosen and authorized to act through a variety of possible formalities whose general purpose was, at least, to slow the haste of human willfulness by compelling propriety, and thus giving trouble to our passions and vices.[26] Machiavelli does the very contrary. He resolves deliberation into decision (in the usage of his time *diliberazione* meant both deliberation and decision), so that a good deliberation becomes one that results in a decision, and a good decision is decisive (*D.* II.15). "Decisive" is a quality known and explained after the fact, and while sudden is not the same as prudent, it is a necessary addition to prudence, as the appearance of willfulness that inspires obedience and makes prudence effectual. Machiavelli's executive cuts through the formalities of which Aristotle was so careful—the formalities, too, of modern constitutionalism. In so doing, he makes possible the creation of republics, such as the Roman was in his interpretation, that do not suffer from the slow motion of excess procedure.

Secrecy

Nowadays, when a committee of the U.S. Congress meets in "executive session," it meets in secret. We have considered the connection between execution and secrecy in Machiavelli's discussion of the Roman office of dictator, who executes not only without appeal but also without consultation (*D* I.33). If execution requires surprise, secrecy is clearly necessary to execution. The surprise is not a happy revelation, of course, but something sinister. Just how sinister execution is may be gauged from the fact that by far the greatest density of "execute" in the *Discourses on Livy* occurs in the long chapter on conspiracies, III.6 (40 occurrences out of 60 in the entire work; 49 together with the related chapters, III.1 and III.3). Whereas Machiavelli speaks only once in his major works of executing a law (*FH* VII.3), he speaks several times of executing a conspiracy (*D* III.6, pp. 201b, 210a; *FH* VIII.5; *Life of Castruccio Castracani*, p. 757b); and he orders his entire discussion of conspiracies in that chapter around execution—before, during and after the deed. As we have seen, the way to keep a conspiracy secret is to hasten its execution (*D* III.6, pp. 204a–b; *FH* II.32). Such an execution perfectly combines the two meanings of execute, to "kill" and to "carry out," since the conspiracy is executed when its object is dead. It is almost needless to add that conspiratorial execution takes place in utter illegality.

What is Machiavelli's reason for removing execution from its subordination to law, where it had been kept in loose tether by Marsilius, and enlisting it in the management of conspiracies? Conspiracy itself must be much closer to the essence of government than had been thought hitherto. One senses this when one is told (at the beginning of *D* III.6) that conspiracies are made not only against the prince but also against the fatherland (*patria*), by the prince. But even this, like so many of his statements, is a mere introduction to his rationale. Government, according to Machiavelli, is the agent of necessity rather than the minister of justice because we cannot afford justice. But we like to think that we can and we demand it, especially for ourselves, and we often see no need for actions that presuppose we will not be able to afford justice—actions that anticipate necessity. This is the popular humor that does not desire to rule (or command, or oppress) but desires only not to be ruled. The desire not to be ruled constitutes a reluctance to face facts, to face necessity. Government has the ambivalent task of bringing necessity home to the people, so that they survive, while concealing it from them, so that they are happy and innocent. Machiavelli's "remedy," we have seen, is to make government seem to come from the people, and for its "wounds" to appear self-inflicted. To do this requires fraud (*P* 18; *D* II.13, III.2, 40) and conspiracy (*P* 19; *D* III.6), not merely as dangerous devices locked away in a cabinet for use by trusted hands, and only in the worst emergencies, but as instruments available generally if not routinely, and to be used without hesitation or scruple.

Those who conspire, Machiavelli says, are either one or more (*D* III.6, p. 201a). But then, he continues, if it is one person, it cannot be said to be a conspiracy; rather it is a "firm disposition arising in one man to kill the prince." Conspiracies, properly speaking, involve more than one person sharing a secret or knowledge together (*coscienza*). The relationship among conspirators is never that among friends, because men usually deceive themselves in the love they judge that others bear for them. You can never be sure of such love unless you test it, and this is most dangerous (*D* III.6, p. 203a). Consequently, at least ordinarily the relationship among conspirators must be that of principals and executives instead of equals. The executive or secretary (the connection between secret and secretary should not be forgotten) may be more capable than the principal, so that it becomes unclear who is using whom (*P* 22). But the inequality of the relationship remains.

To the extent that for Machiavelli conspiracy underlies all politics, we have again reached a fundamental difference from Aristotle, for whom friendship underlies justice and all politics (*NE* 1155a 23–33). The goodness and harmony of friendship are the

145

goal that politics aspires to but cannot attain. Aristotle said that friends do not need justice among themselves, as they are above it. Machiavelli thought that, with the secrets they keep from each other and from themselves, they could not even attain justice.

Uno Solo

Machiavelli praised the Roman dictatorship that gave one man the power to execute his own decisions in order to respond quickly to "extraordinary accidents" (D I.33, 49). But Machiavelli also praised (in D I.9) the original ordering of the Roman republic, attributed by him to Romulus, because it had been accomplished, in consequence of Romulus' fratricide, by "one alone" (*uno solo*). Both the original ordering and the departures from order neces-sary to maintain order—by the dictator and by the memorable executions (D III.1, 3)—must be performed by one person. Why must this be?

Machiavelli gives one reason that turns out to be two. He says that "many" are not adept at ordering a thing "since they do not know what is good for it, which is caused by the different opin-ions among them" (D I.9). Thus, it appears that everything must depend on the "mind" of one man not because he necessarily knows better than many would, but because it is better to have one opinion than many. The prudent "orderer" must therefore, like Romulus, contrive to get all authority for himself, even if he has to dispose of a wiser brother—since Machiavelli says nothing to indicate that Romulus knew more than Remus. It is better to have one opinion and one authority because, with responsibility focused on one, his ambition can be used to promote the common good. If he succeeds, he will have made a lasting state and de-serve glory; if he fails, he can be blamed and "accused" (D I.9), thus purging the hatred of the multitude and perhaps, if he is sufficiently important, serving as a memorable execution. Al-though Machiavelli in his popular humor allows himself some-times to inveigh against ambition (D I.37, II. pr.), his politics makes use of ambition untempered, unabashed, and restrained only by the ambition of others. Glory, like fear, compels men to become aware of their separate individuality, but also enables them to be enlisted for the common good more readily and surely than through the social virtue of justice: "Those who fight for their own glory are good and faithful soldiers" (*D* I.43; see III.30, 35, 40).[27]

If ambition is to be loosed from moral restraint, however, can it be altogether separated from wisdom? It goes without saying that ambitious princes must be prudent, but then prudence for Machiavelli has ceased to be a moral virtue distinct from cleverness (*P* 15; cf. Aristotle, *NE* 1144a24). Must there not be some prudence beyond the ordinary that justifies Machiavelli's corruption of it in the service of ambition—his own *grandi prudenze* (*D* II.26)? If government culminates in conspiracy, and conspirators cannot be equal, must there not be a brain behind the operation, a "rare brain" (*D* I.55), one that does not suffer from "confusion of the brain" (*D* III.6, p. 207a)? Machiavelli, we have seen, was aware of the problem that the one who knows politics cannot "execute" his knowledge by himself (*AW* VII, p. 367b); he can be *uno solo* only in his knowledge.

In fact, Machiavelli was preoccupied with the problem of the relationship between teacher of politics and politician. When he says in *The Prince* that Moses was a mere executor of the things ordered for him by God, he describes God not as an all-powerful Creator but as the "great perceptor" (*gran precettore*). He devotes a chapter in the *Discourses on Livy* to the dangers of being alone against many—(*essere solo*)—in advising something (*D* III.35; cf. *P* 6, 22); and the thirty-ninth example in the chapter on conspiracies (*D* III.6, p. 208a) concerns an unsuccessful attempt by two disciples of Plato to kill two tyrants. In the *Florentine Histories* he describes a poet, inspired by Petrarch, who sought to be the "executor" of a glorious enterprise to free Rome from the popes (*FH* VI.29).

In his own glorious enterprise to bring "common benefit to each" (*D* I. pr.) with the reform of morality and politics, Machiavelli cannot do everything. He cannot be both teacher and prince. But he can put his knowledge into execution, not least with his doctrine of execution, so that princes who follow him become in the deepest sense his executives. This deepest sense of execution is perfectly compatible with the need of each prince to be *uno solo*, because Machiavelli has left space for princes to win their own glory. They can be *determined* executors instead of *mere* executors, and it is not necessary that they realize they are executing his knowledge: indeed, it is better that they do not. Machiavelli foresaw that the enormity of his ambition would obscure it from our view.[28] As he shows in one of his examples, a conspiracy can be executed even when only one person fully knows its object (*D* III.6, p. 204a–b).

So Machiavelli's princes do not rule in the classical sense. They do not begin a policy and continue it in accordance with the beginning so that they can be held responsible for the principle of their rule. His princes are held accountable, not forwards from their principle, but backwards from the effects of their actions. And they win glory or take the blame by virtue of their chance success or their skill in manipulation. Conforming their words to deeds, they do not follow principle but claim to be principled after the fact.

Both Machiavelli and his executives have the ambivalence essential to the modern notion of executive power. They are strong because he has freed them from moral restraint, but they are weak because they act out the roles he has made for them and in the view of those who know, their glory ministers to his. Machiavelli is strong because only he is in charge of the whole reform, but he is weak because he depends on others, or rather on necessity, to accomplish his goal. But to be this person, the true *uno solo*—a god among men—Machiavelli has erased the distinction between his kingship and his tyranny. Like Aristotle's, Machiavelli's king is the political philosopher. Unlike Aristotle, he is by natural necessity a tyrant.

Given the hindsight provided by the subsequent history of liberal constitutionalism, Machiavelli seems to have gone much too far. What he says rings true but his conclusions seem exaggerated, and we often fail to take him seriously. We would like to believe instead that his insights can be retained and his extremism discarded, that his notion of *esecuzione* can be absorbed into the modern liberal constitution without the tyrannical requirement of *uno solo* that may give us a shiver or may merely seem quaint. Machiavelli may have discovered the modern doctrine of executive power, but in his extremism he stopped short of developing doctrines of "power" and of "separation of powers." The doctrine of power, in Hobbes's conception, was to make virtuous princes unnecessary by giving any sovereign, virtuous or not, all the power he could want; and the separation of powers was developed by Locke and Montesquieu to check the prince by law and by formal institutions.

Both doctrines, while accepting much of Machiavellian morality, were directed against the extreme political conclusion that left so much power in the hands of *uno solo*. But we should not be so sure that the development of either doctrine improves Machiavelli's formulation. Knowing our history of constitutionalism, Machiavelli might have chosen not to retract. He could have noted that we have found no substitute for virtuous princes (in his sense), and that every successful organization in our self-congratulating democracy is run by a Chief Executive Officer. He could declare that we obscure the reality with talk of executive power. Yet if he knew our experience of totalitarian tyranny, Machiavelli himself might have shivered.

7

Hobbes and the Political Science of Power

In Machiavelli we find the executive, but not executive *power*. Before executive power could be conceived as one of the equal independent powers of a republican constitution, the very concept of power had to be discovered. This was the work of Hobbes. He created an abstract "power" and made it the centerpiece of political science, where it remains today. When we speak of gaining "power," for example, we use the word to refer to a general capacity abstracted from particular capacities, supposing that power is universal and therefore singular. When we say that someone has more power than someone else generally, and not just to do some particular thing, we imply that different powers add up to more power: the universal concept becomes quantifiable and, in principle, exact. Before Hobbes, "power" was a term of physics, not political science; and it was not used abstractly and universally, as we do.

Hobbes's originality consists, not merely in abstracting—which is something that comes easily to us as denizens of a scientific age—but in conceiving, for political science, the *idea* of abstracting. But what was it he made abstract? Here we must measure Hobbes's innovation against the still greater originality of Machiavelli. With his science of power, Hobbes abstracted from the rich but bewildering detail of Machiavelli's examples, but the message he saved was profoundly Machiavellian—the necessity of acquisition. To be sure, Hobbes universalizes and moralizes that necessity as the right of self-preservation. But the original insight glows through its new formulation. Hobbes was one of Machiavelli's captains, and I shall present his contribution to the doctrine of executive power in the light of his Machiavellian inspiration.

Machiavelli does not sanction personal vengeance in his executives, but he does not oppose it. To approve of cruelty he would have to endorse its expansive form, pious cruelty, and that is something he opposes. But the best way to exclude pious cruelty from politics is to allow men to satisfy their need for personal vengeance. When pious cruelty is appropriated for worldly use, the crusading spirit loses its energy, human hatred is diverted to human advantage, and the personified vengeance of divine anger is reduced to personal vengeance.

Personal vengeance has the two characteristic modes of the two "humors" or classes of men: princes like to gain victories over their rivals, and peoples like to see the great come to grief. Sensational executions satisfy both parties "at a stroke." That is why, for Machiavelli, the executive is revealed in—or rather, *is*—the act of execution. In the beginning is the deed, and deeds are needed to remind us of this fact, lest we try to live in softness and cruelty by the primacy of the word. Machiavelli's prose reflects his point. He writes with examples of venom, indecent triumph, and sardonic humor[1] rather than in generalities composed with scientific detachment. He speaks of executions, not of an "executive power" capable of executions which, as a power or potentiality, it does not actually do.

After Machiavelli, the deeds of execution he promotes are absorbed into an executive power. In scholastic terms, the acts are withdrawn into a potentiality. With the change, the sensations such acts create when they occur as surprises are diminished because they are now regularly expected. *Esecuzioni* are now publicly justified as a feature of sovereignty or even, among constitutional thinkers, as the work of a separate institution. The Machiavellian prudence required to effect them becomes a science containing definitions and rules of application. So the formal executive begins to receive definition in the modern understanding of power. And as a result, despite many individual variations in that understanding, Machiavelli's permission to vent personal vengeance is undermined, and the executive—whatever the hidden reality—at least loses its unscrupulous Machiavellian appearance.

This does not mean, however, that the situation returns to status quo ante—that is, to Aristotle. Once Machiavelli's executive has been expounded and given shape, its advantages are too obvious to forego. And if the costs of tolerating evil can be minimized, then the combination of Machiavellian "good effects" with post-Machiavellian rectitude may seem irresistible. But to come to an unbiased judgment, one must measure Aristotelian natural right, which keeps executive power subordinate, against the new natural right or natural law in Hobbes that eventually allows it to gain a life of its own as an independent institution. For executive power becomes moral through a lowering of the standard of morality from virtue—with all its difficulties—to power, with all its consequences.

Bodin and the Executive as Sovereign

There are two modes in which the executive was regularized before Hobbes conceived all politics, including the executive, as power. These are the absolutism of Bodin, in which the sovereign takes responsibility for execution, and its opposite, the constitutionalism of certain English writers of Hobbes's time, in which a separate executive power first appears.

Jean Bodin (1529–96) was the chief of France's *politiques,* a party so called by its opponents in the Catholic or Protestant parties because it looked upon religious disputes from the standpoint of political necessities. We would call it, more crudely, non-ideological. The *politiques* were accused of being Machiavellian—an accusation they denied and resisted by criticizing Machiavelli. In an early work Bodin had praised Machiavelli for reintroducing the political science of the ancients,[2] but in *Six Books of the Republic* (1576), his major work and a formidable compendium of argument and fact, he takes care in the Preface to denounce Machiavelli's impiety and injustice as "sweet poison."[3] He then proceeds to rescue piety and justice from Marchiavelli's blunder with the Machiavellian argument that they support the state. To confirm his judgment, Bodin invokes Polybius, "considered the wisest *politique* of his age" though an "atheist," and Plato; and he resorts to the "great God of nature," who is all-wise and all-just but not, it appears, all-powerful. So this God avenges his injuries and has his eternal law executed (note the personal attributes of nature's God) by giving government over to wise and virtuous princes, or to say it better than Solomon, to the least unjust and most expert.

These princes had better not behave like tyrants, Bodin warns. If they do, their subjects will rebel and their states will be ruined. Offending their subjects, not God, is what princes have to worry about; they execute God's law without interference from other worldly authority (Bodin means the Church) that may profess to act in God's name. Thus Bodin portrays the sovereign as a strong executive whose task is not exactly to serve as God's agent but to do what God wishes he would do (*Republic* I. pref. 12–14). Here, he is not much different from Machiavelli's Moses, who was said to be a mere executor of God, but who acted with his own virtue in pursuit of his own design. Human sovereignty is thus awarded by God on the same terms by which it might be prudently appropriated by princes.

Nonetheless, Bodin's sovereign is not Machiavelli's new prince: he is both more radical and less. More radical than Machiavelli's respect for the diversity of politics is Bodin's insistence on raising the simple and universal question of sovereignty, "the absolute and perpetual power of a republic" (*Republic* I.8.179). The question of who is sovereign must be abstracted from every political controversy and lifted above the partisan claims that Aristotelian political science takes seriously. Whereas Aristotle examines such claims, and Machiavelli finds a complex interaction of princes and peoples beneath them, Bodin only wants to know who is on top. Instead of principalities and republics, he speaks only of republics as generic sovereign bodies (while also using "state" in a more impersonal sense than Machiavelli). Aristotle uses the generic term "polity" (which means regime) to improve all regimes, but Bodin uses the term "republic" as the primary political identification. As a boat is not a boat without the "form" of a keel, he says, so there is no republic without a sovereign power (*Republic* I.2.41; cf. I. pref. 9–10).[4] Aristotle would want to know what *kind* of boat or regime has this form, and Machiavelli would want to know *whose* form it is, but for Bodin the sovereign form is anything anyone wants it to be. Its abstract nature is its primary reality. The state must be *un seul* (VI.4.178), but this is not like Machiavelli's *uno solo*, an actual, selfish human being. Bodin did not, as Hobbes did later, suppose that the sovereign might be an artificial person. But he does try to maintain a distinction between the person and the sovereignty of the sovereign.[5] Though insisting on the abstract oneness of republics, he does classify kinds of republics in Book II of *Republic*, but any kind is secondary to sovereignty, which itself, as explained in Book I, belongs to no kind. That we speak easily today of an impersonal state or sovereign having no kind and belonging to no one is the result of a radical innovation begun by Bodin and completed by Hobbes.[6]

Less radical than Machiavelli's new prince is the legality of Bodin's sovereign.[7] Its very abstractness permits and requires a retreat from the Machiavellian reliance on one's own arms to the general authority of law. But the generality of law is not found in any actual laws (though Bodin has difficulty with the specific law in the Decalogue, I.8.214, 221–22). Sovereignty can be legal only when its main character is legislation, the power to make laws (I.10.306). While, for Aristotle, deliberation is sovereign, for Bodin it is legislation. Bodin frequently attacks Aristotle, so that no one could mistake him for an Aristotelian;[8] and he specifically criticizes Aristotle for situating sovereignty in something so indeterminate as deliberation (III.2.46; 3.73). The legislative power will never be precisely located if one has to look for men who deliberate; it is safer and surer to look for one who commands. Law is then command, and command is not merely a necessary feature of law (as when Aquinas said that law must be promulgated) but sufficient to define it, regardless of the degree of deliberation or reason that went into the legislation. Of course, in order to command, the sovereign must have arms: "he is master of the state who is master of the forces" (IV.1.30). So the Machiavellian priority of arms over laws is not so much reversed as covered up.

Our modern rule of law asserts the supremacy of the legislative power. To keep the rule of law distinct from the rule of arms we do not claim, as classical political science claimed, that law is reasonable or customary or both. We have forsaken those distinguishing qualities as vague and troublesome. But to avoid governing ourselves by force and fraud as Machiavelli recommends, we resort to the notion of power, either of the sovereign or of constitutional rivals within the sovereign entity. Not yet a theorist of power in the full sense—that we are yet to learn from Hobbes— Bodin nevertheless lays the groundwork for such a theorist with the doctrine of a human sovereignty that is given by God, permitted by God, or taken from God. Not as theoretical as Hobbes, Bodin is neither as academic nor as hostile to lawyers (I. pref. 17–18). As a *politique* he talks to statesmen in their terms, using specific examples rather than a satisfying syllogism. Moreover, in a book too long to be read by busy statesmen, he represents the reasoning of statesmen to scholars and lawyers to induce them to stop using their professional activity to inflame religious passion.

If the sovereign is a strong executive whose legislation executes God's or nature's laws, his officers are weak executives, bound to his command. While Machiavelli's orders are enlivened by extraordinary modes that keep God's laws from inhibiting virtuous princes, Bodin wants to establish the authority of the sovereign over potential rivals, including colleges (the Church? III.7).[9] He calls all magistrates "mere executors" (*simples exécuteurs*), though he introduces flexibility by distinguishing between those with ordinary and those with extraordinary competence (like dictators). Bodin is not above recommending the manipulation of fear in a Machiavellian manner: the need for a new prince to use force and fear (IV.1.27); the prudence of a prince's not executing rebels himself (III.7.199; V.4.98); the use of pardons as a middle between mildness and cruelty (III.7.200); the advantages of public accusations to bring fear to magistrates (IV.4.114); the wisdom of giving benefits little by little, and of doing injuries all at once (V.4.117).

But in place of Machiavelli's sensational executions (cf. III.5.143), Bodin offers the majesty of the sovereign, and accordingly promotes the utility of dignity over fear. Thus he can assert that a magistrate's punishments are not to avenge his personal injuries, but rather (or more!) those of the republic (III.5.137). For Machiavelli, sovereignty is as sovereignty does; the prince makes himself prince (Machiavelli does not say "sovereign") in the display of princely actions. For Bodin, sovereignty consists of those actions withdrawn into their potentiality, into a legal right. Sovereign majesty is the legal right to perform fearful actions, which are then no longer so fearful because they are expected. Bodin's sovereign is thus the strong executive *in potentia*, the legal version of what became, in Hobbes's science, power.

The first book of Bodin's *Six Books of the Republic* establishes that the first requisite of politics is a legal sovereign. But is the legal sovereign also sovereign in fact? If the Machiavellian prince is legalized by being abstracted from fact into law, will he still be able to sustain himself in fact? This is a difficulty for Bodin that we shall see even more prominently in Hobbes. While developing his legal sovereign, Bodin remarks that it is evil to say that the sovereign has the power to do evil; when the sovereign does evil, this is not power but powerlessness, feebleness, and cowardice (I.8.222). So Bodin denies sovereignty to the tyrant and, unlike Machiavelli, maintains the distinction between kingship and tyranny.

But if to act means to act well, it is not enough for Bodin to make his legal argument on the sovereign's behalf. Having abandoned fact for law, Bodin must return to the field of fact; he must show the sovereign how to act well so that the legal claim that he is not a tyrant can be sustained. This Bodin does in the second half of his work, beginning in Book IV, where he discusses the *règles politiques* that keep sovereigns in power.[10] Although he analyzes conspiracies in Machiavellian detail and recommends the use of Machiavellian devices, he emphasizes stability over innovation and growth over renewal. Machiavelli's necessity is a prompter of virtue; Bodin's necessity is almost a determinant of virtue. Like Montesquieu, he provides a theory of climate to see how nature affects the success of sovereigns (V.1).

Bodin's work is an odd combination of legal formalism and politic shrewdness, occupying the middle ground between Hobbes and Machiavelli. We may find it unsatisfactory because it seems to us that the elements Bodin wants to combine remain in conflict. But perhaps we only think so because we have embraced Hobbes, who presents the same combination in a more scientific, hence more extreme, form.[11] In Hobbes, an argument joins the right of the sovereign with the right of self-preservation, which is the right of each to be his own Machiavelli.

The historian Charles McIlwain has been quoted as saying that the "end-product of divine right sovereignty was reason of state."[12] It might be more promising to say the reverse: that divine right sovereignty was the product of reason of state. Bodin does not speak of reason of state, but he shares in the impersonal, academic obscurity of the concept. He maintains that princes are bound by natural law and by God's law (or the law of nature's God), but because of these very laws princes are not bound by human laws. The divine right of kings culminated in the doctrines of Bossuet and Filmer in the seventeenth century, but as Quentin Skinner has said, their basis was laid in Bodin's doctrine of sovereignty.[13]

That sovereignty was little different in effect from what came to be called, soon after Bodin, reason of state. Bodin's sovereign is a legislator who by right does not have to take account of previous legislation: he is Machiavelli's new prince legalized. Reason of state is the justification for Machiavellian advice or precept when it is applied to the benefit of an impersonal state. In Machiavelli's writings the word *stato* always refers to somebody's state—a prince's or an oligarchy's or a people's. After Machiavelli, and already in Bodin, "state" begins to signify an impersonal entity belonging to no one, just as we use it today. Doing something morally distasteful for the state acquires a moral exemption because such actions are no longer selfish. They are, of course, generalized selfishness and specious too, since the state does in fact belong to somebody.

Giovanni Botero is the first and chief theorist of a moral exemption for the state. In his *Of the Reason of State* (1589) he keeps his distance from the "conscienceless" Machiavelli while offering his readers Machiavellism, that is, Machiavellian prudence in particulars served up in the form of rules.[14] For example, in the execution of enterprises, Botero says, quickness is much more important than force; so one should employ cautious men while consulting, but ardent men for executing.[15] Botero says that reason of state, since it deals with matters exceeding ordinary ambition and imagination, cannot be reduced to "ordinary and common reason."[16] Later, Hobbes was to make precisely this reduction. He showed that by reasoning about the state of nature, ordinary reason would give its consent to the sovereign power of an impersonal state, and thus become identical with reason of state as something distinct from ordinary reason. Hobbes made it possible for us to dispose of reason of state. Or is the modern doctrine of executive power uncomfortably close to it?

Hobbes and the Constitutionalists

Executive power, as we have it now, was invented not at a stroke but by stages. Near the end of its development, when the new theory had created a new institution—the American presidency— Alexander Hamilton defined his task in *The Federalist* as disproving the idea "that a vigorous executive is inconsistent with the genius of republican government" (*Federalist* 70). In our day, free government is republican government, or in the case of England, republican with an easily penetrated disguise of monarchy. In Hamilton's day the identity was not yet fact but mere assertion. Republics still had to argue their claim to superiority in freedom against the rival claims of monarchies. To be republican was neither an abstract nor an unopposed preference; it was to be a partisan of republics against monarchies.

How then could good republicans be persuaded to accept, as consistent with their partisan spirit, not merely an aspect of monarchy but monarchy itself? To this theoretical and rhetorical task, classical republicanism (which may be roughly defined as pre-American republicanism) had nothing to contribute. For classical republicanism was partisan republicanism, and partisanship was the problem, not the solution. Classical republicans had to learn a new, nonpartisan republicanism not only from dubious republicans such as Hamilton, but before him from liberal philosophers who made the "moderated" monarchy of England their model for free government.[17] These were Locke and Montesquieu, above all others; and of these two, Locke was the author of the modern executive power.

Yet Locke in his invention had the aid of two political philosophers who were somehow, but not altogether, liberal—Machiavelli and Hobbes. By accepting Locke's invention, therefore, modern republics were admitting a submerged influence from nonliberal as well as nonrepublican sources. Instead of combatting monarchy as an enemy, modern republics have absorbed it and made it their own institution. To do this, they had to learn from thinkers who were not partisan republicans to relax their anti-monarchical animus. Yet, scholars in recent years, intent upon showing the influence of republicanism on modern government, have not taken account of the transformation of republicanism, epitomized in republican assent to executive power—an assent at first suspicious, but soon willing, and even enthusiastic. The transformation occurred against the thought and feeling of the republican spirit, and was not initiated by republicans.

Without such understanding, it might seem incorrect to have assigned to Thomas Hobbes so prominent a place in the development of the doctrine of executive power. For even more than Bodin, Hobbes asserted and argued, without possibility of doubt to the most conscientious reader or of disregard by the sleepiest listener, that the sovereign power in a commonwealth must be indivisible and inseparable. Therefore, according to Hobbes, no separate executive power can or should exist. In saying that sovereignty must be indivisible, he spoke not only against our constitutional notions and practices today, but also against those of his time.

Yet the extreme doctrine of absolute sovereignty contains a paradox which is apparent to all who read him, then and now. Hobbes derives the absoluteness of the artificial sovereign in a commonwealth from the absolute natural sovereignty of each individual in the state of nature, where each has a right to everything and in that sense is free. In Hobbes, the most extreme sovereignty in government is derived from the most extreme liberty in the individual. And liberty in the individual must make way for sovereignty in government, which is given by the individual's free consent so that sovereignty and liberty, identical in the natural individual, are shown to be connected (and opposed) in Hobbes's commonwealth. With Hobbes, power and liberty are not enemies but associates dependent on each other: power depends on liberty for its origin, and liberty depends on power to avoid misery. The paradoxical association holds promise for republicans seeking to strengthen republican liberty. Despite Hobbes's refusal to countenance the notion of a separate executive power, he prepared the way for that institution. To see how he did it, we must see how he differed from his predecessors' thinking on the executive.

For Machiavelli, the act of executing the law against criminals becomes a political instrument. In his conception, *esecuzione* is a sensational punishment by which every state must be refreshed from time to time. The wholesome fear and wonder engendered by the act are enhanced if it is a surprise and not an ordinary consequence of lawful procedure. Machiavelli did not claim to have invented the idea of a political execution emancipated from law, but he was perhaps the first political scientist to endorse it. Hobbes did not do so, despite his insistence on absolute sovereignty. Instead, going beyond Bodin, he formulated a general doctrine of natural law so that every execution would execute a law, the natural law, not a sensational, lawless act of dubious justice. At the same time, going far beyond Bodin, he formulated a general doctrine of power so that its exercise would be regular and apparent to all rather than hidden until made manifest as a surprise.

Yet Hobbes agreed with Machiavelli that execution is not a subordinate issue. In this he differed from a group of writers of his own time, the 1640s and 1650s, who might be called "constitutionalists": John Milton, John Sadler, Philip Hunton, Marchamont Nedham, John Lilburne, Isaac Penington, Sir Henry Vane, George Lawson, Charles Dallison.[18] Holding various opinions, these writers could be found on both the parliamentary and the royalist sides during the English Civil War. But they agreed on the necessity of separating the executive from the legislative power. Like the *politiques*, looking over their shoulder at the fanaticism of religious politics in their time, they struggled to keep human government from being entirely prescribed by divine right. They therefore upheld the sovereignty or quasi-sovereignty of legislative power—*human* legislative power—with some freedom from the commands of divine law so that in practice, government would be in the hands of political men rather than divines.

But once these writers had in various ways established the primacy of legislative power, or the opportunity for legislative power to rule under an inexact and unexacting divine law, they rejected Bodin's absolutism. They found it necessary to distinguish the executive from the legislative in order to make clear that the legislative serves the rule of law, and does not permit the tyranny of ambitious men. Without such separation, the difference between sovereignty and tyranny would be lost—the legislative and executive powers in the same hands would be tyranny, since the law would be bent to the private ends of the legislators. The purpose of separation was to maintain the rule of law by denying the executive the privilege of law-making, and by preventing the legislative from descending too far into particulars. But the effect was to subordinate the executive to the legislative. Sometimes the result was embraced in a republican solution; sometimes a remedy was sought in a "mixed monarchy."

The separation of the executive from the legislative power was readily used to subordinate or check the king. John Milton, in his pamphlet *Eikonoklastes* (1649), says: "In all wise nations the legislative power and the judicial execution of that power have been most commonly distinct, and in several hands; but yet the former supreme, the latter subordinate."[19] Milton supposes that the king executes the law, and hence should have no veto in law-making. John Sadler in *Rights of the Kingdom* (1649) finds three estates in the kingdom—the original, judicial, and executive powers[20]—represented in the Commons, the Lords, and the King; again, the king is reduced to "mere" executive. In *A Treatise of Monarchie* (1643), Philip Hunton speaks to two kinds of power; the architectonic or nomothetical, and the gubernative or executive; the former is supreme. Since, according to him, England is a "mixed monarchy," it must be mixed also in its supreme power, and the king must have some legislative power in addition to executive. Hunton mentions the "speed and secrecy of execution" and the "power of despatching affairs which are of the greatest difficulty and weight" in a manner that confirms his appreciation of the expansive nature of the executive. But he cannot think of a justification for it, and remains embarrassed by the unresolved tension between the supremacy of the legislative power and the practicability of monarchy.[21]

Marchamont Nedham, in *The Excellencie of a Free State* (1656), asserts that one of the cardinal errors in politics is to permit the legislative and executive powers to rest "in one and the same hands and persons." The executive power, he says, is derived from the legislative, and by the latter's authority may be transferred into the hands of one or many for the administration of government. The king is thus a mere executive except on extraordinary occasions when the safety of the state is at stake.[22] Despite many references to Machiavelli, Nedham does not make what Machiavelli made of the concession. Oliver Cromwell's *Instrument of Goverment* (1653) is explained and justified in an anonymous pamphlet, possibly by Nedham, *A True State of the Case of the Commonwealth* (1654), in which it is said that the separation of legislative and executive powers is "the grand secret of liberty and good government." These powers must be kept apart, flowing in distinct channels, except for "transitory extraordinary occasions."[23]

A separate executive could also be advocated as a check against the tyrannical tendencies of both Cromwell and Parliament. So the Levellers, authors of the *Agreement of the People* (1648), complained of imprisonments by Parliament, and attacked it as a confusion of the legislative and executive powers. John Lilburne, imprisoned himself, said in 1649 that "the House [of Commons] . . . was never betrusted with a Law executing power, but only with a law making power."[24] For Isaac Penington, the executive is the life of the law. But what makes execution most certain is "an exact Rule or way" prescribed to those who are to execute. The executive is clearly subordinate, but the superior legislative power should not meddle in it. So, too, Sir Henry Vane, protesting in 1656 against Cromwell's misrule: executive power should be distinct from legislative, but also subordinate.[25]

According to Gwyn, the separation of powers is an invention of seventeenth-century republicans.[26] But these republicans did not solve the problem of how to keep powers separate when one of them, the legislative, was—in accordance with republicanism— clearly superior. The solution was left, as Hamilton claimed, to American republicans in 1787.

The separation of legislative and executive powers was also invoked on the royalist side. Robert Filmer, the supporter of divine right monarchy whom Locke attacked so fulsomely, made the same distinction when opposing an argument for mixed monarchy. He said a mixed monarchy would reduce the king to a mere executive, when in right he had the legislative power.[27] George Lawson's *An Examination of the Political Part of Mr. Hobbs his Leviathan* (1657) argues that civil power is threefold, or has three degrees: legislative, judicial, and executive. Of these three the legislative is supreme, then comes judgment according to the laws, then execution "by the sword" according to judgment. The separation of the judicial from the executive has the effect of dropping the executive from a close second to third in rank. So Lawson's schema is much less an anticipation of ours than might appear from the names he adopted for the three powers. He denies the possibility of a mixed monarchy such as Hunton's maintaining that one supreme will, directed by one judgment and strengthened by one force of the sword, must command, judge, and execute. Lawson gives all three powers to the king and seems to distinguish them in order to promote the legality of the king's sovereignty. The king's judgment makes it possible to unite the distinct legislative and executive powers in the same hands.[28]

In *The Royalist's Defense* (1648), Charles Dallison puts aside divine right and claims that the king is the principal legislator and sole executor. The king legislates with the assent of the two Houses, who play a subordinate role. The legislator is supreme but his power is not unlimited because the judges of the realm determine which acts are binding; but the executive remains subordinate. Dallison says: "He who has the sovereign power of government has the power of sword." The king, that is, has executive power because he has the legislative power; the king is not subordinate, but the executive function is.

In all the constitutionalist writers, whether for or against the king, legislative and executive are separated in order to subordinate the executive. There is no strength in the executive except insofar as the executive, though separate in conception, shares in the legislative power. Republicans and royalists disagreed on the extent of the sharing, but not in their notion of a weak executive.[29]

How different is the executive in Hobbes's thought:

> For in vain would he give judgment, who could not execute his commands; or if he executed them by the power of another, he himself is not said to have the power of the sword, but that other, to whom he is only an officer. All judgment, therefore, in a city belongs to him who hath the swords; that is, to him who hath the supreme authority.[30]

This is the reverse of Dallison's judgment: He who has the power of the sword—the executive power—has the sovereign power. Hobbes specifies two swords—the swords of justice and of war—not of the temporal and spiritual powers. For Hobbes, the latter has no sword.

Hobbes and the Professionals

Why should the sovereign power be placed with the power of execution? Why should the location of sovereignty be decided by the evident fact of its exercise? Why, for Hobbes unlike the various constitutionalists, should sovereignty be indivisible? Because Hobbes believed that England had suffered, and that all nations had and would continue to suffer, when private judgment interfered with sovereignty. Although each of us is endowed with private judgment, some dispense it by vocation and thereby constitute a never-failing, overflowing source of it. These are the professionals—lawyers, priests, and scholars—who claim to help the sovereign with their powers of judgment.

Surely the sovereign needs able counsel? Perhaps. But Hobbes sees such offers of help from private, professional sources as concealed claims to rule resulting only in divided sovereignty. While such men are no doubt eager to help, they are far from disinterested counselors. Accordingly, any separation between the executive and the legislative is made-to-order for the professionals because it allows them to advance and at the same time to conceal their ambition. With institutional or constitutional standing in the legislature, they can demand a hearing and thus impede or thwart the execution of power. And if the professionals are too timid to cause trouble themselves, they can at least encourage others who are bolder. Thus, separation between legislative and executive leads to incompetent execution.

Hobbes's general solution to the problem of institutionalized private judgment is to put the legislative power entirely in the hands of the sovereign, "an absolute and arbitrary legislative power," to quote a phrase that Locke noticed adversely.[31] Both legislative and executive powers (including those we now call judicial) are drawn together, deprived of their claims to rule, and awarded to the sovereign. Because sovereignty comes with executive power, the sovereign must judge himself, allowing no one power to hinder him. Therefore he must make laws with an absolute and arbitrary power.

But is the sovereign to be deprived of help? While excluding the implicit claim to rule of those who want to help, will Hobbes exclude any necessary form of help to the sovereign? What of his own help, for example, the offer of the philosopher's own private judgment? Hobbes's own advice to the sovereign, and what as a consequence the sovereign owes to Hobbes, may lead one to doubt whether Hobbes's sovereign can in fact be absolute. If Hobbes's sovereign accepts help from Hobbes as his superior, why should he not accept the same from others, and from institutions, presumably his inferiors? Hobbes begins with the realistic observation that sovereignty is his who holds the sword, and ends with the formalistic conclusion that sovereignty must remain absolute despite its apparent, actual dispersion in the sovereign's helpers. Hobbes rejects the claims to rule of the professionals who claim to have wisdom, preferring the strength to be found in him who executes. But must he not admit, does he not actually assert in his own case, that wisdom has its own strength? Then how can sovereignty belong merely or entirely to the power that executes?

To answer the question, we may begin with Hobbes's late work, *A Dialogue Between a Philosopher and a Student of the Common Laws of England*, probably written in 1675.[32] Here is a clearer statement of the issue than in Hobbes's systematic presentations of his political philosophy. We find a dialogue between a (Hobbesian) philosopher and a lawyer who defends the common laws. The philosopher quickly gets him to say that the laws he defends are not dead letters but laws "living and armed," that is, capable of being executed, regardless of who pens or devises them (*Dialogue*, p. [10]). There may, then, be an author or deviser of the laws in addition to the sovereign. But the sovereign needs money for arms in order to execute the laws, and for this he must not be made dependent on Parliament. Yet though the King has the right to levy money for armies, he should not do so rashly; he should consult with military men, even with Parliament. "God made Kings for the People, and not People for Kings,"[33] declares Hobbes's philosopher, and it is in the King's own interest to make such laws as the people will endure, keep without impatience, and live under in strength and with courage to defend the King and the country against potent neighbors. The interlocutors agree that even an Act of Oblivion, or general pardon, should not be made without the assent of Parliament (*Dialogue*, pp. [44, 187–90]). On the one hand, the philosopher contends that "it were in vain to give [Soveraign Power] to any Person that had not the power of the Militia to cause it to be executed" (*Dialogue*, p. [158]). But on the other hand, precisely the "power of the Militia" induces the sovereign to seek the consent, or good will, of his subjects in order to raise money for it and in general to keep them content.

Hobbes's *Dialogue* consists of arguments by his philosopher against the interference of lawyers in the sovereign power. Lawyers justify their public use of private judgment with the doctrine of the chief lawyer, Sir Edward Coke, who supports the lawyer's artificial reason over every man's natural reason. Hobbes's philosopher defends natural reason. According to him natural reason teaches us, first, to adopt the principle of absolute sovereignty, and second, to apply sovereignty with restraint while seeking counsel and consent. Not only does natural reason justify absolute sovereignty. It also makes itself available for use by absolute sovereignty. For the philosopher's natural reason, unlike the lawyer's artificial reason, holds that reason should not interfere in sovereignty. So the philosopher, unlike the lawyer, will not use his private judgment to judge the sovereign, but instead will leave the sovereign's politic judgment free to decide in his own interest and according to his habit. By going the route to the extreme of absolute sovereignty, natural reason discovers its own principle of restraint and becomes the silent partner of politic reason. For Hobbes, unlike Bodin, the politic philosopher should be silent rather than offer politic advice, for politic advice from philosophers will only encourage politic advice from other professionals, among them lawyers. And rather than instructing lawyers how to give advice, Hobbes, unlike Bodin, wants them out of the picture.

Yet the sovereign still needs the philosopher's advice, and in particular the philosopher's arguments against the use of courts of equity, supported by the lawyers. The King's politic judgment must prevail over the lawyer's artificial reason.[34] Moreover, the sovereign needs the philosopher's warnings against laws punishing heresy. Finally and above all, the sovereign depends on the philosopher in the battle against lawyers because not only is someone like Coke at their head, but behind them is Aristotle, furnishing lawyers their definition of justice (*Dialogue*, p. [9]). Hobbes, it now appears, was a political philosopher who insisted that philosophy could reform politics and law, while claiming no political role for the philosopher and no legal status for political philosophy. The philosopher judges without becoming a judge and without authorizing others to become judges. His philosophy tells him, contrary to the self-styled "professional philosophers" of our day, that philosophy must not become a profession. In politics at least, if not in private, the professions produce greater effects from their talk than from their learning: they encourage a regime "where the most ignorant and boldest talkers do commonly obtain the best preferments."[35] To make the point, and to explain political philosophy's extreme shyness, Hobbes reluctantly permitted himself some bold talk.[36] Aristotle, we saw, also kept the political philosopher private. But he constituted his philosopher a cautious unofficial judge of the professional politicians—that is, of the rest of us. Hobbes's political philosophy is non-judgmental with a fierce passion.

Legal and Actual Sovereignty

In his three treatises of political philosophy, Hobbes speaks in his own name and with little self-effacement, but the difficulty of

combining sovereignty with the executive comes out in the am-
bivalences of his system, not in direct attack on his professional
enemies. In the *Elements of Law* (completed in 1640) Hobbes concludes very emphatically that sovereignty is indivisible. To reach
the conclusion, he describes the three powers somewhat as we
know them today—legislative, judicature, and administrative or
executive ("the carver")—which were thought to compose a
mixed regime.[37] But the component parts are not three sorts of
sovereignty, he says, and sovereignty is not a mixture of them,
although in the administration of sovereignty we may find them
subordinate to the sovereign.

Sovereignty comes from union, which Hobbes defines as a
union of wills, not of reason (*Elements* I.12.8, 19.6). The principles
of reason, or natural law, are nonetheless in accord with what
wills may will in union (I.5.5, 12, 14.14). Hence the faculties of
will and reason that constitute the three powers do not appear as
different or in conflict. Powers are faculties, involving will *and*
reason, but since these are not essentially in conflict, neither are
the three powers (I.1.7–8, 6.9, 8.4, 12.7–8). Since reason does not
judge the will, the judicature has no basis for judging the legislature. Reason accords with will, and reason must be consistent,
coherent, and consequential from its own beginning; reason is
not the application of a higher standard or ground found in nature (I.14.13–15.1, 17.11–12, 18.1). Nothing in men's nature or
souls makes impossible or even difficult the union of wills in sovereignty: reason dictates peace (I.18.1, II.8.13).

Yet, according to Hobbes in the *Elements,* a tension remains between the principles of reason or the laws of nature and the art
of government (I.9.1). The duty of a sovereign is to govern the
people well, for which he needs the art of government as well as
the principles of reason. A wise or prudent sovereign compre-
hends the art of government; so it becomes the duty of a sovereign to be wise or prudent. But of course an unwise or imprudent
king is no less sovereign. Hobbes's problem in the *Elements* is that
the indivisibility of sovereignty is defined by will alone, but also
requires reason, and not only the principles of reason but the art
of government.[38] The legal, formal definition of sovereignty as a
union of wills is not sufficient, yet it cannot be corrected without
danger to the actual union of sovereignty.

In *De Cive,* published in 1642, Hobbes does not retain the subversive distinction between principles of reason and the art of

government. We hear no more of this art which implies the need for Machiavellian prudence in the world of chance particulars. Now human art seems to work by principles or dictates of right reason, which are the laws of nature.[39] But a similar distinction reflecting the same difficulty now appears between wisdom and right reason. Wisdom is defined as "the perfect knowledge of the truth in all matters whatsoever."[40] Right reason is not an infallible faculty for Hobbes, but the act of reasoning that is peculiar and true: peculiar because it is the rule of every man's own actions, and also the measure of another man's reasoning in what concerns the first man; true because it is derived from true principles rightly framed (*De Cive* II.1, p. 123). In effect, "peculiar" means "common" as it appears to each individual. So the principles of right reason would be the true principles every man can see and frame for his own conduct, and expect from others: this falls far short of wisdom.

Now principles of right reason do not include the "justice of single actions," which is determined by civil as distinct from natural laws (pref., p. 104). Civil laws are rules and measures, but not of right reason or natural law directly; they specify or determine generalities in natural law. They may vary or even conflict: for example, "that copulation which in one city is matrimony, in another will be judged adultery" (VI.16, p. 186). Yet civil laws are universal, since law is a generality. They aim at the "welfare of the most part," which means, according to Hobbes's uncompassionate definition of the Welfare State, "that no man suffer ill, but by his own default, or by some chance which could not be prevented" (XIII.3, p. 259). Civil law would be the product of the knowledge or judgment of good and evil in the sovereign which private men surrender when they join the commonwealth. This law, the word of the sovereign, is the "reason of the *city*" (XIV.17, p. 283; XV.17, p. 304) as opposed to right reason, which is available to private understanding. Clearly the civil law could be better or worse than the natural law: better if the "Justice of single actions" is determined by a sovereign's wisdom, worse if the determination is wrong.

To help sovereigns, Hobbes has written Chapter 13 of *De Cive*, "Concerning the Duties of Them Who Bear Rule," stating how they ought to behave toward their subjects. He does not mention, much less supply, an art for fulfilling kingly duties, and seems to think that they are contained in right reason rather than wisdom.

Anything additional to right reason is "left to the political practices of each commonweal" (XIII.1–2, p. 258). But of course such practices might be well- or ill-suited to the performance of sovereigns' duties, and in stating those duties Hobbes has supplied, if not an art to fulfill them, then a set of criteria for judging the efficacy of the civil laws and practices of sovereigns.[41] To be sure, the efficacy of civil laws does not determine their justice; but this is a strange conclusion to an argument that begins by uniting sovereignty and execution.

To summarize: in the *Elements* and in *De Cive*, Hobbes attempts to draw all power into sovereignty to give the sovereign the supreme power of making laws. But he cannot quite succeed in giving the sovereign a legislative power that also includes executive and judicial powers. Not every law that can be executed will pass judgment, and not every law might pass judgment can be executed.

The Sovereign Power

In *Leviathan* (1651) we find a new view of the problem and a new solution for it, one that has been fundamental to modern executive power, to modern constitutionalism, and to the modern understanding of politics. We do not find here a distinction between science or philosophy and art, as in the *Elements*. In his introduction Hobbes says that art, his art, imitates nature, which is the art of God and the object of scientific study. The commonwealth, or artificial man, is made by art, or (one may say) by science, a branch of the same science that studies natural man.[42] Nor do we find a distinction here between right reason and science or wisdom, as we do in *De Cive*: Hobbes says in *Leviathan* that reason is right reason, and the development of reason to perfection is science.[43]

We do find in *Leviathan*, as we do in the *Elements* and *De Cive*, a distinction between science and prudence. Science is specifically human and conditional, the knowledge of consequences; prudence is shared with beasts and concerns fact. Although Hobbes does not apply the distinction with Kantian strictness, prudence is based on experience and deals in probabilities, but science expands our experience by conceiving new possibilities.[44] What then does Hobbes the scientist have to impart to the prudent sovereign? His science instructs prudence through a discourse on power. A thematic discussion of power was lacking in the *Elements* and in *De Cive*, but, since *Leviathan*, modern political discourse, including that describing the "powers" in modern constitutions, has used "power" in its Hobbesian sense.

Hobbes defines power in chapter 10 of *Leviathan*: "The Power of a Man, (to take it Universally,) is his present means, to obtain some future apparent Good" (*Leviathan* X, p. 66). This is a neutral definition: a *means* to, *some, apparent* good. Why does Hobbes not specify *which* good and that it be *truly* a good? It might seem that only certain goods give men power and only if they are truly good. One would seek these goods as ends, not merely as means to unspecified objects. But Hobbes takes power "universally" instead of, in the Aristotelian manner, particularly, with regard for the distinct powers of different things to produce different goods.[45]

For Aristotle, power or potentiality (*dunamis*) is always related to actuality (*entelexeia* and *energeia*), though always distinct from actuality. Power is the power of something to realize itself; each power has its own actualization. Hence for Aristotle there can be no abstract power, and no "love of power" such as we today, under Hobbes's influence, attribute to politicians. Tellingly, Aristotle discusses power not in his *Politics* but in his *Physics* and *Metaphysics*. In the latter, he distinguishes between power exercised with reason (*meta logou*) and without (*alogon*)—between, for example, the power of medicine and that of heat. Though heat always works, and without anyone's applying thought to the matter, medicine, which uses reasoning, may by chance produce disease instead of health. Powers that are humanly directed may fail; they are indeterminate. When they succeed, we say they are done *well*; we do not say that heat works well or badly. In Latin, the difference was sometimes, though not always, reflected in the use of *potentia* for power that works without fail (e.g. God's power) and *potestas* for power that works through human intention, hence imperfectly.[46] *Potestas* can therefore refer to moral or legal power, but the usage seems inconsistent.

Hobbes's intent was to construct a political science that would not trust or tolerate indeterminate powers, but would give such human powers the reliability of non-human power—that would impart to *potestas* the unfailing exactness of *potentia*. His intent becomes clearer if we compare it to Machiavelli's, which also aimed to reduce human dependency on fortune. Both attempted to actualize human power by removing the opportunity for chance to intervene between potentiality and actuality. Machiavelli's way was to advance potentiality into actuality; Hobbes's was to withdraw from actuality into potentiality. Machiavelli's way led to the *act* of execution, Hobbes's to executive *power*. For Machiavelli, the potentiality of forms of government to behave in their intended manner is unreliable; all such forms need to be reduced to their "effectual truth" by acts of execution that bring glory to princes, and salutary fear to peoples. The honor or pride of maintaining one's constitution regardless of its success is rejected in favor of efficacy from the viewpoint of more elemental motives.

For Machiavelli, acts of execution thus no longer reflect intended ends: they no longer merely "carry out" an order or a law. They are now ends in the sense of outcomes, effects that invigorate governments whatever their intended forms: effects that serve as causes. Of course, the prudent executive stands behind these effects, planning them as surprises, and in that sense they are intended. But it is the creation of form, the act of becoming a new prince, that matters—not the form that has already been created. Instead of political power being the cause of political acts, the acts create the power.

Hobbes takes the opposite course, however, following Bodin and radicalizing his work. He creates the executive as a regular, formal office, duly authorized with power that attaches to the office, not the person. With the same Machiavellian purpose of reducing chance in politics, Hobbes draws attention away from the exercise of power and turns to power itself, regardless of what it does. Hence arise the questions of sovereignty, legitimacy and authority that are featured in all discussion of Hobbes and in all politics influenced by Hobbes. These questions can be decided exactly, only if they are abstracted from particular forms of government and their intended ends. Particular forms must yield to the sovereign form, to sovereignty itself. Hobbes's sovereign governs through the sovereign passion of fear, the passion to be reckoned on, not the virtues relied on or hoped for by particular governments to achieve their ends. Even the virtue in execution—Machiavellian *virtù* in gaining glory—is reduced, as Leo Strauss has shown, to the motive of fear.[47] Whereas Machiavelli worries that executors will lose their nerve when it comes to the deed,

Hobbes fears that they will go too far and counsels them to conserve their power by avoiding vainglorious enterprises.

Hobbes's reason for taking power universally is, again, that the distinct powers of different things cannot *assure* men that they will produce their various effects. Riches, honors, commands cannot be assured, hence they are not assuredly good; so men are compelled to seek one good after another. No stopping point will be reached at which men can rest in assured happiness; there is no highest good, no utmost aim, no furthest end (*Leviathan* XI, p. 75). And since the highest good is lacking, no good can be good in its place or rank. Without a highest good, no natural hierarchy of goods, and of powers to produce goods, can exist. Hobbes takes a frankly anthropocentric, even a popular, view. "The object of man's desire," he says, is to have assurance of the goods he seeks (XI, p. 75). Instead of reproving the vanity of this desire, he accepts it and accordingly demands that "good" mean only "good for us human beings." But since nothing good has the power to assure good to us, we are entitled to seek power without reference to the goods or ends of particular powers, thus turning every unassured good in nature more surely to our advantage as it appears to each of us. Since we cannot be assured of satisfaction from nature or God, we must deny that we receive *any* help from powers outside ourselves, and attempt to assure our own power. This is power pure and simple, taken "universally."

To supply men's desire for power, they have a natural propensity for science, by which they seek causes. They seek the causes of the good things they want to be assured of; so in Hobbes's view the propensity for science is hard to distinguish from self-preservation. But in seeking causes they stop at the first cause, or the highest good, as they think it—this being an invisible power responsible for all good things. Since there are grounds for mistrust of such an invisible power, if it exists it must be feared. That fear is the natural seed of religion (XI, p. 81)—and also of rebellion, because the invisible power allows for private interpretation, and for private judgment separate from the sovereign's. The natural illusion of a *summum bonum* and its personification in God are, by this reasoning, the cause of the *summum malum* in human society, civil war. Men only have themselves to blame for their laziness in seeking causes, and their complacency in finding assurance; but they are led into error by the professions that embody and encourage an aristocratic vanity of knowers, who in fact presume upon nature's goodness to justify their privileges. To counter them, Hobbes adopts and promotes a democratic vanity that doubts all goods but human power.

"So that in the first place," Hobbes says, "I put for a general inclination of all mankind, a perpetuall and restlesse desire of Power after power, that ceaseth onely in Death" (XI, p. 75). Hobbes *puts* this inclination first. It is not so much an observed as an imputed restlessness, and being futile and intolerable, it requires a remedy of assured power other than the invisible highest good. The remedy is a visible common power, rather than a highest power. To establish a remedy, Hobbes's science must find a fact that brings the restless desire of power after power to a halt, or at least redirects it so that men seek greater power over nature (in accordance with democratic vanity) instead of power over one another. Science must find some substitute for the natural hierarchy of goods made possible by an alleged highest good. This substitute is an ultimate fact, the state of nature, "the condition of mere nature" in *Leviathan* in which men are equal—in which indeed men and women are equal, since equality means equal ability to kill wherein cunning makes up for strength. Hobbes has difficulty in proving men equal, then finally gives up the attempt and says that men must be admitted equal because they think they are equal (more democratic vanity, XIII, p. 95).

It might seem, as many today would say, that "nature" is just another invisible power arbitrarily crowned by Hobbes as the first cause. But for Hobbes, nature is visible because nature is this-worldly. The state of nature according to Hobbes could not possibly be confused with the Garden of Eden, which if not otherworldly itself, implies the existence of the otherworldly. What is visible in nature are one's own self and one's self-preservation (intro., p. 10); and what is reasonably imaginable are threats to that security. Nature so understood is reason. Science, which is concerned with conditions rather than facts, shows the condition of mere nature or prescribes it. And that condition is readily conceivable and must be taken as fact: the fact from which methodical reasoning begins. Thus we are told in chapter 17 that the final cause of men's subjecting themselves in commonwealth is the "foresight of their own preservation, and of a more contented life thereby" (XVII, p. 128). The foresight is of the visible, which is reasonably imaginable. What are visible, then, are presumed equality and the natural laws deduced from it. Both lead to the institution of sovereignty: or are these only generally appreciable by our democratic vanity in a vaguer sense than "visible"? The surely visible, not to say sensible, power is the sword or executive power of the sovereign.

Power is the end that is not an end, the end we determinedly pursue because we lack an end from nature or God. By our experience or imagination of the state of nature, power is transformed from end into means, the means to peace. Peace, the necessary condition of any end, becomes the final end for Hobbes. Thus the Machiavellian "art of government," to which Hobbes has recourse in the *Elements*, whose end is acquisition, is swallowed up in *Leviathan* by the science of justice or natural law, whose end is peace. In maintaining and increasing his power, not wasting it in vainglorious conquests, the sovereign achieves peace. Perhaps peace in the sense of private ease cannot be the sovereign's end as much as it is for his subjects, but peace in the sense of security is his end and his subjects' together.

Besides having a neutral end, power is also neutral with regard to its components, which are will and reason. Since Hobbes's generalized power is not the power to do something in particular, it does not mean the power to do well, and so does not imply the dominance of reason over will. Such neutrality reflects or reveals the undesirability of separate institutions based on the need for will to be judged by reason—a legislature that wills, or a judiciary that judges, for example. It also opposes a separation of powers that would obviate the dangerous dominance of will over reason by establishing institutions that check each other. The first reason for the separation of powers expects too much nonpartisanship from judging; the second reason allows too much partisanship in all institutions. Hobbes did not draw power together in the sovereign merely in order to separate it into visible, institutional "bodies" of will, judgment, and discretion, as Locke did. For Hobbes, power must be neutral as to form, so tha' 't can be neutral as to its end, or effective in securing the neutraı end of peace. No visible rival or impediment to executive power can be tolerated. Although England's constitutional parts should remain, as the *Dialogue* makes clear, they must be understood either as sovereign or as counsellors and officers of the sovereign.

Hobbes's Formalism

The difficulty we have seen throughout between the justice and the wisdom of the sovereign remains in *Leviathan*. To describe the proper conduct of the sovereign, Hobbes says in chapter 20: "The skill of making, and maintaining Commonwealths, consisteth in certain Rules, as doth Arithmetique and Geometry; not (as Tennis-play) on Practise onely" (XX, p. 160). Here the certain rules set down in Hobbes's system of justice seem to account for the skill of a sovereign. But, in chapter 19, Hobbes speaks of "The unskilfulness of the Governours, ignorant of the true rules of Politiques" (XIX, pp. 151–52; see XXV, p. 200), where, from the examples given, the true rules of politics do not seem to be included in the certain rules of justice. In chapter 24 Hobbes discusses the *use* of sovereignty in the "Nutrition and Procreation of a Commonwealth." Is this discussion part of natural law, and hence required of the sovereign as sovereign? Or is it part of wisdom, as considerations which the sovereign would be wise to entertain, but which are superfluous to his sovereignty?

In chapter 25 Hobbes distinguishes command from counsel, leaving counsel at the sovereign's discretion. "A man that doth his businesse by the help of many and prudent Counsellours, with every one consulting apart in his proper element, does it best, as he that useth able Seconds at Tennis-play, placed in their proper stations" (XXV, p. 202). So tennis is not rejected after all! Divided counsel gets in the way of execution, Hobbes says. If it is necessary to take counsel, the sovereign must take it in the proper way; and the proper way is from tennis, not from natural law. In chapter 26 Hobbes makes an express distinction between a judge of right and wrong and a judge of what is commodious to the commonwealth (XXVI, p. 216). And in chapter 30 is the well-known distinction between a good or needful law and a just law (XXX, p. 268).

In sum, for Hobbes legal power is placed with actual power in the hand that executes, but legal power is not identical to actual power. The legal sovereign may be unskillful, forget to do what is needful, and botch his job while still obeying the certain rules of natural law. Natural law points in the right direction, but following its guidance does not guarantee success, particularly, one may suppose, against another sovereign taught by Hobbes. Legal power does not guarantee actual power: so after all, that power *cannot* be placed with actual power. Some discrepancy will remain between the legal and the actual sovereign, between the form and the reality of power, and this is the formalist aspect of Hobbes's realism.

Some discrepancy between the form and the reality of power seems to be necessary to the modern doctrine of executive power, as a quick look at Spinoza can verify. Hobbes admitted that Spinoza had been bolder than he, as if Spinoza's bad example might excuse his own habit of behaving like a naughty boy. But in executive matters, Spinoza was all innocent. Hobbes thought Spinoza bolder because his science of power referred to its actual exercise in the Machiavellian manner, rather than to potentiality or legal sovereignty. Hence for Spinoza the famous equation of might with right. But the political consequence is not the rule of one or few by means of fraud; it is democracy and public openness, since Spinoza argues that most men will insist on being heard and on knowing what the government does. Since power is power in fact, the form of government is not different from the reality; and since there is no legalism or formalism, there can be no secrecy, no fraud—and no executive. There is, in short, no mask for the executive to hide behind, and the boldness of Spinoza's political science therefore leaves no room for the cunning.[48] Machiavelli's realism is bold but still cunning, and Hobbes's is bold but still legal.

Because there is a discrepancy in Hobbes between legal and actual sovereignty, it is hard to say that Hobbes's executive is either strong or weak. Hobbes certainly seems to be a proponent of the strong executive, and his argument for placing sovereignty with executive power is intended to teach that free government can and must be strong. But then Hobbes gives his sovereign an "absolute and arbitrary legislative Power." The legislative power gives the law over to Hobbes's executive, both legalizing and subordinating it. Now Hobbes's executive seems weak: He cannot go beyond the law, and not merely for the formal reason that every act of the sovereign is by definition legal, but also because the sovereign as sovereign does not have an extraordinary power beyond the rules of justice, for which he might employ the "art of government," or the "true rules of Politiques," or a statesman's discretion.[49] There is no prerogative power in Hobbes as there is in Locke. The very union of legislative and executive power weakens the executive by leaving the impression that government consists in passing laws that obey the rules of justice. Hobbes's simplification of power—a founding act of modern politics—brings power to the fore, yet at the same time obscures it. Although eager for a strong executive, by uniting it with the law-making power he does not escape the republican difficulty of weakening the executive by separating it from the legislative.

To expose a distinction that Hobbes was anxious to conceal, one could say that he gives his sovereign access to his science, but not to his wisdom. The sovereign and his subjects, Hobbes says, need the "help of a very able Architect" (XXX, p. 247)—modestly not naming himself—to define power, gather it in the sovereign, and combat false doctrines that have the effect of dividing it. But if such help is needed, has Hobbes really combined sovereignty with executive power? Isn't there an unofficial power in the very able architect?

In chapter 10 of *Leviathan*, Hobbes says: "The Sciences, are small Power; because not Eminent. . . . For Science is of that nature, as none can understand it to be, but such as in a good measure have attayned it" (X, p. 67). He seems anxious to deny the existence of *any* invisible power, including or especially his own. He makes his science or wisdom visible in his simplified doctrine of the wise, for natural right so understood is the power behind tent that modern sovereigns are Hobbesian, then, are they not his executives and thus weaker than they appear? In his simplified doctrine of natural right, Hobbes presumes that all men are equal and that they consent to a sovereign who represents them. With it he opposes above all the classical tradition of the natural right of the wise, for natural right so understood is the power behind the presumption of the learned. At the same time, through the help of a very able architect, he draws on the natural right of the wise and thus vindicates the very principle he opposes. Free governments may thereby be reminded that they need the strength of wisdom as well as that of the sword.

III

The Constitutional Executive

8

Constitutionalizing the Executive

With John Locke we come to the constitutional executive we think we know. We think we know it because it is familiar to us, but its very familiarity restricts our knowledge because it hinders our imagination. In fact, we know no other than the constitutional executive—except his alter ego, the unconstitutional executive.

But what exactly *is* a constitutional executive? It is often thought to be an executive subordinate to the constitution. But could it not also be considered an ambivalent, submissive recognition of the need for a strong executive? What then is the precise relationship between the constitution and this executive power? Locke's political science shows that the modern constitution and the modern executive are mutually dependent and yet antithetical. Each needs and opposes the other.

The Modern Constitution

We have seen the modern executive develop in two modes after Machiavelli's invention of *esecuzioni*. For Machiavelli, the executive lies in the awe-inspiring act of execution. He is so confident of the need for fear that he abandons all concern, vital in the Aristotelian tradition, for the distinction between the tyrant and the king who rules justly. When nature is understood as such necessity, the ground for such a distinction disappears. The good prince has the same need to be cruel as does the bad, and he will be less cruel only when it is prudent; that is, when necessity

181

requires. After Machiavelli, the necessity for the executive to act as a tyrant was reconceived as the need for a sovereign, by Bodin and Hobbes; or else it was effectively dismissed or depreciated in the form of a separate and subordinate executive power, as described by constitutionalist supporters of the rule of law.

In the first of these modes, almost any act of the sovereign was considered legal; and the necessity of tyranny was thereby embraced and baptized. The intended result, especially evident in Hobbes, is to make all men aware of the necessity, and therefore to throw very cold water on the ardent hopes they have cherished for any notion of justice that would oppose necessity. Once aware of the need for an absolute sovereign, men will no longer complacently set themselves up for Machiavellian surprises. With a new notion of justice as incorporating necessity, politics and morality will be brought into alignment—and hence, so will princes and peoples. Fraud will no longer be perpetrated because sovereigns will stop promising to be good. Further, the Machiavellian conclusion recommending cruel and tyrannical executions can be denied on the Machiavellian premise of anticipating necessity. No unscientific excess of evil-doing will sully the name of Leviathan.

The second mode refuses the necessity of tyranny. Instead, a constitution is drawn up, or an implicit form of the constitution is found, that claims to rule justly without resort to tyranny. We have encountered this thought in the English writers of the 1640s who distinguished between legislative and executive powers. Notably, the original separation of powers was twofold, not three-fold, and it was made for a double purpose: to separate the executive (which usually included the judiciary) from the legislative, and to place the executive in a subordinate role. In both respects the end was to maintain the rule of law. The separation was intended to prevent those lawmakers from applying it to suit themselves, and the subordination was meant to prevent the executor of the law from changing it in his own interest. Since the executive in Britain was the king, he was by implication reduced to subordinate status. If he retained any part of the legislative power so as not to be subordinate, he compromised the principle of separation. Thus, when separation of powers was adopted in defense of the king by moderate royalists such as Dallison and Lawson, it had to be combined with some version of the mixed regime in order to elevate the king from the rank of mere executive. So the notion of separation of powers, despite its seemingly impartial devotion to the rule of law, had from its origin a republican bias.

A further example of republican resistance to the necessity of tyranny can be found in the work of James Harrington, whose constitutionalism opposed a strong executive but did not make a point of separating it from the legislative. Harrington (in his utopian tract *The Commonwealth of Oceana*, 1656) presents himself as a foe of Hobbes and a friend of Machiavelli.[1] His book abounds in praises of the latter, to whom he is an eager but incompetent guide, for Machiavelli would not himself have approved of such indiscreet compliments. For Harrington, Machiavelli is the defender of the rule of law in "ancient prudence," Hobbes the promoter of rule by private interest in "modern prudence." Machiavelli defends the rule of law by insisting on an armed citizenry capable of maintaining the laws (*Oceana*, p. 162); Harrington believes, on his own, that this citizenry can be brought into balance through an agrarian law regulating property to make it more equal (*Oceana*, pp. 162, 180). With a well-ordered people, the "superstructure" of government can also be balanced because it is drawn from the people in a complicated "ballot" providing rotation in all offices. This balance in people and government will make an immortal commonwealth immune from Polybian decay without resort to fearful Machiavellian executions (*Oceana*, p. 321).

To make the promise, however, Harrington refers to Machiavelli; indeed, he includes a dictator among the officials of *Oceana* and mentions the "necessity" of providing beforehand for actions that will have to be sudden and secret (*Oceana*, p. 254).[2] He also speaks of the need for one man to act alone in reforming a state as legislator, though not in maintaining it as executive; his executive is plural (*Oceana*, pp. 207, 281, 286).

All this would seem to recognize the necessity of executive tyranny. But in fact it does not. Harrington's Machiavelli is really a benign populist reminiscent of recent scholarly understanding; the fear, the fraud, and the shock are gone, rendered unnecessary by Harrington's contrived balance in people and property. Harrington admits that his commonwealth cannot stand if Machiavelli is correct that enmity between the nobles and the people cannot be removed (*Oceana*, p. 272). On that fundamental point he differs from the man he calls the "greatest artist in the modern world . . . the prince of politicians" (*Oceana*, p. 274).[3] The unwise venture into disagreement permits him to omit fraud from the necessities of politics and to suppose that the interests of the people can be brought into accord not only in one state but for the whole of mankind. He rests his case for justice on the ease with which "two silly girls" could divide a cake (*Oceana*, p. 172).[4] His executive "is answerable unto the people that his execution be according unto the law; by which Leviathan may see that the hand or sword that executeth the law is in it, and not above it" (*Oceana*, p. 174).

Harrington's visible, instrumental executive has little of Hobbes and less of Machiavelli.[5] Harrington wanted Hobbes's certainty without his monarchism. So he turned to Machiavelli, determined to find freedom without risk and bloodless strife. He has been called a classical republican, but in truth the presumptuous constitutionalism of his balanced state is almost as far from Machiavelli as it is from Aristotle. It takes account neither of Machiavelli's discordant humors of nobles and peoples, nor of Aristotle's competing claims of justice. In fact, Harrington's balanced people is a poor substitute for Hobbes's state of nature as a ground for agreement on a sovereign: Harrington could not figure out how to combine the state of nature with constitutional government.

Locke was finally to show us this important combination. We shall see that the supposedly innocent Locke was able to grasp the Machiavellian principle of anticipating the necessity of executive tyranny better than the supposedly Machiavellian Harrington. One cannot identify Machiavellians merely by counting references to the name of Machiavelli, useful as that may be. A better test is to look for who comes out on top not quite smelling like a rose. Rightly and tellingly, Harrington never had Locke's influence.

The English constitutionalists who rejected the necessity of tyranny were not Aristotelians, but, unlike Bodin and Hobbes, they had not freed themselves from Aristotle. It will be useful now to draw a contrast between Aristotelian and modern constitutionalism, so that we can appreciate the change Locke wrought. For Aristotle, the form of the constitution or regime is its visible order, which indicates who rules. "Take me to your leader," the Aristotelian political scientist requests. The end of the regime is thus identical, or almost identical, to its form, since the end of a society is simply to live as it is ordered. And naturally, each regime claims to be ordered for the best life. Aristotle takes hold of any claim and examines it by the implicit standard it contains, the standard of nature. Applying this standard, Aristotle (despite his practicality) prefers what is intrinsically best over what is merely necessary in difficult circumstances. Survival is not enough if the regime does not survive either as it is or as improved. Nor is stability recommended, as in our contemporary political science, regardless of what is kept stable.

The Aristotelian political scientist examines the claim or principle of each regime by the standard of nature and finds it to be partisan and biased, typically toward either democracy or oligarchy. To understand a regime is thus to see how it is biased, and therefore how it might be corrected. By understanding partisan regimes, the political scientist corrects them toward a mixed regime; if he reflects on what he does, as we have seen, he also corrects them toward monarchy. Every regime is a mixed regime, and a monarchy; and insofar as it is biased, it is neither. But in any case, every regime takes its chances with necessity; it is exposed to the possibility, hence to the ultimate inevitability, of its own destruction. A healthy regime is willing to take risks in its own defense, but it does not know how to be "altogether bad," in Machiavelli's sense, for the sake of survival (Machiavelli, *D* I.27). For Aristotle, there are certain foul deeds even a tyrant will not commit simply in order to survive.

The modern constitution, as Locke established it, is less defiant of necessities that keep us from doing what we would like or feel is right. Modern constitutionalism begins from Aristotle's, or any philosopher's, observation that the claims of justice made by regimes are partisan. But rather than argue with such claims in order to improve them, modern constitutionalism forces the claimants to abandon their partisanship by confronting necessity. Necessity as revealed in the state of nature will compel partisans to consider what is essential, their self-preservation, and to forsake their partisan opinions about the good or godly life.

Locke therefore adopted and improved upon Hobbes's state of nature in order that politics might begin from pre-political necessity. Like Hobbes, he obviates all claims to rule proceeding from existing groups that might be used to justify a mixed regime. Harrington also makes clear his fundamental kinship with the modern political science, asserting that his skill consists in "raising such superstructures of government as are natural to the known foundations" (*Oceana*, p. 202). But Harrington's foundations had no certainty because they were not located in a state of natural necessity wherein men could choose nothing else; they depended on an arbitrary balance in conditions such as one would have to wish for. Instead, Locke used the "known foundations" that Hobbes had discovered and established for all modern men.

Yet unlike Hobbes, Locke believed that men can be successfully governed by "declared laws." Necessity does not compel them to consent to any government regardless of its lawlessness. The rule of law that the constitutionalists desired but could not deliver can be achieved and sustained. Locke thought he could safely define the legislative power as supreme, rather than insisting, like Hobbes, that every act of the sovereign be considered a law. Rule of law in Locke's understanding becomes rule by the law-making power, thus giving it exactness; for one knows by looking at that power which laws have been declared. And the reverse is also true: rule of the legislature becomes a rule of law, so that only standing laws, not just the sovereign's decrees, have legal status. Locke's rule of law protects each person; it satisfies the reasonable desire of each to know what is his and to keep it secure. But just as important, Locke's rule of law contains a principle that responds to our innate desire to be both free and safe. One cannot choose to remain in the state of nature, but one can create the means of leaving it. For Locke's rule of law is the rule of a legislative power that each has *constituted* out of the state of nature. When the legislature makes a law, its activity results from and extends this constitution, which was originally the (more or less) free act of each person. Unlike Hobbes, Locke does not insist that men surrender their freedom to the government when they leave the state of nature. True, men no longer make laws for themselves, but the laws are made by a legislative power they have constituted. The lawmaking power must therefore also be representative; by its constitution, and because it was so constituted, it must be created through elections.

The modern constitution, then, was produced by Locke's combination of Hobbes's political science with the constitutionalist opinion favoring the rule of law. Its peculiar character reflects the manner of its birth because the two elements combined in it remain recognizably distinct, even conflicting. When a legislative power has been constituted, it represents both the act of its creation and the end it was created for. Those two things are only partially the same. In the Aristotelian regime, the form is the end because the form (for example, democracy) reflects a certain choice of end (to have democracy). But in the modern, Lockean constitution, the form is not *what* is chosen but the *act* of choosing, or freely constituting. It is therefore perfectly proper, and in a sense "constitutional," for the people to replace one constitution by another. The people would do so if they decided that another constitution better served their end. Hence the form and the end are only partly identical. They are identical insofar as the legislative power continues the collective act of free self-government in constituting that power, but different because the practice of that form may not serve the end for which it was constituted.

What is that end? For Locke, it is self-preservation combined with the preservation of one's property. This is the end men pursue in the state of nature, before they have a "common judge" or government. That end is pre-political, unattached to any form of government, and it retains that character once a government has been formed. In the modern constitution, therefore, the government is judged partly by an intrinsic political end and partly by an extrinsic, nonpolitical end. We want to know whether a government is free and also whether it protects us.

If we return to the question of the need for tyranny posed by Machiavelli, we recall that Hobbes accepted that necessity, hence denied the rule of law, while the constitutionalists rejected it precisely to *maintain* the rule of law. Locke accepts the necessity but works it into the constitution: he *constitutionalizes* the necessity of tyranny.

Where is the necessity in the constitution? Fundamentally, it lies in the end of self-preservation. Self-preservation is in fact the tyrant's end of self-aggrandizement, but it has been transformed by being placed in the state of nature. There it is attributed to all men, thus made universal, equal, and modest—and then found moral. When the people think about whether the government they have constituted serves its end, they use the test they must apply to any government, the test of natural necessity that all governments of whatever partisan hue must face. In this regard a free government can claim no advantage in efficacy or legitimacy from its freedom or from its having been freely constituted; to this extent the modern constitution is Machiavellian. But in the act of constituting and by the activity of free government, the

187

modern constitution is in part Aristotelian. For freedom and government by consent are considered good in themselves without regard to whether they succeed in the end that any government must accept. Aristotle himself would have wanted to know to what end freedom was used, but by regarding the exercise of freedom (which is indistinguishable from the exercise of power) as good in itself—that is, by departing from Aristotle in this one respect—Locke manages to retain part of Aristotle's constitutionalism in his own, namely the notion that the constitution is an end in itself as well as a means to an end.

In constitutional politics, therefore, it matters *how* an end is achieved, as well as *whether* it is achieved. Thus, for example, it is as important to try the guilty correctly as to convict them. For Machiavelli, to the contrary, it is as important to violate regular procedure as to remove inconvenient rivals: the end alone is sovereign, and that end is to shock. But Locke's constitution is not judged by its success alone. Indeed, one could say that resisting tyranny, and reforming or replacing a failed constitution, are themselves as constitutional as forming a government and making it work.[6]

Locke does not provide such an analysis of his own constitution. For one thing, he was not eager to claim kinship with Hobbes, much less with Machiavelli.[7] For another, he was too prudent to expose his kinship with them by boasting of new inventions in political science. When he does produce a novelty, a law that every man executes, he immediately admits it will look "very strange" to an observer (*Two Treatises of Government* II.9, 13). His use of "constitution" in the *Two Treatises* suggests a writer who has stumbled upon a word he finds he likes. He first uses "constitution" without reference to the act of constituting (I.51, 168; II.76). Then, in the chapter on the "forms of a commonwealth" he uses "constitute" as a verb (II.132) while also using verbs such as uniting, placing, erecting, and establishing; after that, he moves to "Constituted Commonwealth" before essaying "original Constitution" (II.153); he repeats that several times and finally, though still incidentally, defines "constitution" as the act of constituting (II.157) after his experimentation seems to have succeeded. Locke is a very entertaining writer, once one realizes that one is being entertained.

The act of constituting, then, contains both the principle of free government in action, and the standard by which to judge its success, the necessary end of self-preservation. But the two elements, always potentially at odds, are also to be found *within* the modern constitution. Here enters the executive in Locke's political science, where it assumes an importance that deserves notice even in works not devoted to executive power.[8] When a people constitutes a government, Locke says, it places the legislative power in certain hands. The legislative power extends the principle of free government first expressed in the act of constituting. Placing supremacy in the legislative power, Locke frequently insists, assures the rule of law and prevents the exercise of arbitrary power. But there is also a need for discretion, since laws do not always attain the desired end. That end is the public good, understood as the protection of life, liberty, and property: the same end for which the legislative power is constituted. That power therefore represents the principle of free government, but the executive applies the principle to the ends of society, and thus enforces the discipline of necessity. It is by virtue of the executive power that necessity is constitutionalized in Locke's constitution. Within that constitution are the principle or the form represented by the legislature, versus the end or necessity maintained by the executive.

Such a constitution has a power of self-criticism through the working of its separated powers that is unlike the Aristotelian regime, where criticism comes from outside (to be sure, in answer to the claim of each regime to be best). Locke's constitution admits the possibility of failure; so it imports within itself an executive power to remind a possibly overconfident legislature of all those chance necessities that get in the way of human intentions. The executive has the power of prerogative, which Locke defines as the power—left by the people in the executive's hands—of doing public good without a rule (II.163, 166). Then he goes so far as to say casually, in a parenthesis, that this is an "arbitrary" power (II.210)—the very thing his constitution was formed to prevent. Prerogative power is not arbitrary in the sense of unaccountable to the people, to be sure, but it is unpredictable. Moreover, Locke explains the original act of constituting as being the execution of the law of nature in the state of nature. When each person consents to form a government, he executes the law of nature that requires him to seek his own preservation and that of the rest of mankind. So the rule of law in Locke emerges from an executive act and can end in an executive act. The necessity of executive power seems to surround the rule of law and thus to sum up the problem of modern constitutionalism. Is it better for the constitution to keep that harsh necessity at bay, following Aristotle and his tradition, or to give it an uneasy welcome according to Machiavelli's insights?

The Model Constitution

The modern constitution is a model constitution. It is designed to be applied beyond the circumstances of its conception, if not everywhere. The demonstration that it has been applied in one place will teach others that they too can enjoy its benefits without fear of attempting the impossible. The modern constitution is not utopian in the classical sense of being the best regime in the best circumstances (or even in the sense of being impossible, above the best circumstances). It is meant to be the best practicable regime. But the description does not imply that the modern constitution will always aim at being the best it can practicably be, for such an attempt would require the prudence of a political scientist or statesman who could discern the practicable best in any circumstances. For that degree of prudence we would need, if not Plato or Machiavelli, then the deputy of Plato's philosopher-king or the captain of Machiavelli's commission. Locke's constitution has greater fixity; it is, as we now say, institutionalized. But to be so, it needs principles, since institutions do not survive on inertia. Locke's constitution proclaims a doctrine of natural law that distinguishes it as much from the classical utopia in respect to law as from Machiavelli's prince-driven republic with regard to morality. With legal definition to hold on to, and with morality to inspire, this doctrinal constitution can serve as a model for effectual action. It is neither an object for yearning nor a lesson in tyranny.

Yet Locke's constitution (and our modern constitution follows him in this), is not an abstract doctrine, as one sees in Hobbes and in some of his contemporary constitutionalists. When Locke constitutionalizes necessity, he does not merely theorize or universalize it in the scientific manner of Hobbes. His constitutional doctrine embraces English constitutional practice, especially (but not only) in the executive. "Executive power" in Locke's *Second Treatise* is a thinly veiled description of an institution in an actual regime, the English constitutional monarchy. Locke never says that his executive is the English king, but he makes it clear that the English monarchy is not merely a "fresh example," as Machiavelli would say; it is *the* example, the model. It is the executive as it ought to be "in all moderated Monarchies and well-framed Governments" (II.159). As a model, England's constitution offers reassurance to others that Locke's doctrine is applicable and sound. And using Locke's rationalized version, others can imitate it without feeling envy or suppressing their own pride. Locke's presentation avoids boasting, and it offers as much indirect rebuke as praise of his own country; his doctrine could not be accused of patriotism or parochialism.

Locke also avoids the paradoxes of Hobbes, in particular the central paradox of raising sovereignty to an unprecedented pitch in theory by rejecting the claims of all actual sovereigns. Locke assimilates the English tradition of constitutional law to his political philosophy, and thus makes possible an appeal to the authority of writers who preceded him. Locke's theory could use the knowledge of statesmen and especially of lawyers, and they in turn could become purveyors and defenders of his doctrine. Indeed, by combining political philosophy and constitutional doctrine, Locke was able to effect a further combinition within English constitutional doctrine, which was so far from harmonious that the country had come to civil war. In any case, Locke combined royalist and commonwealth notions with a success that has eluded previous compromisers. In his doctrine of separation of powers, Locke accepted the actual monarchy with its presumption of prerogative, while also accepting the commonwealth doctrine of legislative supremacy. Here Locke's political science is very difficult to grasp because he seems to follow a path of convenience that sometimes coincides with that of reason, sometimes with that of custom, and sometimes with both. He is more theoretical than if he were totally absorbed in matters English, and his political science cannot be read, as it often is by historians and historicists, as a mere comment on disputes of the moment. Even where he does comment, one can err by underestimating his theoretical elevation. Locke's position, for example, was not to be found in the politics of the Exclusion Bill. From what I have just noted about his synthesizing, one could surmise that he wanted to retain a monarchy that would attract the likes of King William as well as the Tories; in short, Locke is closer to Halifax the Trimmer than to Shaftesbury the Exclusionist Whig.[9] Yet Locke is also less theoretical than if he had ignored English politics; or perhaps one should say that it is necessary to find a theoretical interpretation for his use of them. Most professors of political philosophy today prefer paradoxical Hobbes to judicious Locke, because, unlike the latter, judiciousness has no place in their schemes.

While Machiavelli conceived the modern executive, Locke gave that executive his modern form as the "executive power." Locke's contribution, we have seen, was to introduce two changes in the Machiavellian executive that made him more acceptable and palatable. On the one hand, he gave him a principle in the doctrine of the separation of powers, in which the executive appears as one power. Political power, for Locke, is composed of powers (plural) in civil society, so that political power and its powers depend on the distinction between the state of nature and civil society. In Locke's thought, this distinction gives right or legitimacy to both legislative and executive powers in civil society. Locke thus transforms Machiavelli's sensational criminality into a doctrine of right, and divides Hobbes's absolute sovereignty into powers with legitimate lives of their own. On the other hand, Locke referred his reasoning continuously to England. For him, "executive power" referred to, or was based on, the English king, just as today it refers to the American presidency. Present-day discussion of "the executive" is actually focused on a particular office; it is almost always less theoretical than it seems and more informal than it knows or admits.

The two reversals in Machiavelli's conception of the executive, working in complementary fashion, produce Locke's model constitution. Recall that Aristotle's notion of kingship was argued from unnoticed tendencies of actual regimes, but was found to be the cause of unity in the best regime. Machiavelli's political science was presented partly in cautionary "fresh examples" from his own time, but its model was the Roman republic, an actual regime that was not a living regime. Harrington reasoned about England as a thinly disguised "Oceana." But Locke gave modern political science the basis of an actual, living, undisguised regime; and in his choice of England he was followed by Montesquieu and a number of constitutional writers in the eighteenth century. *The Federalist* and Tocqueville attempted to switch regimes from England to America, and met with some success. Whether the model is England or America, we observe that the practical, institutional basis for modern political science, its "effectual truth," not its claims and pretensions, is limited monarchy, hereditary or elected. Machiavelli would not be surprised that the choice comes down to an old prince or a new one, nor to see that the new prince wins out.

Executing the Law of Nature

In Locke's thought, the executive receives a foundation both in right and in practice. To see how this occurs, we must engage the vexing question of what Locke means by the "law of nature," for executive power first appears in Locke in relation to that law. Today, because of the influence of Kant (who radically separated the realm of freedom from that of nature), or thanks to the lazy assumption that freedom exists because we want it to, we either reject or ignore natural law as the possible foundation of free government. We know Locke as the great advocate of government by consent, but we do not really understand that he presents such consent as executing the law of nature.

Locke supposes that men are free and equal in the state of nature (II.4), which he defines as living together according to reason without a common power (II.19). "According to reason" is according to the law of nature, which affirms that man has a duty to preserve the rest of mankind, as much as he can (II.6). What makes this law effectual is not a natural inclination to sociability (see II.77), but an "executive power" of every man to carry out the law of nature in the state of nature. That power gives him both the right of self-defense and the duty of punishing offenses against the law of nature. Given the lack of a natural inclination to support the law of nature, men must be made to obey it. Hence the emphasis on punishment. Locke admits or asserts that his is a "very strange doctrine"—a law that every man executes, and by which every man becomes judge in his own case (II.9, 13; cf. I.80, II.180).[10]

Natural executive power includes, or consists of, the judicial power. Every man is by nature his own judge and executioner, because in the state of nature all are equal and none has political power over anyone else, political power being a common power, only produced by consent. However, executive power generates political power. The natural power which men have, by right, to protect other men, generates a political power that can ensure that protection; for every man's being his own executive in his own case leads to great inconveniences (II.13). Guided or instructed by the law of nature, then, men consent to the political power that creates civil society. Political power is not natural but arises from man's execution of natural law.

Politics would appear, then, to be fundamentally unfree because it arises not out of human choice but by the execution of a law we have not made. And yet Locke speaks of the "perfect freedom" of men in the state of nature, living within the bounds of the law of nature (II.4). Perhaps Locke's freedom may be found in the doctrine that each man executes the law of nature for himself: although executing nature's law, one is set free by the necessity of doing so oneself. In short, Locke's idea of freedom seems to imply what we have called executive ambivalence. Weak insofar as it recognizes man's submission to the law of nature, it is strong insofar as the execution requires discretion and assertiveness. In this ambivalence we see again the two elements of the act of constituting—the end of self-preservation established by the law of nature, and the form of consent by which we execute it.

Why does Locke discover executive ambivalence in his version of the law of nature? The ground must be sought once again in his need to confront the religious issue. We have seen the same ambivalence referring to the same issue in Machiavelli and Hobbes. But it is hardly possible to exaggerate the importance of the religious issue for modern politics, and Locke's particular solution has formed our understanding of government by consent. When Locke says that human beings are bound to execute the law of nature, one reason could be that the law of nature is God's law and human beings are God's property. In his most prominent statement on the subject (II.6), Locke says that men are the property of him whose workmanship they are, the servants of one sovereign master; hence bound to preserve both themselves and others. It is hard to see how this line of thought leaves them perfectly free (II.4), or free enough to be capable of instituting political power, which Locke has just distinguished from the power of a master over his servant (II.2). It is still harder to see how the statement that men are God's property can be consistent with Locke's assertion that "every man has a property in his own person," which is the premise of his argument defending private property (II.27).[11]

Clearly Locke did not wish the premise that each person belongs to himself to stand unsupported by the theological idea that each belongs to God. And Locke uses both together whenever he can. But clearly, too, the latter premise does not carry as much weight as the former. If man is God's workmanship, he is bound to preserve himself as his maker's property and *equally* bound to preserve the rest of mankind, also God's property: but how can he also put himself first, as required for him to exercise the *right* of self-preservation? In the very place where Locke says that men are God's property he limits their obligation to other men with the significant qualification: ''when his own Preservation comes not in competition'' (II.6). Where is there any authority for that loaded phrase to be found in the Bible, or even in Locke's rationalized version of Christianity? In a longer discussion of Locke's natural law, this first, entering question might turn out to be the conclusion as well.

If Locke does not want to do without some kind of divine sanction for his argument, he also wishes to limit its political consequences. If men are regarded as God's property, they may be governed by whoever can persuasively claim to be His vicar. Such a claim might easily be made for fathers, both spiritual and physical; thus Locke wrote the *First Treatise* to establish the distinction between paternal power and political power, a distinction he insisted on throughout the *Second Treatise* as well. Locke wished to oppose and prevent any claim of divine right for political power through the medium of paternal authority.[12] To reduce the power that operates through generation or hierarchy, then, Locke conceived his very strange doctrine that we establish governments by the execution of a law of nature. If government were established merely by uninstructed consent without such a law to execute, then clearly a majority religious opinion might suffice to justify a government of divine right—in fact, this was the ground of government that prevailed literally everywhere before Hobbes and Locke set to work. Locke's natural law gives human consent the instruction it needs to avoid both slavery and strife.

Nature's lesson according to Locke is imparted in the form of a certain necessity: man is mortal, a finite being who must necessarily have a concern for his own survival; and lacking the instincts of a beast, he uses his reason to preserve himself. As with Hobbes, the law of nature is identical with reason when it comes to human necessity, through not when it reaches to the complete human good. The principal advantage of natural law so conceived appears when one takes the religious issue into account. For the necessity that applies to men applies with equal force to God as the Maker of men. If God wanted to make men, He had to implant in them a strong desire of self-preservation (I.86, 88, II.56). Thus, God as a workmanlike Maker obeys the same necessity men do when they execute the law of nature. So God the Maker can be used to confine and humanize the omnipotent Biblical God who creates by miracle without regard to human necessity. In executing the law of nature, men are merely following their own necessity, not Scripture.

Locke distinguishes the law of nature from revelation, or the "positive law of God" (II.52), but he does not point out the differences between the two, except to a careful reader.[13] Thus Locke prefers to remark upon the coincidence of reason and revelation. But this does not alter the fact that revelation comes when reason calls it to minister to human necessity. In the battle against enslavement to divine commandments and to the rulers and priests who interpret them, Locke's weak executive who obeys a law of natural necessity becomes a liberating weapon.

But it is characteristic of Locke not to rely too much on this weapon. Machiavelli and Hobbes continue to identify the strong executive with the prince and the sovereign; the prince's people and the sovereign's subjects must bow to his representations of their necessity. Their spirited naysaying resistance to necessity dissolves in fear as they tremble at the prince's executions and the sovereign's sword. For Locke, such reliance on visible fear smacks of the fear of invisible powers exploited by advocates of divine right. So he retains and encourages spiritedness in the people. Not only prince and sovereign but the people too become strong executives. In Locke's version of the state of nature, every man executes the law of nature as he judges to be necessary, so that the law reflects in its execution the very freedom that its content might seem to deny.

One must not forget that Locke adopts the state of nature from Hobbes. Locke agrees with Hobbes in allowing each man the natural right to use any means whatever to preserve his life, and to be the sole judge of the necessary means. It was Hobbes who, with the concept of the state of nature, first equalized and universalized Machiavelli's prince. Tyranny became a natural right, provided that the opportunity for tyranny was extended to every man. Machiavelli, observing the actual circumstances of politics, had seen that opportunity for only a lucky few, and had concluded only that these few could not reasonably be blamed. Hobbes's political science rendered Machiavelli's insight more dependable and more moral; and Locke's argument depends fundamentally on Hobbes's attempt.

Nonetheless, Locke's state of nature differs from Hobbes's in two contrary ways. It is more moral, because each man's executions punish violations of natural law—they do not merely anticipate possible transgressions in a state of mistrust for which nobody can be blamed, as in Hobbes (II. 7–10, 28; cf. 16–17; cf. *Leviathan* XIII, p. 95). Yet Locke also allows for the release of Machiavellian venom in such punishments. Whereas for Hobbes the law of nature is not properly a law in the state of nature, because it is not executed (*De Cive* VI.8; *Leviathan* XVII, p. 128), Locke has every man executing, and doing so as if he were exterminating a lion, a tiger, a wolf, or a polecat (II.10, 11, 16, 18, 93; cf. II.181).[14]

Thus Locke permits everybody to possess the freedom of strong executives. That freedom is not an uncaused effect in the manner of Kant, but neither is it a freedom identical to necessity as for Hobbes. Locke's freedom is prompted by the necessity that reason sees, yet it is not reduced to mere acquiescence. This qualified freedom—less than choice, more than subjection—appears in Locke's famous discussion of property, where he argues that property can become private while men are still in the state of nature: property gives men something to preserve besides their naked bodies when they constitute civil society; so they consent to be governed in an act of self-preservation that is more spirited than fearful, though fear is not absent. By virtue of pre-political private property, men acquire an interest that stands for the exertion of honest industry as distinct from quaking fear. So even though they are "quickly driven into society" (II.127), and are not really free to withhold consent, it cannot be viewed as submission. Thereby they keep their dignity. It is not enough to consult a man's interest, because that can be satisfied by his submission and without his consent.[15] But consent, when prompted by an interest in property that one has labored for, yields a motive for consent that is neither too low and servile nor too high and

mighty. Private property is indeed intended by Locke for the provision and enrichment of mankind, given the inadequacy of divine providence; but it also offers unfailing encouragement to
submissive spirits, given the overbearing tyranny of divine commands. It is easy to see bourgeois interest, and also too easy to
dismiss bourgeois virtue, in Locke's argument for private property.

The ambivalence surrounding the execution of natural law reveals a further ambivalence concerning reason and consent. To
the extent that the law of nature is identical with reason, it requires an assent that could not be withheld without fault; to the
extent that the law of nature is consensual, it leaves men free to
do what they "think fit" (II.106). Locke says that the freedom
men have in the state of nature is the "Foundation of all the rest"
(II.17), but he also says that the "Freedom . . . of Man and Liberty of acting according to his own Will, is grounded on his having Reason" (II.63). Freedom as the foundation makes government by consent; reason as the ground denies legitimacy to
governments wrongly consented to. Locke combines them in typical fashion (apparently woolly-headed, actually canny) when he
speaks of "the consent of Men" as "making use of their Reason"
(I.6). Making use of this faculty is not necessarily making correct
use of it.[16] A people must be presumed to be "a Society of Rational Creatures" (II.163). But the presumption means that they
are equal to their rulers, not that they submit to rulers who are
more rational than they.

If Locke were to insist on the correct use of reason, he would
have to give government over to the best reasoners, as Aristotle
ultimately does. Or if these proved difficult to identify, then government would have to be given over to one reasoner, following
Hobbes. Locke's notion of tacit consent (II.50, 74, 119, 122, 131,
164), often criticized by those who do not understand his problem
(which is unwittingly their own), stands midway between reason
and consent; it is the consent that one can reasonably infer. Infer-
ring consent honors the right of consent when its fulfillment is
impossible or unreasonable; not to infer it would disjoin reason
from consent either by too much consent or too little. "Thus we
are born Free, as we are born Rational," he says (II.61); that is,
we are born perfect in neither regard but as safe as we can be
when these are brought together, each controlling and bounding
the other.

Executive Power and Legislative Power

For Locke, in executing the law of nature—weakly and strongly—men in the state of nature constitute political power. Let us now see how this characteristic ambivalence reproduces itself in civil society in the form of the modern executive power.

As soon as political power exists, it is divided into legislative and executive powers for the making of known, settled, standing rules in legislation, and for employing the force of the community both to punish crimes at home and to repel and avenge foreign injuries (II.88). Since the legislative power makes standing rules, Locke concludes that neither absolute monarchy nor the absolute prince is a true form of government (II.90). No single person, that is, can have both legislative and executive power in civil society, as every person does in the state of nature. No one can have both natural power and political power.

Thus the natural executive power belonging to *every* man in the state of nature can exist in no single man in civil society. The natural executive from which legislative power has been subtracted becomes the civil executive. And to enforce the division of executive and legislative power in civil society so that all persons are subject to the laws, Locke says the legislative power must be placed in collective bodies of men (II.94). Here he does not specify the number of the civil executive, but clearly he rejects both the Machiavellian prince and the Hobbesian sovereign. Machiavelli did not distinguish the state of nature from civil society; Hobbes did, but not correctly. Hobbes thought that the natural power of every man remains in the hands of the civil sovereign, who may be one man. Locke has it that natural power is divided when it becomes political, and therefore it no longer exists. This does not mean that, for Locke, political power is any less comprehensive than it is for Hobbes (see II.87). Nor does it mean that natural executive power vanishes after the creation of civil society. Rather, it remains wherever political power is ineffective, for example in the right to resist a robber who threatens your life (II.19).

Next, in chapters 8 and 9 of the *Second Treatise*, Locke gives an account of how political power might have arisen—a much more realistic story than at first might be implied by the idea of the social contract. By Locke's account, political power begins with the father, and others in the family who have cooperated with, or submitted to, his executive power. He became the law-maker in effect, and at a later state might have been the elected head of an extended family, thus a monarch whose chief function was to command the army. Early monarchy is the seedbed of the "federative" power (the power of war and peace in foreign affairs), whereas legislative power is the basis of civilization. There seems to be a historical progression from the executive power of every man in the state of nature, to the federative power of the monarch-general in primitive society, to the more civilized modern legislature, while the three powers of Locke's constitution appear as three stages in its development.

In chapter 10 Locke says for the first time that legislative power is the supreme power, and shortly thereafter that "the first and fundamental positive law of all commonwealths is the establishing of the legislative power" (II.134). The rule of law for Locke clearly means the rule of the law-making power, not the ascendancy or inviolability of certain laws; it is the rule of the men who make the laws. The legislative power is supreme as with Bodin and Hobbes, the defenders of sovereignty; but as opposed to them, it is not arbitrary, because it is ordered to the public good as defined by standing rules.

Executive power is the natural power, which is replaced in civil society by the supremacy of legislative power. By asserting this supremacy, succeeding the supreme executive power in the state of nature, Locke established the weak, theoretical executive conformable to the anti-monarchial animus of his day, and characteristic of constitutional formalism in ours. In civil society, where the legislative power is supreme, the executive would be dutiful and subordinate. It executes not the law of nature, but laws made by the legislative power. Yet from here on in the *Second Treatise*, the weak, theoretical executive is built up, casually as it were, to the more powerful practical or informal executive we know today. But Locke casual is Locke furtive; and when he unveils the extent of the executive's prerogative, the surprise is somewhat Machiavellian.

The legislative power is supreme, but it exists only in collective bodies. In "well-ordered commonwealths" that power will be put into the hands of "diverse persons" who assemble and then separate, so that they too, as private men, are subject to the laws (II.143). One cannot simply leave it to the people to put the legislative power "into such hands as they think fit," as Locke said earlier (II.136). But a "perpetual execution" is necessary to the laws, and because the executive is always in being and the legislative is not, "the legislative and executive power come often to be separated" (II.144). Not with a fanfare of asserted principle, then, but out of practical experience which Locke approves only at third mention (II.153, 159), does he advance the separation of powers.[17] Then he defines the federative power (II.147), which cannot be managed by settled, standing laws; and he says (II.148; see II.108) that though the executive and federative powers are distinct, yet they can hardly be placed in distinct persons. Both require the force of the society for their exercise, and that force cannot be placed under different commands. A practical alliance is thus observed between the executive and federative powers that overrides their theoretical distinctness. And, with the federative power, Locke quietly introduces the need for prudence outside the laws. At first he apparently maintains that the executive can be directed by the laws (II.147; cf. II.158); but as the argument proceeds, the need for prudence in foreign affairs carries into domestic affairs, and helps inflate executive power even further.

Next, while continuing to speak of the supremacy of the legislative power, and insisting that the executive "has no Will, no Power, but that of the Law" (II.151), Locke uses the phrase "Supream Executor of the Law." The executive, soon dubbed "Supream Executive Power," will be visibly subordinate and accountable to the legislature unless also given a share of the legislative power. This share of power proves to be the veto (II.152). The point is introduced as if it were a concession to the actual English monarchy, and Locke does not state as a principle that the executive should not be visibly subordinate. Executive *power* is subordinate, but the executive *person* may not be.

Incidentally, is the executive person singular or plural? To say it is singular would set the stage for Machiavellian vivacity; plural would help maintain republican subordination. When speaking of the federative power, Locke mentions "those whose hands it is in," as if he had in mind a squad of officials (II.147); then he declares that the executive and federative powers can hardly be placed "in the hands of distinct Persons" (II.148), a statement that tends in the direction of a singular executive but distracts us from the number of persons to the number of hands. Next, he tells us that only the "Supream Executive Power vested in one, who [has] a share in the Legislative" is exempt from subordination, as if to mention an accidental characteristic of the English King (II.152). Locke soon refers to "his Prudence," meaning the executive's (II.154), and then gives a reason why the "first Framers of the Government" would have trusted the power of convoking the legislature "to the prudence of one" (II.156.) Did Locke immediately after say "the prudence of some?" Yes, but the power is to be placed "in his hands" (II.156). When we reach the chapter on prerogative, we are told that the good of society requires that "several things should be left to the discretion of him, that has the Executive Power" (II.159). We note that executive *prudence* has become *discretion*. In the next section (II.160) that same prudence is "latitude . . . to do many things of *choice*," a power justified by Locke rather than merely picked up as an interesting custom. Later this is improved to the rulers' *own free choice* (II.164). We today take for granted that the executive must be *uno solo* and that monarchy is a bad thing. This small sample of the intricacy of Locke's argument (which is not less fine on any other point) shows him at work to insinuate the soundness of our opinion despite its seeming inconsistency.

After the executive gains a legislative veto, we learn that the legislative body which assembles and disperses is representative. Locke offers no proper justification for representation, as does Hobbes, but he awards to the executive the power of convoking that assembly, and also of correcting its representation, should it become obsolete or corrupt. When discussing the power of convoking, he mentions the executive's prudence, not brought from foreign into domestic affairs (II.154). Correcting outdated representation gives him occasion to remark on the constant flux of "Things of this World" (II.157), which reminds us of Machiavelli's observation that "all human things are in motion" (*D* I.6). Thus executive power acquires standing in the nature of things: we legislate to hold things as we should like them, but when they slip from our grasp we need a strong executive.

Locke's reconstruction of the executive is completed in chapter 14, "Of Prerogative," defined as doing public good without a rule, not only between the laws but against them if necessary. So the executive is not, after all, directed by law, as was said at the beginning of the discussion (II.147). This power, later called "arbitrary" (II.210), is said to have been "always largest in the hands of our wisest and best princes" (II.165) or "God-like Princes" (II.166); and with this blatant appeal to Tory sentiment, Locke allows the people to hand it over to the executive.[18] An appeal to Tory sentiment, however, does not require the use of Tory argument. Locke's practical objection to the supremacy of the legislative power arises from the changeableness of things—a Machiavellian consideration—rather than from the generality of law that does not allow for the best case, as with Aristotle. Rather than building a case for absolute monarchy from the claim of the godlike prince, Locke explains it away as an instance of tacit consent. The people will acquiesce in an action of executive prerogative when they see it has done good; if it has not done good, they will limit prerogative or exercise their right of resistance. Locke gives his executive access to the prerogative of bygone kings, with a promise of success, but also with a warning of failure (II.165). He leaves it to the executive to infer that he has no choice but to run a risk.

Executive power in its prerogative gives effect to the "fundamental law of nature and government, *viz*, that, as much as may be, all the members of the society are to be preserved" (II.159). Even the guilty are to be spared, Locke specifies, if there is no harm to the innocent. Thus he deduces the power of pardoning, an important feature of the modern executive also traceable to Machiavelli. Political power aims at "the preservation of the whole" (II.171), that is, of the whole society. Natural power has a broader end, the preservation of all mankind, but it is ineffectual. Political power confines itself to the preservation of one society, one Body Politick, and it consists partly in making laws for this society (II.3, 14, 89). But its end is the preservation of men, not the laws. So the executive must be very powerful, if need be overriding the laws or the legislature.

Locke asserts the supremacy of the legislative power, but also the supreme executive: the theoretical sovereign and the practical sovereign. There must always be a sovereign, but to use a Machiavellian distinction, there is an *ordinary* sovereign—the legislature—that makes standing rules, and an *extraordinary* sovereign—the executive—who stands perpetually ready to go beyond the rules, responding to the motion of human things. Locke's commercial, technological society makes possible a great increase in human power, a power controlled by the theory of separated powers combined with the people's rights of constituting and resisting. Locke could not dispense with the theory because it also supports legislative supremacy, the ordinary sovereignty of laws.

And yet, the theory is never adequate, because society cannot do without the natural executive power, which is the origin of the modern informal, or practical, executive.

Locke's theory encompasses what cannot be subject to theory; it anticipates changes that cannot be anticipated; it contains the extraconstitutional within the constitution. The essential characteristic of the modern constitution, I have argued, is its combination of reason with the necessity that resists reason. Locke's unsystematic presentation of his three powers might seem to cast doubt over the constitution that comprises them. Is this the constitution of reason, a model for other peoples, or is it merely what the English people might consent to, a collection of new and old, a haphazard compromise between theory and custom?

Locke makes clear that his constitution is the model for a "Society of Rational Creatures" and not merely for Englishmen (II.163). But it is precisely rational creatures who deserve the right of consent. Locke's very presentation imitates the difficulty of obtaining consent in politics, a difficulty that consists not in getting the people's agreement to the rule of their betters, as with Aristotle, but acquiescence to necessity, as with Machiavelli. One can gain consent by showing them that they have consented to these powers in the past as being necessary, while retaining for themselves the right of resistance that they have also exercised. This approach to the people is like Locke's to his readers, a rationalization and refinement of actual events. By gradually introducing his readers to the scope of executive power, Locke uses reason to help them appreciate that element in humanity which is not amenable to reason. The people generally will use less reason than Locke's readers, who may include a few students of the law of nature (II.12, 124).[19] The people will acquiesce in necessity rather than appreciate it. In either mode, Locke teaches us how to "be practical," that is, how to respect necessity. His rational constitution includes the irrational, but as a form of compensation it also includes the need for persuasion to reason, so compromised.

The Self-Criticism of the Modern Constitution

The supreme executive power in its personal strength, set off against the supreme legislative power with its formal sovereignty, constitutes a structure for self-criticism within the regime. With the separation and balance of these powers, Locke establishes two views of the constitution: the formal view of the legislature that the constitution is designed to make the laws that the people, through their representatives, think right; and the realistic view of the executive—with its Machiavellian "looking to the end" (*P* 18)—that the constitution must keep the people secure. The legislative view, we have seen, maintains the people's freedom by promoting its own process of legislation, and the maintenance of the constitution generally, as an end in itself; the executive sees to security by holding legal and formal procedures to the standard of effectiveness, and by not hesitating to violate procedure, when necessary for the public good.

The liberalism that prevails today in the ruling circles of philosophy distinguishes these two points of view as deontological (the primacy of rights) and utilitarian (the primacy of the end). Under the influence of Kant, various philosophers have found them incompatible. Locke's liberalism, however, finds both views necessary and compatible in a constitution where both are represented, precisely by being kept apart and in conflict. Rights without security are worthless; security without rights is slavish. A philosophy that cannot find equal standing for rights and security amounts to a deconstruction, or rather the destruction, of liberalism.

This is not to say that we should be satisfied with Locke's solution because he understood the problem better than we. Locke establishes a clear distinction between the power concerned about freedom and the power concerned about necessity, between the form of the constitution and its end. But since freedom is as much an end as self-preservation, the end as a whole is unclear. Is it your preservation or your free opinion? Locke wants both together, but to get both he encounters moral and political difficulties that I shall consider briefly.

Locke's determined amplification of executive power brings into focus the famous troubles raised by his conception of natural law.[20] As a weak executive in the state of nature, each man obeys his own necessity. Such obedience is described more fully in Locke's *An Essay concerning Human Understanding*, published at the same time as the *Two Treatises* (1690), but under Locke's acknowledged authorship.[21] In the *Essay*, Locke says frequently and in his own name that a demonstrative moral science is possible that would be as incontestable as mathematics and more surely scientific than Newton's natural philosophy (IV.3.18, 12.10). But he does not actually demonstrate that science. He goes a certain distance toward it and then stops. If one turns to the *Two Treatises* to complete the demonstration, one finds complication rather than satisfaction, and even resistance to the possibility of such a demonstration. For the principle of the *Two Treatises* is nothing if not government by consent; yet consent implies the possibility of choice, and scientific demonstration denies it.

In the *Essay* Locke argues that "Morally Good and Evil . . . is only the Conformity or Disagreement of our voluntary Actions to some Law, whereby Good and Evil is drawn on us, from the Will and Power of the Law-Maker" (II.28.5). The good and evil made effective by the lawmaker are reward and punishment, which Locke reduces to pleasure and pain. He adopts this hedonist premise so that his morality, unlike those of Christianity and of the "old Heathen Philosophers," will have an effective sanction. The ancients promoted a virtue without sanctions that would be practiced for its own sake; Christian morality, on the other hand, depends on invisible sanctions—such as conscience and rewards and punishments in the next life—which are ineffective (I.3.5–8). Virtue for the sake of gaining pleasure and avoiding pain in this life, however, will be effective.

Locke's hedonism, which supports his morality, is in turn supported by his empiricism. For Locke, the "simple ideas" of unmixed pleasures and pains (as well as other sense perceptions) are true and adequate, but "complex ideas" that aggregate the simple ones are questionable composites. The reason is that since all simple ideas are true, none is truer than another; hence none is essential. We do not see things or beings as wholes; instead, we construct complex ideas without any guide from the senses or from nature about what is essential. The idea of "man," for example, is a complex idea that must be conceived without any prior notion of what is essentially or specifically human, since all we know are the simple qualities we observe which are all equivalent. Morality aims at happiness, which Locke understands as pleasure or at least as the removal of uneasiness (II.21.42–4). Since the highest pleasures are the most complex and dubious, not they but ordinary ones give us the utmost enjoyment we are capable of.

Morality, therefore, can be demonstrated because it rests on the reality of pleasure and pain. But it is real only because it is radically individual and necessitated. Each person's happiness is uniquely his own; no common or specifically human definition is possible. And because happiness occurs only in moments, each person's happiness is momentary, and his reality or identity as an individual over time is called into question. The "self" whose preservation is the key to Locke's political philosophy is scattered into real, but instantaneous, sense impressions by his moral philosophy. The Machiavellian principle of *uno solo* is carried to the extreme at which the individual becomes isolated from himself and almost vanishes into impersonal instants too fleeting to belong to him. Such moments of happiness are real precisely because we do not choose them. We receive them according to three sorts of law—divine, civil, and the law of reputation. Locke does not say which of them, or what combination, would constitute his demonstrative morality. None of them is natural law, and none would be obeyed for its own sake or because it is reasonable. The law of reputation is the virtue of the ancient philosophers, modernized by Locke and given an added inducement and sanction. In the *Essay*, morality appears to be the pursuit of happiness, or following one's natural and necessary interest in pleasure and in avoiding pain.

But when we cross the boundary[22] of the *Essay* and enter the *Two Treatises*, where Locke speaks anonymously, we find a different landscape featuring natural law, and doctrines of rights and consent. These seem to promise a morality that is not imposed by necessity, but is chosen for its own sake. Natural law appears transgressable, hence it is a guide to men rather than an imposition on them. Rights in this view are specifically human, requiring a fixed essence of man; and consent reflects, if not unqualified pride in human reason, the satisfaction with one's portion of reason, and an assertion of one's freedom to exercise it. We should note the moral implication of the strong executive as he appears in the *Two Treatises*. Morality as described here cannot be mere legality or obedience to law, since it issues in wide executive discretion to violate the law if necessary. Society is a "politick Body" (*Two Treatises* II.93, 131), to be preserved as a body, containing individuals whose selves must be preserved by a passionate defense rather than cool calculation. Thus, morality in the *Two Treatises* seems not demonstrable, not radically individual, and not necessitated. Executive power limits consent by recalling necessities we would rather forget; but it also reminds us of consent by the very power of executive discretion.

To make morality effectual, Locke lessens its claims upon us and allows our pleasure and pains to determine our duties. But then, as if to recognize the value of the pride we take in freedom, he gives us rights that we must exercise, and selves we must preserve. Strangely, after scattering the self into individual moments of pleasure in the *Essay*, here in the *Two Treatises* he seems to adopt the proud perspective of the self, which strongly resembles the democratic vanity we have seen in Hobbes. Yet Locke allows such vanity expression not only in the instituting of a government but also in the actual system that makes government accountable to popular opinion. This recognition, too, is designed to make morality effectual.

One can understand self-preservation as a means to the pursuit of happiness, since one must be alive to be happy. But to preserve oneself, one must be willing to risk that happiness: practically, then, one must regard self-preservation and the liberty that helps us preserve our life as ends in themselves. To be effective as means, in other words, life and liberty must appear as ends. When Locke puts our origin in the state of nature, he plunges our lofty moral and religious notions into the cold bath of necessity. He shows us that we are not so noble as we like to think. But when he proposes that we constitute civil society, he asks us to rebound from necessity, for which he must preserve the warmth of our good opinion of ourselves. After deflating our pretensions by confronting us with our probable behavior in the state of nature, he must reinflate them to get us out of that state.

Locke's morality—now ours—contains opposite and complementary elements. To cool the ambition of religious fervor and replace it with decent calculation of self interest, Locke sketches out a demonstrative morality according to which we are wholly absorbed in meeting our necessities. By this view we shall find it in our interest always to consult necessity and live as we must without taking on the risks of enterprise. Such a notion of virtue is of course opposed to classical and Christian conceptions that do not accept the sovereignty of human necessity, but it also differs from Machiavellian virtue. While eager to anticipate necessity, Machiavellian virtue nonetheless leaves room for the influence of chance necessities or fortune. Machiavelli left this door open so that his princes could be free to take enterprising risks and so receive glory or blame; whether or not he could have produced a demonstrative morality, in fact he did not. Virtue for him is thus more consistently animated than it is for Locke, whose scheme is scientific, universal, and determinate so as (oddly) to be more humane. Locke does not leave peoples at the mercy of princes. But then, in order to escape the cruelties that attend princely glory, he risks the inconvenient possibility that men who feel no challenge may afterwards lapse into passivity and dependency, enslaving themselves to a system—of government, or of morality—if not to individual princes.

Locke seems aware of the risk—we may call it the risk of scientific risklessness—and so he adopts contrary measures to put men on their mettle, to engage their love of liberty, and to reward their industry. But he cannot escape the moral ambivalence that amounts to a conflict between passively following one's interest and actively defending one's liberty. The debate we hear today between utilitarian and deontological liberalism reveals the corruption, rather than the cooperation, of the two elements. The deontological liberals demand that rights be seen as trumps: any one can enforce his individual right against the majority, and even against the common good. The utilitarians want to satisfy interest regardless of the opinions of those whose interests they want to satisfy, thus transforming free citizens into passive beneficiaries. Neither tendency is normally carried to its extreme, and both are often found together, unreconciled, even in the elaborations of philosophy professors. The folly of the one theory is usually balanced by the folly of the other.

To leave room for his demonstrative morality, and thus to make the chief work of reason the exclusion of revelation from political life, Locke lets go of prudence (see *Essay* IV.17.1–5, 19.14). Prudence, for Aristotle, is the reason that assesses particulars with a view to the whole, combining private interest with the common good by governing the virtues for the sake of both. But Locke divides prudence into following one's interest and claiming one's right—kept together and divided at the same time. On the one hand, Locke does not endorse any rights whose exercise would destroy society, and he gives the trump card to the executive power when it acts against individual rights and existing laws to preserve society as a whole—that is, the majority. He also gives the same trump card to the majority in its right of resistance to tyrannical government, should his constitutional precautions fail—though he does not authorize mere individual expression. On the other hand, his emphasis on the exertions of liberty and the virtue of industriousness adds spiritedness to the concept of interest.

But when one listens to the debate of people who might be regarded as Lockean moralists today, one might conclude that his division of prudence into right and necessity has defeated his expedient attempt to keep them cognizant of each other. We are now taught to claim our rights regardless of interest, or to follow our interest regardless of rights; our opinions are encouraged to become inflexible, and our sense of self-preservation is allowed to become unprincipled. For Locke, right and necessity were held together by the convention of Property, in which the need to work was answered by the virtue of industry, and in which the right of each depends on the right of everyone else.[23] But our experience shows that Locke's convention could not cohere. Despite Locke's appeal for the preservation of Property as a whole, your property does not engage my interest as much as mine, and, more tellingly, my spirit may be more readily engaged by the attack on Property than by its defense. Locke's arrangements are therefore vulnerable to the impact of Marx as well as to the analysis of Kant.

Locke's constitution is devoted to the preservation of Property, in the extended sense that property includes life and liberty. Though it calls on political passions attending the practice of liberty, and when necessary, the defense of one's life, the constitution is devoted to the preservation of something other than itself because it is representative. It represents the members of society, and their ends, as much as it promotes its own end. Accordingly, it suffers always from a divided mind. The constitution is not "rule" in the Aristotelian sense of a part giving form to the whole, but instead is separated into two powers (since the third power, the federative, is effectively combined with the executive), neither of which has responsibility for the whole.[24] The legislature can deliberate about laws but cannot act; the executive can act but cannot change the settled, standing laws. In practice, perhaps the power of acting will attract the legislature's capacity to deliberate, especially since the executive has a veto over legislation. The executive will then acquire the capacity and habit of setting a program of "extensive and arduous enterprises." But this is Alexander Hamilton's phrase (*Federalist* 72), not Locke's.

Locke stresses the versatile, emergency character of executive power and leaves the fixing of intent to the supreme legislature. Thus he builds a divided mind into constitutional government. Its separated powers are not yet "bodies" sufficiently independent of one another to have separate wills; this we shall find in Montesquieu. But in Locke the constitution or regime can no longer be likened, as with Plato and Aristotle, to an individual soul. Locke, it is true, declares that the legislative "is the Soul that gives Form, Life and Unity to the Commonwealth" (*Two Treatises* II.212; see 239), but the executive has a countervailing prerogative, and the two powers are placed in distinct hands. By "soul" Locke means the principle that animates, not the principle that directs. Men cannot take their bearings from their humanity alone but must proceed with their attention divided between desire and necessity. Loss of a sense of responsibility for a whole that comprises both is the price of rejecting the possibility of Aristotle's "kingship over all."

9

Moderating the Executive

"Executive power" became a common term in the eighteenth century as the influence of Hobbes and especially of Locke expanded. Even a writer such as Jonathan Swift, whose politics owes little to them, uses the term prominently. Swift begins *A Discourse of the Contests and Dissensions between the Nobles and Commons in Athens and Rome* (1701) with the assertion:

> 'Tis agreed that in all Government there is an absolute unlimited Power, which naturally and originally seems to be placed in the whole Body, wherever the Executive Part of it lies.

But he goes on to describe an Aristotelian or Polybian mixed state in which the natural and reasonable claims of the one, the few, and the many are harmonized—very different from the Lockean executive who derived from each person's executive power in the state of nature.

Meanwhile, David Hume's Toryism—that, unlike Swift's, was not at all indebted to the ancients—leaves room for a somewhat more Lockean executive. Commenting on the government of Britain, he remarks that "the executive power in every government is altogether subordinate to the legislative,"[1] and draws the Lockean conclusion that the executive needs informal strengthening through what was called the Influence of the Crown, or the practice of awarding offices and emoluments to Members of Parliament by which means the king could make a part of the legislature dependent on his favor.[2]

Still another Tory, Bolingbroke, leading the so-called Country party of those who either refused or were not offered such temptation, attacked the practice as corrupt. In political debate with the opposing court party of Whigs, he developed a doctrine of the separation of powers into the three we know today—namely, the legislative, executive, and judicial. The legislative power, he held, was distributed among all three branches of the English constitution, while the executive resides in the king, and the judicial in the Lords. With this rather simplistic design, Bolingbroke hoped to block the Influence of the Crown from undermining Parliament, and so he emphasized the independence of the three powers from one another in making their own resolutions, while arguing their mutual dependency in the controls they maintain over one another. Thus the ambivalence of the executive was denied; Bolingbroke asserted that no secret, informal, or subconstitutional power was necessary to the proper functioning of the constitution.

In a later work Bolingbroke posited an ideal Patriot King who would preside over a constitution open to public view, and not requiring any manipulation of interests to make it work.[3] The scheme of separated powers that Bolingbroke advanced for the sake of his own party has since been cited as a source for Montesquieu's profound analysis, because the terms he uses are the same, and the notion of tripartite independence is common to both. And the two men did meet when Montesquieu visited England in 1729, almost twenty years before his *The Spirit of the Laws* was to be published.[4] But one can recognize Bolingbroke as a source for Montesquieu only in retrospect, and with the latter's achievement in view, very much as a geographer might trace the mighty Mississippi back to a tiny rivulet. The true sources of Montesquieu's greatness lie in himself and in others greater than Bolingbroke.

Yet Montesquieu's greatness is not obvious, and his fame today is mainly based on his association with the principle of the separation of powers, a doctrine which he claimed to have discovered, not invented. He is also known for an antique—or is it rather an inimitable—elegance of style. Although a philosopher far more profound than Hume, he does not hold an equal place in the history of modern philosophy. But the reason is simply that his philosophy is self-effacing. He announces no great "philosophical" principle that purports to be the independent ground of morals and politics, such as Descartes' *cogito*, Hobbes's state of nature, Locke's and Hume's empiricism. Instead, Montesquieu's philosophy is political because he allows it to manifest itself in the politics, morals, and manners of the diverse nations that appear in his book as characters of a sort. His philosophy is political philosophy, but neither in the classical sense of the search for the best regime, nor in the modern sense of Hobbes and Locke who wanted to establish a government whose rule is clearly legitimate. But in fact *The Spirit of the Laws* is the most comprehensive modern book on politics, exceeding in range and complexity any that appears before or since, excepting Aristotle's *Politics*.[5] Its range of examples covers the entire world and all of history to the author's day, and its brilliant formulations show throughout a penetrating and sympathetic insight, as well as a cosmopolitanism that knows how to appreciate other nations without falling into relativism, and a worldly morality that never lapses into cynicism.

At the beginning of *The Spirit of the Laws* Montesquieu remarks that the role of philosophers is to "warn" men by means of the laws of morality so that they do not forget themselves; and legislators return men to their duties, using political and civil laws (I.1; cf. Locke, *Essay* II.28.7–11). This careful statement distinguishes the philosopher from a legislator, while still connecting them. the philosopher in Montesquieu's conception does not legislate for legislators by laying down the principles of their laws in a natural law, but rather causes the "spirit" of their laws to emerge by considering each set of laws as a whole. His understanding of the laws as legislated and executed reminds us of Machiavelli's *verità effettuale*, the truth that is evident in its effect or outcome. Machiavelli's philosophy, too, is unappreciated because it is not presented as philosophy, but is rather embodied in an interpretation of institutions and laws found in actual regimes, not philosophical utopias. But Machiavelli has an evident political principle, the acquisition of honor in this world by "one's own arms." The principle enables or compels him to promote a new conception of virtue, which is sometimes ambiguously, sometimes aggressively, immoral. Montesquieu has no such principle; he has, instead, a non-principle—moderation—that cautions men against the extremism produced by simplified principles (V.14, VIII.8, XI.4, XXIX.1).

The "warning" issued by the philosopher Montesquieu reminds men of their own customary morality, lest they forget themselves and surrender their freedom to legislators who will seek to reform them according to a principle. While allowing and even encouraging (by his own example) a carefully contrived nostalgia for the ancients, Montesquieu takes the side of modern politicians who do not accept the force of virtue, but speak only "of manufactures, commerce, finances, riches, and even luxury" (III.3). Yet he does not respond to Machiavelli's call for "new modes and orders," and he does his best instead to reduce the intensity of the drama of modernity. Rather than defeat the ancients in open debate, Montesquieu shows that they defeated themselves as the contradiction in their notion of virtue became manifest in historical fact. And he therefore shows that modernity did not begin as a heroic project, but rather established itself insensibly through a series of unplanned, unlegislated causes.

By assembling this picture of modest beginnings, Montesquieu seeks to induce us to believe that the essence of modernity itself is moderation. And in no aspect of the question is his attempt more impressive than in his method of taming the modern executive:

> We begin to cure ourselves of Machiavellism and will cure ourselves every day. One must have more moderation in counsel. What we formerly called *coups d'état* would be today, independently of their horror, only acts of imprudence (XXI.20).

These *coups d'état* Montesquieu also calls *grands coups d'autorité* ("great strokes of authority") referring to the sensational executions recommended by Machiavelli.[6] Does he mean to imply that Machiavelli's own project of changing the world by a great stroke of authority was somehow unnecessary?

Although Montesquieu does not seek to abolish fear from political life, he rejects it as the "passion to be reckoned on" to make government effectual. Accordingly, the principle of separation of powers for which he is famous establishes for the first time anywhere the independence of the judiciary, creating the three powers as we know them today. Unlike Locke, and contrary to previously accepted custom, Montesquieu subtracts the power of punishment from the emergency and foreign policy powers of the executive. He thereby separates punishment from politics, and so prevents or constrains the political use of punishment devised by Machiavelli and extended (in more legal fashion) by Hobbes and Locke. Montesquieu establishes a strong executive that need not be terrible, and he demonstrates how a free government can manage its affairs without having to frighten its own people. That free government is not a soft one, by our standards, but it is mild compared to Locke's, and Montesquieu's executive is sovereign neither in pretension nor in act. Since Montesquieu does not have a sovereign principle from which to infer the nature of the executive directly, he must proceed by indirection, allowing his point to be made gradually, apparently against his will. He does not create a mild executive, but rather tames the ferocious one that he finds already on the scene. And he does it not by any action of his own but by permitting the beast to do its worst so that we in the audience can draw the moral lesson ourselves.

The Obsolescence of Republican Virtue

To tame the Machiavellian executive, Montesquieu had to dissipate the fear that he first inspires and then manages; in other words, he had to oppose and replace Machiavellian *virtù*. Would he have to return to the classical virtue that Machiavelli himself had opposed and replaced? Not in the least. Although Montesquieu praises classical virtue repeatedly for its noble elevation of the human soul, his praise is in the spirit of a connoisseur's appreciation for an inimitable object of a bygone age, a beautiful museum piece. His strategy is really to replace classical virtue *without* opposing it—indeed, while praising it eloquently.

Machiavelli too had praised *antica virtù* but had condemned the imaginary republics and kingdoms in which the ancient philosophers had displayed it, the better to appraise it. In Machiavelli's view of acquisitive deeds, ancient virtue has a different look: its politics has been transformed from justice and moderation into courage and prudence, and its mode is understood not as trust or gratitude but fear. Only thus transformed, Machiavelli believed, can classical virtue be revived. And when the change has been accomplished, ancient virtue is Machiavelli's virtue. His successors Hobbes and Locke no longer spoke of a revival of classical virtue, but announced instead a modern politics of rights, interests and institutions. By making sovereignty or legitimacy their first question, they indicated that the basis of this new politics was fear—for only in a state of fear does one forget about the good and scramble to safety under a sovereign.

In the preface to *The Spirit of the Laws* Montesquieu remarks that in an enlightened age one trembles even to do great goods, while in an age of ignorance no one hesitates to do the greatest evils. One trembles because although one feels the old abuses of the ignorant age and sees how they are corrected, one also sees the abuses wrought by their correction. To see the abuses of enlightenment without renouncing enlightenment is Montesquieu's essential task. The abuses of enlightenment arise from the decision of modern philosophers to oppose classical virtue. Perhaps they were compelled to do because they were unable to assume the moderate role recommended by Montesquieu, lacking their own revolutionary extremism to react against. Whatever their excuse, though, Montesquieu does not follow them. Unlike Hobbes and Locke, he does not oppose classical virtue; unlike Machiavelli, he does not attempt to revive it, by means of a cunning reinterpretation. He does indeed reinterpret classical virtue, but only in order to show that it is out of date.

In the first book of *The Spirit of the Laws,* "Of the laws in general," Montesquieu corrects the early moderns who had themselves corrected the ancients. We therefore see Montesquieu's posture toward both. His beginning is very abstract and contains no concrete examples, unlike his later books, which are full of them. The first book gives some promise that it may set forth the ruling principle of nature and government, but in fact it discloses that no such principle exists. According to Montesquieu, it is merely an abstraction that shows the futility of abstraction.

The first chapter, which considers law "in the most extended sense," seems Aristotelian or scholastic in its assertion that the "primitive reason" present in all things refutes the "blind fatality" alleged by unnamed modern philosophers—perhaps such as Spinoza.[7] But men's access to this primitive reason is limited; unlike material objects, intelligent creatures do not behave according to constant, unvarying laws, and are subject to error. Judged by the principle of reason, then, men appear as inferior beings, feeble, forgetful, and erring. Montesquieu does not address, as Aristotle does, the human faculty of speech by which men form opinions about the whole and align themselves with its ruling principle. Men appear merely as "possible " beings with the potential for just relations—a feeling of gratitude when they have received a benefit, a feeling of retribution when they have been harmed, and so on.

Retribution, viewed as a reaction to injury rather than an act of obedience to natural law, is Montesquieu's only hint of human freedom in this vague account. In striking contrast to modern philosophers who maintain that man begins in perfect freedom, Montesquieu subjects him from his origin to laws, with no mention of freedom. He implies that the freedom posited by the modern philosophers is overwhelmed by the necessity, amounting to blind fatality, to which they must subject human beings in their attempts to free them from an enslaving gratitude to God. Yet Montesquieu, who mentions gratitude, does not describe much that men in all their weakness should be grateful for. He does not say, for instance, that men share in God's reason.[8] From what he does say it appears that men are essentially reasonable or intelligent rather than free—aligning him with Aristotle and the scholastics—but also that they are not *very* reasonable, which rather aligns him with Hobbes and Locke. So it appears that freedom is not the foundation of political life, and human reason is a weak foundation.

Montesquieu speaks next "of the laws of nature" derived from the constitution of our being. These are actual laws, as distinct from the possible relations of justice and the philosophic laws of morality he has mentioned (I.1). Montesquieu agrees with the modern philosophers that men at first care nothing for speculation, and concern themselves only with self-preservation: passions and fear are more fundamental than reason and gratitude. But in explicit disagreement with Hobbes, he denies that fear would necessarily lead men to dominate others. Instead, it would fill them with timidity (that is, with neither the gratitude nor the retribution he has mentioned). Hobbes makes the mistake that Rousseau would also notice of importing the social passion of domination back into the state of nature. Yet if men at first are timid, they form society in a spirit of timidity, not freedom. Montesquieu finds freedom neither in the "extended sense" of law, where it is necessary to know whether law is from God or is blind fatality, nor in natural laws based on human passions (not requiring speculative knowledge). Will he find it in "positive laws," the third and last part (I.3) of his search for a beginning principle?

In society, says Montesquieu, men lose their sense of weakness and the state of war begins. War then arises from security, not security from war; so the desire for domination was present in men at the beginning, but unawakened. In that case the formation of society was not an act of freedom—not the establishment of a sovereign or the making of a constitution. The whole question of legitimate right by consent, central for Hobbes and Locke, is passed over in silence by Montesquieu. He does not derive politics by reasoning from man's reasonable nature, as does Aristotle, nor by reasoning from man's conflictual nature, like Hobbes and Locke. In fact, Montesquieu does not derive politics from anything pre-political. And he denies that the rule of "one alone" is most conformable to nature, since paternal power does not suffice for government and must be supplemented by the power of "several." The summary dismissal of patriarchy—an argument that Locke took seriously enough to oppose in Filmer—leaves no standing for Aristotle's monarchy of reason according to nature (cf. V.10). "It would be better to say"—Montesquieu does not quite assert it—that the government most conformable to nature is one whose particular disposition is best related to that of the people for whom it is established.

Montesquieu continues to clear out of his inquiry the rival extremes represented by the ancients and the moderns, so that his own moderation can emerge. The *disposition* of a people, he says, is *its reason*. But it is not a reason that accords with the reason of nature, as for Aristotle, nor with natural law, as for Hobbes and Locke. Montesquieu's distinction between political and civil right implies his rejection of the legalism in both. Political right, he says unites the particular *forces* of a society; civil right unites its particular *wills*. For Hobbes and Locke, the legal sovereign unites the forces of society by representing its will; but Montesquieu does not believe that law can accomplish such a union on its own, employing a universal reason based on natural law (see X.3). While admitting that a union of particular forces requires a union of particular wills, he finds that it is achieved through a complicated set of relations between laws that are willed and physical laws (laws "in the extended sense"), a relationship he calls the "spirit of the laws."

Hobbes and Locke first posit a natural freedom in the state of nature and then immediately take it away by requiring men, under natural law, to submit to a sovereign. Montesquieu sees no liberty for men in nature: if they are not subject to blind fatality they are subject to God. And he does not think it sensible to encourage the delusion that liberty is natural. In the first book he mentions "liberty" just once when he refers to "the degree of liberty that a constitution can suffer"; he does not promise the liberty to constitute a government that Locke endorsed and that

Americans were soon to exercise. Instead he speaks of the government most *conformable* to nature, not of one that is *according* to nature (which would imply that nature can guide political action). Both human freedom or will and what opposes it are natural, but only the former is subject to reason. Thus law in the extended sense (beyond human law) with its "primitive reason" may be distinguished from the positive law that "in general, is human reason" (I.3; cf. XXVI.1). The latter treats the *relations* of human law (representing human will) to nonlegal phenomena (things not legislated by men). Because of his care for the nonlegal, Montesquieu has had to suffer the indignity in our day of being praised as sociological; but he is certainly opposed, as we shall see, to the formalism, as well as legalism, of the earlier liberals. He does not *assert* liberty, either in regard to the natural freedom of man in the state of nature or in the free act of a people removing itself from that state. Instead, he shows how liberty *emerges* in a whole which mixes the law with what we would call its conditioning factors in a series of "relations" *(rapports)*.

In considering these relations Montesquieu retreats from the exaggerated claim of earlier liberals that free government can arise and be maintained by consent. Consent is compounded of the things we will or wish for and the things we must accept, and the latter element cannot be either willed or wished away. It is too strong for the formalistic subterfuges of representation and tacit consent by which Hobbes and Locke attempted to transform what we inherit into autonomous creations. Rather than exaggerate *consent*, Montesquieu brings *opinion* to the fore—actual, everyday opinion about government as opposed to grand, legitimating acts of consent that are rare, such as constituting governments, or infrequently repeated, such as elections. Hobbes and Locke tried to remove opinion from politics because they held it responsible for partisanship, and especially religious partisanship. They did not share the serious concern we have seen in Aristotle for what can be elicited from partisan opinion. Bypassing opinion, they went directly to human nature, to the passions that move men as opposed to the boastful speech by which they justify their actions.

In this manner, Hobbes and Locke gave recognition to the things we must accept. But having recognized the need for fear, they then disguised it with the ambiguous term, "consent." Thus they asserted a claim to liberty that was belied by their dependence on necessity. Montesquieu returned to Aristotle's concern for opinion, but by a different route. He did not examine the truth of partisan opinion, nor seek to dignify its partial statements about the common good or the whole. Instead, combining ancients and moderns, he looks to our opinions about our fears—to our sense of security. Opinion reflects confidence; fear shows the lack of it. Our opinions regarding our security are in fact many individual opinions about each one's own security, reflecting confidence in his own worth and fear that it will not be sustained by his fellows or in general by nature. The confidence and the fear together reveal Montesquieu's mode of encouraging our boastfulness—the democratic vanity with which we assure ourselves that each one of us matters. It is still very much our mode today, the mode of life insurance: the responsible person must assume that he is indispensable!

If liberty need not be asserted, free government need not be based on fear, and the executive need not terrify. In its civil aspect (the relations of citizens to one another) government needs to terrify criminals, but, politically, it no longer needs to terrify its citizens in order to inspire respect.

Montesquieu has now dealt with the ground of classical virtue and its modern "correction." But it would be more accurate to speak of their groundlessness: classical virtue cannot establish a ground in reason, while modern freedom cannot find a ground in nature. It was a mistake for the moderns to substitute one ground for another: forsaking virtue for the sake of freedom, they built on the passion of fear; but fear produces timidity and results in a surrender to necessity. Far from being conducive to freedom, it is the principle of despotism (III.9).[9] But having made this point, Montesquieu shows how classical virtue can be grounded in politics, if not in nature:

> Greek politicians, who lived in popular government, recognized no other force that could sustain them than that of virtue. Those of today speak to us only of manufactures, commerce, finances, riches, and even luxury. (III.3; cf. VII.1)

This statement, which at first seems so disdainful of modern politicians, introduces us to Montesquieu's characteristic theses regarding classical virtue.[10] Such virtue is Greek, hence as "singular" as it is admirable (IV. 6, 7; XIX.16) and on the whole democratic rather than aristocratic; it is political rather than philo- sophic; and it is a means to sustain the state rather than the end served by the state. In every way Montesquieu depreciates classi- cal virtue as he appraises it, offering its politics as the effectual truth of its philosophical intention or pretension. So understood, classical virtue becomes the sole "executive" force of a popular government. In a monarchy, Montesquieu says, he who executes the laws judges himself to be above them; hence monarchy has less need of virtue than popular government, where he who exe- cutes the laws knows that he too must submit to them (III.3). With this comparison—unflattering to both because it implies that virtue is not voluntary—Montesquieu presents classical virtue, not any modern institution, as the executive power of govern- ment. This would presumably be a tame, subordinate executive if it worked at all, but would it?

Montesquieu begins by drawing a distinction, foreign to Aris- totle, between the nature of a government and its principle.[11] Its nature is the particular structure that defines it; while its principle is the human passion that causes it to *move*. For Aristotle, a gov- ernment is defined by its form, and it moves toward that form as its end; a democracy, for example, must behave democratically in order to be democratic. But for Montesquieu, apparently, the form of government has insufficient power to move democratic citizens to behave democratically. "Ruling" in the Aristotelian sense that combines the nature or structure and the principle of motion is impossible according to Montesquieu. As with Locke, therefore, the end of government does not vary according to its diverse forms; security is the invariable end of government (I.3, III.6).

Montesquieu and Locke both accept a fundamental tension be- tween the form and the end of government, a tension characteris- tic of modern constitutionalism as opposed to Aristotle's notion of the regime. But Montesquieu departs from Locke when he finds a principle of motion peculiar to each government whose structure he defines. Although the end is invariable, no single motive leads to it. The supposedly universal motive of fear, which Hobbes said was the "passion to be reckoned on," is, as we noted, the principle only of despotism for Montesquieu; and the love of liberty, a motive for citizens who, apart from the benefits of free government, desire to live freely, does not exist and does not accord with Montesquieu's distrust of whatever is purely formal. He will present the English constitution as the constitution of liberty, but "this beautiful system," as he calls it, was found in the woods of Germany and was not itself freely constituted (IX.6).

In a republic, the people—either in a body (democracy), or in part (aristocracy)—hold sovereign power. But since the sovereign power does not maintain itself for the sake of its sovereign form or structure, it must call on the executive power of virtue: only a virtuous democracy maintains itself. The "fundamental laws" of a democracy, in contrast to despotism, are not self-executing (II.2, 4, 5). This executing virtue is called a "passion"; it is not what Aristotle describes as a habit in accordance with reason. Like all such principles of government, it is a spring *(ressort)*, that is, a reaction to something, rather than self-driven to a chosen end. Even the despot's prudent fear of the ambitious is a reaction; he cannot afford to be lazy, turning over his affairs to a vizier who may plot against him (II.5; III.9). A democratic republic by its nature has the people's will for its sovereign; its principle of motion is the virtue that reacts against this will, the public-spirited virtue of self-renunciation (IV.5, V.2, 12).

Republican virtue is austere, even ascetic; Montesquieu compares it to the love of monks for their order (IV.6, V.2, XIV.7). Just as monks, deprived of ordinary objects, give themselves up to a passion for the very rules that bind them, so a republican people finds satisfaction in general passions when particular ones are denied. But we know that Montesquieu also considers republican virtue to be the classical virtue of the ancient philosophers; the laws of Plato are nothing but the "correction," or, on second thought, the "perfection" of the laws of Sparta (IV.6, VII.16). Montesquieu could have called them more correctly a "refutation" of those laws, but he is interested in Plato's effect, not his intent. He directs attention only to the repression found in classical as well as Christian virtue, taking no notice of the higher ends—love of knowledge and love of God respectively—for whose sake the lower passions were repressed or redirected.

Higher and lower in the ancient philosophers and in Christianity reappear as general and particular in Montesquieu. Reducing the higher ends to general passions permits him to ignore the fundamental differences between philosophers and monks in favor of the self-renunciation that, to our eyes, they appear to have in common. This deliberate vulgarization is only unfair to the pretensions of philosophers and monks, not to the political effect of those pretensions. The philosophers in particular may claim that their proposed repression of our base passions is in the service of our higher nature, so that their virtue is "according to nature." But in its Christian "correction," classical virtue is popularized and simplified. In this version, our higher nature is understood as pure and speculative, hence detached from the body, hence at home only in the next world (I.2, IV.8, XIV.7). The effectual truth of virtue "according to nature," then, is virtue "contrary to nature."

Montesquieu provides a smokescreen for his politicization of classical and Christian virtue by insisting, in the "Advertisement of the Author" at the very beginning of his book, that when he says virtue he means only political—not moral or Christian—virtue. But in practice he does not sustain this professed distinction. When discussing education in a republic, he says that "all the particular virtues" display nothing but the continual preference of the public interest over one's own ("Advert.," III.5 note, II. 6 and note, IV.5, V.2, 4): yet these are simply moral virtues politicized, not (as Montesquieu maintains) moral virtues left intact by the creation of an unrelated political variety.

Once classical virtue has been politicized, it may be attached to the classical *polis*, and Montesquieu can reveal its defects without having to criticize them himself simply by contemplating the troubles and historical fate of the ancient city. My summary of Montesquieu's intricate presentation cannot do justice to his ambitious strategy of disillusionment. To begin with, he makes the illusion bright enough. Montesquieu remarks that the ancient peoples "astonish our small souls" with the things they did when their virtue was effectual (IV.4). In the corruption of modern times the republican virtue we see today, in such communities as those of William Penn (the Lycurgus of Pennsylvania) and the Jesuits in Paraguay (IV.6), is less impressive. Virtue, the principle of democratic government, requires more education than do fear and honor, which are the principles of despotism and monarchy. Ancient republics therefore sought to harden men by teaching them disdain for servile occupations such as agriculture and commerce, and by occupying them with gymnastic exercises that made the Greeks a "society of athletes and combatants." But then it was necessary to temper their hardness by music that would sweeten and soften their "ferocity": such is the "paradox" of ancient education (IV.8).

Beneath the paradox one finds a contradiction: virtue made men worthy of self-love, but only by teaching them self-renunciation. What, then, was the end of virtue—to promote the self, or mortify it? By ignoring the difference between lower and higher things in the self, Montesquieu changes the status of virtue from end to means—from the end for which the republic should be maintained to the means of maintaining it. Aristotle said that virtue is both a means and an end, and as his argument in the *Politics* moved toward the best regime, the status of education in virtue was elevated from means to end (1310a12–14; 1337a22–26). But Montesquieu, having redefined virtue as passion, politicizes it and thus leaves republican education incoherent. Why did it harden men only to soften them again? But it appears that republican ferocity was not successfully tempered: even when they were uncorrupt, Greek republics depended on fear of the Persians to sustain their laws (VIII.5), and the Romans used oaths, depending on religious fear (VIII.13). In practice, then, republican virtue was really based less on love than on fear, the principle of despotism.

Montesquieu presents the element of love in republican virtue first as love of the laws and of the fatherland (IV.5), then as love of the fatherland leading to good customs (*moeurs*). By this, he means the monkish preference for general passions over particular ones (V.2). In a democracy, the principal motive is love of equality, understood as hostility to ambition (V.3; see III.3). Here is the first appearance in Montesquieu's work of equality. What is for Hobbes and Locke the fundamental condition of men in the state of nature (see VIII.3) is, for Montesquieu, the consequence of the principle of one regime. And in his treatment, love of equality is associated with love of frugality. Each maintains the other to maintain itself, since riches will always nourish inequality (V.4–6). But the force that would be needed to maintain these virtues ensures that if democracy is not corrupted by their loss, it will be so by the extremism necessary to enforce them (VIII.2, 8). In the latter outcome, the people will wish to do everything by itself, lacking respect for the magistrates and the Senate. Disobedience will spread among women, children, and slaves—Montesquieu reminds us of the slavery in ancient republics

(VI.17, VIII.2)—and virtue is lost. While it existed, Roman virtue was the virtue of *not* exercising power; this was the proof of their magnanimity, Montesquieu says (VIII.12). But since the people, as republicans, are hostile to ambition, the nobles they defer to are constrained to use their riches in support of "admirable institutions," such as public festivals, to show that their burdens are equal to those of the poor (VII.3). Yet how are such institutions to be distinguished from the flattery by which nobles corrupt the people, or by which the people corrupt themselves? (VIII.2)

When a people is virtuous, few punishments are necessary (VI.11, 15). But in practice, zeal for the public good leads to the situation Locke describes as the state of nature where each man is an executive, though in this case for the public good, and not in self-defense (VI.8). Ancient republics did not separate judge from prosecutor, just as they did not distinguish political right from civil right. Citizens could accuse one another, and sycophants prospered under the encouragement to virtuous men to be zealous for the public good. This we moderns do not have, Montesquieu says in a tone of congratulation (VI.8). Thus republican virtue, which is supposed to execute republican laws, needs itself to be maintained by laws that lead it to an extreme spirit of equality, and therewith to anarchy and tyranny at the expense of individual security.

Nor do the troubles of republican virtue end there. The frugality needed to maintain equality compels republics to pass sumptuary laws directed against luxury. Such laws are difficult to enforce, and have the effect—contrary to their intent—of preoccupying men with glory, since other forms of excess are prohibited (VII.1–3; VIII.4, 11). In the ancient republics, women were free by law and constrained by custom; since rules of modesty were not enshrined in codes of law, the punishments for violating them were necessarily arbitrary (VII.8–13). Thus we see again that, contrary to Montesquieu's assurance, republican virtue was not merely a political virtue but a moral virtue politicized.

The greatest difficulty of republics lies in foreign affairs. It is in the nature of a republic to have a small territory where fortunes are small, and where citizens do not believe they can be happy, great, or glorious without their fatherland (VIII.16). But in addition to great successes that unexpectedly bring empire, like the victory at Salamis to Athens (VIII.4), small republics often become large on their own. Their virtue is martial, hence easily translated into pride, and then into a desire for glory (VIII.16). Such ambition is helped, when the republic is uncorrupt, by the fusion of civilians and military that infects the army with republican pride (IV.8; V.19); and when the republic is corrupt, or weak, ambition abroad is a cure for divisions at home (IV.8). In Book IX, on "defensive force," Montesquieu assures us that "the spirit of a republic is peace and moderation" (IX.2), but in the following book on "offensive force" he tells us about conquering republics among the ancients (especially the Roman) and speculates that the right of self-defense may indeed enforce aggression (X.2, 3, 6, 7; see XI.5). To be sure, Montesquieu does not permit a general right of anticipation as do Machiavelli and Hobbes; and to deny that right he does distinguish between defense and offense. But the distinction, and the concept of international law it implies, are the occasion for his "homage to our modern times" (X.3). Finally, since uncorrupt republics are small, they are more likely to need to attack in order to defend themselves (X.2).

I have extracted and connected Montesquieu's scattered remarks on republican virtue. He himself has left them inconclusive, though his most notable summary statements are admiring. He says, "I am strong in my maxims when I have the Romans for me," when he claims that their punishments were mild in accordance with the natural spirit of a republic (VI.15). But this contradicts his earlier statement that the republican spirit in Rome produced the sort of zealous accusations encouraged by Plato but unsuitable today (VI.8). "Rome was a vessel held by two anchors in a storm: religion and customs" (VIII.13)—here he does not mention virtue.

As I interpret Montesquieu's account, the fundamental difficulty in republican virtue, which brings it to its heights and its depths as well as causing it to spend itself in excess, is the conflict between its nature and its principle. Its nature is the form or structure that makes the will of the people sovereign, and its principle is the virtue needed to execute that will. But that virtue becomes a restraint on the will that, without a higher justification, cannot help but appear contrary to the will of the people. At first the people may obey the laws and defer to the magistrates; but in time the very popularity of the magistrates will suggest to the people that the magistrates are the people's instruments, and that virtue is the people's executive. Then the people, abandoning the restraint of virtue, will take government into their own hands or give it to a tyrant. Virtue politicized is virtue democratized. The moderation that Montesquieu calls the principle of aristocracy cannot last. Either the nobles must be harsh—hence immoderate—in order to maintain their power, or they must do favors for the people, flatter and corrupt them, and finally induce them to overthrow the nobility (VIII.2, 5). Moderation is the proximate goal of politics for Montesquieu; political liberty, the higher goal, is found only in moderate states (XI.4). In Books II–VIII, on the natures and principles of governments, where his theme is the difference between republican government and one-man rule, another distinction is gradually brought to notice—the distinction between moderate states whose principle is security, and despotic states whose principle is fear. And since monarchies can be moderate and republics despotic, the new distinction undermines the previous one and casts doubt on republican virtue (III.10; V.14, 16, 19; VI.1, 2, 9, 12, 16, 19; VII.17).[12]

Whereas the despotic principle of fear is corrupt in itself (VIII.10), and the monarchical principle of honor may be corrupted by bad policy (VIII. 6–9), Montesquieu does not say (but lets us think) that republican corruption is—or better, *was*—inevitable. Although he does not like extreme democracy, he does not blame either people or nobles for the corruption that brings it about. His discussion of republican corruption, like Machiavelli's, is not flavored with the moral disapprobation of a republican partisan or of a classical political philosopher. According to Aristotle, a regime becomes corrupt when it no longer aims at the common good, as it claims to do by the form of government that is both "nature" and "principle" in Montesquieu's terms. The cure for corruption is a mixed regime that does not merely restrain partisan excess, but improves the city in a manner consistent with partisan ambition. If democracy is the government of all, why not provide a special place for the rich who, as rich, are part of "all"? (*Politics* 1318a19–b6).

Montesquieu, as I noted, finds little partisan attachment to a form of government as such; so he does not propose to reform or to cure corruption in accordance with the regime's desire to be itself. He takes for his principle the desire for security which is common to moderate states: such desire is neither specific to a regime, as it is in Aristotle and in Montesquieu's own provisional classification (in II.1), nor is it pre-political, as in Hobbes and

Locke. Montesquieu takes England for his model—a nation, he has told us, "where a republic is hidden under the form of a monarchy" (V.19). Here the executive is not virtue, but a "power" derived from monarchy. Before analyzing the constitution of liberty in England, Montesquieu speaks "of the promptitude of execution in a monarchy," and notes its great advantage over republican government because its affairs are conducted by *un seul* (V.10).[13] Such a Machiavellian advantage must be made safely available to republican government without depending on despotic virtue, and without periodic recourse to despotic strokes of authority. Despotic power is communicated with no loss of authority, so that every officer of a despot is a despot himself. This should remind us of Locke's executive power of the law of nature, which gives effectual sovereignty to the momentary will of every man. But monarchical power, Montesquieu says, is distributed so that the monarch retains a greater part than he gives (V.16). The monarchical principle of distribution can also be applied to the powers of a republic so as to make it both safe and efficient, while leaving the people's will supreme. Such a republic would have liberty as its direct object (XI.5), rather than virtue as its principle.

The Constitution of Reason

The most famous discussion of constitutionalism in the history of political thought is Montesquieu's chapter on "the Constitution of England" in *The Spirit of the Laws* (XI.6). Following Locke, Montesquieu adopts England as his model for constitutional liberty, an actual regime that serves as a model attainable by others. Also following Locke, he keeps his model at a certain distance from historical fact. Although he names England in the chapter title, he describes English institutions or makes unmistakable allusions without naming them, and his arguments are repeatedly phrased in the conditional mood. In what sense, then, is the author's would-be England a model for others?

In Montesquieu's description, England's "extreme political liberty" may "mortify" those who enjoy only a moderate liberty (XI.6, end). Montesquieu denies any intention to disparage other governments. He does not claim to decide whether England actually enjoys the liberty whose constitution he examines; and he proceeds to discuss "monarchies with which we are acquainted" (XI.7) where the three powers are not founded on this model. The difficulty inherent in political liberty is that men believe it means doing what they will, when in truth that liberty must be limited (XI.2, 3). But how can an "extreme" political liberty be limited? Montesquieu objected to virtuous republics on the grounds that they were extreme, not moderate: "Even virtue has need of limits" (XI.4). Hence political liberty exists only under moderate governments. He then sets forth a constitution of liberty that he himself calls "extreme."

Montesquieu poses the problem in a short chapter (XI.3) in which he gives two quite different views of "what liberty is," after having denied that it means doing what one wills.[14] Liberty, he says, can only consist "in being able to do what one ought to will and in not being constrained to do what one ought not to will." One sentence later, he says that "liberty is the right to do all that the laws permit." But not being constrained to do vice is different from being permitted to do anything legal. It is the difference between law that makes morality possible, while not getting in its way, and law that does not care about morality. The first is a moral view of liberty that reminds us of Kant's dislike of paternalism; the second seems to be taken from Hobbes. Montesquieu seems unwilling to settle for either view. He wants to permit virtue, but not to enforce it—an aim he shares with both Kant and Hobbes. But instead of reasoning his way to absolute sovereignty, like Hobbes, or to the single constitution suitable for rational beings, as Kant would do, Montesquieu equivocates.

Men are neither simple power-seekers nor *a priori* moralizers, according to Montesquieu, but they abuse power *when they have it*, whether they mean well or not.[15] One cannot build a rational constitution on either the Hobbesian or the Kantian assumption, for it is dangerous to let either will or virtue hold sway unopposed. Rather than make a point of the difference between them, therefore, Montesquieu looks merely to the powers men may hold, and tries to arrange a "disposition of things"—an order not derived either from human will or human virtue—by which "power checks power" (XI.5). The disposition produces a constitution defined negatively as one in which "nobody will be constrained to do things to which the law does not oblige him, and not to do those that the law permits him" (XI.5).

Such is the constitution of reason when reason does not inquire into either the origin of power in will or the end of power in virtue, but rests content with examining its exercise regardless of its origin or end. Reason so confined not only remains consistent with human liberty but also goes to the limit of what is reasonable. Any statement of the *principles* of our actions to try to specify a guide for them would be as arbitrary in reason as it would be intolerable to our liberty. But the *constitution* of reason is neither arbitrary nor intolerable. It is extreme because it carries liberty as far as it can, and it is moderate because it is a constitution of limits. It is not the best regime, because the regime of virtue has been shown to be willful in practice, with aspects of despotism. Reason requires, then, that one "find" this constitution rather than "seek it out." So Montesquieu introduces his famous chapter, and at its end he brings up his complaint against Harrington, who, he says, *sought* for the extreme of liberty when he could have *found* it under his nose (XI.5, 6, end).[16] The English constitution does have "principles," but Montesquieu, instead of seeking them in nature and human nature, finds them in "one nation in the world." If the principles of this unnamed nation's constitution are examined and found good, liberty will appear in it as in a mirror (XI.5).

You can see liberty, Montesquieu seems to say, only if you look at its image in politics, not if you seek its foundation in nature, as did the ancient and the earlier modern political philosophers. The image has the status of opinion as contrasted to knowledge, but, as William Kristol says, it makes liberty *look* real.[17] Indeed, the fundamental principle of such a constitution is the *opinion* each individual holds regarding his own security. That opinion cannot be grounded in nature, for nature is indifferent to human liberty. Nature at best is partially friendly to liberty because it does not have any ruling principle to which we must subordinate our will, and partially unfriendly because human will—a natural endowment—often turns despotic. For Montesquieu, the task of reason is to analyze itself and assess its own effectual truth, as seen in laws actually made in diverse nations. England does possess the constitution of reason, but it is neither more natural nor more original than other, less reasonable ones. "This beautiful system was found in the woods" (XI.6, end); that is, not in ancient philosophy, but in the practice of the barbarian Germans, in a society which resembles the state of nature (I.2; XIV.3; XVIII.23; XXX.19). So we are told, Montesquieu says, not by a philosopher but by Tacitus, the well-known stalking horse for Machiavelli. Thus reason's search for the grounding of liberty runs to earth in the Germans, who supplant the ancients as the antecedents of modern liberty.

Montesquieu happens on England, as it were. England does not have founders, as Sparta, the paradigm of ancient republics, had Lycurgus. Montesquieu will "perfect" England, as Plato perfected Sparta, but not by developing an inherent founding intention (see XII.19, XXI.7). He does not refer to Locke, much less Bolingbroke: nor does he celebrate the great Whig lords, as Edmund Burke could do.[18] The only sources of design he mentions are Sidney and Harrington, two republicans not involved in the English constitution. Sidney he praises for an observation about representation; Harrington he scolds for missing the point by "seeking" instead of "finding" (see XXIX.19). But "finding" England does not mean consulting its founding. Rather it means listening to what English laws and institutions tell us by their practice, without distorting interference from their founders' protestations. Thus we do not see the constitution of England constituted, as we do with Locke.

As a whole, the English constitution, which is also the constitution of reason, replaces the principles of regimes that execute laws. In particular it replaces virtue as the executive principle of republics. But this constitution consists of a distribution of powers, among which the executive is but one. In a sense the whole constitution executes the will of the people; in another sense only one power does this. Consequently, and in contrast to Machiavelli, Hobbes, and Locke, no power is clearly supreme for Montesquieu, either in law or fact. He does not return to Aristotle's subordinate executive, but, unlike his modern predecessors, he broadens the executive without concentrating it in one person.

Montesquieu begins the chapter on the English constitution with two different accounts of the powers of government, and then proceeds at length to a third. He says first that in each state there are three sorts of powers (*pouvoirs*): the legislative power (*puissance*), the executive[19] power over things depending on the right of nations, and the executive power over things depending on civil right. Here is a formal definition valid for each state, not only for a free one, with no mention of sovereignty, or law, or hierarchy among the powers. It represents what each state would want—the primacy of right, especially right among nations, enabling each state to establish its own civil right. But Montesquieu immediately restates the powers in practice: by the first, the prince or the magistrate makes laws for a time or for always, and corrects or repeals those already made; by the second, he makes peace or war, sends or receives embassies, establishes security, and prevents invasions; by the third, he punishes crimes or judges differences among particular persons. The first power is an assertion of sovereignty without the name and without reference to right; the second demonstrates the easy and serene execution of the right of nations; the third raises the question whether punishing is executing law or civil right. The second sort of power becomes the "executive" in Montesquieu, and the third becomes the "power of judging." In the informal restatement, there is unity in the "prince," but "right" disappears; there is still no hierarchy in the functions, which are not defined or described, and there is no reference to a free state. The natural constitution of each state must be applied to a free state in its twofold aspect: three powers yet one "prince or magistrate," and unity without despotism.

Montesquieu tells us next what political liberty is. In a citizen, he says, political liberty is that tranquillity of spirit which comes from the opinion that each has of his security. The government must be such that one citizen cannot fear another. Free government respects the present opinion of citizens about their security regardless of an original promise or contract, as in Hobbes and Locke. Only in an attenuated sense, we shall see, is free government self-government. So it is the separation, not the authorization, of power that makes a state free. Montesquieu asserts emphatically and absolutely that when the legislative power is united with the executive in the same person or body, there is no liberty; for one could fear that a monarch or senate might make tyrannical laws so as to execute them tyrannically. This is separation of powers in its original, republican meaning. But then he declares that if the power of judging is not separated from the other two, there is also no liberty. If it were joined to the legislative, the judge would be legislator; if joined to the executive, he would have the force of an oppressor.

Montesquieu's scheme of separation is the new one, though more in theory than in fact, since he acknowledges that in most of the kingdoms of Europe the prince holds the first two powers and leaves the third to his subjects (XI.6, 11). In his rational constitution, Montesquieu also locates the power of judging in the people, to be exercised by persons drawn from the body of the people who form a temporary tribunal lasting as long as necessity requires. Thus the power of judging, so terrible among men, becomes "as it were invisible and null." Men do not have judges continually before their eyes; and they will fear the magistracy, rather than the magistrates (therefore, not other citizens).

Montesquieu seems to have English juries in mind, though he does not name them; and he seems to have forgotten English judges. He appears to be anticipating or even inspiring Tocqueville's discussion of juries in America as an institution of self-government. But Tocqueville argues that juries serve to instruct a democratic people in justice and responsibility, that they increase the influence of the lawyers and judges who expound to them, and that they permit the "legal spirit" to penetrate to the lowest ranks of society.[20] Tocqueville reproduces in democratic conditions the Aristotelian notion of the independence of judging, according to which it represents a check on human government, or a calling to account in the light of an external standard, either law or nature. Accordingly, judging in Tocqueville's view demands the independence of detachment and criticism.

But with Montesquieu, judging is independent of the other powers of government, not of government as a whole; and he makes it independent precisely so that the people will *not* have the terrible sense of being judged. The detached judge who embodies law and justice must be rendered as it were invisible and null, because the standard he enforces (ancient virtue) is too high or too low (modern fatality), and in either case is fearsome. In the constitution of reason, the *opinion* each has of his own security must be sheltered from the reason of judges who might demand too much of us, or who might remind us of our insignificance. We may conclude, therefore, that judging is placed in the people precisely in order to sever its connection with philosophy.[21] The general opinion of security must be partly a delusion, but Montesquieu protects it by not confronting citizens with judges, or at least minimizing the confrontation.

Montesquieu opposes the political use of punitive justice that forms the leading characteristic of Machiavelli's notion of the executive, but he agrees with its central idea of making government indirect, thus invisible and less odious. The *chef-d'oeuvre* of the legislator of a free people is to know well how to place the power of judging (XI.11). Placing it well means placing it where it does not attract odium, precisely with the people to whom it would otherwise becomes odious. Montesquieu reverts to Aristotle's concern that the need for punishment not make government odious, in contrast to Machiavelli's notion that sensational punishment makes it impressive. Nor does he share Locke's opinion, that the people must both relinquish their natural power to the executive and retain it when that executive is not effectual. But Montesquieu does share the concern of Machiavelli and Locke for the security of the individual, and defines political liberty in this way. This is very unlike Aristotle's argument that nature permits men a free, self-sufficient life of virtue. So, while Aristotle refers judging to an intelligible standard according to which men judge, Montesquieu understands it to be grounded in each man's private opinion of his own security. The difference is that Aristotle seeks moderation because nature supports it; Montesquieu seeks it, because nature does not.

With judicial power removed from view, the two remaining visible powers are the general will of the state and the execution of that will, neither of them exercised on individuals. Montesquieu respects individuals as the objects of government, but not as its originators. He says:

> Since in a free state every man who is considered to have a free soul ought to be governed by himself, it would be necessary that the people in a body have the legislative power. (XI.6)

An individual that a free state regards as having a free soul is at some distance from Locke's description of perfectly free men in the state of nature. And then Montesquieu flatly denies that it is possible or suitable for the people to hold the legislative power. They are incapable of discussing affairs, and representatives should do for them what they cannot do for themselves; only the choice of representatives is within their reach. Although Montesquieu is careful to protect the people's self-esteem from the power of judging, he is so frank about their political incapacity that he does not attempt to justify the resort to representation as authorized by popular consent, in the manner of Hobbes and Locke. Montesquieu does not preserve even the appearance of popular sovereignty; those considered to have free souls must yield to reason.

It was a great vice in the ancient republics, he says emphatically, that the people made active decisions, requiring "execution," of which they are entirely incapable. We recall that the executive "principle" of republics was popular virtue in the people, and such popular virtue is now ruled out here. Even the representative body should not make an active decision, since this is an executive, not a legislative function. Montesquieu further maintains, against the sovereignty of the people, that those distinguished by birth, wealth, or honors must not be confused with the people, and should have a hereditary body to preserve their prerogatives, which in a free state are always endangered. That concession to the nobles leads him to state a distinction between what seem to be two legislative faculties: that of enacting (*statuer*) and that of preventing (*empêcher*). Enacting means ordering a measure by oneself or correcting the order of another; preventing is the right to block the decision of another. The power of veto is called the power of approval, and derives from prevention because it signifies not exercising the power to prevent.

Although the preventing faculty in the House of Lords defends the body of nobles in England, Montesquieu cites also the preventing power of the Tribunes in Rome, thus generalizing that faculty to the practice of a democratic body. The executive veto, he says later, is also a preventing faculty within the legislative power. Sovereign deliberation, as in Aristotle, and supreme legislation, as in Locke, are divided by Montesquieu into enacting and preventing. In effect the division means that the constitution permits or encourages its bodies to prevent without enacting. The independent faculty of prevention preserves human naysaying in the form of a simple negative; it "prevents" any Aristotelian requirement that those who veto should take the responsibility of affirming or choosing something positive.

The legislative body endowed with the faculty of enacting is the body representing the people. We should note that the legislative "power" has almost imperceptibly become a "body" or "bodies." Today we speak of governmental "bodies" as a matter of course. But Hobbes and Locke stressed that political power is united in only "one politic body," and although Locke insisted on a separation of powers, he did not call them separate "bodies." Aristotle's three functions (deliberation, offices, judging) are neither powers of one body, nor separate bodies, but functions of the rational soul. Montesquieu calls the powers "bodies'' in order to give them separate wills. He remarks that "a body is not considered to have any will except when it is assembled"—which is another argument against the fictive will of the social contract. Montesquieu appropriates the defensive impulse characteristic of animal bodies to create will for these assembled (but still fictive) "bodies." Aristotle spoke of political institutions as "forms," a term that endows them with distinctiveness but not with a defensive capacity. His discussion of the three functions depicts them as separate but not in conflict. As soon as Montesquieu calls the powers "bodies," however, he shows them in conflict and in need of self-defense against the others, who will be "brought to abuse" their power. With this question we have arrived at the concern displayed by Blackstone and the American founders for the "encroachment" of one power upon another.[22]

The executive power must be placed in the hands of a monarch—"one alone"[23] because its use requires sudden action. The executive is limited only by its own nature, and it is useless to try to limit it by human contrivance. In Rome, the Tribunes could not only prevent legislation but executive actions as well, a power that Montesquieu condemns as "vicious." The preventing faculty belongs to the legislative power, not the executive, even though it is given to the executive; for execution of the law cannot be understood as preventing the law from being enacted. Nonetheless, the executive in fact receives a share of legislative power that it can use in the aristocratic or democratic interest according to need.

The law-making (or enacting) power is vested in the representatives of the people, but it can be checked by another part of the legislature using the faculty of preventing. The executive power cannot be checked. Montesquieu says that the law is both clairvoyant and blind—clairvoyant, we may suppose, because it claims to foresee everything, and blind because it sees the general principle but not the particular case. Legislative power is therefore limited by the nature of law, and the limitation is visible in the preventing faculty within legislative power, as well as in the need for unhindered execution of the laws. What then is the relation between legislation and execution? Montesquieu says in a famous passage—famous as much for its obscurity as for its importance—that in the "fundamental constitution of the government of which we speak," the legislative body consists of two parts, each restraining the other by their mutual faculty of preventing. Both are bound by or connected to (liées) the executive power, which is itself bound by or connected to the legislative. These three powers might be expected to come to rest or inaction by mutual restraint, but since the necessary movement of things constrains them to proceed, they must proceed together.

How may the passage be understood? It appears that the executive is the one that prevents but cannot be prevented. When he prevents, he acts within the legislative power; and once again the executive has more power in practice than in theory. The executive is the active power, dealing with contingencies. Since we are told that things necessarily move, the executive power would be the natural power, because it cooperates with the natural motions of human affairs. Montesquieu speaks next of the executive powers in war and peace, and as commander-in-chief of the army *versus* the legislative power to enact taxes—said to be the most important power. Foreign danger keeps government tense and in motion, and Montesquieu insists that the army depend immediately on the executive power, since by its nature it involves more action than deliberation. For Montesquieu as for Locke, questions of war and peace are decided by the executive; Aristotle had left them with the sovereign deliberative part precisely so that "action" would be ruled by "deliberation." But it would be dangerous, Montesquieu continues, to have the army depend on the legislative body, because the army would not respect the latter's caution. Moreover, the people would be likely to side with the army in such circumstances. "It is in the manner of thinking of men that they make more of courage than of timidity"—a Machiavellian generalization very favorable to the executive.[24] Montesquieu's example seems to suggest a typical instance of inaction or deadlock between the legislative and the executive, and shows how it might be resolved by the "necessary movement of things."

In Book XI, Montesquieu shows how to make the executive serve liberty rather than military glory, as was the case in Rome; and elsewhere he recommends the spread of commerce to the same end. And if the executive is the active power, the legislative essentially does the preventing. We note that in the passage on the "fundamental constitution" Montesquieu makes no reference to the enacting faculty of legislation. The reason may be that enacting is a kind of preventing.[25] The enacting faculty was said to be that of ordering or correcting an order, but given the necessary motion of things, an order seeks to make things stop, to create stability, as do Locke's "standing rules." Stability is necessary to liberty, that is, to the security of the individual. But it is not achieved merely by being steady, as Montesquieu would seem to indicate by the active character of the two verbs, "enacting" and "preventing."

Legislation seeks stability: it is a "general will" applied against the necessary motion of things, or in other words, against nature. But one must be active to have an effect against nature. "Enacting" and "preventing" thus refer to the law-making power, not to the fixed laws of a tradition. For Montesquieu as for Locke, a government of laws means a government of active legislation; but unlike Locke, Montesquieu sees legislation as less of an assertion than an adjustment. In continually ordering anew and correcting ifself, legislation uses executive energy to establish stability, so far as stability is possible.

The Self-Executing Constitution

"This beautiful system" (XI.6) is so involved with itself that when its bodies move, they move together; and due to the "necessary movement of things," the system must move. It does not require the virtue that Montesquieu first said was characteristic of democracies, defined as a devotion to the common good. The citizens of this constitution are not said to have virtue, or to be devoted to a system that is "beautiful" only to the observer who sees the whole. The system does not need their virtue to execute their will; it is self-executing. Such execution requires neither a grand exertion nor discipline of human will. Nature in the mode of harsh necessity, calling for the spirited Machiavellian executive who makes his own necessity for others to obey, has been replaced by "what comes naturally" in the sense of easily and automatically. Montesquieu's system is a mechanism.

As such, however, the system takes responsibility for the discrepancy between the form and the end of the liberal constitution. Locke constructed a self-critical constitution that contained both the form of liberty and the end by which it may be criticized. On one side is the exercise of constituting reflected in the supremacy of the legislative will; on the other is the end of self-preservation protected by the discretion of the supreme executive. Instead of attempting to overcome the discrepancy, Locke puts it into his constitution in order to preserve it. For him, the constitution is a system in tension, hence one that must be judged as a whole by the people in case it fails and needs to be replaced. It has no mechanism that substitutes for this judgment, and hence no assurance that its form will move on its own toward its proper end. The people must play the role of an umpire between the legislative and the executive because the two elements are *not* bound to move in concert.

The tension, caused by the discrepancy between the form and the end of the constitution, reflects Locke's conception of nature, which is harsher and more Machiavellian than Montesquieu's. For Locke, nature is man's enemy. Locke finds him in the "state of nature" whose great inconveniences can only be remedied by an assertion of will.[26] The legislative sovereignty that results has to be counteracted by a sovereign discretion in the executive. But for Montesquieu, nature's indifference to man need not be remedied with an assertion of right or sovereignty, and so does not result in a contest for supremacy between the legislative and the executive powers. Thus, instead of importing the contest into the constitution, he regards it as a problem to be resolved. Locke does not expect the form of the constitution to achieve its end. Indeed it is intended to remain merely formal in some degree so that the actual exercise of freedom in society is not determined by the free constitution itself.[27] For if the end or content of a free society were specified in advance by its form, the constitution would not be free to specify the end in the course of its operation. Montesquieu's constitution is not determinedly formal in this way; that is why his political science, as we have seen, is not formalistic but "sociological." The end of his constitution is security, or a secure liberty, as it is for Locke. But unlike Locke, he regards this end as naturally moderate, and not as one that justifies a claim to legislative supremacy or unlimited executive power.

"It is the triumph of liberty when the criminal laws draw each punishment from the particular nature of the crime" (XII.4; see XIX.14). Here is no assertion of will or liberty, no claim to right or sovereignty, but rather a calm statement that liberty can *triumph* when the actions of the free constitution follow nature— or better, particular natures—to a satisfactory end. According to Montesquieu, the form of the free constitution moves automatically, or with the unobtrusive aid of his political science, toward its end. This does not mean that the form is identical with the end; if it were, it could not move toward identity. But Montesquieu states as a problem what one often hears today as a reproach—that the constitution may be free but the citizens under it not free, that a constitution may therefore be free in right but not in fact (XII.1; see XI.18).[28] Montesquieu does not tolerate such a discrepancy, much less regard it as a virtue; he says that it requires him to consider not only the constitutional distribution of powers, but also actual mores, manners, received examples, and certain laws, to show how the latter favor political liberty.

Montesquieu's political science resembles Aristotle's in its attempt to bring the form of government toward its end, but the differences between the two are more instructive. For Aristotle, the form of a regime constitutes a claim to rule by the citizen-rulers in accordance with their (partisan) understanding of the end of government; the regime, therefore, has a certain intent, a characteristic self-motion toward its end. For Montesquieu, the end of government is not virtue or happiness but security, and citizens have no devotion to any particular way of arriving at it, hence no devotion to any particular regime. Citizens are not rulers; they do not take responsibility for moving the regime as a whole towards its end. Rather, as citizens they remain distinct from the constitution; their freedom is not guaranteed by its freedom. But constitutional freedom moves on its own or by the necessary movement of things toward their freedom, which Montesquieu defines, not as security precisely, but as the general *opinion* of security (XI.6; XII.1, 2). If it were necessary to motivate the free constitution, this opinion would be its "principle"—following Montesquieu's distinction between the (executive) principle and the nature of a regime.

But in fact the opinion is more the result than the animating principle of that constitution. A citizen's opinion of his security is part will—the democratic will (II.2), now tamed and deprived of its desire to rule others—and part remnant of virtue, now understood as toleration. To achieve it, government must avoid the punitiveness recommended by Machiavelli, Hobbes, and Locke. Montesquieu's necessity is not the brutal harshness to which Locke appeals when he compares punishing human beings to eliminating wild beasts. It is necessary to respect the opinion of necessity we commonly entertain, thus to respect our sense of shock (XII.4) and our desire to be free from fear. Our opinion of our own security must be respected with mildness (*douceur*) in government, lest that security come to consist in trembling at the power that protects us. Mildness is the face of moderation, which avoids advancing heady claims of either virtue or sovereignty.

Montesquieu therefore turns from such claims to the laws that actually provide security, always remembering that security is an opinion, not necessarily an objective condition that may override opinion. "It is on the goodness of criminal laws that the liberty of the citizen principally depends" (XII.2). Montesquieu sorts crimes into those that shock religion, mores, tranquillity, and security, and he proceeds to look at the first three in terms of the fourth.[29] We are not surprised that he dwells on the crime of *lèse-majesté*, which results from sovereign claims, human and divine (XII.7–18). This is the crime of offending a higher power, particularly with one's speech. Montesquieu opposes higher powers that tyrannize men, but he needs one himself, indeed he needs a *principle* apart from virtue, as a standard against which to measure criminal laws. That principle is security, the desire for self-preservation in the form of opinion. Security is not "offended" by speech or thought, but crimes against security have to be understood as *lèse-majesté* precisely because Montesquieu cannot prove that any principle is above human law. Security is violated or offended only by what opposes human advantage, or by what is contradictory in our arrangements for it.[30] Montesquieu does not speak of the social contract as the origin and guarantee of security, for as we have seen in Hobbes and Locke, the social contract begins and ends with a fearful executive action by the people.

Book XII of *The Spirit of the Laws,* on the political liberty of the citizen, considers the problem of will in the constitution of reason: specifically, he asks, how will the rational conclusions as to right *(droit)* agree with citizens in fact *(fait)*? Montesquieu has to substitute his own treatment of will for the self-denying restraint of ancient virtue that issues in the harsh punishments denounced in Book VI. Human will cannot simply deny itself, as in ancient virtue, nor can it simply be denied from outside by the "blind fatality" of modern philosophy (I.1). Rather, Montesquieu must show how the mechanism of the rational constitution comes to terms with human will, which resists being reduced to mechanical responses. His answer is, that it comes to terms insensibly by degrees. Since the constitution is not made by a founder, it need not be reformed by one; it changes by correcting or corrupting itself (XI.13). But lest "corrupting" seem too harsh a judgment or suggest a sensational Machiavellian renewal, Montesquieu defines it amorally as a loss of animating principles. Mildness, then, is the means as well as the end of politics, which seeks to reconcile reason and will.

After Book XII on the will of the citizen, Montesquieu presents a series of Books, XIII–XVIII, considering the relationship between liberty and slavery, or between human will and its constraints. By Book XIX he is ready to speak of the laws and principles forming the general spirit, mores, and manners of a nation. Mores and manners are distinct from laws; mores refer to the interior and manners to the exterior conduct of men as men, and not citizens. The natural way to improve mores and manners is not by violence, through laws, but mildly, through mores and manners themselves (XIX.14, 16, 21). For this one must respect the general spirit of a nation—not the willfulness of human nature in general, but its collective manifestation in particular nations, each possessing a distinctive general spirit.

Here is the culmination of Montesquieu's political science, at the point where the philosopher-legislator has shown how the mechanism of the free constitution mechanically, yet freely, sets itself in motion. But we are only at the end of Part I; Part II begins with a meditation on commerce, which Montesquieu considers the motive force behind both freedom and moderation, and continues with an historical account of the mechanism of progress. At the start of Book XX he salutes his readers with an invocation to the muses, a poem of his own. The self-executing constitution needs to be set to work with a flick of its author's finger.

In XIX.27 Montesquieu returns to the English constitution as his example of how the laws contribute to forming the mores, manners, and character of a nation. This example illustrates the constitution of reason in motion, as compared with the static view of XI.6. We are told that for the constitution to work, it does not matter whether individuals reason well or ill; it is enough that they reason. They become partisans "to give effect to their independence as they please." This is precisely the independence of will earlier distinguished from political liberty (XI.3), and set aside as "philosophical liberty" (XII.2).[31] It appears that the constitution of reason must contend with the reasoning of its citizens as partisans, wherein "each [regards] himself as a monarch." Such citizens are neither cowed nor calm, as they might be if they had used their reason to consent to a sovereign (Hobbes), or to constitute the legislative power (Locke). They have no loyalty to the constitution as a whole, and they are brimming with partisan hatreds and fears, passions to which their reason is a minister. Apparently, Montesquieu has a Machiavellian appreciation for the nature of parties in a free state.[32]

Montesquieu's description of the parties, however, is more familiar to us than Machiavelli's because Montesquieu constitutionalizes them. Instead of the nobles *versus* the plebs, whose contest Machiavelli described in classical terms, Montesquieu speaks of parties that collect around the two visible powers in the constitution—the legislative and the executive. Like Machiavelli, he praises the vigor of partisan passions; a state without them would be like a man overcome with sickness who has no passions because he has no strength. But unlike Machiavelli, Montesquieu does not try to quiet partisan hatreds with the fear induced by occasional, sensational executions. The hatred between the parties will last, he says, because it is always impotent: if one party gets on top, it would soon be brought down as citizens rally to raise up the other. Hatred is impotent, his reasoning suggests, because citizens can be relied on to be more active in frustrating or "preventing" the other party than in promoting or "enacting" their own view. And each individual, feeling himself independent, will often change parties, forsaking his friends and binding himself to his enemies. Rather than authorize or support a sovereign, he can be expected to desert any party that seems likely to gain sovereignty.

Montesquieu preserves the negativity of human naysaying in his free constitution; he does not attempt to transform it and make it responsible for a positive course. Living by one's own will consists not in imposing it on others but in denying the imposition of others' wills. Freedom consists in impotence, not in power. It is more satisfying to say, "You can't boss me around!" than it is to actually boss others around. When united in a free society, such individuals regard themselves as monarchs and are rather "confederates" than "fellow-citizens." It follows that the opinion of security established by a free constitution leaves the people, paradoxically, in constant unrest. They believe themselves in danger when they are really most secure, since only

245

then are they free to imagine false terrors. But false terrors contribute to avoiding true perils. The people therefore forestall the perils by exaggerating their fears; they gain security, in other words, by freely expressing a false opinion of it.

Impotent hatred, false fears: Montesquieu has adopted Machiavelli's popular humor as his own and thus tamed Machiavelli's prince. The executive has become one partisan representative of the people—no longer is it a nonpartisan, discretionary check on legislative will, as in Locke. Since in Montesquieu nothing (or everything) is extraconstitutional, the executive has lost its link to executive power in the state of nature. The partisan, representative executive is both more perfectly constitutional and more reliably self-executing than the natural prerogative held by Locke's executive—not to mention Machiavelli's prince.

10

Republicanizing the Executive

From its conception in Machiavelli's prince, the modern executive has been implicitly republican or popular: Machiavelli's prince followed a policy of winning over the people; Hobbes's sovereign was authorized by all; Locke's executive power was derived from each man's natural executive power, and in civil society corrected the legislative in the interest of preserving all its members; Montesquieu's executive satisfies the people's desire for security, along with their appetite for partisanship. But the American president is expressly and publicly republican, as opposed to popular or anti-aristocratic merely in policy. He is elected by the people, hence republican; and he is a single executive with ample powers not elected by the legislature, hence strong. The American president can handle emergencies, but he is not an emergency device, like the Roman dictator and the Florentine *balìa*;[1] he can provide energy and unity but is not an alien monarchical element like the Roman consul, Venetian doge, or Cromwellian Protector.

In sum, the American Constitution establishes the first republic with a strong executive that is consistent with republicanism. Here the theory of the executive emerges from the shadows cast by existing or previous practice. The American president is neither a revived Roman dictator nor a moderated British monarch; he is one main feature of a new experiment in self-government which will attempt to found the first successful republic. The novelty of the executive, dating from Machiavelli's ''new modes and orders,'' now becomes fully explicit in a new office of a new republic. The theory had of course been intended from the first to

247

be applied in practice and to produce the great benefits expected of a new style of indirect government. But now the theory has, if not an incarnation, a formal embodiment in an office. No longer merely a theory created for practice, executive power becomes a theory in practice—an office consciously understood and variously interpreted by the presidents holding it. With that development, the theorist's responsibility for his creation is quickly and smoothly assumed by the practitioner. After the transfer has occurred, it is possible to forget that it even took place.

The new office of president was framed in the Constitutional convention of 1787; it was explained and justified shortly afterwards in *The Federalist*, on which I shall rely to prove its novelty. We know what the Framers did and what *The Federalist* said; but what is the relationship between deed and word? In my study of the doctrine of executive power, I cannot attempt to perform the historian's task of discovering what influenced the Framers; I have tried to show what existing doctrine was available to them and I shall try to show what new doctrine they produced. Up to now, I believe, the historian has performed his office without full awareness of the nature of executive power or the history of its doctrine. Above all, the origin of executive power in Machiavelli is unknown; hence the need to look for Machiavelli's influence among the constitutionalist writers where one would least expect to find it is unappreciated.

Only when the tradition of thinking about executive power is better known will the question of its presence or absence at the Constitutional convention become more clear. Full understanding is probably impossible: common deliberation on a practical matter, even one so comprehensive as a constitution, is not a theoretical inquiry. The issues most discussed (for example, the "Great Compromise" between the large and the small states) are often not the most important, because they have involved securing consent to the Constitution rather than the question of how it will operate, while the reasons offered in discussion are often those intended to persuade others, not those that persuaded the speaker. One suspects Madison, for example, of deferring to Edmund Randolph in his apparent hesitation over the value of a strong executive at the beginning of the Convention.[2] One may also be persuaded by a reason that one does not fully understand at the time. And a later explanation from the principals involved may be simply a rationalization in which one boasts of having known what he was doing—the usual assumption of historians; or it may truly supply the meaning of an action as time reveals its implications.[3]

I believe *The Federalist* is of this latter characrter. It is surely a partisan document, but it is partisan for a Constitution, not merely for a transient issue of the day. There is a higher and a lower sense of "partisan"—the responsible partisan versus the one who seeks his own advantage. Although *The Federalist* does not record the hesitations of the Framers over the executive, and the long process of coming to agreement, it does report the principal difficulty. This was the "idea . . . that a vigorous executive is inconsistent with the genius of republican government" (*Federalist* 70). Knowing this, we can make sense of Madison's insufficiently explained remark, in a letter to Jefferson after the convention, that the executive was a "peculiarly embarrassing" subject for the Framers.[4]

We are also not surprised to learn that the two main proposals for a constitution submitted for discussion at the beginning of the convention, the Virginia plan and the New Jersey plan, provided for a weak executive as though it were required by the genius of republican government. The Virginia plan proposed an executive elected by the legislature but not eligible for reelection, with authority to execute the laws (and somewhat more), and leaving the number of executive, single or plural, unspecified. The New Jersey plan offered a plural executive, elected and removable by a congress, and not eligible for reelection. It was not until nearly the end of the convention that a strong executive independent of the legislature was decided upon, though most of the Framers were searching throughout for ways to accomplish just that.[5] Far from distorting the work of the convention by giving a false impression of unanimity, *The Federalist* enables us to understand why the Framers found a strong, republican executive to be "peculiarly embarrassing."

In the course of the eleven papers Alexander Hamilton (as Publius) wrote in *The Federalist* on the executive (67–77), he says briskly that "a government ill executed, whatever it may be in theory, must be, in practice, a bad government" (*Federalist* 70).[6] The executive, it seems, is sovereign in the realm where practice is not subject to theory—where, if strength is not always good, feebleness is bad. We may recall that the best modern commentator on the executive—Richard Neustadt—had also located it in a region far removed from the "literary theory" of the Constitution. Yet it was precisely in regard to the executive that the Constitution was most in need of the theorizing of political science, and most indebted to it.

Publius implies that, in theory, government might have a feeble executive. The theory he had in mind was republican theory, ever hostile to anything smacking of monarchy, and never stronger than among Americans who had just fought themselves to independence from a King. As historians have shown, Americans had come to recognize during the course of the Revolutionary War that the executives they had instituted in the states in 1776 were too weak.[7] After the war, the national government under the Articles of Confederation had also shown itself to be weak not only in domestic crises like Shays' Rebellion but especially in facing hostile actions from foreign powers, such as the taking of hostages by the Bey of Algeria. Such weakness suggested, as John Jay remarked to Thomas Jefferson, the lack of an executive capable of secrecy and swift response.[8] But American republicanism seemed to offer no remedy, and left Americans bewildered at the claim of fact against their notions of legitimacy. The task of political science in *The Federalist* was to show that an energetic executive could be republicanized. That we take the completion of the task for granted today is a sign that it was well done, not that it was superfluous.

Publius and the Republican Tradition

Earlier in *The Federalist* (Nos. 6, 9, 10, 14), Publius had scathingly criticized all previous republics, including the celebrated republics of the ancient world, for the alternating anarchy and tyranny of their popular majorities. In *Federalist* 10 he formulated the sorry experience as the problem of majority faction and proposed, as the basis for a solution, to "extend the sphere" of the republic, and thus to overthrow the republican prejudice in favor of a close, homogeneous people and against imperial size. An extended sphere, however, requires an energetic government at the center to "preserve the Union of so large an empire" (*Federalist* 23); so the republican prejudice against energetic government must also be abandoned, together with that against diversity and size. And what is energetic government but an energetic *executive*?

250

Publius does not at first make clear that the American people must give up their instinctive hostility, not only to the imperial size that often goes with monarchy, but also to the very idea, to the actual person, of one-man rule. He says that the "great and radical vice" of the Articles of Confederation is the principle of legislating for states in their collective capacities rather than for the individuals within them (*Federalist* 15). He explains patiently that a law is not a law without a sanction, and concludes that we have a choice between coercion by the magistracy ("the courts and ministers of justice") and coercion by the military—thus presenting civil sanctions, while not mentioning "executive power," as the alternative to "military execution." Since coercion is necessary, be glad, he seems to say to republicans, that it is civil coercion. "The measures of the Union have not been executed," and a new constitution is needed to do so.

Publius remarks on the effect that good administration has in bringing the people to become attached to, not merely to obey, their government. Executive administration is a "great cement of society" (*Federalist* 17). The state governments now have the advantage here, but the national government may in time win over the hearts of citizens by a better performance. Publius displays the concern of modern theorists for an effective executive, but in his own way. Contrary to what Machiavelli says, the people will be impressed more by steady administration than by sensational examples; and contrary to Hobbes, Locke, and the republicans, the people's consent to obey is not effective enough. They must like their government, rather merely obey it, if it is to be effective. And they will like it more for its good administration than because it is derived from their consent. Publius elevates the modern demand for results to a requirement of good performance. Thus the Machiavellian "effectual truth" by which government is judged need not require or excuse criminal deeds. The stage is set for a new kind of responsibility in executives—constitutional and republican.

The necessity of union having been shown, Publius considers in the series *Federalist* 23–26 how much power is necessary to the union, and upon whom that power should be exercised. But he saves for a later series the consideration, which is almost the disclosure, of *by* whom that power should be exercised. In this early section he appeals to necessity and to the recent history of the union under the Articles of Confederation—an experience of necessity—against the "idea of governing at all times by the simple force of law" (*Federalist* 28). The idea, which Publius identifies as republican, "has no place but in the reveries of those political doctors whose sagacity disdains the admonitions of experimental instruction." Again, Publius draws no pointed conclusion recommending an energetic executive; he only prepares the way by reminding his readers of the force of necessity. In the language of the "necessary and proper" clause of the Constitution, even laws are the means of *executing* the legislative power (*Federalist* 33).[9]

It seems to be a particular characteristic of republican sagacity that it is impervious to the instruction of necessity.[10] The long, sad, horrifying experience of republics has taught republican theorists nothing, it appears; for though they write at length of Sparta, Rome, and Venice, they look for remedies in details and have not absorbed any general lesson about necessity. Their influence readily confirms the partisan prejudices of republican peoples who are hostile to monarchy, and remain heedless of all experience but the recent cause of that hostility. It sometimes seems that for *The Federalist*, republican theory causes nothing but trouble for republics, and that nothing else causes more trouble. At the least, it must be clear that its impervious sagacity cannot be refuted by experience alone, that it must be met on its own level as theory, and that executive power in the American Constitution, though mainly preoccupied with the demands of necessity, did not arise simply in response to practical necessity.[11] Peoples generally, and especially those instructed by republican doctors, do not respond automatically to what seems necessary to later generations gifted with hindsight. But the creation of executive power was made possible, indeed it was created, by a recognition—new to republican theory and contrary to previous republican theorists—of the power of necessity. As we have seen with Harrington, republican theorists could be devoted to Machiavelli without taking his main point.[12] They did not see that Machiavelli's republicanism was neither partisan nor anti-monarchical, but eager to use princes for the purpose of acquisition. Publius recognizes necessity, but does not draw the Machiavellian conclusion. As we shall see, this recognition does not become an excuse for doing ill, but an incentive for doing better than what is merely necessary.

When Publius does approach the matter of *by* whom necessary power was to be exercised, he admits that he has to face the "aversion of the people to monarchy" (*Federalist* 67). Hardly any part of the Constitution ("the system") was more difficult to arrange than the executive, he says, and perhaps none has been criticized with less judgment. Then he denounces the misrepresentation of the critics and exposes one flagrant, but typical, example of it.[13] Neither the section of *The Federalist* on the legislature nor that on the judiciary begins with a comparable blast at the Anti-Federalist critics of the Constitution, and we are easily led to suppose that the difficulty in arranging the executive arose principally from the same source as the criticism of the result: "that maxim of republican jealousy which considers power as safer in the hands of a number of men than of a single man" (*Federalist* 70). Publius could and did appeal to politicians and statesmen celebrated for their sound principles and just views, who have "declared in favor of a single executive and a numerous legislature" (*Federalist* 70). But these are identified neither as republican nor, though they may consist of men like Locke, Hume, and Montesquieu, as theorists.

A quick look at the Anti-Federalist critics of the new executive reveals the obstacle Publius had to confront. At the Constitutional Convention Edmund Randolph had pronounced a single executive to be "the foetus of monarchy,"[14] and Luther Martin, another non-signing framer of the Constitution, declared that the president could, when he pleased, become King in name as well as substance.[15] During the ratification debates, comparison of the American president to the British King became an Anti-Federalist theme. Cato, whom Publius attacked in *Federalist* 67, asked how the president, with his powers and prerogatives, essentially differed from the King of Great Britain; and Tamony, the target of a footnote in *Federalist* 69, asserted that the president will "possess more supreme power than Great Britain allows her hereditary monarchs."[16] Some recognition of the need for an executive of such power could be found in the lesser-known Cato of South Carolina, but with the requirement that it be held for a short term without reelection.[17] The Federal Farmer, praised in *Federalist* 68 as the most plausible of the Constitution's opponents, conceded that "in every large collection of people there must be a visible point serving as a common center in the government, toward which to draw their eyes and attachments," but—or therefore—insisted on the ineligibility of the president for reelection.[18] Thus, when the Anti-Federalists were not railing against monarchy, they were relunctantly bowing to it.[19] They had no way to justify it as republican.[20]

Nonetheless, despite these loud fears (and quiet concessions), bullheaded (or bewildered) republicanism was not merely an obstacle to the framing and the ratification of the Constitution. It provided the animating spirit and determined the general character of the new government. *The Federalist*, after all, is preoccupied with the diseases of republicanism because it has chosen republicanism.[21] On the first page of *The Federalist*, Publius adopts an opinion frequently heard, as he says, that Americans will decide, by their conduct and example, whether mankind is capable of establishing good government from reflection and choice, or whether it must always depend on accident and force. Good government by reflection and choice cannot help but be republican, for if the people are not sovereign, good government must depend on the accident of a good monarch or aristocracy to rule them well—and probably against their will, by force. But popular sovereignty should not be understood here in the traditional sense of a government ruled directly by the people. The Constitution differs from traditional republicanism by being wholly representative or wholly elective. This means that although all parts of government are derived from the people, they are also *withdrawn* from them. No part of the government, such as a popular assembly, *is* the people (*Federalist* 63). By choosing representative government, the people choose to limit themselves; they choose not to govern themselves directly, but instead to have a government whose working is determined as much by its internal structure as by its dependence on the people—thus they choose to have a constitution. For representative government without a constitution would merely be an awkward delegation from direct democracy, liable on any difficult occasion to succumb to the evils of direct democracy.

Yet the Constitution remains definitely republican because it is "wholly popular" (*Federalist* 14, 39). All its branches are derived from the people, not just the "lower" house of the legislature. All branches reflect the people's choice through elections. And no favored class with a greater sense of honor or a superior faculty of reasoning than theirs is postulated and endowed with power to check the people's choice. The American Constitution is not a mixed constitution giving different classes separate powers, nor does it make any concessions to this idea (as did John

Locke and Montesquieu) by accepting, while modifying, traditional institutions not based on consent, such as the British monarchy and House of Lords. Nor was the American Constitution a
government formed by a single act of consent, as in Hobbes's
theory, wherein the people's "choice" is made once and for all,
with no possibility of change or specification. A single consent
of this kind is more submission than choice. The Constitution is
republican because it rests on the capacity of *mankind* in general,
not on that of any particular class or race, for self-government.

Yet the people would not choose to limit themselves in a constitution if there were not difficulties in their choosing. A choice to
limit choice implies potential trouble in what is typically chosen.
Traditional or primitive republicanism, with its dependence on
a small territory, a homogeneous people, and cultivated virtues,
exaggerates the possible extent of human choice. The task of "reflection" (in Publius's phrase, "reflection and choice") is to take
account of things in nature and in the realm of chance that cannot
be chosen, and to match them with things that can. A republic
might prefer to live in isolation under a homogeneous majority,
and imbued with virtues to keep it moderate. But a regard to the
necessities of international relations, and of human nature generally, will demonstrate that these desirable things are often beyond
choosing. Reflection, then, in the form of political science, will
teach a republic not to choose what is abstractly most choiceworthy, but to be content with, or indeed make the best of, a large
territory, a diverse people,and a spirit of interest and ambition.

It is characteristic of the American Constitution, by contrast to
republican tradition, to *constitutionalize* necessities in the manner
of Locke. Those necessities limiting our choice, which we would
like to wish away, are brought into the Constitution so that the
people, through their government, can choose how to deal with
them after having anticipated the necessity of doing so. That is
how reflection enables choice to contend with "accident and
force," which cannot in fact be removed from human affairs. Traditional republicanism might admit as much, but still choose to
keep its republican faith intact and take its chances with events
even if that faith were frequently frustrated. Such a choice would
account for the strength of republican faith despite the disasters
of republican experience. But the Constitution constitutionalizes
the necessities of republican experience—and in no respect more
obviously than in the executive. In its "energy" or quickness, the

executive deals more than any other branch with the accidents and force that may thwart or disturb republican choice. By dealing with such necessities, the executive actually represents them in the Constitution. The provision for a strong executive thus reflects a realistic recognition by the people, in ratifying the Constitution and electing a President, that emergencies will arise that may confound their choices.

The essential distinction, then, in *The Federalist*, as spelled out in *Federalist* 9, 10, and 14, is the distinction between a democracy and a republic. A democracy is "pure" democracy (or it could be a mixed republic) when it is small, homogeneous, and (it hopes) virtuous; a republic is large, diverse, and ambitious. A republic represents the necessities of being large, diverse, and ambitious in its constitution; in a word, it *constitutionalizes* the necessities. *The Federalist* appropriates the name "republic" from the republican tradition, then reassigns it the less respectable name of "democracy," which tends to be dominated by "demagogues." Publius agrees with Montesquieu's critique of ancient republics, but by calling them democracies he saves the reputation of republics and applies this good name to the government framed by the Constitution. The deliberate theft can perhaps be justified if *The Federalist* shows that by constitutionalizing the limits to republican choice, it has improved republican choice, and is thus entitled to sole possession of the name.[22] This it does by arguing that the virtuous majorities in which traditional republicanism puts its faith are often factious in deed, and are always potentially so. Thus the people's choice in such republics amounts only to the people's will or ruling passions. The purpose of the Constitution is to transform the people's will both by settling it into a determined intent (a "cool and deliberate sense," *Federalist* 63) and by elevating it from whim to deliberate choice. Such is the work of reason, and it is "the reason, alone, of the public that ought to control and regulate the government. The passions ought to be controlled and regulated by the government" (*Federalist* 49). Madison specifies the reason of the *public*, not of philosopher kings, as that which ought to prevail.[23] He therefore remains a republican, but a better, more sophisticated one than the primitive republicans or democrats who invite anarchy and tyranny with their reliance on popular will, or their trust in virtue too weak to restrain popular passion.

Republican choice is improved by the same forms in the Constitution that represent, or constitutionalize, necessities. Through the elections of representatives, the legislature not only distances itself from the people's momentary inclinations but also calls forth the people's virtue (it does exist there) and sets it to work (*Federalist* 55, 57). Similarly, the Senate is both a "salutary check" on government and a source of positive virtues, such as firmness, wisdom, stability, responsibility, and a sense of national character (*Federalist* 62–63). Meanwhile the judiciary uses its independence not only to remove partisan choice from criminal justice but to ensure, through judicial review, that the legislature—and the people themselves—keep to the fundamental law they have chosen (*Federalist* 78).

But it is especially in the executive that republican choice acquires new capability. For the executive not only makes decisions in emergencies as one ingredient of "energy," but also, as another ingredient, supplies the consistency in administration that makes possible "extensive and arduous enterprises" (*Federalist* 72). Such enterprises are familiar to us today as the long-term programs of legislation and administration—the New Deal, the Reagan Revolution—which always have their origin in the executive branch. Precisely the branch that most recognizes the limits to human choice arising from emergencies, also best extends human choice in the capability to set a general direction for policy now and in the future.[24] An able executive will improve upon the occasions of his decision. He will make his quick reactions consistent with his general program, so that his quickness is not merely willful but somehow adheres to his lasting intent.

The Federalist, then, constitutionalizes the republican tradition. By finding a place for the necessities of government within the framework of government itself, the Constitution corrects the foolish optimism of republicanism which thinks, in essence, that men can live by the laws they choose and never have to bow to the necessities they do not choose, or learn from their experience of them. But in teaching republicans to bow to the necessities represented especially in the need for executive power, *The Federalist* also shows them how to choose better, because more lastingly, while not departing from the republican principle that all government should be derived from the people. Thus it teaches republicans to be better republicans.

257

Publius and the Separation of Powers

To teach republicans about executive power, the Framers had to borrow from the constitutional tradition of Locke and Montesquieu. But in that tradition, executive power was not "strictly republican." Rather, it was still held by an hereditary monarch though perhaps advised, as in Britain, by ministers selected from the House of Commons. If the Constitution was to borrow the British monarchy as understood in the constitutional tradition for its executive, it was necessary not only to limit monarchy but also to republicanize it. In *The Federalist* we see the republican tradition constitutionalized and the constitutional tradition republicanized. A brief comparison with Locke, the founder (because he was the conceiver) of the modern executive power, will make the point clear. Just as *The Federalist* makes better republicans by constitutionalizing republicanism, so it improves the Constitution by republicanizing it.

In Locke's constitution we have seen two supreme powers, one representing law, the other representing extralegal discretion. Locke leaves the two powers in open, unresolved conflict, and since the legislative power appeals to Whig republican sentiment and the executive to Tory regard for prerogative, one might conclude that Locke has imported a moderated but still lively version of the English civil war into his constitution. Indeed, as the party of discretionary prerogative, the executive is not altogether within the constitution. For in Locke's conception, the constitution goes only so far as law extends. There is no fundamental or constitutional law above ordinary law; hence the prerogative power of the executive can be exercised as much against the constitution when necessary as against the law. Locke's constitution attempts to contain a power that admittedly cannot be contained. The executive is limited only by the end for which it is entrusted by the people, which is the public good as they interpret it.

Such an arrangement can be criticized from the standpoint of *The Federalist*. To allow a prerogative power so defined is to set the public good as a standard *against* the constitution; it is to make the constitution "self-critical." Locke thus implies that the constitution is merely a means to the public good, not a part of it. He thereby encourages in the public, perhaps against his intent, an instrumental attitude toward the constitution hardly compatible with the "veneration" that even a republican constitution cannot do without (*Federalist* 49).[25] Moreover, he leaves no place in the constitution for the executive's program, a combination of law and discretion in which the choice of legislation is guided by a long-term choice of policy. No doubt there will be parties such as Montesquieu foresaw, gathered around the executive and the legislative powers as they conflict. But it does not seem wise to permit one of them, the party of prerogative, to continue as an extra-constitutional party and the other, the republican, to regard the constitution as its own.

For *The Federalist*, the political situation was different because America had no Tory party defending prerogative. But as we have seen, it was necessary to face the truth in the argument for prerogative (which in Locke was to be the need for extralegal discretion as distinguished from divine right). To do so by setting law and prerogative against one another would have the further disadvantage, in the view of *The Federalist*, of not overcoming but actually aggravating republican distrust of the executive. It would confirm their conviction, ironically shared with their Tory opponents, that energy is inconsistent with the genius of republican government.[26]

The strategy adopted by *The Federalist* of republicanizing the executive through election brings the dispute between law and prerogative into the Constitution: it does not end that dispute, but it makes both parties to it republican. The consequence is to improve the contitutionalism of Locke's constitution. Without denying the need for something like a prerogative power, that need may not be satisfied outside the Constitution.[27] This does not mean that the Constitution will not become an issue in the conflict between the two powers, but it does ensure that both sides can cite the Constitution on their own behalf. *The Federalist* preserves Montesquieu's improvement on Locke's constitution, so that both the executive and the legislative parties are constitutional. But by contrast with Montesquieu, *The Federalist* combines a constitutional executive with the principle of popular sovereignty. The new constitutional executive is thus openly republican, and Montesquieu's England, a disguised republic, is replaced as the model for free government by America, an avowedly republican experiment.

So Publius is not concerned merely with the abuse of power, whether by the government or by the people. Such an experiment in the capacity of mankind for self-government requires a positive attitude toward virtue in the capacity of the use of power. Indeed, it suggests that abuse of power is as much a sign of weakness and incompetence as of ruthless skill in tyranny. American's most recent experience under the Articles of Confederation has produced no Napoleons, but a number of good men, endowed with talent and virtue, had been frustrated and disgusted. Tyranny must be prevented, but not by choking off virtue. Montesquieu, who said that even virtue has it limits, has constructed a constitution aimed at preventing the abuse of power, one that moved with the nature of things: in short, a mechanism. Following Montesquieu, Blackstone made the point explicitly: "Like three distinct powers in mechanics, [the branches] jointly impel the machine of government in a direction different from what either, acting by itself, would have done; but at the same time in a direction partaking of each, and formed out of all; a direction which constitutes the true line of the liberty and happiness of the community."[28]

But the American Constitution is not such a mechanism, according to *The Federalist*. Those who say it is have taken *Federalist* 10 and 51 for the whole of the work and have also mistaken the mechanistic aspect of those papers. Setting *Federalist* 10 aside, I shall make a few remarks (guided by William Kristol) on *Federalist* 47–51, where Publius discusses the separation of powers in general before undertaking the study of each particular power.[29]

Here Publius defends the Constitution against the Anti-Federalist charge that it violates the maxim of free government that the three powers ought to be separate and distinct. It turns out that "separate" and "distinct" are two different elements of the problem. Keeping the powers separate presupposes that they have first been distributed as distinct. But Publius does not explain or justify this prior distribution in *Federalist* 47–51, and in the later papers on the powers in particular he again does not say directly what legislating, executing, and judging are, though he makes one valuable remark in *Federalist* 78. In *Federalist* 37 he says that "no skill in the science of Government has yet been able to discriminate and define, with sufficient certainty, its three great provinces, the Legislative, Executive and Judiciary," but in *Federalist* 48 he speaks of "discriminating . . . in theory the several classes of power" as if this could be done. The most difficult task, he says, is to keep the powers separate by giving them practical security against invasion by the others. But perhaps, as Kristol suggests in keeping with *Federalist* 37, the real trick would be to discriminate the powers in theory.[30]

As we look back on our theorists, we can see that none after Aristotle succeeds in distinctly defining the functions of the three powers. In Aristotle we do find a distinct separation between deliberation and judging, with "offices" in-between. Deliberation is choosing, hence engaging in politics and taking responsibility for one's actions. Judging, to the contrary, means disengaging from politics in order to call these choices to account. Judging presupposes a standard—the law, or, ultimately, nature. But for the modern theorists, the standard of judgment becomes the necessity that determines choice. Nature does not enable us to judge how well we have done, but in her aspect of necessity she robs us of choice and compels us to act decisively. Then, since we had no choice, no one can pass judgment on the event. When Aristotle's deliberation becomes Machiavelli's decision (*diliberazione*), the deed anticipates necessity and covers over subsequent judgment; men learn to "look to the end" and to judge by success. The laws are subordinated to the will that makes laws, and that will wants to be decisive, though always in obedience to necessity. The ambivalent executive, willful yet obedient, takes over from the deliberative legislator and takes with him the sober judge. Thus the three powers converge in the power to execute, or rather, in the act of executing.

As against this Machiavellian convergence, Hobbes, Locke, and Montesquieu attempt to resurrect the laws, or the law-making power, as supreme. But in practice the sovereign turns out to be the one who has executive power. When Locke and Montesquieu try to separate the executive from the legislative, to prevent tyranny in the legislature, they run into difficulty. Locke sets up a contest for supremacy between the legislative power, representing human willfulness, and the executive power, representing necessity. But since the laws aim at anticipating necessity and the executive acts willfully to remind men of necessity, it is hard to see how legislating and executing can be distinct functions. If the constitution fails, the people shall be judge, and they may exercise their right to alter or abolish the constitution and institute a new one.

But what would be the basis of this popular judgment? Merely an opinion about what is politically necessary, no different in character from those of the legislative and executive powers. As opposed to the trial for supremacy staged by Locke, Montesquieu arranges a defensive contest between these powers to prevent invasion of one by the other, like that in *The Federalist*. Montesquieu then separates the judicial power from the executive, but he does not elevate the law to serve as its standard; his judging is done, as it were, by juries—Locke's extra-constitutional people brought piecemeal into the constitution. The standard for the three powers is the same, an avowedly subjective opinion of security. How then can they be defined as distinct?

Publius shares the modern doubt that any solid basis for Aristotle's distinction between deliberating and judging can be found. Judging is merely another choosing, because men are not capable, or not reliably so, of the required detachment from their own interests and necessities. Judging is a political surrogate for philosophy, and philosophy or "skill in the science of government" cannot find a standard in nature by which to judge human partisanship without sharing in it. To deprecate the power of judicial review in the Supreme Court, Publius in *Federalist* 78 makes a distinction in function between judgment and will; but that distinction, apparently, cannot be established in science.[31] Or perhaps the monarchical implication of virtue that Aristotle brings to light in his theory of kingship cannot be stated openly in an argument addressed to republicans.

Thus the separation of powers in *The Federalist* must be advanced without the prior demonstration that the powers are distinct, that is, without the Aristotelian kingship of virtue that grounds their distinctiveness. Simply assuming that the powers are distinct, Publius explains how to keep them separate, which requires giving them a will of their own, and then powers of self-defense against encroachment by the other branches of government. Such additional powers—inventions of prudence rather than political science, according to *Federalist* 51—will necessarily embroil them with these other branches. Separation thus compels involvement, just as Montesquieu predicted. Since the legislative branch will usually predominate in a republic, the executive must be "fortified" with non-executive powers like the veto. Locke, too, fortified his executive, but more for the sake of prudent discretion than to keep him equal to the legislature. *The Federalist*, we shall see, gets executive discretion without expressly asking for it.

262

The principle of separated powers is stated in a famous formulation that seems to describe a mechanism: "Ambition must be made to counteract ambition. The interest of the man must be connected with the constitutional rights of the place" (*Federalist* 51). Note that interest is identified here with ambition, even though the risks of ambition are not necessarily in one's interest. Note, too, that the constitutional office is *connected* to the interest of the man, not *determined* by it. Ambition must be accommodated but at the same time it must be appealed to. And ambition does not answer the appeal automatically but is called forth by rival ambition. Ambition is more like a knight answering a challenge than a merchant seeking gain.[32]

"The constitutional rights of the place" form the interest of an ambitious person into a specific shape, so that he wants to be a good Senator, Congressman, or President, and not merely to gain more money or "utility" in general. But the office only forms and appeals to his desire to excel; it does not guarantee, in the manner of an economic incentive, that he performs it well. Publius describes the approach as one of "supplying by opposite and rival interests the defect of better motives." Opposite and rival interests are not private economic interests, though they are also not the best motives. To understand the passage one must not only consider office in the light of interest but also interest in the light of office. Publius does not appeal to virtue, wary as he is of virtue in both republican and aristocratic form. But he also avoids reliance on the base motives of greed and vanity as well as common gain.

Whereas for Blackstone separation of powers is a mechanism giving direction to government unintended by any of the powers, and for Montesquieu it is a mechanism without direction but moving with the movement of nature, in *The Federalist* it is a structure that serves in the first place as an "auxiliary precaution" to dependence on the people for controlling the government. For the purpose of control it has the aspect of a mechanism, though it does not work with mechanical certainty. But separation of powers has another purpose—to appeal to virtue. Powers that are separated in order to control each other are thereby withdrawn from the people, as we have seen: to use ambition one must allow it to operate, hence one must loosen republican constraints on it.[33] When Publius comes to describe the particular powers, especially the executive, we shall see that the mechanism of separated powers gives opportunity to virtue as much as it supplies the lack of virtue.

The Office of the President

Publius begins his treatment of the executive power in the Constitution[34] with a discussion of its mode of election, which is its republican character (*Federalist* 68). Publius describes the mode of election in a beautiful distinction as "if not perfect, at least excellent." It has not been criticized, he notes. We, however, cannot help but be aware that it has not lasted either, and soon had to be revised in the Twelfth Amendment, because parties took over the designation of presidential candidates and mounted "campaigns" to elect them. Nonetheless, it is worth considering what and how much was expected from the mode of election.

Avoiding any mention of what might be necessary, Publius speaks only of what is "desirable" in the choice of the president. It was "desirable that the sense of the people should operate in the choice": no more than the *sense* of the people (which is ambiguous—their good sense or their general sentiment?) and no more than *operate*. So much for the sovereignty of the people; this is to be a republican government unlike all previous republics—one in which the people choose not to be sovereign. But the realistic alternative to the electoral college in 1787 was not direct election of the president, which had been proposed in the Constitutional convention by Gouverneur Morris but voted down after receiving little support.[35] The realistic alternative—election by the Congress—was meant to render the executive subordinate to the legislature. Such dependency, required by classical republican theory, was a feature of both the Virginia and the New Jersey plans in the Constitutional Convention. In Publius's satisfaction with the new Constitution's mode of election, no trace remains of the long and difficult debate in the Convention by which delegates were brought to see the necessity of a president made independent of the Congress by his own connection to the people.[36] In 1787 (and for us today) it was significant not that the president's election was indirect, but that the election was conducted by the president's own Electoral College and not by Congress. The Constitution does provide that the House of Representatives (voting by states) will choose a president among candidates who have failed to receive a majority in the Electoral College, and opponents of a strong, independent executive in 1787 may have believed that the provision would operate frequently.[37] But if so, they were deluded, and in any case the process of election would prevent domination of the president by Congress.

It was equally desirable, Publius continues, that the immediate election of the president be made by capable men in circumstances favorable to deliberation; it should not be made by the people either dispersed or gathered in assemblies. This mode of election is a "process" of two stages, wherein the people choose the choosers who meet once for that purpose only. Such a process has the negative virtue of preventing or combatting the tumult and corruption typical of republics when they have finally had to admit their need for one-man rule. The American Constitution anticipates the need by a regular process which also has the positive virtue of providing a better choice. It affords the "moral certainty"[38] that a president will have more than "talents for low intrigue and the little arts of popularity." These arts might gain him the election in a single state, that is, in a small republic, but not in the whole union. And today we still speak of the need for a candidate to appear "presidential," or somehow of a size to fit the office, the reverse of petty and small-minded.

Publius goes on to predict a "constant probability" that the office will be filled by "characters preeminent for ability and virtue." Such characters are important not merely because they serve well in emergencies, but because they make the difference between good and bad administration. "The true test of a government is its aptitude and tendency to produce a good administration." Here Publius allows that the executive will have an undefined share in administration; later he asserts that administration in the most usual and precise sense is peculiarly executive (*Federalist* 72, 76). Thus, even though the genius of republican government exists in the legislature, the test of whether the republican form produces good government is entrusted to, and performed by, the executive. Republican government needs preeminent characters, and as we shall see, needs to give them sufficient powers in order not merely to pass the test at some minimum level, but to excel in it. That necessity—chosen or honorably determined (*Federalist* 39) by the American people when it decided to make their Constitution an experiment of the capacity of mankind for self-government—is very different from the necessity of survival in emergencies, though it may comprehend that more immediate justification for executive power. To excel as good government, the American republic must remain a limited, constitutional government, which does not mean a passive or minimal government that governs best by governing least. Rather, it is government that uses and engages the virtue and ability of preeminent characters. Contrary to the republican animus against such characters, republics not only need them to survive, but depend on them in order to excel. Yet in keeping with republican theory, the Constitution does not directly designate these characters as if they were a class requiring or deserving political recognition. Instead, it sets the people to the task of seeking them out. By the "process of election" the people identify those whom they choose, not merely as preeminent, and not as their superiors, but as preeminent characters capable of making an indispensable contribution to the public good.

Hamilton does not mention the right to vote in his discussion of election. Obviously he takes this right for granted as guaranteed by the states, though he does not believe it includes the right to vote on the final choices of candidates—the right to vote *for president*—as we assume today. The Electoral College as originally intended results in a president whom the individual voter cannot regard as his own, because he has not voted directly for that person. The distance between the voters and the president is a republican remedy against the influence of image and charisma, a remedy that we have today decided to do without. We complain about the manipulation of voters, but we forget that the right we insist on—to have voters make the final choice—makes manipulation easier. The process of election, and Publius's presentation of it, are meant to shift attention from the right to vote as an individual expression ("having one's say") to the exercise of that right toward an end. In any case, the right to vote for President presupposes that an energetic executive should exist. But Publius could not presuppose what is now simply accepted, and had to establish the point.

In *Federalist* 70 Publius introduces the fundamental problem of republican aversion to executive power. He proclaims that "energy in the executive is a leading character in the definition of good government," and remarks sardonically that "enlightened well-wishers" to republican government had better hope that a vigorous executive is consistent with the republican genius, because if it is not, their principles are doomed.[39] Publius will show them how to save their principles, but to do so he must reinterpret both the principles and the object of their aversion.

What is energy in the executive? Energy is not something good in itself; it is not virtue. In the thematic discussion of *Federalist* 37, energy and stability appear as the two modes of political power in the definition of good government, but stability comes first because energy seems to be needed for the sake of stability rather than the reverse, and also because the people appreciate stability more.[40] "Energy" and "stability" are terms in physics, only just entering into political science and political discourse with *The Federalist*. Like Hobbes's use of the word "power" itself, they represent qualities in government that are neutral as to regime. And clearly it was an advantage to Publius's argument that executive power could be described with a term that abstracts from its origin in monarchy.[41] "Energy" also abstracts from the virtue that justifies a monarch's claims to rule. It is merely a mode of power that may be used for good or ill, and a subordinate mode too, rather than a ruling principle.

Yet if energy is not virtue, in the American Constitution energy leads to virtue. Publius's argument progresses from the neutrality of energy—as it answers the necessities that any government must face—to the indispensable contribution energy makes to the goodness of republican government. In *Federalist* 70 he discusses unity, the first ingredient of energy because it ensures unanimity in the "most critical emergencies" when a decision—any decision—is "most necessary." In such circumstances differences of opinion can be fatal. While dissensions may often promote deliberate choice in a legislature by bringing every consideration into view, they cannot be tolerated in the executive. A plural executive, therefore, is simply a misplaced legislature.

The partisan dispute Publius wants to avoid between monarchy and republic has been transformed into a separation of functions (or a separation of powers arising from a separation of functions) within a republic between the executive and the legislative powers. The most delicate aspect of executive power, the unity in which it most resembles monarchy, is justified at the lowest, but most universal, level as what is necessary—especially to a republic—when there is no time for choice. A plural executive, Publius continues, not only cannot act but also destroys responsibility by concealing faults, as the several executives accuse one another. A single executive, however, can both keep secrets and maintain open and public responsibility, for when one person has to shoulder the blame, it does not matter who advised him, and one does not have to inquire into the "secret springs of the transactions" to find the culprit. One accountable man can be more narrowly watched than a numerous body whose members have no individual responsibility.[42] Publius therefore directly denies the "maxim of republican jealousy which considers power as safer in the hands of a number of men than of a single man" (*Federalist* 70)— as it applies to executive power, that is, in emergencies. The neutrality of energy at its most exigent forces a change in the maxim of republican jealousy, but a beneficial one in the interest of republics that teaches republicans how to be more effectually jealous.

Even in emergencies, where necessity is paramount, there may be time for a quick choice following on quick thinking, as when the executive seizes an opportunity—one of the "tides" in the "affairs of men" (*Federalist* 64)—to make a treaty or to exercise his pardoning power.[43] To be quick on such occasions it is not enough simply to decide; the executive must decide well and possess the necessary virtue. But when Publius comes to the second ingredient of energy, duration, then virtue comes to the fore. Duration is of course connected to unity, because what is meant is the consistency of a single executive, of *his* personal firmness (the topic of *Federalist* 71) and of *his* system of administration (*Federalist* 72). Publius could have argued for unity in duration from the first, instead of presenting the case for unity separately. This would have pleased political scientists today, who take executive power for granted and want to see more discussion of the president's program than Publius supplies. But that would not have pleased republicans in Publius's day, to whom such an initiative smacks of monarchy. So Publius first proves the necessity of unity in quick response to emergencies, then shows the advantage of duration for the unity that we have accepted for the opposite reason—its quickness.

"Personal firmness" will result from extended duration in office because "it is a general principle of human nature that a man will be interested in whatever he possesses, in proportion to the firmness or precariousness of the tenure by which he holds it" (*Federalist* 71). Thus, an executive with long tenure will act with more firmness than one whose tenure is kept short by republican jealousy. The long-term executive will not be tempted into "servile pliancy" to a prevailing current of opinion, either in the people or in the legislature. Publius endorses the "republican principle" that the "deliberate sense of the community" should prevail in its government, but that republican principle requires a firm executive, precisely contrary to the maxim of republican jealousy, to see to it that the people's deliberate sense is defended against their "temporary delusion." This is his duty, Publius says.

Personal firmness is also needed in standing up to the legislature, which is most likely to reflect popular delusions, and in republican governments tends to absorb the executive and the judiciary. Separation of powers requires independence in the powers, and above all, in practice, firmness in the executive, since the usual danger in republics is legislative domination and usurpation of the executive and judicial powers. Publius makes the executive the guarantor of separation of powers, as well as the defender of the republican principle. All this is in the executive's "interest" as we have seen in *Federalist* 51, if he has the character to be willing or eager to take risks in public affairs. If he does not, his interest is likely to be a course of "servile pliancy," giving him an easy time in office no matter how long it lasts. Publius understates the virtue required of the executive by calling it "interest." If it is a man's interest to procure the "lasting monuments" of popular gratitude reserved to men who had "courage and magnanimity enough to serve the people at the peril of their displeasure," then one might as well call interest "duty," as Publius does.[44]

In *Federalist* 72, the subject shifts from a four-year term for the president to his indefinite reeligibility for election, and the argument moves on from there. Those who believe their interest lies in taking risks are brought into the open; they are called the "noblest minds," whose ruling passion is love of fame.[45] Instead of cautiously advancing the advantage of including them in the Constitution, Publius speaks of the disadvantages of *excluding* them (as if a one-term presidency were equivalent to ostracism). In doing so he sums up the reasons for constitutionalizing executive power. To try to keep the executive weak, like the republicans, or to allow a strong executive to escape the constitution, as Locke did, is to *exclude* the noblest minds. For from their point of view—and Publius now adopts this perspective—exclusion from reelection would diminish the inducements to "good behavior," by which he means not correct deportment but planning and undertaking "extensive and arduous enterprises for the public benefit." And negatively, it would tempt the risk-seekers to "sordid views, to peculation, and in some instances, to usurpation." The community would be deprived of experience, a quality that is more desirable in governors than any other. Such exclusion would banish from office men who might be absolutely necessary at that time; and it would establish a constitutional prohibition against stability in administration. In this impressive passage, republics are not merely instructed in the uses of ambition, but actually warned of the dangers of thwarting it. It appears that consideration of the noblest minds introduces us to necessities to which only they have, or are, the answer. With all due respect for virtue in ordinary citizens, it is really these extraordinary men who will make or break the republic. And "make or break" refers not to mere survival or stability, but greatness. When the recognition that the republic can survive in emergencies only with the aid of such men is incorporated in the constitution, it becomes the recognition that republics really employ their preeminent virtue and abilities in order to become great. Here the constitutionalizing of necessity is elevated to the appreciation of greatness.

Yet republics do not thereby become mere vehicles for the noblest minds and their would-be imitators. Concluding his survey of energy in the executive (*Federalist* 77), Publius says he has shown how the office combines energy and republican safety. Energy includes republican safety because, despite his first statement that "energy in the executive is a leading character in the definition of good government," Publius argues the case for energy within republican government. He does not mean that republican government is identical with good government, but he reminds us that good government must assume *some* form. Thus energy must, after all, be of a certain kind, appropriate to a specific regime. He had said that "republican safety," which is something less than the "genius of republican government," consists of two things: a due dependence on the people, and a due responsibility to them (*Federalist* 70). But as the argument proceeds, due dependence is elevated to due responsibility.

"Responsibility" is a term apparently coined by Madison (see his use of it in regard to the Senate, *Federalist* 63) to mean not only "accountable" or "responsive" to the people, but also responsible on their behalf: responsible politicians in this sense do for the people what they cannot do for themselves, but *can* form a judgment about.[46] To republicans, responsible government had always meant many citizens governing for short terms, because that form of government is closer to the people. But when one considers what government has to do, especially to get energy from the executive, it appears that one man with a long term can be more reasonably responsible for both quick responses and systematic administration. He can *do* the job more capably, and he can more readily be *seen* to have done it, or not to have done it. When many govern for short terms, "due dependence" on the people is a delusion because responsibility cannot be fixed; any individual in the government can always excuse himself because of the shortness of his term and the number of his collaborators.

When one looks to the end of government, even to the end of *republican* government, some adjustments to the republican form and some resistance to the republican genius become necessary. Precisely for the sake of republican safety, understood as a secure liberty, or stability, republican government must leave room to maneuver for an energetic executive (and, one must add, a responsible senate and an independent judiciary). A republican people must conceive the republican form as a method, not merely for finding the culprit and fixing blame, but more for giving the rewards of reelection, esteem, and lasting fame to those who appear to deserve them. The Machiavellian priority of punishment over reward is reversed. Fame would go most fittingly to those who had "courage and magnanimity enough to serve the people at the peril of their displeasure," but it is the American Constitution that makes such fame possible by making it republican, and makes it republican by making it constitutional.

After discussing the ruling passion of the noblest minds in *Federalist* 72, Publius returns to the mundane in *Federalist* 73 with the third ingredient of energy in the executive, an adequate salary. "Stern virtue is the growth of few soils," he observes. So most presidents will need a salary guaranteed against legislative manipulation if they are to maintain independence of will. This thought introduces the last ingredient of energy, "competent powers." Six constitutional powers of the president are considered, though none of them is what one might consider the primary executive function—executing the laws.

The first and most important, the president's (qualified) veto, is not, by a dictionary definition, an executive power at all. The executive's veto is perhaps the most apparently anti-republican feature in the Constitution, originating in the British King's power to thwart the will of the legislature. But Publius treats it primarily as necessary to the separation of powers, a republican invention in politics designed to keep the legislature from executing its own laws. Again he takes the opportunity to teach republicans a lesson in republicanism, or to reiterate a previous lesson. Madison (as Publius) had established in *Federalist* 51 that separate powers must be independent if they are to remain separate, and to be independent they must have constitutional means of defense, especially against the legislature, which is likely to dominate a republican government. He particularly mentioned the need for a "fortified" executive. Now Hamilton shows that the executive must be fortified with a power so far from strictly executive as to be legislative. The veto, moreover, as David Epstein has pointed out, is an element of "energy" designed to slow down the government,[47] contrary to the necessity of emergency action that first justifies a strong executive. That the veto is qualified by the possibility of being overriden by two-thirds of Congress, Hamilton remarks, only makes it stronger, because it will be used oftener than the British King's absolute veto.

Yet the veto has a further use, not only as a "shield to the executive," but as "additional security against the enaction of improper laws."[48] Publius calls this use "secondary" to the primary one of enabling the executive to defend himself, and he denies that it turns upon the "supposition of superior wisdom or virtue in the executive." But, in the excess of lawmaking typical of republican legislatures, he finds a reason to suggest why the executive might often show more "due deliberation" than the legislature. His office, situated and fortified as it is, calls for a certain virtuous behavior from the office-holder—a virtuous behavior which is, as it were, accidental to the virtue or lack of it in his person.

At a lower level, as in the "primary" use of the veto power, the office-holder's "fortitude would be stimulated by his immediate interest in the power of his office" (*Federalist* 73), which might be quite different from his personal interest. Even Neustadt, who makes a theme of the difference between the formal office and the actual behavior of the president, says: "no one else sits where

272

he sits."[49] In other words, how you act partly depends on where you sit. Characteristically and for good reason, *The Federalist* puts forward the lower interest as "primary" and leaves the higher virtue to be "secondary." To do the reverse would imply the need to identify a class of men of higher virtue instead of allowing them to emerge as individuals through the process of republican choice. Keeping process before substance, Publius discusses the presidency in terms of constitutional formalities: mode of selection, number, length, and powers of the office. He does not try to say what "executing" is.

When men of higher virtue emerge as office-holders, safeguards remain against any president who "might sometimes be under temptations to sacrifice his duty to his interest, which it would require superlative virtue to withstand" (*Federalist* 75). Publius speaks of the possibility when he considers the treaty-making power shared between the president and the Senate. The president, he says, does not have sufficient interest in a four-year office, as might an hereditary monarch, to warrant being trusted with the entire power of making treaties. That power, since it deals with contracts between sovereigns, is neither executive nor legislative in nature, though if anything more the latter. Yet foreign negotiations require executive "qualities." Still, because the responsibility is so great (and less visible than in domestic matters), and because treaties operate as laws, participation of the legislature, or a part of it, is called for. Thus again virtue is seen through interest in the office, while the checking function is regarded as a positive contribution.[50]

Constitutional republicanism is based on self-interest, but really, one is forced to add, on self-interest properly understood. That form of government relies on the interest of the people, rather than on their cultivated virtue, because their interest leads them to think that it is better to confine themselves to choosing or electing their governors, while their virtue might lead them to desire to rule on their own in accordance with primitive, preconstitutional republicanism. Most notably in *Federalist* 10 and 51, Publius opposes interests deriving directly from "human nature" to virtues cultivated artificially and undependably by particular regimes. This has led some to say that the Constitution, according to *The Federalist*, is based on self-interest understood as what is lowest in human nature. But one must not mistake lessons in political necessity, intended specifically for primitive or "classical'' republicans, for the whole of political science. As a system of self-government the Constitution presupposes that men can rise above what is lowest in them. The Constitution, says *Federalist* 39, is based on a ''honorable determination . . . to rest all our political experiments on the capacity of mankind for self-government.'' How may this be done?

What is lowest in human nature includes not only the love of gain and the need for security, but also the desire for liberty (*Federalist* 10). To lift the latter low desire (for liberty can mean nothing more than having your way) to the level needed for self-government requires honorable determination, because success is not certain and one must therefore risk one's honor in the attempt. But the constitutionalized republican form can make success possible, if not guarantee it. It can construct or ''model''[51] an executive office that has a ''constant probability'' (*Federalist* 68) or ''bids fair'' to be filled by capable men. That probability arises from the qualities associated with the quantities of the office—its unity in one person as opposed to the character of ''any numerous body whatever'' (*Federalist* 73–77) and its length of tenure which appeals to men ambitious of fame as well as power (*Federalist* 72). In the Constitution, virtue appears not in its own name but under the rubric of qualifications for office. The people, whose interest is to elect rather than rule, must have the wisdom to appreciate virtue and the judgment to trust it. But when they elect constitutional officers, their virtue is not—or does not appear to them to be—virtue deferring to greater virtue. They find virtue in their fellow-citizens by looking for those who are qualified for office[52]— originally, in presidential elections, for those qualified to be electors; now, for qualified presidential candidates. Meanwhile, candidates for office claim to have, not superior virtue, but the necessary qualifications. These are not stated formally in the Constitution, nor could they be; but they must rather be inferred, as in *The Federalist*, from bare quantities, and by reference to the plan of the whole. Whether men with the requisite qualifications can be found is in some measure up to us; whether they will succeed is in some measure up to them. By republicanizing the executive, the Framers tried to ensure that no one was overqualified for the job. Their success can be concluded from the fact that while previous republics were fearful of great men, Americans are proud of their ''great presidents.''

The Constitutional Debate Between Pacificus and Helvidius

As a formal possibility, Aristotle's kingship of virtue remains in the Constitution. Nothing in it prevents the emergence of such a king, except for the same practical problems that stand in the way of Aristotle's king elsewhere. The Constitution adopts that which precludes kingship in order to create a republican executive rather than a king; nevertheless, constitutional powers broad enough to meet necessities may also be strong enough to satisfy virtue. The Machiavellian principle of anticipating necessity by the use of *virtù* may be interpreted in the interest of virtue. Just as the people may elect rather than rule, so those with outstanding virtue may run for election and act within constitutional restraints instead of ruling. In a rare case such a person may rule *through* the contraints, that is, may succeed in using them to serve his virtue. What Aristotle understands as the interest of the regime—the partisan tendency in every regime whose preservation constitutes survival of the whole—is America's republican genius, according to *The Federalist*. That republican genius is as much a brake on virtue as it is virtue itself; "republican virtue" (of which one hears so much today) is primarily directed and often exercised against outstanding virtue. But perhaps those few men of outstanding virtue would accept the restraint, the more so because they have a Constitution in which the presidency, as *The Federalist* explains it, sometimes allows their virtue to escape the jealousy of republican virtue under the unprovocative name of "interest."

The Constitution formalized the ambivalence of virtue—republican or super-republican—in the ambivalence of executive power, weak or strong. The ambivalence is exemplified in the person of "Publius," named after an outstanding man who saved the Roman republic. But the weak and strong executives are one in theory only. In practice, the very formality of the office leaves open to partisan interpretation which of the two executives should prevail at any particular time. Thus in 1793, when President George Washington by executive proclamation declared America neutral in the war between Britain and France, Hamilton and Madison, the two principals writing as Publius, disagreed with each other. They had already clashed over other issues; this time, in a deservedly famous debate, Hamilton, writing as Pacificus, defended the proclamation, and Madison, as Helvidius, attacked it.

This was a *constitutional* debate of a kind characteristically American. When an Aristotelian regime is formalized in writing, as it is in the American Constitution, the claims of justice advanced by its rulers become claims of constitutional propriety advanced by competing partisans. Rival constitutional claims can be made because of the formality with which the Constitution states its powers, leaving open a range of actual relationships; and the debate between them maintains this formal character. A constitutional debate invests the occasion for it with the significance of a precedent which may return to haunt one party or both later on. A strong executive, for example, may become useful to Republicans, baneful to Federalists. Constitutional politics achieves its long view and its flexibility at the cost of inconsistency in its partisans, as they capture offices they had previously opposed or face difficulties they had previously minimized. But Hamilton and Madison were not scramblers for constitutional advantage. Together as Publius they had explained the ambivalence of a republicanized executive, and separately they were founders of both sides of the constitutional debate over the powers of that office.

Hamilton argues that since Washington's proclamation was neither a legislative nor a judicial act, it must be "of necessity" executive. By this he means political, not logical, necessity. Hamilton implies that since the government must be able to do anything, if two of the branches do not possess a power, it must reside in the third. That is the branch possessing "the executive power" under Article II of the Constitution, not the enumerated legislative powers in Article I. The executive power, in the singular, can be illustrated, but it cannot be enumerated because it cannot be exhausted. Therefore executive power, unlike legislative power, is more than the sum of its parts. The reason is not so much that contingencies of every kind cannot be foreseen, but rather that the executive branch, not the legislative, is "the organ of intercourse between the United States and foreign nations."[53] Executive power must therefore be a whole because it acts for a whole in relation to other wholes. The Senate's power to ratify treaties and confirm appointments, and Congress's power to declare war, are exceptions out of executive power, and accordingly should be construed strictly—that is, minimally.

Here Hamilton, unlike Publius, shows little concern for the sensitivities of the republican genius or for the necessity of counteracting ambition. Instead, he emphasizes the concurrent authority of each branch to perform its own duty. Consequently, we learn something not taught by Publius—that executing includes interpreting. "He who is to execute the laws," Hamilton says, "must first judge for himself of their meaning."[54] Perhaps for only this occasion, Hamilton seems to derive executive power from the power to deal with foreign affairs, Locke's federative power. He makes explicit, as Publius did not, that the preservation of the Union is the work of the executive (cf. *Federalist* 23). Thus, executive power becomes a whole, hard to limit because hard to define, defending the nation and serving the end of the Constitution. Its place in the form of structure established by the Constitution is determined by its duty to that end.

On Madison's side of the debate, the reverse holds: the end of the executive is determined by its place in the structure. "The natural province of the executive magistrate is to execute laws," he says. "All his acts, therefore, properly executive, must presuppose the existence of the laws to be executed."[55] Madison indignantly rejects the "extraordinary doctrine" that the powers of making war and treaties are executive by nature. If a treaty is not precisely a law, nevertheless it has the force of law, and should be carried out by the executive. To make a treaty is not in the "natural province" of executive power, even though the Constitution awards it to the executive branch; consult *Federalist* 75 (written by Hamilton), Madison says pointedly. To declare war is a legislative act, because it represents sovereign power. And precisely because in carrying on war the executive is *not* executing law, its power in war should be construed narrowly. The executive has indeed a propensity to war, but this must be kept in check.

Hamilton, calling himself "Pacificus" and keeping in mind the purpose of the Neutrality Proclamation, had associated Congress with declaring war and the President with keeping peace. Madison displays a republican suspicion of the power to be assumed by the executive in war, and he begins his first Helvidius letter by exciting the very republican sentiment which, as Publius, he had attempted to cool. Pacificus, he says, has been read, "with singular pleasure and applause by the foreigners and degenerate citizens among us who hate our republican government."[56] Madison represents the republican genius, the interest of the republican regime that wants a weak executive duly restricted to its "natural province." He denies the executive any discretion, even—or especially—in foreign affairs; his only responsibility is to execute the laws faithfully regardless of the consequences.[57]

When Hamilton speaks expansively of the nature of the executive, and Madison speaks slightingly of its natural province, we see why Publius avoided the controversial issue. Not only *The Federalist* but the Constitution too avoided making a list of executive powers—to say nothing of a definition of executive power. Prompted by the Constitution's silences, Edward Corwin notably remarked that the Constitution is "an invitation to struggle for the privilege of directing American foreign policy."[58] Events will resolve the prevailing voice, he said; but, one may add, the abilities of the contenders will also determine who decides. An invitation to struggle is an incitement to excel. In practice the issue of the nature of executive power must be addressed, and the debate between Hamilton and Madison was not only the best of many to come but also an archetype. In the American Constitution the office of executive permits and encourages a continuing dispute about the nature of executive power.

Every president has to define the office for himself and face the definitions of his partisan detractors. Thus the Constitution does not determine the behavior of those who govern under it, and is not intended to do so. A Constitution that operates unfailingly does not work well, because it leaves nothing to the virtue of the participants. After 1793, American history was to reveal many possible variations on the theme of executive power, some better than others, and all of them debatable. The lack of an official definition allows each president to become responsible for his own. When executive power is made constitutional and republican, it gives Machiavellian necessity its due by maintaining some of the maneuverability and flexibility of the prince. But it does so, at its best, without loss of responsibility for acting with virtue.

11

Conclusion: The Form and the End

As executive power comes to be accepted as a normal and essential feature of government, all manner of men get in on the act. Not only new thinkers of various kinds, but now doers— real executives reflecting on what they intend to do—use and develop the concept invented by Machiavelli. Among the leading thinkers are Tocqueville, Hegel, Marx, Nietzsche, and Weber; some prominent doers include Robespierre, Napoleon, Andrew Jackson, Abraham Lincoln, Woodrow Wilson, Lenin, Hitler, Franklin Roosevelt, and Winston Churchill.

In our century, totalitarian governments have arisen, executing millions of people in order, they claim, to execute the will of the people. New forms of evil, undreamt of by Machiavelli but aided by his political science, have become realities. Executive power, we have seen, was at its inception deliberately neutral regarding the distinction between principality and republic, because Machiavelli thought his new doctrine would bring men more glory and security in no matter what regime. That neutrality as to form enabled the Machiavellian executive to be borrowed and suitably transformed by those who fashioned modern sovereignty (Bodin and Hobbes), by constitutionalists (Locke and Montesquieu), and by the American constitutional republicans. But of course a neutral executive could also be democratized, perhaps for good and surely for ill.

In America the distinction dear to Publius between a republic and a democracy has been lost to sight, though the Constitution based on that distinction continues in force. Publius understood executive power as a nonrepublican device intended to energize the republic and thus secure it from the weakness and division of democracies; we now see the executive as the leader who gets his strength from the democratic element and strengthens it in turn. Whereas in *The Federalist* a strong executive holds out against the people, with us his strength is with and for the people. That change is perhaps beneficial, and at any rate difficult to reverse. But the modern totalitarian use of the strong executive surely raises a fundamental doubt about the neutrality of the original concept. Should we not now reevaluate a doctrine that has escaped its constitutional or republican constraints and proved so useful to the worst enemies that liberty has ever known?

For we know now that Machiavelli was wrong: religion is not liberty's worst enemy. Machiavelli stole the idea of the executive from what he took to be the worst enemy and tried to fashion it for the advantage of human liberty. He found it in the pretense of Christian or other priests to rule men as mere executors of divine will, and he appropriated it for use by secular authorities by substituting human necessities for divine will. But we have learned that these necessities can serve as an incitement and excuse for greater evils than Machiavelli ever saw in religion. And it is precisely this ground in human necessities that gives the idea of the modern executive its peculiar neutrality. For the modern executive is not politically neutral, in the way that those who claim to execute the will of God do so regardless of the needs of a particular regime. Nor is it theoretically neutral in the sense of Aristotle's political science, which analyzes the parts of regimes—deliberating and judging in particular—that are indeed to be found everywhere. Of course, there is no guarantee that a ruler will deliberate and judge well. One who does so will be a good man. Despite all the difficulties in this view (recall the problem of the good man and the good citizen), Aristotle is somehow confident of it.

But Machiavelli's neutrality has a sinister tendency, since one can hardly imagine a good man doing well the wicked tricks he recommends. In contrast, Aristotle's mixed regime is edifying; it teaches us a neutrality that loosens the grip of our partisan attachments and permits us to improve them. Machiavelli's prudence is nothing but cunning, and his principality or republic (each of which is a mixture of both), when prudently understood, inspires its princes or citizens to abandon all loyalties impartially, save the one to themselves. It appears that, for Machiavelli, a good executive must be a bad man. His evil remains even after it is excused by his necessities—and are those necessities truly such, or are they merely arguable anticipations of what may or may not become necessary? Does the excuse given to evil really derive inevitably from impersonal necessity, or is it issued by Machiavelli himself—spokesman for the Devil? Thus a certain evil cunning clings to the neutrality that allows Machiavelli's executive to be appropriated in the liberal constitution.

Even if it is true, as I argue in chapter 10, that ambition for the offices presented in the American Constitution can call forth virtue, still it is a hindrance to virtue to have to go by the name of ambition or interest. Virtue's splendor is obscured by these terms, a certain meanness of spirit is excused, and the possibility of evil is discreetly covered over. When ambition is set to counteract ambition, it is harder—though still necessary—to denounce demagogues. Over time, Machiavelli's sinister neutrality has emerged in the value-neutral behavioralism of professional political scientists, whose categories do not permit them even to recognize demagogues, much less denounce them. Following the example of Hobbes, their science universalizes, democratizes, and therefore sanitizes the tyrannical actions of Machiavelli's prince. But if they were pressed, they might have to admit that wicked men would be more effective than good ones in the explanatory schemes they derive from their innocent analyses of nice-guy American presidents.

Perhaps, then, the modern totalitarian regimes offer the most revealing view of the contemporary executive. In those regimes Machiavelli's neutral conception comes down to its effectual truth, so that we can judge its success by its own test. There we see executive formalism and informality at their worst. The formalism is in a numbing, careless bureaucracy, which might at first seem rule-bound for no reason and to no discernible end, in a way reminiscent of Kafka—but which after some experience proves to be oppression in the interest of a very obvious ruling party. As Montesquieu said about the servants of despotism, totalitarian bureaucracy transmits the tyranny of the leader undiminished to the arbitrary petty official, who uses the rules to make himself into a miniature boss. Formalism of that kind does not truly respect the forms and formalities which prevent arbitrary rule, but on the contrary multiplies them as an instrument of tyranny. Rather than following Machiavelli's rule of "injuries all at once, benefits little by little," totalitarian bureaucracy prolongs the pain it inflicts, compelling its subjects to wait in line interminably and sometimes to suffer excruciating torments.

Thus it is quite consistent with formalism at its worst to find executive informality also at its worst in the totalitarian leader. That leader makes a virtue of his revolutionary will, acting on behalf of either the *Volk* or the proletariat and representing the anger they are meant to feel against the enemies that have been pointed out to them. In the paradigmatic case, the leader has his own charisma, as with Lenin and Hitler; but when the system falls into routine, and the leader is no more than the leading apparatchik, it becomes necessary to rely on the inspiration of a dead man's will. The Marxist science of impersonal historical forces very easily becomes a cult of personality.

The formalism and formlessness of totalitarian regimes are two kinds of neutrality, claiming to signify that no one rules. The bureaucracy belongs to the state, which is the impersonal servant of the party; and the party supposedly represents interests not only above the interests of present incumbents but also beyond any qualities they might have to recommend them as rulers. Neither Nazi nor Communist ideology shows much concern for the class of the ambitious, as did *The Federalist.* Caring only for racial consciousness or material interest, their analysis lacks the introspection characteristic of the political science that supports constitutional regimes. Whether the bureaucrats are fanatical ascetics or, more likely, eager claimants of privilege, their ideology systematically evades the question of who rules with bland assurances of impersonality and unbelievable assertions of universality.

The formlessness of the totalitarian leader is a reaction and counterweight to the impersonality of the bureaucracy, but it has a neutrality of its own. The leader supplies will to a structure that allegedly has more of its own or, if it does, only a will to resist motion. The leader gives a partisan tone and direction—a party line—that would otherwise be lacking. But the strength of will for which he is praised serves the mission for which he is destined at his time. For like all other individuals, the leader is an agent of historical forces that are larger than man not because they are divine, but because they are more powerful than any particular man or group of men. The leader represents the people or the class that will regenerate mankind. In that sense his will receives its form from outside and has no truly inner direction: however belligerent he may be, in his claim to be history's representative he is at bottom a weak executive. As history's executive, the totalitarian leader goes where he is told, like the bureaucrat. His triumph is that of his people or his class, not really his. Since he does not confront his own necessities but only assists in the working out of historical necessities, he never gets the individual glory of Machiavelli's prince. What recognition he receives depends on the needs of his successor, who may throw him on history's rubbish heap—all for the good of the material cause.

Two kinds of neutrality, formalist and formless, agree in disclaiming responsibility for what happens. The bureaucracy is mere form without an end, and the leader, who provides the end, merely passes on what he gets from history. Neither rules responsibly, but each attempts to make up for the irresponsibility of the other with its own characteristic irresponsibility. Thus we have seen monstrous evil done and somtimes avowed, but never claimed—and this not because of the human propensity to offer excuses but precisely because totalitarian doctrine permits no excuses. "It was neither an accident nor a mistake," said the Soviet spokesman about the shooting down of a civilian passenger aircraft. The principle of the regime does not allow accidents or mistakes. Totalitarian evil is not without malice, but it does not appear to be ruled by malice. Its neutrality marshals the great power of superhuman forces, but the regime lacks the human interest and the occasional grandeur of traditional tyranny. Its irresponsibility is all the more chilling for that.

The totalitarian executive raises the question of responsibility for evil which Machiavelli's doctrine was designed to evade. But in the working of its own neutrality—in the interaction of leader and bureaucracy—we also find the problem of the executive as most people see it today in the liberal democracies. Although some flavor of dislike for the demagogue remains in the popular contempt for "politicians," we no longer denounce demagogues, as in Publius's day. Now we denounce "bureaucracy." To us, the executive's problem is not a demanding people easily flattered by demagogues but a sluggish, unresponsive bureaucracy. The executive must make government move, so that it can care. To do this, the executive must have "charisma."

Charisma is a technical term of social science that was imported from Germany and now has become the most frequently heard expression of praise for American executives. The "dynamic" executive is long gone. Certainly a charismatic leader is difficult to distinguish from a demagogue, not to mention a tyrant. But despite the trend of social science, any democracy still needs to identify and denounce demagogues and tyrants—for they are still its enemies. A considerable loss of discernment has occurred from the long-term consequences of the thought of Machiavelli, a most discerning man. The neutrality that served his x-ray vision of hidden motives and blundering goodwill has become a so-called scientific objectivity that is deliberately obtuse to distinctions necessary in constitutional politics.

''Charisma'' was a concept invented by Max Weber in the spirit of Nietzsche's revolt against rationalism. Its current use constitutes an unconscious return to the Machiavellian appetite for the sensational, as opposed to the solid benefits of constitutional administration promised by Publius. In the search for charisma, a democratic people is asking to be fooled, and justifying in advance the levity and irresponsibility of its leaders. As a concept, charisma is scientific neutrality bored with itself and looking for excitement from any direction—it cares not where. The consequence, however, is to prefer the executive who offers excitement, the demagogue.

What did Machiavelli intend to accomplish with his neutral executive? Men become complacent in the arrangements that please them, the orders that reflect their partisan wishes and desires, the existing form of government. The purpose of Machiavelli's executive is to remind men of their fear. A sudden and sensational execution recalls to mind the origin of such comfortable orders and also their end, which is to provide security against the objects of their fears. Such executions give them a glimpse of the necessity for government, along with a vivid picture of the consequence of disobedience. In these truly Machiavellian moments, the form of government is returned to, and judged by, its end in the sense of an outcome or result. All partisan forms of government must pass this neutral test: does it make me secure?

But a direct appeal to popular feeling was also intended by the various democratizing movements that have followed the framing of the American Constitution. In the constitutional republic, ways have been found to return to the people the very government which by its form was originally withdrawn from them. The appeal is not the sobering, Machiavellian recall of popular fear, however. On the contrary, the early democratizing modes include political parties intended to express a people's republican pride in governing on its own—precisely the appeal to popular passion over public reason that Publius warned of in *Federalist* 49. Of late, the trend has accelerated and changed in character. Instead of appealing to an existing popular pride, it has seemed necessary to awaken and stimulate the passion of a passive and dependent people that scarcely bothers to vote. Hence the call for charisma to excite the people. Hence, too, the resort to opinion surveys, television, and presidential primaries to say for the people what they seem unable to say for themselves. The "little arts of popularity" that Publius despised (*Federalist* 68) have acquired the status of science, and the function of explaining a people to its government and to itself.

Whether passionate or not, the democratizing modes have invaded the space and disturbed the calm that constitutional offices were supposed to protect. On this point Tocqueville's foresight is better than our hindsight:

> Men living in democratic centuries do not readily understand the utility of forms; they feel an instinctive contempt for them. . . . Forms arouse their disdain and often their hatred. As they usually aspire to none but facile and immediate enjoyments, they rush impetuously toward the object of each of their desires, and the least delays exasperate them. This temperament, which they transport into political life, disposes them against the forms which daily hold them up or prevent them in one or another of their designs.
>
> Yet it is this inconvenience, which men of democracies find in form, that makes them so useful to liberty, their principal merit being to serve as a barrier between the strong and the weak, the government and the governed. Thus democratic peoples naturally have more need of forms than other peoples, and naturally respect them less (Tocqueville, *Democracy in America* II.iv.7).

The democratic propensity to put the end, or object of desire, before the form is precisely what the American founders meant to contain by means of the Constitution, and especially with their republicanized executive. The American president was to protect the Constitution from bouts of rampant enthusiasm in the people and the legislature. He, not they, would have emergency powers, and his long-term enterprises would attract an enduring approval from the people, so that he would be less subject to their impetuous exasperation.

Conversely, impatience with forms was just what Machiavelli meant to release with his fearful executive. With the democratization of the executive that is epitomized in the word "charisma" we seem to have returned to Machiavelli's prince, though without his expedient "cruelties well used." Governments today appear to be divided between those incapable of deliberate cruelty, and those incapable of anything but; none is correctly Machiavellian. We seem to be doubtful of our constitutionalism, yet unwilling to embrace the Machiavellian consequence of "looking to the end" (*The Prince* 18). Something might be wrong, then, with the modern doctrine of executive power. To see where we are now, we need a review of where we have been. In reviewing I shall bring to the fore the problematic relationship between form and end, which is the essence of executive power.

The modern doctrine of executive power begins by reacting against Aristotle's theory of kingship, whose central idea is the assumption by human beings of responsibility for ruling. Ruling is accomplished through an order or a form of government that aims at and moves toward its end. The democratic form, for example, moves its citizens toward a democratic life. But true democracy cannot be realized unless men are naturally fit for such a life. If, as turns out to be the case, they have elements of oligarchy as well as democracy in their natures, mere democracy will not satisfy them, and unanswered claims will remain. Only the claim of the best man, who is both democratic and oligarchic but also better than both, will be fully satisfied; thus only in the kingship of this best man will the form of government attain its end.

But, having concluded with a kingship or aristocracy resembling Plato's philosopher-kings, Aristotle backs away from it. Weighing the practical difficulties in the way of such a king, he finds a useful surrogate for him in the mixed regime. Here he takes a constitutional view in the modern sense, and looks for ways—"barriers" in Tocqueville's sense—to inhibit the movement of the form toward its inevitably partisan end. But the kingship of the political philosopher remains effectual behind the scenes, always attracting or directing reform of the imperfect regimes toward the best regime; the direction of compromise, therefore, is upward. Responsible rulers accept human imperfection, so as to be useful, but with a view to what is noble they do not accept every imperfection as given. For Aristotle, nature permits, but does not guarantee, the success of human virtue; thereby nature induces and compels us to take responsibility on our own to make her enigmatic promise bear fruit.

For Machiavelli, nature is no friend to human virtue. She presents us with necessities, not gifts, and the necessities must be managed with a transformed virtue. Machiavelli's *virtù* is self-assertion in search of glory, but it also, through the executions that revive states, reminds men of their paramount end, the need for security. Machiavelli advises us not to assume responsibility for perfecting ourselves, still less for perfecting nature. That responsibility, as interpreted by Christianity, enslaves men by forcing them to become executives of divine will, cruel on God's behalf and weak on their own. Instead of trying to be responsible for a delusive perfection, Machiavelli shows us how to assume responsibility for our own human necessities. With his executions, the prince submits government to the test of success, and measures the form by the end in the sense of outcome. The prince forces this responsibility on the government, or on himself, and the test suits very well the popular or human penchant for judging by the outcome. But its very suitability suggests that Machiavelli's prince in fact *evades* responsibility when he matches form and end. For in effect he tells the people: this is your end; I am acting for you; I merely make you aware of the conflict between your (partisan) want and your (neutral) necessity. For ''human necessities'' are each human being's necessities, hence not the responsibility of the ruler. Executive ambivalence resides in this simultaneous embrace and avoidance of responsibility.

These human necessities become the foundation of representative government in Hobbes, and here the taming of the prince begins. Hobbes formalizes the prince. He does not make examples of the actual deeds of princes, as does Machiavelli. Rather, he draws a picture of the state of nature, a condition rarely seen in actual experience but very easily inferred from it. The state of nature shows each man to be his own prince, formally, because we can use our imaginations and do not actually have to behave as princes. The principle of each man his own prince is formalized as the natural right of self-preservation, that being a defensive, moderate, universal, theoretical, and hence moral restatement of Machiavellian acquisition. Thus, when the sovereign power is authorized by each man's natural right, the form of government is created according to the end and under its discipline. This was also true for the governments created by Machiavelli's princes, but Hobbes's scheme is less chancy, or more scientific, because it does not rely on actual deeds of execution and the prudence required for them. The formal advantage here is accompanied by the disadvantage of formalism, a continuing discrepancy between form and reality in Hobbes's political science. The form and the end are together for him, but only formally. An actual sovereign could follow all of Hobbes's rules and still fail. In other words, legitimacy does not guarantee success. But the constitutional view of executive power after Hobbes is precisely an attempt to guarantee adequacy through legitimacy. If an executive office can be properly defined in law or theory, it will call forth the abilities needed to perform in it—while restraining those abilities that are too great for it.

Hobbes's attempt to regularize the disciplining of the form by the end was taken up and enhanced by Locke. Locke improved the Hobbesian authorization of sovereign power by constituting it with a certain structure, a "constitution." By adopting the structure of separate powers, the form of government becomes more than a merely formalized prince or tyrant. And because the form is no longer a mere formality, the act of constituting the government acquires a certain dignity it could not have in Hobbes's political science. The form becomes part of the end; the free choice which brings security becomes a test or feature of security. Locke retains the end of security as a test of the form in two ways: one is the extra-constitutional right of the people to alter or abolish or institute a new form of government; and the other is the constitutional prerogative of executive discretion. Within the constitution, then, the form and the end are in tension, rather than in harmony as for Aristotle. The form of government is the legislative power in which the rule of law is constituted; the end is represented by the prerogative power of doing "public good without a rule." Locke's executive—and ours—is thus ambivalent, because he serves both form and end. As minister to the legislative power he is subordinate; as critic he is equal or superior.

Montesquieu is not satisfied with the formalism that holds form and end apart. A liberal constitution requires a liberal society, or it will be corrupted and perverted to illiberal ends. Indeed, on its own the form of a free republic (its "nature") will contradict its end (or "principle"), as Montesquieu shows in his subtle critique of the republican virtue of the ancients. And with the modern philosophers, the legitimacy of the sovereign (Hobbes) or the dignity of the constitution (Locke) is maintained by reliance on the despotic principle of fear. A mutual adjustment of form and end must be sought, an essential aspect of which is an executive without the power to punish in criminal matters, so that government and society can live together on speaking terms. When the parts of society speak to one another, they dispute each other through parts of government, forming parties around the legislative and the executive powers. The parties represent will and nature, or the form and the end, respectively. But despite his adjustments Montesquieu does not succeed in making form and end identical. His liberal constitution is an open-ended process of adjustment.

According to Publius, the American Constitution puts its own form before the end it serves, because that form is part of the end. This was also Locke's constitutional paradox. To serve the people, the Constitution must control the desire of the people for mastery; to do this, it must be in a sense the master. A government rules constitutionally only when the people do not compel it to rush precipitously toward the objects of their desires, regardless of constitutional restraints—because the people put the constitutional forms of structure, procedure and rights before their own ends, which they perceive as the ends of the Constitution also. But to achieve that, the people must cherish or "venerate" the Constitution as an end whose preservation merits their devotion.

Paradoxically, the Constitution cannot serve the people well when they regard it merely as their instrument. It is of course possible for a few to subvert or overthrow the Constitution, but in a popular government, Publius reminds his republican brothers, this is not the main danger. The main danger comes from within, that is, from a majority faction of the people itself; since the few who subvert are most likely to be demagogues with popular backing. Publius does not excuse the American people from responsibility for their affairs simply because they do not actively and directly govern. The people are responsible for choosing their governors well, and for permitting and requiring them to govern by the forms of the republic. Their veneration for the Constitution should encourage in them what one might call an active forbearance from governing, which may be readily distinguished from apathy or submission. The federal system, with many offices to man, permits a sizable few to govern. So no one who insists on governing personally need forbear from doing so. But all are responsible for governing constitutionally.

The American Constitution is Lockean, but it is milder than Locke's because fitted with Montesquieu's separation of powers, dividing judicial power from executive. Since all of its branches derive from the people, the Constitution rests on the people's pride rather than on their fear or on the majesty of a king. It is subject to amendment, but only in accordance with its own forms, constitutionally. It is theoretically subject to replacement when the sovereign people wishes, but in time the sovereign people, having chosen to ratify and live by the Constitution, becomes the constitutional people. Its end ceases to be outside the Constitution, neutral to its fate. That the people might abandon the Constitution becomes unimaginable, because having formed the Constitution, the people are now formed by it. Rather than merely bringing the discipline of necessity to the forms of the Constitution, the end of the Constitution serves as a reminder of its excellence and a challenge to maintain it. Form and end are related as in an Aristotelian regime, at least in part: the form of a constitution directed to itself as the end. Thus forbearance from rule becomes a kind of rule. The people are the judge of the Constitution, but they have been formed by the Constitution to judge it well.

This welcome development, however much or little it has been realized in American history, is threatened by the direct appeals to the people increasingly evident in contemporary politics. The direct appeals result from a combination of democratic restlessness and doctrines on both Right and Left that encourage impatience. Such appeals are most obvious in totalitarian governments, which claim to improve the people without bothering (or stooping) to ask their consent. Totalitarian governments pretend to be closer to their peoples than any other; hence they have no need for constitutional formalities. Yet as a result of that pretense, they are the most pretentious governments the world has ever known. Although dedicated to the truth, they lie more freely than all other governments. They are filled with the preposterous dignity of their science, which they allege will reform the human race; and they are far more self-assured than the governments of divine right which modern constitutions were designed to defeat.

Yet, in constitutional democracies today, one can discern the same tendency to sacrifice form to end. Constitutional rights in America are often interpreted according to the outcome of their exercise, as in the notorious phrase ''equality of result,'' without respect for the constitutional means or procedures by which that result is reached. Within American government, activism can be found in all three branches, not just in the executive where it belongs. It is as if the spirit of the strong executive had escaped its constitutional bounds, and all three branches were ready to claim the prerogative power of doing public good without a rule. The constitutional executive might seem to have the advantage in a competition of prerogative where all behave like executives. But the larger territory he covers, extending beyond the legislature and judiciary to where law cannot reach, is more exposed to intrusion from the other branches. When the branches and political parties dispute constitutional powers and limits, they accept the need for definitions, and they consent to live together under the Constitution, and within its spirit, despite their partisanship. But when parties do not admit the need for definitions or interpretations, the Constitution begins to lose authority.

This would not matter, perhaps, if the Constitution did not define our responsibility. But it does: we know what to expect from our government and from ourselves through the powers and duties defined in the Constitution. When all branches or even all citizens have a prerogative power, no one has responsibility because no one has a *definite* responsibility. Loss of constitutional definition leads to loss of responsibility. The Constitution must define neither too little nor too much. But it is in defining *executive* power, the power that most resists definition, that the problem lies. For a constitutional people, nothing is more difficult, nor more necessary, than to define what executive power is.

If the executive and the people for whom he acts are capable of acting responsibly, we need a political science capable of discerning responsibility. Such a political science is essentially Aristotelian, opposed to the Machiavellian political science that invented the modern executive. A responsible political science joins the form of government to its end so that it can see how well the form performs. Like a responsible person facing a problem, it ''sees it through to the end." It is not content with either value-free description, leaving a people free to hang itself if it wishes, or value positing regardless of consequences.

The best and only true political science takes responsibility for consequences, but does so in accordance with a principle. It recognizes necessity, but does not merely submit; even when it sees men dealing with natural necessities, it looks for the human choice in how they do so. Aristotelian political science seeks a reconciliation between nature and choice (or end and form), not the Machiavellian mastery of nature that turns out to be submission to necessity. Only that reconciliation makes men responsible: if their choice is set against nature, they can always disclaim responsibility for their actions by declaring, with pompous woefulness, that the result was fated. We wanted democracy, but we had to accept tyranny—it's not our fault!

So the political scientist must become a philosopher and a teacher of responsibility. Teaching responsibility to others is very different from taking it on oneself. To teach it, one must leave room for others to claim their due and exercise their choice. The teacher must not try to do everything himself, leaving nothing for his pupils to attempt. He may show that the claim of virtue leads to kingship, but he himself must not try to become a king. Like Aristotle, he must allow himself, a man of outstanding virtue, to be democratically ostracized from politics. The American founders did something similar with their Constitution because they wanted it to belong to the American people. Some believe that the founders set up a system of interests because they were afraid of letting others be responsible for themselves, but in fact they allowed interests to represent virtue because they wished to encourage responsibility. That is the only responsible thing to do. Since one cannot oneself rule everything—either directly, like Alexander the Great, or indirectly, through a mechanism—it is irresponsible to leave no responsibility to others.

Aristotle and Machiavelli both wished to make the philosopher less conspicuous in politics. Aristotle thought that Socrates's philosopher-king was too daunting to the gentlemen to whom Aristotle promised rule. Machiavelli believed that any show of philosophy, even in a contemplative life at a good distance from politics, would disrupt the worldly preoccupation of his beloved princes. So he cut them loose; he taught them—and us—how to evade the responsibility of improving politics. We would learn to conceal our choices by representing them as necessities and ourselves as executives. But Machiavelli was more intrepid than his successors, who were as much frightened by his insight as grateful for it. In one sense, they radicalized his thought as they developed his political view of necessity into science and epistemology; in another, they put a brake on his recklessness by taking measures to tame the prince. The latter element of their strategy could be interpreted as a return to Aristotelian responsibility.

The process began with Hobbes, who brought philosophy or science into the open. He saw that Aristotle's philosophy had become public in scholastic guise, and that a new science was necessary to supplant it. The risk, however, was that sovereigns would seem to become executives of scientists, a risk Hobbes sought to minimize with his attacks on political interference from professionals. He himself hid from sight under the cover of his diversionary fire on others. Locke retained the idea of a public political science but amended it to include a defense of freedom so that free peoples would be indebted, but not subject, to him. But while positing a "perfect freedom" in practice (the *Two Treatises*), he denied it in theory (the *Essay Concerning Human Understanding*); and Montesquieu, with greater reticence in both regards, did much the same. The modern philosophers of freedom in politics—and this holds true in our day—do not take responsibility for their bleak view of freedom in theory. They hardly provide the needed reconciliation of nature and choice. So they alternate between not enough freedom—realism—and too much—idealism.

In practice, responsibility in politics today is to be found only in executive leadership. The modern division of Aristotle's deliberative function into legislation and execution has not succeeded; it has left the legislature too far from the scene of action, ignorant of what it needs to know in order to legislate. Everywhere but in America the legislative function has fallen into the hands of the executive, and in America, Congress has sustained its not-quite-equal position only by invading the sphere of the executive by means of its committees and their staffs. One notes that, in the private sector, no business finds it useful to separate legislation from execution. That the separation of functions has not worked does not mean that the separation of powers should be abandoned or that the American way of confusing the functions should be exchanged for the British one. But Locke's intended

293

division of responsibility between generalizing by law and using discretion has been overcome and—not surprising to anyone schooled by Machiavelli—to the advantage of the power closer to the deed. As a sign of this universal tendency, one may remark that it is quite possible to use the term "leadership" without seeming to favor monarchy. In executive leadership, bygone partisans of monarchy do not quite have all they ever wanted, but they have enough to satisfy them that modern republicans have unwittingly admitted much truth in the monarchist cause.

To succeed, executive leadership must be principled. For only a principle permits an executive to ride out the bad fortune that is sure to come and by which he will be brought down if his only measure is success. "Stay the course," said a recent American president to his partisans when things were not going well for him. That was an appeal to virtue as opposed to the calculation of one's interest: when all else fails—and it will—be virtuous. After pragmatism collapses, virtue is the last resort of the pragmatist.

This is the modern version of Aristotle's responsible rule, and it is disclosed only by a modern version of Aristotle's political science. Periods of executive leadership such as the Reagan Revolution show what American government means. They bring together the form of government and its end so that those who govern can be held responsible not merely for their ideas or their deeds but for both together. The Reagan Revolution, for example, promised to produce a certain America, peopled by a certain kind of American with certain virtues—not just the same America better off or more secure. Of course, all such "extensive and arduous enterprises" in our age must take place within the bounds of the "pursuit of happiness." They play variations on the broad themes of security and liberty that modern democratic peoples insist on; any appeal to daring, sacrifice, or nobility is ruled out, except in the gravest and most obvious emergencies. Not even Alcibiades could convince a modern democracy to launch the Sicilian expedition that he persuaded the Athenians to undertake. In this regard, every modern executive is weak. Yet variations on the pursuit of happiness represent the kinds of virtue that we call by their partisan names—liberal, conservative, radical, reactionary. Hence they constitute claims to virtue and can be analyzed by an Aristotelian political science using kingship and the mixed regime. Who is the liberal produced by the New Deal, and could he be king over all? If not, what qualities would have to be mixed with his to make perfect virtue? And how can this be done politically? These questions are still necessary to ask, and possible to answer—if not in such archaic terms. I leave the task of finding appropriate terms to others or for another occasion.

I conclude with a few lessons for political scientists and a piece of advice for executives.

Political scientists should, first, be mindful of the origin of their questions. They need to know whether the phenomenon they study is natural to politics and coeval with it—thus inevitable—or artificial, invented for a purpose, and changeable. Executive power, we have seen, was invented; but it has a natural basis in monarchy which it both reflects and attempts to repress. To appreciate the power of political science to affect politics, political scientists must be aware of the history of their discipline: in practice, they must learn the difference between the Greeks, who saw politics so well and so calmly, and the bolder, more inventive moderns. Political scientists today come in at what they believe is the end of the question, wrongly assuming that their point of entry is the culmination of human science. They study "the executive" in the behavior of the American president today. In that particular attribution of universality, they are correct: the American president *is* the critical executive. If only they were less parochial, they would realize how they have chanced upon a truth.

Second, political scientists should study politics through the claims of political partisans, as Aristotle advised. Of course such claims, being words, are equivocal. They are often deceiving or self-deceiving; they are usually difficult to interpret; and so their meaning may be impossible to agree upon. But turning to deeds in order to understand politics, in the hope of finding an unequivocal measure independent of faithless, unreliable words, is chasing a phantom. This unconsciously Machiavellian move, characteristic of all kinds of behavioralists, would not have impressed Machiavelli. He knew that deeds by themselves are dumb and that they make sense only by imputing necessity to them. Our behavioralists imitate that imputation when they speak of "interest" or "rational choice" or concoct any other value-neutral term. But "necessity" is a word, and so are its variants. Applying that word to the deeds of political actors is more arbitrary than examining the words one hears from their mouths, because in doing so one confounds necessity and choice and thus deliberately robs both of their meaning. Nothing in this lesson denies the common sense of judging words by deeds to see how seriously they were spoken. It is the methodical dismissal of political claims that is objectionable.

Next, if words matter, political scientists should pay attention to the choice of words they find in politics, not assume that they are the only ones who use words advisedly. (I have mentioned their neglect of the word "executive.") Such terms may have been introduced by a political scientist of the past, a possibility which should command their respect; or popular discourse may have hit upon a revealing name for an interesting feature of the political landscape. It is remarkable that today's political scientists, themselves so partial to democracy, should think the political speech of common people so valueless in understanding politics. When, for example, one hears executives praised as "charismatic," that is not only a phenomenon to be explained but also a perception to be assessed.

Fourth, political scientists should not assume the possibility of formal analysis. Studying the executive, whose stubborn essence is an informal power necessarily greater than any definition can anticipate or systematize, would be a good cure for behavioralism or other methodological disease. (But to get better, the patient must know he is sick.) Where it is a case of one prince and his glory, there is not much for the quantitative expert to count. And the little rules of executive behavior, precisely because they are systematic, apply only to the mediocre in competition with one another. In modern politics, the executive stands for what is singular, individual, and particular. Any science that does not recognize those qualities but insists on counting, aggregating, and formalizing will not comprehend executive power.

Last, political scientists should not believe that democracy is the only regime. To be a thinking partisan of democracy, one must be able to compare its merits to those of other regimes. Quoting Winston Churchill's quip that democracy is the worst regime except for all the others does not suffice for a political scientist—especially since it is clear that Churchill himself had reflected on the question. Only with practice in comparing regimes does one become aware of the degree to which modern democracy is a compromised democracy, a mixed regime. Above all, in the presence of executive power political scientists should not marvel at the veneration for monarchy in unenlightened times, or wonder where it has gone in ours.

Some years ago it was still a question whether executives would do better by being trained in a science or by learning in the "school of hard knocks." Now it is clear that the business schools and their methods have won a victory: the executive has been professionalized. Professionalized means collectivized. Today's executive is so packaged by consultants and confined by bureaucracy that he yearns atavistically to do something on his own, by himself. That is the Machiavelli in him. He wants to be alone—if he is president, on the summit. At the summit, a president is on top because he is alone and alone because he is on top. In other words, it is a delusion to confuse loneliness with singularity and singularity with excellence. The desire to be alone could be misinterpreted as a wish for charisma—which is in truth its very opposite, the desire to be popular. But if there is one clear result of our study, it is that the perceived need for executive power constitutes an admission of the need for virtue. All authorities on the topic confirm that no law or system can actually ensure the behavior it summons without depending on an executive who is at least in part outside the law and not explained by the system. Whatever is not self-executing is in the realm of virtue. But what is virtue, you ask? Perhaps it is the perfection of the soul—not an easy thought in these times, but bracing, refreshing, restorative.

Notes

PREFACE

1. For a discussion of this term, see ch. 8, p. 187; ch. 10, p. 255.
2. Machiavelli's thought was also appropriated, if not exactly domesticated, in Marxism; see the work of Antonio Gramsci, especially *Note
   sul Machiavelli* (Turin: G. Einaudi, 1974).
3. J. G. A. Pocock, *The Machiavellian Moment* (Princeton, NJ: Princeton
   University Press, 1975); Quentin Skinner, *The Foundations of Modern
   Political Thought*. 2 vols. (Cambridge: Cambridge University Press,
   1978).
4. Less simply, the difference is between virtue as both means and
   end, and virtue as a means only; see Aristotle, *Politics*, 1310a12–22;
   1337a10–23; 1338a9–12.
5. Pocock, *Machiavellian Moment*, pp. vii–ix, 524–26, 544–45.
6. For Skinner, the essential discovery of modern political thought was
   the modern state, and this he defines with reference to Max Weber,
   not to Machiavelli; Skinner, *Foundations of Modern Political Thought*,
   I. x, II. 358.

Chapter 1
INTRODUCTION: THE AMBIVALENCE OF EXECUTIVE POWER

1. Article II, section 3.
2. Kant, *Metaphysik der Sitten, Rechtslehre*, II. 45.
3. *Pacificus*, no. 1 (June 29, 1793); *The Papers of Alexander Hamilton*, Harold C. Syrett, ed. 26 vols. (New York: Columbia University Press,
   1961–79), XV. 33–43; *Federalist* 70.
4. See Richard M. Pious, *The American Presidency* (New York: Basic
   Books, 1979), p. 45.
5. Kant, *Metaphysik*, II. 48: the executive in the syllogism is a "per-

son''; as coordinate, he is a "moral person." The question of executive power provides a useful vignette of Kant's political and moral philosophy.

6. Chester Barnard's use of the phrase has not caught on. For him, "executive process" is the only way to speak of the executive's sense of the whole organization. That process is "non-logical" but cooperative rather than imperious. Barnard's is a mild, organizational executive, but the "sense of the whole" claimed for him holds the possibility of decisive action. Chester I. Barnard, *The Functions of the Executive* (Cambridge, MA: Harvard University Press, 1938), ch. 16. One might also find "the executive process" in Hobbes's definition of deliberation as an alternation of appetite and aversion; but the last appetite is called the "will," a more decisive but more whimsical execution than Barnard's. Thomas Hobbes, *Leviathan*, W. G. Pogson Smith, ed. (Oxford: Clarendon Press, 1909), ch. 6, pp. 46–47. For another instance, see Paul H. Appleby, *Morality and Administration* (Baton Rouge, LA: Louisiana State University Press, 1952), p. 87.

7. See also Clinton Rossiter, *The American Presidency* (New York: Harcourt, Brace and World, 1956).

8. Nor is C. Herman Pritchett, "The President's Constitutional Position," in Thomas E. Cronin and Rexford G. Tugwell, eds., *The Presidency Reappraised*, 2nd ed. (New York: Praeger, 1977), pp. 3–23. See also Joseph Bessette and Jeffrey Tulis, eds., *The Presidency in the Constitutional Order* (Baton Rouge, LA: Louisiana State University Press, 1981); and Pious, *American Presidency.* The phrase "literary theory" is from Walter Bagehot, quoted by Woodrow Wilson (*Congressional Government*, New York, 1956, p. 30), and used by Richard Neustadt, *Presidential Power* (New York: John Wiley & Sons, 1962), p. 43; see 14 below.

9. Corwin, *The President: Offices and Powers 1787–1957*, 4th ed. (New York: New York University Press, 1957), p. 291. Cf. Corwin, "The Progress of Constitutional Theory between the Declaration of Independence and the Meeting of the Philadelphia Convention," *American Historical Review*, vol. 30 (1925), p. 521.

10. Arthur M. Schlesinger, Jr., *The Imperial Presidency* (New York: Popular Library, 1973), p. 169; Theodore J. Lowi, *The Personal President* (Ithaca, NY: Cornell University Press, 1985), p. 211.

11. Corwin, *The President*, p. 307.

12. Neustadt, *Presidential Power*, pp. 7, 9–10, 179, 183. The presidency is the "greatest of all" offices, the only one that commands "a view of the whole ground," said Thomas Jefferson in his First Inaugural Address.

13. Ibid., pp. 31, 198n1.

14. Ibid., pp. 33, 43. Surely the "literary theory" is not adequate to the forms of the Constitution if it means that the president should be a mere dictionary executive. But see the literary theory in *Federalist* 47. In the 1976 edition of *Presidential Power* Neustadt again comes close to acknowledging my point: "the need to bargain is a product of a constitutional system that shares formal powers among separate institutions" (p. 12).

15. For Neustadt's book, first published in 1960, was recognized to be the most formative in the creation of what Thomas E. Cronin has called "the textbook presidency," which shows that even realism may be, indeed must be, formalized in a doctrine. Cronin, *The State of the Presidency* (Boston, MA: Little, Brown, 1975), ch. 2. Lowi treats Neustadt's book expressly as a "new governmental theory." *Personal President*, p. 57.

16. Neustadt, *Presidential Power,* pp. 38, 46.

17. A comparative study of presidential style is in fact much needed and sadly lacking in the literature.

18. Ibid., pp. 9–10.

19. Fred I. Greenstein, *The Hidden-Hand Presidency* (New York: Basic Books, 1982), pp. 5, 121n, 234–35.

20. Pious, *American Presidency,* p. 422.

21. Ibid., p. 333. The "Rule of Constitutional Construction" given on pp. 41–46 would serve beautifully for scholars of philosophical texts as canons of overinterpretation.

22. "The irreducible core of presidential power lies with the constitutional prerogatives of the office." Ibid., p. 63.

23. The presidential and congressionalist parties began in the Philadelphia convention, Pious notes; ibid., pp. 26–27, 213. Montesquieu, *The Spirit of the Laws* XIX. 27; see ch. 9.

24. Pious, *American Presidency,* p. 38.

25. Ibid., pp. 15–17.

26. James D. Barber, *The Presidential Character: Predicting Performance in the White House* (Englewood Cliffs, NJ: Prentice-Hall, 1972).

27. Ibid., p. 11; Erwin C. Hargrove, *Presidential Leadership: Personality and Political Style* (New York: Macmillan, 1966), p. 3. This active-positive executive, with characteristic executive ambivalence, frequently pops out of the matrix in which he is merely one among four possibilities to become the standard by which all executives are judged. Cf. James H. Qualls, "Barber's Typological Analysis of Political Leaders," *American Political Science Review,* vol. 71, no. 1 (March 1977), p. 192; Lowi, *Personal President,* pp. 136–37.

28. Hargrove, *Presidential Leadership,* p. 72.

29. See the account of Erwin C. Hargrove, "What Manner of Man?" in James D. Barber, ed., *Choosing the President* (Englewood Cliffs, NJ: Prentice-Hall, 1974), p. 18.

30. Harold D. Lasswell, *Power and Personality* (New York: Viking, 1948), p. 54. See the similar statement in Aristotle, *Politics,* 1325a34–37.

31. Lasswell, *Power and Personality,* p. 108.

32. Ibid., pp. 9–16, 174, 181. Note how the discussion of power in this book moves from the giving and taking of cues to something rather more punitive.

33. Ibid., pp. 58–89. One should not miss his celebrated, lively portraits of Judges X, Y, and Z, pp. 64–87.

34. Hargrove, *Presidential Leadership,* p. 153.

35. M. J. C. Vile, *Constitutionalism and the Separation of Powers* (Oxford: Oxford University Press, 1967), pp. 2, 17, 33–34, 101, 135, 143; W. B. Gwyn, *The Meaning of the Separation of Powers,* "Tulane Studies in Political Science," vol. IX (New Orleans, 1965), pp. 26, 37, 108.

36. As Herbert J. Storing has said, "the administrative principle, while calling for the executive's independence, implies executive subordination to the legislature; the political principle, on the other hand, implies an equality (in not, indeed, a superiority) of the executive in the constitutional scheme. The beginning of wisdom about the American Presidency is to see that it contains both the principles and to reflect on their complex and subtle relation." Introduction to Charles C. Thach, Jr., *The Creation of the Presidency 1775–1789* (rev. ed., Baltimore: Johns Hopkins University Press, 1969), p. vii. Also Doris Kearns: "the analytical problem is to understand not only where the president is too strong but also where he is too weak; to delineate what is meant by strong and weak and to describe the curious relationship between the two." "Lyndon Johnson's Political Personality," in Cronin and Tugwell, *Presidency Reappraised,* p. 131. And see Edward S. Corwin, "Some Aspects of the Presidency," *Annals of the American Academy of Political and Social Sciences,* vol. 218 (1941), pp. 122–31.

37. *History of the Decline and Fall of the Roman Empire.* 6 vols. (New York: Everyman ed. n.d.), I. 1; cf. I. 370, IV. 131.

38. In the justly famous exchange of views on executive power between Roosevelt and William Howard Taft, Roosevelt proclaimed, with a view to his rival, that "every executive officer . . . was a steward of the people, bound actively and affirmatively to do all he could for the people, and not to content himself with the negative merit of keeping his talents undamaged in a napkin." Theodore Roosevelt, *Autobiography* (New York: Macmillan, 1913), p. 389. Yet what is the

phrase "steward of the people" but a napkin to keep TR's talents undamaged so that he can exploit them? It is hardly bolder than Taft's claim that the president is the "Chief Agent" of the people. William Howard Taft, *Our Chief Magistrate and his Powers* (New York: Columbia University Press, 1916), pp. 139–44, 157. Roosevelt and Taft differ on the question whether, as Taft put it, the president can "exercise no power which cannot be fairly and reasonably traced to some specific grant of power." But the specific grant in the Constitution is wide, perhaps wider than TR's unspecific claim which in our day might make him a prisoner of surveys of popular sentiment.

39. Cf. Pious's chapter on "domestic program innovation," *American Presidency,* pp. 147–75. Lowi brings out the less attractive Machiavellian aspect of Neustadt's "initiatives," *Personal President,* pp. 137–38.

40. Sheldon S. Wolin, *Politics and Vision* (Boston, MA: Little, Brown, 1960), pp. 221–24.

41. On the distinction between ruling and representation, see Harvey C. Mansfield, Jr., "Hobbes and the Science of Indirect Government," *American Political Science Review,* vol. 65 (1971), pp. 97–110; and Harvey C. Mansfield, Jr. and Robert Scigliano, *Representation: The Perennial Issues,* pamphlet published by the American Political Science Association, 1978, pp. 15–23.

42. This is implied in Thomas E. Cronin, "The Presidency and its Paradoxes;" Cronin and Tugwell, *Presidency Reappraised,* pp. 69–85; but one should consider whether the Constitution is indeed "of little help in explaining any of this" (p. 69).

43. Neustadt, *Presidential Power,* p. vii.

44. Plato, *Crito,* 50d–51c.

45. *Federalist* 78. For judicial power as "executive," see John Locke, *Two Treatises of Government,* II. 130; and Montesquieu, *Spirit of the Laws,* XI. 6 (beg.).

Chapter 2
ARISTOTLE: THE EXECUTIVE AS KINGSHIP

1. Plato, *Laws* 871d–e, 872b–c. A convicted murderer can be killed, if he returns from exile, by a relative of the one he murdered, by the first citizen he meets, or by the rulers who judged him. There is no office of executive except for the slave who murders, and then it is implied that the public executioner is himself a slave (872b8).

2. *Laws* 853b2–c3; or is it "shameful in some way," that is, in a way assuming human responsibility?

3. *Laws* 875c–d; see 876c–d, 914a, 925e–926b, 962d.

4. Xenophon, *Cyropaideia* III.1.27, 29 (trust the gratitude of those whom you spare from punishment more than that of those whom you have favored); III.3.56 (pin the responsibility for timid advice on the adviser); V.4.20 (fight with all your resources); V.4.51 (attack the weaker to intimidate the stronger); VIII.2.27 (let those who are to be judged choose their judges).

5. See the useful survey of scholarship by Renato Laurenti, *Genesi e formazione della "Politica" di Aristotele* (Padova: Cedam, 1965), pp. 5–42. Richard Robinson says: "The fact is, probably, that the Politics is a collection of long essays and brief jottings pretending to be a treatise." *Aristotle's Politics, Books III and IV*, R. Robinson, ed. (Oxford: Clarendon Press, 1962), p. ix. Cf. Jean Aubonnet, ed., Aristote, *Politique* (Paris: Les Belles-Lettres, 1971), II.4; C. H. Rowe, "Aims and Methods in Aristotle's *Politics*," *Classical Quarterly*, vol. 27 (1977), p. 160; and Carnes Lord, "The Character and Composition of Aristotle's *Politics*," *Political Theory*, vol. 9 (1981), pp. 459–78. For Ernest Barker it is also a "fact" that the *Politics* is "a collection or conflation of different essays rather than a single treatise," but he warns that "differences of tone and emphasis . . . may well be merely the differences inherent in different contexts." Barker, trans., *The Politics of Aristotle* (New York: Oxford University Press, 1962), pp. xxxvii, xlvi. W. D. Ross, *Aristotle* (London: Longman's, 1923), p. 236; W. L. Newman, *The Politics of Aristotle*, 4 vols. (Oxford: Oxford University Press, 1902), II xxix–xxxii.

6. On Book III of the Politics, see Leo Strauss, *The City and Man* (Chicago: Rand McNally, 1964), ch. 1; Harry V. Jaffa, "Aristotle," in Leo Strauss and Joseph Cropsey, eds. *History of Political Philosophy*, 2nd ed. (Chicago: Rand McNally, 1972), pp. 64–129; Delba Winthrop, "Aristotle and Political Responsibility," *Political Theory*, vol. 3 (1975), pp. 406–22, and "Aristotle on Participatory Democracy," *Polity*, vol. 11 (1978), pp. 151–71; Egon Braun, "Das dritte Buch der aristotelischen 'Politik': Interpretation," *Sitzungsberichte der Österreichischen Akademie der Wissenschaften*, philos.-hist. Kl., 247.4 (1965).

7. The error of the pre-Socratics. See Aristotle's reference to Socrates' "second voyage" in Book III, *Politics* 1284b19.

8. If we are nature's property (*Politics* 1254a12–17), then all human beings are natural slaves; if nature belongs to us (1256b20–22), men are free to acquire without limit. Thus slavery and acquisition are the two topics of Book I, reflecting the ambivalence of Aristotle's teleology.

9. Aristotle, *Metaphysics* 1012b34–1013a24.

10. See *Politics* 1301a29–30, at the beginning of Book V, where the ab-

soluteness of the democratic and the oligarchic claims is emphasized.

11. *Politics* 1275a35. For a recent consideration, see Robert A. Dahl, *Dilemmas of Pluralist Democracy* (New Haven, CT: Yale University Press, 1982), p. 98.

12. Perhaps the good man will also wonder about this, unless he is in a regime where he can be the statesman. His occupation is with necessities, and his situation, if ruled by others, is comparable to that of the banausic. Note that Aristotle restates his conclusion on the good man and the good citizen after discussing the banausics. *Politics,* 1278b1–5. Harry V. Jaffa, "Aristotle," in Strauss and Cropsey, *History of Political Philosophy,* p. 100.

13. Aristotle indicates his appreciation of the democratic objection by distinguishing next the correct regimes from the deviants on the basis of freedom. Correct regimes aim at the benefit in common, but those aiming only at the rulers' advantage are despotic; and the city is a community of the free. That the benefit in common does not *require* democracy we see from the example of the trainer and the pilot. *Politics* 1279a1–28; Strauss, *City and Man,* pp. 35–37.

14. In the next section Aristotle contrasts wealth and the oligarchical city based on commercial contracts with virtue, whereas previously he had contrasted freedom with virtue. *Politics* 1280a26–1281a9, cf. 1278a10.

15. See Harvey C. Mansfield, Jr., "Constitutionalism and the Rule of Law," *Harvard Journal of Law and Public Policy,* vol. 8 (1985), pp. 323–26; R. G. Mulgan, *Aristotle's Political Theory* (Oxford: Clarendon Press, 1977), pp. 82–88.

16. *Politics* 1283a16, 1283b29–31. Aristotle changes the verb for "claim" when it becomes clear that a claim against another party is a claim over all.

17. *Politics* 1285a7–15. Delba Winthrop, *Aristotle: Democracy and Political Science* (unpublished doctoral dissertation: Harvard University, 1974), pp. 341–43.

18. *Politics* 1286a10–16, cf. 1287a17, 34; 1269a18–25. The example refers to the law regarding the arts in ultra-conservative Egypt, which permitted a doctor to change his treatment after four days; but that *law* could not be changed.

19. *Politics* 1286a16–20. See also 1286b3, 1287a15–16.

20. *Politics* 1286b2–4, 1282a39. Here the multitude is made moderate by dividing it through formal institutions.

21. *Politics* 1287a10. The emendations here should be rejected.

22. See W. R. Newell, "Superlative Virtue: The Problem of Monarchy

in Aristotle's *Politics*," *Western Political Quarterly* vol. 40 (1987), pp. 175–76.

23. *Politics* 1287a33; *De Anima* 414b2–3, 432b3–7; cf. 433a23–27. See P. A. VanderWaerdt, "Kingship and Philosophy in Aristotle's Best Regime," *Phronesis*, vol. 30 (1985), p. 260.

24. In the inquiry on kingship one finds hesitations at 1282b23, 1284a4, 1284a37, 1284b17, 1284b38, 1286a21, 1286b8, 1286b34, 1287b37, 1288a5, 1288a32.

Chapter 3
ARISTOTLE: THE ABSENT EXECUTIVE IN THE MIXED REGIME

1. Vile, *Constitutionalism and the Separation of Powers*, p. 22. See Barker's warning, *The Politics of Aristotle* (New York: Oxford University Press, 1962), p. 193n; Newman's discussion, *The Politics of Aristotle*, IV.236–38; and Eckart Schutrumpf, *Die Analyse der Polis durch Aristoteles* (Amsterdam: Gruner, 1980), p. 240n4.

2. For the first two forms of tyranny, the barbarian and the ancient Greek, Aristotle mentions only unaccountability as the criterion of tyranny; in the third, modern form, he adds the lack of benefit to be ruled. Thus he flatters the free men of his day for their resistance to tyranny, while illustrating his point that men must be flattered because even when inferior to others, they will consider themselves similar or better.

3. *Politics* 1295a3; 1293b29. My translation of 1295a3 follows that of Thomas Taylor the Platonist. Besides being one of the regimes, tyranny is a part of regimes.

4. This is a concern of the gym coach or political scientist (1288b16), who tries to transform the desires of his charges into acceptance of what is fitting for them.

5. The failure of the Spartan mixed regime has just been explained, *Politics* 1294b12–39.

6. Cf. Plato *Laws* 757b–3. The Athenian Stranger accepts the necessity of lot reluctantly and with a prayer, not preserving the standpoint of human recalcitrance.

7. In our day this democratic attitude has been expressed by John Rawls:"No one deserves his greater natural capacity nor merits a more favorable starting place in society." *A Theory of Justice* (Cambridge, MA: Harvard University Press, 1971), p. 102. How then does a human being deserve his lot? In this view, "human" rights as a whole, which depend on man's favored place in nature, must be undeserved.

8. There is some doubt that ruling is part of the rational soul because, as we shall see, it is connected to *thumos* in the irrational soul.

9. See Harvey C. Mansfield, Jr., "The Absent Executive in Aristotle's *Politics,*" in T. B. Silver and P. W. Schramm, eds., *Natural Right and Political Right* (Durham, NC: Carolina Academic Press, 1984), pp. 169–96, for a longer version of the following analysis of Book IV.

10. The soul is more a part than is a body (*Politics* 1291a24) because it is a part of several possible wholes. See also 1278b8.

11. Earlier in Book IV, at 1291a27–31, Aristotle speaks of deliberating and judging as parts of the soul but not as ruling; here he discusses them as ruling and together with the offices, but not as parts of the soul.

12. Again, in 1291a27–31, it is shown that deliberating and judging may be done in separate parts of the city or in the same part, but the offices, the element of polity, are lacking. In the intervening argument Aristotle shows that it is necessary to mix, and how this may be done.

13. *Politics* 1297b38. Thus, as Barker says (*Politics of Aristotle,* p. 188n), Aristotle fulfills the next-to-last item on the program given near the beginning of Book IV at 1289b13–26. Cf. Newman, *Politics of Aristotle,* IV.235.

14. See Pierre Aubenque, *La prudence chez Aristote,* 3rd ed. (Paris: Presses Universitaires de France, 1986), pp. 26, 111–17; and Larry Arnhart, *Aristotle on Political Reasoning* (Dekalb, Ill.: Northern Illinois University Press, 1981), pp. 55–57, 71–75.

15. To study an Aristotelian list, one must make an accurate translation with special attention to the prepositions and conjunctions that create sets. Aristotle says: "The deliberative is sovereign about war and peace and alliance and dissolution, and about laws, and about death and exile and confiscation, and the audits." (1289a4–7) The three "abouts" give three sets; the "ands" and the sense give five sets; and the items are nine. "Laws" are in the center of each.

16. *Politics* 1291a28, where the context would suggest joining the necessary and the noble.

17. See esp. *De Anima* 426b8–427a15, 432a16; *Metaphysics* 990a24, 995b2–4, 1008b2–1009a5; *Nicomachean Ethics* 1118a28, 1134a31, 1165a34; *Politics* 1289b11, 1291a40, 1321a30.

18. In general, men cannot rule by one of the possibilities alone. This finding is confirmed by the lists of several democracies, oligarchies, aristocracies, and polities that Aristotle has supplied earlier in Book IV. In these lists it is shown that the several democracies and oligarchies can be understood together as either all democracies or all oli-

garchies, depending on the standard of judgment applied to them. Just as all regimes can be found in each, so each can be found in all. See 1291b30–1292b10 and 1292b10–1293a35.

19. See *Politics* 1294b11 and 1273a18, 1317b21. Hobbes has it that lot (in view of the lot of primogeniture) is an aristocratic principle; *De Cive,* III 18. See note 7 above.

20. Aristotle makes it explicit at the end of this section that his discussion has served to delimit both deliberation and sovereignty, *Politics* 1299a2–3; see *Nicomachean Ethics* 1112b33.

21. On priests, see *Politics* 1322b18, 1328b11, 1329a27, 1331b5; on chorus-sponsors, see 1276b5, 1309a19. Aristotle does not explain why priests et al. are not rulers (Aubonnet, *Politique* II.326n3 and Newman, *The Politics of Aristotle,* IV.256), because the matter is a delicate one.

22. Aristotle directs this inconclusive discussion to a "dianoetic inquiry." See *Eudemian Ethics* 1249b10–17; *Metaphysics* 982a18, 1072b2–14; *Physics* 184a15.

23. Hence Aristotle speaks next of aristocratic offices, *Politics* 1300a4–6.

24. *Federalist* 72.

25. Plato, *Republic* 557d.

26. *Politics* 1300a20; cf. 1294a35–1294b40. See G. J. D. Aalders, "Die Mischverfassung und ihre historische Dokumentation in den *Politika des Aristoteles,*" Fondation Hardt, Entretiens sur l'Antiquité Classique, vol. 11 (1965), p. 209.

27. This addition is reflected in Aristotle's addition of the democratic and oligarchic modes. He says: "And so the modes become twelve, apart from the two combinations." The twelve modes can be counted with this key: 1) all 2) some 3) from all 4) from some 5) vote 6) lot 7) in turn. Thus: 135, 136, 145, 146, 175, 176; 235, 236, 245, 246, 275, 276. 145, 146 and 275, 276 are not given but ought to be counted: all from some and some from a section in turn. The two "combinations," a) some in turn and some from all, and b) some by vote and some by lot, reflect the two standpoints of the chosen and the chooser: democracy and oligarchy. They are to be set apart because their separateness is overcome in aristocracy.

28. Newman, *Politics of Aristotle,* IV.269.

29. See also *Politics* 1281b31–1282a24, 1287a10–26; *Nicomachean Ethics* 1112b32, 1141b34. John Locke, *Two Treatises of Government,* II.7–13.

30. *De Anima* 926b8–927a15; *Metaphysics* 995b2–4, 1008b2–1009a5; *Rhetoric* 1354a36–b8. Winthrop, "Aristotle on Participatory Democracy," p. 170.

31. Beauty of soul is not separable from beauty of body; and so Aristotle

says, with some understatement, that it is "not easy to see" beauty of soul; *Politics* 1254b39.

32. The two final causes given are gain and honor, but gain is indicated to be a cause by comparison with others, that is, when it is a matter of honor; *Politics* 1302a32–1302b2.

33. On democracy: *Politics* 1317a11–1320b17. On oligarchy: 1320b17–1321b3. Aristotle does not cite the example of Solon, who came from "the middle citizens" and founded a democracy; 1296a19. See *Ath. Const.* 12–13.

34. Literally, for one or two or three days—perhaps in the dialogues of Plato? *Politics* 1319b33–37.

35. *Politics* 1321a36–40; *cf.* 1318b17. Note that this virtue leads to the second necessary office of maintaining buildings that are falling down; 1321b20. It is also interesting that the gods do not maintain their own houses, and the eleventh office must be assigned this among other similar duties; 1322b22.

36. *Politics* 1321b8: *oikeisthai,* implying the management of one's own; this is something of a private task for the honor-lovers. It can also mean "settled in."

37. *Politics* 1321b41–1322a2. This office is *almost* the most necessary and difficult, because the first office could be held to be so if "markets" are taken in the most extended sense as the traffic of human beings with all things.

38. *Politics* 1322a7; *Nicomachean Ethics* 1180a21. Newman (*Politics of Aristotle,* IV.557) refers to Plato, *Crito,* 50b.

39. In Book VII Aristotle says that judges are the most necessary of the necessary tasks in the city, 1328b13.

40. *Politics* 1322a10; cf. 1322a1. This strange category may include those who write about the *archai* in the more elevated sense; for in writing about the beginning principles of nature and men they can hardly avoid identifying them with the gods, as can Aristotle with his ambivalent writing.

41. *Politics* 1284b31. The eleventh office here is men caring for the gods, but not executing their decrees; 1322b19.

42. *Politics* 1322a23–26. The base can make great profit out of guarding prisoners if, to do this, they rule, 1322a3. On the base, see 1254b1. Though more explicit than Aristotle, Montaigne has captured his spirit if not his tone in the following superbly sardonic passage. Note that for all his realism, Montaigne betrays no Machiavellian confusion as to who is virtuous and base:

> In every government there are necessary offices, not only abject but also vicious; there the vices find their place and are

employed in making the seam of our union, like poisons for the preservation of our health. If they become excusable since they answer our need and the common necessity effaces their true quality, one must allow this part to be played by the more vigorous and less fearful citizens, who sacrifice their honor and conscience for the salvation of their country, as others of old sacrificed their lives. We who are weaker take up roles that are more easy and less hazardous. The public good requires that one betray, lie, and murder; let us resign this commission to men who are more obedient and more supple. (Montaigne, *Essays* III.1.)

43. See Tocqueville, *Democracy in America* II; IV.7; Harvey C. Mansfield, Jr., "The Forms of Liberty," in Fred E. Baumann, ed., *Democratic Capitalism? Essays in Search of a Concept* (Charlottesville, VA: University of Virginia, 1986), pp. 1–21.

Chapter 4
PROTO-EXECUTIVES

1. Likewise the somewhat surreptitious praise of the early Athenian tyrants to be found in Thucydides and Plato. Thucydides I.20; VI.54–55; Leo Strauss, "On the *Minos*," in *Liberalism Ancient and Modern* (New York: Basic Books, 1968), pp. 74–75.

2. See Pierre Manent, *Histoire intellectuelle du libéralisme: dix leçons* (Paris: Calmann-Levy, 1987), pp. 18–19.

3. "A system of automatic checks," F. W. Walbank, *Polybius* (Berkeley, CA: University of California Press, 1972), p. 150; see also Kurt von Fritz, *The Theory of the Mixed Constitution in Antiquity* (New York: Columbia University Press, 1954), pp. 183, 219; Polybius, *Histories* VI.11–18. But cf. VI.10.6, where Polybius refers to a mixture of *virtues* in Lycurgus's mixed regime.

4. Polybius, I.2.8, 35.9; III.47.8; VI.5.2; IX.2.4; XII.25e1, 27a1; XXX.17.1; XXXIX.1.4. See Walbank, *Polybius,* pp. 56–57, 66–73; Walbank, *A Historical Commentary on Polybius* (Oxford: Clarendon Press, 1957), pp. 6–16; Paul Pédech, *La Méthode historique de Polybe* (Paris; 1964), pp. 25–29; von Fritz, *Mixed Constitution,* pp. 40–44.

5. Machiavelli appropriates Polybius's account with significant changes, *Discourses on Livy* I.2; see Harvey C. Mansfield, Jr., *Machiavelli's New Modes and Orders* (Ithaca, NY: Cornell University Press, 1979), pp. 32–41. Montesquieu, *Spirit of the Laws,* IV.8; see also *Oeuvres complètes de Montesquieu,* Andre Masson, ed., 3 vols. (Paris: Nagel, 1950) II.493, III.1218.

6. Polybius, I.1–2, 4.11; VI.2.8–9. Cf. Walbank, *Polybius*, p. 28; Pédech, *Méthode*, p. 30.

7. Polybius, VI.5.1–4. This confession did not save Polybius from the charge in our time of not knowing Plato's work directly or of not caring about it; Walbank, *Commentary*, pp. 2, 645, 650, 657; *Polybius*, pp. 32–33.

8. *Caput civilis prudentiae;* Cicero, *Republic* II.25.45.

9. Polybius mentions inbred pests such as rust in iron and worms in wood: natural virtue and natural degeneration from it; VI.10.3.

10. Polybius, VI.10.6, 13–14; cf. Aristotle, *Politics* 1324b5–10.

11. On Polybius's mixed regime see von Fritz, *Mixed Constitution*, chs. 4, 8; Walbank, *Polybius*, pp. 144–50.

12. See Polybius, I.1.5, 3.4, 4.1–2 (cf. I.63.9); VI. 2.3.

13. Polybius's understanding of *kata physin* is often misinterpreted as a necessary or determined law of nature in the modern sense; see VI.10.12–14, 57.1. Walbank, *Polybius*, pp. 142, 145–46; von Fritz, *Mixed Constitution*, p. 84. The "necessity of nature" (*tēs physeos anankē*, VI.57.1) is decay and change, but the regularity of the cycle, while foreseeable by a statesman, is not predictable by a (modern) scientist. The fact that cyclical changes take place "necessarily and naturally" (*anankaios kai physikos*, VI.10.2) does not mean that necessary is identical to natural for Polybius.

14. See Polybius, VI.48.2–3, regarding Sparta, but he does not comment on Roman education. Cf. Cicero, *Republic* IV.3: Education of the young is "the one thing of which our guest Polybius blames the neglect in our institutions."

15. Polybius, unlike Aristotle but like Plato, does not look for the best regime in actual regimes; so the three parts of the Roman regime cannot correspond to three functions of an individual soul, as in Book IV of Aristotle's *Politics*. Cf. Polybius, VI.48.3, on the legislation and foresight of Lycurgus.

16. Cicero, *Republic* II.16.30, 21.37.

17. Cf. Walbank, *Polybius*, p. 149, who takes a sensibly sceptical view of this "archeology," unannounced by Polybius and imagined by scholars today on the basis of a few "miserable remains" of text (Pédech, *Méthode*, p. 313). Because Cicero sometimes acknowledges the help of Polybius, it is supposed that his account of the early history of Rome (*Republic* II.1–37) is based on Polybius, though this is not only not acknowledged, it is even denied, by Cicero (II.1.3, 11.21). Cicero's unacknowledged borrowing can then be used to fill out Polybius's unannounced archeology! This is what happens

when ingenuity, in establishing a text, replaces reflection on the text.

18. Polybius, VI.19–42 on the army, as compared with VI.11–18 on the regime.

19. "Polybius is apt to identify success with moral worth." Walbank, *Polybius,* p. 178.

20. Polybius compares Sparta with Crete (VI.45–47), and Rome with Carthage (VI.52–56), but not Sparta with Rome.

21. Machiavelli says, in the passage he appropriated from Polybius and transformed (*Discourses on Livy* I.2), that a state would rarely go through the changes of the cycle because it would soon fall victim to a better–ordered neighbor—that is, to a neighbor ordered for acquisition.

22. Rousseau, *On the Social Contract* IV 6; Marx, *The Civil War in France,* Intro., III; *Critique of the Gotha Program,* IV; letter to Joseph Weydemeyer, March 5, 1852.

23. See the references (s.v. "dictatorship") in Herbert J. Storing, *The Complete Anti-Federalist,* 7 vols. (Chicago, IL: University of Chicago Press, 1981).

24. Carl Schmitt, *Die Diktatur,* 3rd ed. (Berlin: Duncker und Humblot, 1964), pp. 6–13.

25. The Roman dictator had a precedent in the *aisymnetai* of the Greeks, whom Aristotle discusses as elective tyrants (*Politics* 1285a29–42, 1295a11–17). These he appears to deprecate for being characteristic of "ancient Greeks," hence obsolete, and similar to the monarchies found among barbarians, who are slavish and willing to put up with irresponsible rule. Aristotle himself, we have seen, held a much subtler view that takes account of the element of tyranny in all rule while refusing to formalize or encourage it in any way. Cf. Machiavelli, *Discourses on Livy* I.34.

26. For the phrase "one alone," see Machiavelli, *Discourses on Livy* I.9, 33. The quotation from Bodin is in the English translation of Richard Knolles (1606). Jean Bodin, *The Six Books of a Commonweale,* K. McRae, ed. (Cambridge, MA: Harvard University Press, 1962), p. 716. The French original is less apt for our purpose: *faire* instead of "execution" and *un personnage* rather than "one alone."

27. The Tacitean original is in the *Annals* I.6 (my thanks to Eve Adler for the reference). In Tacitus, the remark refers not to great exploits but to a sordid murder, not to a dictator but to the emperor, and it is made not in Tacitus's name but in that of a self-interested counsellor. Tacitus shows his disdain for this "first crime of the new principate," done through fear and stepmotherly hatred in just the situation that Machiavelli might have exploited.

28. The incompleteness of Polybius's Book VI does not detract from the significance of omitting the dictator at this point.

29. Livy, II.18, 30; III.20.8; IV.17.8, 26.6, 56.8; VI.38.3; VIII.32.3.

30. See also Plutarch's "one strong mind" to describe the dictator, *Life of Camillus* 18.6.

31. Romans 13:4, KJV. *Dikonos,* the New Testament Greek for "minister" here, is used by Aristotle to denote menial service; *Politics* 1333a8.

32. Ernst H. Kantorowicz, *The King's Two Bodies* (Princeton, NJ: Princeton University Press, 1957), pp. 89–93, 456, as interpreted by Manent, *Libéralisme,* p. 29n.

33. "The concept of an Emperor of the Romans served the pope as an instrument of creating an assistant on a universal scale, an *advocatus,* the strong arm to execute his program." Walter Ullmann, *A History of Political Thought: the Middle Ages* (London: Penguin Books, 1965), p. 95.

34. Ibid, pp. 32, 45–47. Walter Ullmann, *The Growth of Papal Government in the Middle Ages,* 3rd ed. (London: Methuen, 1970), pp. 31–36. Norman H. Baynes, *Byzantine Studies and Other Essays* (London: The Athlone Press, 1955), pp. 48–50, 55, 168–72.

35. Ullmann, *History,* pp. 65, 93–95, 39; *Papal Government,* p. 1. Robert Folz, *L'idée d'empire en Occident du Vᵉ au XIVᵉ Siècle* (Paris: Aubier, 1953), pp. 17–18, 29.

36. Ullmann, *History,* pp. 60–63; Folz, *L'idée d'empire,* pp. 19–21.

37. *Papa a nemine judicatur,* Ullmann, *History,* pp. 29, 106; *Papal Government,* p. 48.

38. Machiavelli, *Florentine Histories* I.11, cf. I.9. Despite his sardonic criticisms, Machiavelli had great respect for the papacy. Indeed, one might say that he masked his respect with his criticisms; see *The Prince,* 11.

Chapter 5
THE THEOLOGICO-POLITICAL EXECUTIVE

1. The following exposition owes much to Ernest L. Fortin, "Natural Law and Social Justice," *The American Journal of Jurisprudence,* vol. 30 (1985), pp. 1–20.

2. Natural law and the virtues are connected, yet kept distinct, in *Summa Theologica* Ia IIae 94.3

3. It is dated between 1260 and 1265 by I. T. Eschmann in his introduction to St. Thomas Aquinas, *On Kingship,* G. B. Phelan trans. (Toronto: The Pontifical Institute of Medieval Studies, 1949), p. xxx.

4. Aquinas himself is a kind of founder; he writes a book, he says in the dedication to *On Kingship,* out of his ability (*ingenium*), which relies on the help of God for the beginning, progress, and accomplishment of his work.

5. R. W. and A. J. Carlyle, *A History of Medieval Political Theory in the West.* 6 vols. (London: Blackwood, 1903), V.348–54. Thomas Aquinas, *Summa Theologica* IIa IIae 60.6.3.

6. See Ullmann, *History of Political Thought,* p. 110.

7. Ernest L. Fortin, *Dissidence et philosophie au Moyen-Âge* (Paris: Vrin, 1981), pp. 98–99; and see Dante, *Monarchy* III.9, on the doctrine of two swords.

8. This is the ninth argument for the thesis advanced in Book III of *Monarchy, the* argument from reason which reveals that the two authorities, pope and emperor, necessarily confuse substantial and accidental form; so the appeal to reason suffices neither to sustain nor to overthrow any particular authority.

9. See Fortin, *Dissidence,* ch. 5, and the literature cited there.

10. Fortin, *Dissidence,* p. 126.

11. Note Dante's new word for imperial rule, *imperiatus,* in *Monarchy* III.11. See Fortin, *Dissidence,* pp. 99–100; Kantorowicz, *Two Bodies,* p. 458.

12. See Larry Peterman, "Dante's *Monarchia* and Aristotle's Political Thought," *Studies in Medieval and Renaissance History,* vol. 10 (1973), pp. 3–40.

13. But note the use of *typo* in *Monarchy* I.2, beg.; in I.3, form is presented as the consequence of the end.

14. Cf. Etienne Gilson, *Dante the Philosopher* (London: Sheed and Ward, 1948), p. 178.

15. As in Thomas Aquinas, *Summa Theologica* Ia 79.11.

16. Dante refers to Averroes's commentary on Aristotle's *De Anima* at *Monarchy* I.3, but he himself goes beyond actualizing intellectual virtue in a multitude of philosophers to actualizing both intellectual and moral virtue in a political multitude. On Dante's Averroism in *Monarchy,* see Fortin, *Dissidence,* pp. 99–102; Gilson, *Dante,* pp. 168–71; Bruno Nardi, *Saggi di filosofia dantesca,* 2nd ed. (Florence: La Nuova Italia, 1967), pp. 229–44; and Dante's fourteenth-century opponent, Guido Vernani, *De reprobatione Monarchiae* (1327).

17. The problem is indicated in one small difference of phrasing. Dante announces that his purpose in Book I is to show that temporal monarchy is "necessary for the good of the world" (I.2), and ten of the eleven proofs he supplies repeat the formula or say that monarchy "appears necessary" for the good of the world (I.9), or is necessary

for "the best of the world" (I.11, 13). But in the sixth (and central) proof concerning the need for adjudication between any two princes we find merely that monarchy is *necessary* for the world. Is human virtue the fulfillment of nature's goodness, hence indebted to nature, as Dante's formula implies? Or shall we take our cue from the central proof and suppose that human virtue is necessary to the world, hence that nature is indebted to human goodness?

In the latter possibility, the "principle" of nature imposed on man is turned around and made the principle of man's freedom and self-rule. As in Aristotle, the agency of self-rule is man's capacity for ordering; and the importance of formal cause, that seems at first so much reduced in Dante's *Monarchy* in contrast to Aristotle's *Politics*, is introduced carefully—and less prominently, lest it signify too much freedom—into Dante's argument. A full study would have to explain the progress from the second argument (*Monarchy* I.6), where forms appear as the consequence of the final cause (as in I.3), to the ninth argument on ruling (I.13), in which the agent desires to make manifest his own image (cf. I.8, III.15). Dante's eleven arguments are not separate and unconnected; there is an argument of the arguments.

18. See the discussion of the meaning of *omnia* in *Monarchy* III.8.

19. To guide government, Dante says little of natural law in *Monarchy*. Natural law is not so much an authority over human law, as we tend to think it today when dismissing it, as a protection for human law against the intrusion of divine law. See *Monarchy* II.7, III.13, where natural law is distinguished from divine law; and the reference in I.14 to a common law not said to be natural.

20. Fortin, *Dissidence*, pp. 100–101.

21. In *Monarchy* II.3 we learn that nobility is partly convention; in III.4, that authority is never equal to its source; in III.12, that "father" is an accidental form.

22. Note the *two* ends of man ordained by Providence, abruptly stated in *Monarchy* III.16. Here Dante's natural teleology is restated in the light of the need for conventional authority.

23. Dante never proposed the indignity for the pope that Machiavelli calls for in the place where he explains the meaning of "altogether bad," *Discourses on Livy* I.27; Fortin, *Dissidence*, p. 176. Cf. Marsilius of Padua, *Defender of the Peace* II.28.29. On the question of Dante's relationship to Machiavelli, see Larry Peterman, "Dante and the Setting for Machiavellianism," *American Political Science Review*, vol. 76 (1982), pp. 630–44.

24. John P. Gibbons, *Marsilius of Padua's Defender of the Peace* (unpublished doctoral dissertation, Harvard University, 1981), p. 53; I am

much indebted to this excellent study. Marsilius comes close to quoting Aristotle's definition of man when, in *Defender* I.4.3., he quotes Aristotle's conclusion that everyone has a natural impulse toward politics (*Politics* 1253a29). But Aristotle shows immediately thereafter that this natural impulse is not enough, since someone must still constitute the city. See Antonio Toscano, *Marsilio da Padova e Niccolò Machiavelli* (Ravenna: Lungo ed., 1981), p. 49; Alan Gewirth, *Marsilius of Padua*, 2 vols. (New York: Columbia University Press, 1951) I 90; Georges de Lagarde, *La Naissance de l'esprit laïque au déclin du Moyen-Âge*, 5 vols. (Paris: Beatrice-Nauwelaerts, 1956–70), III 323; Marino Damiata, *Plenitudo Potestatis e Universitas Civium in Marsilio da Padova* (Florence: Studi Francescani, 1983), pp. 148–49.

25. Thomas Aquinas, *Summa Theologica* IIa IIae.50.1 ad 1; 58.1 ad 5; 60.1 ad 4.

26. Thomas Aquinas, *Commentary on Aristotle's Ethics* VI.7, 1197–99; cf. Aristotle, *Nicomachean Ethics* 1141b24–27.

27. Hervaeus Natalis, *De iurisdictione* (Munich: Max Hueler, 1959), p. 15; Brian Tierney, *Religion, Law, and the Growth of Constitutional Thought, 1150–1650* (Cambridge: Cambridge University Press, 1982), p. 45.

28. Gewirth, *Marsilius* I.232–34, cites Giles of Rome, *De ecclesiastica potestae* III.5; James of Viterbo, *De regimine Christiano* II.8, 10; Augustinus Triumphus, *Summa de ecclesiastica potestate* I.1, 7; Alvarus Pelagius, *De planctu ecclesiae* I.13.

29. On *pars valentior*, see Gewirth, *Marsilius* I.182–99; Lagarde, *Naissance* III. 141–45; Damiata, *Plenitudo*, pp. 166–69; Jeannine Quillet, *La philosophie politique de Marsile de Padoue* (Paris: Vrin, 1970), pp. 93–99; Strauss, *Liberalism*, p. 191.

30. See the citations in Gewirth, *Marsilius* I.3–6; Ewart Lewis, "The 'Positivism' of Marsiglio of Padua," *Speculum*, vol. 38 (1963), pp. 541–82.

31. Priests are a part of the city, according to Aristotle, but not as teachers; *Politics* 1328b11. See Strauss, *Liberalism*, p. 187.

32. Note the phrase "within the confines of political philosophy," several times repeated by Strauss, *Liberalism*, pp. 185–201.

33. *Defender of the Peace* II.16.17, as remarked by Strauss, *Liberalism*, p. 201n8. "Sect" appears 13 times in *Defender of the Peace*.

34. *Defender of the Peace* I.5.13; II.11; Gibbons, *Marsilius*, p. 78.

35. *Defender of the Peace* I.17.10 might be a reference to Dante; at least Marsilius's mention of the utility of wars and epidemics makes clear the difference between the high road and the low road. See Gewirth, *Marsilius* I.127.

36. See *Defender of the Peace* I.5.9, where acquisition is called treasury, i.e., keeping rather than gaining, and slaves are not mentioned.

37. See the misreporting of Aristotle in *Defender of the Peace* I.5.8, and note the absence of slavery in I.3.3–4, 7.1, and the mention of "beast or slave" in I.4.1 as if slave were subhuman. Gewirth, *Marsilius* I.177–78.

38. Cf. Mario Grignaschi, "Le rôle de l'aristotélisme dans le *Defensor Pacis* de Marsile de Padoue," *Revue d'Histoire et de Philosophie religieuse,* vol. 35 (1955), pp. 310–11.

39. See note 24 above; and *Defender of the Peace* I.1.6

40. *Defender of the Peace* I.9.5; note that the discussion of Aristotle, *Politics* 1295a15 here ignores the element of tyranny in consent that we have considered in ch. 3.

41. On these two words for power, see ch. 7, pp. 171–72. Hobbes was to identify *potestas* and *potencia* systematically.

42. See Carlo Pincin, *Marsilio* (Turin: Giappichelli, 1967), p. 75. The king called Theopompus was one of two Spartan kings, ruling at the same time, Aristotle notes (*Politics* 1313a25); so Theopompus did not have *plenitudo potestatis* to begin with. That Marsilius speaks of the king *called* Theopompus shows how he read Aristotle and how Aristotle is to be read: with attention to names and details. On how to read Marsilius, see his great Dutch opponent Albertus Pighius, *Hierarchia ecclesiastica* (1538), who delivered this accurate assessment: *Fuit homo Aristotelicus magis quam Christianus.* Gibbons, *Marsilius,* p. 19; Gregorio Piaia, *Marsilio da Padova nella Riforma e nella Controriforma* (Padua: Atenore, 1977), p. 294.

43. The "soul" spoken of in *Defender of the Peace* I.6.9 consists of the defensiveness that emanates from the body.

44. These are not necessarily the same as those *called* prudent (*Defender of the Peace* I.12.2), who have leisure.

45. On *Defender of the Peace* I.14, see Gibbons, *Marsilius,* ch. 3.

46. *Defender of the Peace* I.14.10. Marsilius therefore makes little of the Aristotelian dilemma whether to prefer a prudent man or a man of moral virtue in office (*Politics* 1309a33). See Gibbons, *Marsilius,* p. 175.

47. *Defender of the Peace* I.16.7, 21. I.16.21 contains the fourth of seven quotations from Cicero, in addition to the one reference to Cicero the consul in I.14.3. Cf. Machiavelli's criticism of Cicero, also in regard to sedition by the ambitious, but less favorable to it, *Discourses on Livy* I.52. See also Toscano, *Marsilio,* pp. 93–94.

48. Gibbons, *Marsilius,* p. 75.

49. Or is judging—in the second sense of knowing political science—between knowing and ruling? *Defender of the Peace* II.2.8. The prominence of judge over legislator in Discourse II, by comparison with Discourse I, accords with the greater evidence of nature and natural right in Discourse II.

50. Note that Marsilius does not mention the virtue or the knowledge of the best man here; cf. *Defender of the Peace* I.9.7, 15.3; II.8.6.

51. Skinner, *Foundations of Modern Political Thought* I.18–22, 52–65. For Skinner, Marsilius provided "ideological backing" for the Italian republics (I.18). It is strange that he does not comment on Marsilius's relationship with Ludwig of Bavaria.

Chapter 6
MACHIAVELLI AND THE MODERN EXECUTIVE

1. Leo Strauss, *Thoughts on Machiavelli* (Glencoe, Ill.: The Free Press, 1958). For the reception of this book, see Harvey C. Mansfield, Jr., "Strauss's Machiavelli," *Political Theory*, vol. 3 (1975), pp. 372–405. When Pocock published his book *The Machiavellian Moment* in 1975, he could not bring himself to make a single reference to Strauss. But for Skinner, the progress of Strauss's influence is evident in the contrast between his single, inaccurate reference in *Foundations of Modern Political Thought* (1978), I.137, and his later book, *Machiavelli* (New York: Hill and Wang, 1981), which begins and ends with Strauss. In the earlier work, Skinner first vulgarizes Strauss and then accuses Strauss of "vulgarization." The later book takes Strauss more seriously, though not to the extent of recommending his book in the bibliography. The first scholar to offer a serious appreciation of Strauss's book was Claude Lefort, in his *Le travail de l'oeuvre Machiavel* (Paris: Gallimard, 1972), pp. 259–305.

2. Machiavelli, *D* II.5; *FH* V.1. See Harvey C. Mansfield, Jr., *Machiavelli's New Modes and Orders; A Study of the Discourses on Livy* (Ithaca, NY: Cornell University Press, 1979), pp. 55–56, 60–61, 202–6, 299–300; and "Machiavelli's Political Science," *The American Political Science Review*, vol. 75 (1981), pp. 301–2. Machiavelli's works will be cited as *P, The Prince; D, Discourses on Livy; FH, Florentine Histories; AW, The Art of War*. Page references are to Niccolò Machiavelli, *Tutte le Opere* (Florence: G. Barbèra, 1929).

3. St. Augustine, *City of God* I.1, 7; Letters 137, 138. Ernest Fortin, "St. Augustine," in Strauss and Cropsey, *History of Political Philosophy*, 3rd ed., pp. 198–203.

4. Machiavelli implies that Brutus made this sacrifice for his own private good; Dante says that he did it for the common good. Dante,

Monarchy II.5; see Mansfield, *Machiavelli's New Modes and Orders*, pp. 309–12. On Machiavelli's ferocity, see the useful reminder by Conor Cruise O'Brien, "The Ferocious Wisdom of Machiavelli," in O'Brien, *The Suspecting Glance* (London: Faber and Faber, 1972).

5. Mansfield, *Machiavelli's New Modes and Orders*, p. 400.

6. Alfonso Tostado (1400–1455), quoted by Ernest Nys in James Scott, ed., *De Indis et De Iure Belli Relectiones* of Francisco de Vitoria (Washington, DC: Carnegie Endowment for International Peace, 1917), p. 17.

7. Henry Higuera, *The Empire of Love; The Problem of Christian Politics in Don Quixote*, unpublished doctoral dissertation, University of Toronto, 1982. I am also indebted to Higuera for the interpretation of Vitoria that follows.

8. Vitoria, *De Indis*, pp. 166–75. See Skinner, *Foundations of Modern Political Thought*, II.16–73; J. H. Parry, *The Spanish Theory of Empire in the Sixteenth Century* (Cambridge: Cambridge University Press, 1940), pp. 19–26; Lewis Hanke, *The Spanish Struggle for Justice* (Philadelphia: University of Pennsylvania Press, 1949), pp. 31–36; J. A. Fernandez-Santamaria, *The State, War and Peace; Spanish Political Thought in the Renaissance, 1516–1559* (Cambridge: Cambridge University Press, 1977), pp. 58–119.

9. See *P* 15; *D* I.2. See also Strauss, *Thoughts on Machiavelli*, pp. 13, 30, 59, 222, 236, 290; Claude Lefort, *le Travail de l'oeuvre Machiavel*, p. 301; Gennaro Sasso;, *Studi su Machiavelli* (Naples: Morano, 1967), pp. 50–65.

10. Machiavelli speaks of "natural virtues" in *D* I.56. Such virtues might belong to "intelligences in the air" which might come to the defense of mankind by issuing warnings and signs. See Mansfield, *Machiavelli's New Modes and Orders*, pp. 164–66.

11. Cf. Harold D. Lasswell's "Safety, income, and deference," in *Politics, Who Gets What, When, How* (New York: Meridian, 1958), pp. 13ff.

12. So I call it, not to say that Machiavelli ever made scientific or academic use of terms that do not equivocate, but rather to suggest that his favorite phrases deserve study.

13. Aristotle wanted to keep the priests "fifth," not "first"; *Politics* 1322b20–21; 1328b11.

14. Anticlericalism in Marsilius and Machiavelli is perfectly compatible with the fact that both saw priests as their primary addressees. For both, politics can be cured through the channels by which it is infected. See Mansfield, *Machiavelli's New Modes and Orders*, pp. 295, 394–95.

15. Machiavelli transforms the seemingly similar Epicurean conclusion into a political doctrine. See Leo Strauss, "Notes on Lucretius" in *Liberalism Ancient and Modern* (New York: Basic Books, 1968), p. 105.

16. Mansfield, *Machiavelli's New Modes and Orders*, pp. 299–305; Pocock, *Machiavellian Moment*, p. 167.

17. Compare the voluntary exile of Giano della Bella in *FH* II.13 with the forced exile of Dante seven chapters later. Both were in the situation of Fabrizio; neither knew how to solve the problem as Machiavelli solved it.

18. But precisely on "commissions," see Machiavelli's praise for the Roman Senate's grant of "very great authority" to Fabius in the mysterious Ciminian forest affair; *D* II.33. Strauss, *Thoughts on Machiavelli*, pp. 106–7; Mansfield, *Machiavelli's New Modes and Orders*, pp. 293–96.

19. Machiavelli also uses *seguire* (e.g., *FH* II.20) and *mandare ad effetto* (*FH* I.24, II.10, VII.23, VIII.5, 23) in the sense of "execute."

20. Cf. Aristotle, *Politics* 1285b1–4.

21. See Schmitt, *Die Diktatur*, pp. 7–13.

22. The use of the term "coalitions" by current political science to describe gatherings of citizens as well as groupings of states is an instance of hidden and unconscious Machiavellism.

23. Plato, *Laws* 690a–c; Aristotle, *Politics* 1280a8–23, 1283a23–b35.

24. Pocock and Skinner do not state this fundamental issue clearly in their treatments either of Machiavelli or of republicanism. They do not seem to have absorbed Aristotle's distinction between a city *(polis)* and its regime *(politeia)*; so in describing republican virtue they overlook the interest of the regime as distinct from the city. Pocock, *Machiavellian Moment*, pp. 212, 306; Skinner, *Foundations of Modern Political Thought*, I.165, 176, 180; *Machiavelli* (New York: Hill and Wang, 1981), pp. 52, 64.

25. Thus for Machiavelli to conceive the dictator as commissioned was not in contradiction to his conceiving the prince as sovereign, as Carl Schmitt says; sovereign by commission is the essence of executive ambivalence. Schmitt cites *D* I.3 but not *D* III.1. Schmitt, *Die Diktatur*, pp. 6–9.

26. Cf. Plato, *Apology* 37a–b.

27. Dante also speaks of the need to be *solus*, but to be so with justice so as to give justice more power. *Monarchy* I.11.

28. Compare Marsilius on Theopompus (*Defender of the Peace* I.11.8) with Machiavelli on Junius Brutus (*D* III.2–3); Machiavelli does not accept the status of "voluntary poverty" (*Defender of the Peace* II.12–14).

Chapter 7
HOBBES AND THE POLITICAL SCIENCE OF POWER

1. See the outrageous example of "Madonna Caterina," the woman who chose career over family, in Machiavelli, *D* III.6; *P* 20; *FH* VIII. 34.

2. Jean Bodin, *Methodus ad Facilem Historiarum Cognitionem*, VI (beg.). Ignoring the claims made by Machiavelli in the Dedicatory Letters to *The Prince* and the *Discourses on Livy*, Bodin complains that Machiavelli would have done better had he known more of the writings of the ancient philosophers and historians.

3. Jean Bodin, *Six Livres de la République*, 1576 ed., 6 vols. (Paris: Fayard, 1986), I, pref. 12. References are to volume, chapter, and page in this edition. Cf. Bodin's defense of Tacitus against charges of impiety, *Methodus*, IV; see Girolamo Cotroneo, "Le Quatrième Chapitre de la *Methodus*," in Horst Denzer, ed., *Jean Bodin* (Munich: Beck, 1973), pp. 101–3. On Bodin and Machiavelli, see Pierre Mesnard, *L'Essor de la philosophie politique au XVIe siècle* (Paris: Boivin, 1936), pp. 475, 538–42; William F. Church, *Richelieu and Reason of State* (Princeton, NJ: Princeton University Press, 1972), pp. 47–51, 59; G. Cardascia, "Machiavel et Jean Bodin," *Bibliothèque d'Humanisme et Renaissance*, vol. 14 (1943), pp. 129–62. Cardascia says: "Bodin, by intention anti-Machiavellian, is a Machiavellian who did not know it. One should certainly not believe that he made himself the detractor of Machiavelli, but approved him in his heart of hearts. This would be cleverness useful to a prince: this attitude, credited rightly or wrongly to Frederick of Prussia, may not be understood in anyone other than a Chief of State" (p. 151). But Bodin said in his preface that a person in his situation had to help out the chief of state (I, pref. 9; see II.4.111, 7.189), and Cardascia had himself shrewdly remarked (p. 152) that Machiavellism is more repellent in principle than in deed. I was directed to Cardascia's excellent article by its recommendation as "impossible" by W. F. Church (p. 50n). Surely intellectual history will remain in the Dark Ages until it abandons the childish presumption that every writer is always sincere. The quality of Bodin's understanding of Machiavelli can be judged from his remark about Machiavelli's lifting Cesare Borgia to heaven (I pref. 12).

4. See Mesnard, *L'Essor*, p. 483; J. W. Allen, *A History of Political Thought in the Sixteenth Century* (London: Methuen, 1960), p. 414; Nannerl O. Keohane, *Philosophy and the State in France* (Princeton, NJ: Princeton University Press, 1980), p. 67.

5. Cf. n. 26 in ch. 4: When Bodin attributes the word *un seul* to Tacitus

(VI.4.181) he approves it; when he attributes it to Machiavelli, he calls it tyrannical (VI.4.148). The difficulty regarding the person of the sovereign can be seen in the fact that Bodin, as contrasted to Hobbes, does not speak of the *office* of the sovereign: the sovereign as such is above all offices.

6. Skinner, *Foundations of Modern Political Thought,* II.290–93; Julian H. Franklin, *Jean Bodin and the Rise of Absolutist Theory* (Cambridge: Cambridge University Press, 1973), p. 108; Janine Chanteur, "L'Idée de la loi naturelle dans la *République* de Jean Bodin," in Denzer, *Jean Bodin,* pp. 210–12.

7. Friedrich Meinecke, *Die Idee der Staatsräson* (Munich: R. Oldenbourg, 1957), pp. 66–69.

8. Bodin, *Methodus,* VI.

9. "The Church is strangely absent from the works of Jean Bodin." Chanteur, "L'Idée," p. 209.

10. Cf. Skinner, *Foundations of Modern Political Thought* II.291–92. Skinner's very useful discussion of Bodin begins with an analysis of Bodin's book as a book. I agree with his statement of the two parts of the argument but would reverse the order: the positing of legal sovereignty precedes the induction of the actual sovereign.

11. Cf. R. W. K. Hinton, "Bodin and the Retreat into Legalism," in Denzer, *Jean Bodin,* pp. 303–13.

12. Church, *Richelieu,* pref.

13. Skinner, *Foundations of Modern Political Thought* II.301.

14. Meinecke, *Staatsräson,* p. 78. Machiavelli himself sometimes indulges in Machiavellism, vulgarizing himself. See, for example, the mode in *P* 22 "that never fails," and then fails; and *D* II.13, as interpreted in Mansfield, *Machiavelli's New Modes and Orders,* pp. 225–28.

15. Giovanni Botero, *Della Ragion di Stato* (Bologna: Cappelli, 1930), pp. 67–70. Cf. Francis Bacon: Boldness "is ill in Counsell, good in Execution." *Essays,* XII, "Of Boldnesse."

16. Botero, *Ragion,* p. 9.

17. Locke, *Two Treatises of Government* II.159; Montesquieu, *Spirit of the Laws* XI. 5–6.

18. See Francis D. Wormuth, *The Origins of Modern Constitutionalism* (New York: Harper, 1959); Gwyn, *Meaning of the Separation of Powers,* chs. 3, 4; Vile, *Constitutionalism and the Separation of Powers,* chs. 2, 3.

19. John Milton, *Eikonoklastes,* in Don M. Wolfe, ed., *The Complete Prose Works of John Milton.* 8 vols. (New Haven, CT: Yale University Press, 1962), III.413.

20. John Sadler, *Rights of the Kingdom* (London, 1649), p. 86; Vile, *Constitutionalism*, pp. 31–32.

21. Philip Hunton, *A Treatise of Monarchie* (London, 1643), pp. 5, 9, 26, 44. Vile, *Constitutionalism*, pp. 40–42.

22. [Marchamont Nedham], *The Excellencie of a Free State* (London, 1656), pp. 212–13. See Vile, *Constitutionalism*, p. 29; Gwyn, *Meaning*, pp. 32–33.

23. [Nedham], *A True State of the Case of the Commonwealth* (London, 1654), p. 9; Vile, *Constitutionalism*, pp. 49–50.

24. Quoted by Vile, *Constitutionalism*, p. 44; see Gwyn, *Meaning*, pp. 37–51.

25. Isaac Penington, *A Word for the Commonweale* (London, 1650), pp. 8–10; Gwyn, *Meaning*, pp. 52–53, 56–63.

26. Gwyn, *Meaning*, p. 27.

27. Quoted by Vile, *Constitutionalism*, p. 42.

28. George Lawson. *An Examination of the Political Part of Mr. Hobbs his Leviathan* (London, 1657), pp. 8, 30–34, 113–14. Separation of the judicial power from the executive in the modern sense begins with Montesquieu, or perhaps with Bolingbroke, when the *independence* of the judiciary is established. Cf. Vile, *Constitutionalism*, pp. 55–56.

29. [Charles Dallison], *The Royalists Defence* (London, 1648), p. 99. To quote an excellent remark from Julian Franklin: "The modern idea of separated powers depends on the rather subtle, and at first sight curious, thought that executive power can be simultaneously independent and subordinate." Franklin, *Jean Bodin*, p. 29. See Gwyn, *Meaning*, p. 47; Wormuth, *Origins*, p. 72.

30. Thomas Hobbes, *De Cive*, VI.8, p. 178 in the edition of Bernard Gert, *Man and Citizen* (New York: Doubleday, 1972).

31. Hobbes, *Leviathan*, W. G. Pogson Smith, ed. (Oxford: Clarendon Press, 1909), Rev. and Concl., p. 550; Locke, *Two Treatises of Government*, II.137, 139.

32. Hobbes, *A Dialogue between a Philosopher and a Student of the Common Laws of England*, Joseph Cropsey, ed. (Chicago: University of Chicago Press, 1971). Cropsey's introduction has been a great help to this inquiry. Page references in brackets are to the first edition.

33. *Dialogue*, p. [15]; see p. 21, Introduction.

34. See Cropsey's discussion of Hobbes's use of Bacon's arguments, *Dialogue*, Introduction, pp. 12–15.

35. *Dialogue*, p. [21]; cf. Hobbes, *De Homine*, XIV.9, p. 76, Gert ed.; *De Cive*, XII.12, p. 253.

36. *De Cive*, pref., pp. 105–6; *Leviathan*, Rev. and Concl., p. 557.

37. Hobbes, *The Elements of Law,* F. Tönnies, ed. 2nd ed. (New York: Barnes and Noble, 1969), II.1.16.

38. *Elements* II.8–9 contain directions for the art of government mixed with principles of sovereignty; see also II.10.10.

39. *De Cive* II.1–2, pp. 121–22. On the lack of an art of government, see pref., pp. 98, 103, and XIII, pp. 257–70; but note Hobbes's references to the "political practices of each Commonweal," XIII.1, p. 258, and to "vision political," XIII.7, p. 261. On the denial of right reason in *Elements,* see *Elements,* p. 188.

40. *De Cive,* let. ded., p. 90; pref.; p. 105; XII.12, p. 253.

41. Unless the sovereign fails in his duty deliberately and properly, out of prudence; see the interesting admission of prudence, *De Cive* VI. 13, p. 181n.

42. See the chart of science in *Leviathan* IX, where political science appears twice, as an original branch from philosophy and as the last part of natural philosophy.

43. *Leviathan* V, p. 33. This is nothing new, but a decision to leave that term to those who abuse it by claiming more of it.

44. *Leviathan* III, p. 22; IV, p. 28; V, pp. 37–38; see Harvey C. Mansfield, Jr., "Hobbes and the Science of Indirect Government," *American Political Science Review,* vol. 65 (1971), p. 105.

45. The following discussion is indebted to Leo Strauss, *Natural Right and History* (Chicago, IL: University of Chicago Press, 1953), pp. 194–96.

46. Aristotle, *Metaphysics* 1046a36–1046b29; 1048a10–11. In Thomas Aquinas, *Summa Contra Gentiles* III.31, there is a shift from *potentia* to *potestas* when Aquinas speaks of rational powers in accordance with Aristotle's distinction. But in his commentary on this passage, Aquinas uses *potentia* throughout. *In Metaphysicam* IX.2.1789.

47. Leo Strauss, *The Political Philosophy of Hobbes* (Chicago, IL: University of Chicago Press, 1952), pp. 113–14.

48. Spinoza, *Political Treatise* I.4; IV.4; V.7; VII.2, 5; VIII.20–5; X.1, 8–9.

49. See *Elements* II.9.6 for extraordinary power the sovereign may delegate.

Chapter 8
CONSTITUTIONALIZING THE EXECUTIVE

1. James Harrington, *The Commonwealth of Oceana,* in J. G. A. Pocock, ed., *The Political Works of James Harrington* (Cambridge: Cambridge

University Press, 1977), pp. 161–62; cf. pp. 341, 423. Further page references will be to this edition.

2. Zera S. Fink, *The Classical Republicans*. 2nd ed. (Evanston, IL: Northwestern University Press, 1962), pp. 66–67.

3. Charles Blitzer, *An Immortal Commonwealth* (New Haven, CT: Yale University Press, 1960), pp. 296–97.

4. Harrington expects the result to be: *cuius divisio, alterius electio*. But instead, as his contemporary critic Matthew Wren remarked trenchantly: "The stronger girl gives the other a piece of cake to fetch her some water to drink after it." Quoted by Pocock, Introduction to *Political Works*, p. 87; and see pp. 415–19. J. A. W. Gunn, *Politics and the Public Interest in the Seventeenth Century* (London: Routledge and Kegan Paul, 1969), p. 124; Blitzer, *Immortal Commonwealth*, pp. 149–52.

5. See Blitzer, *Immortal Commonwealth*, pp. 155–58; Fink, *Classical Republicans*, p. 56.

6. Locke does not mind ending his *Two Treatises of Government* with a chapter, not on the success, but "Of the Dissolution of Government," in which, with a certain levity, he encourages resistance to government by a people both to avoid slavery and to preserve itself (II.220, 222, 239). See Nathan Tarcov, "Locke's *Second Treatise* and 'The Best Fence Against Rebellion,'" *Review of Politics* 43 (1981), pp. 198–217, and Harvey C. Mansfield, Jr., *Spirit of Liberalism*, pp. 78–80, 86.

7. "Locke is closer to Machiavelli than he is generally said or thought to be." Leo Strauss, *What is Political Philosophy?* (Glencoe, IL: Free Press, 1959), p. 218. Locke "could perhaps be looked upon as Machiavelli's philosopher." Peter Laslett, Introduction to his edition of John Locke, *Two Treatises of Government* (New York: Mentor, 1969), pp. 100–101. See also the study of Locke's Machiavellian art of governing on the level of education by Nathan Tarcov, *Locke's Education for Liberty* (Chicago: University of Chicago Press, 1984), p. 6 and *passim*.

8. On Locke and the executive, see Martin Seliger, *The Liberal Politics of John Locke* (London: Allen and Unwin, 1979), pp. 324–72; John Dunn, *The Political Thought of John Locke* (Cambridge: Cambridge University Press, 1969), pp. 148–64; Richard H. Cox, *Locke on War and Peace* (Oxford: Clarendon Press, 1960), pp. 82–84, 118, 123–30; Vile, *Constitutionalism*, pp. 60–67; Gwyn, *Meaning*, pp. 69–81.

9. Peter Laslett: "*Two Treatises* as an Exclusion Tract," Introduction, *Two Treatises of Government*, p. 75; criticized by Dunn, *Political Thought of John Locke*, pp. 47–57; and by Michael P. Zuckert, "The

Recent Literature on Locke's Political Philosophy," *The Political Science Reviewer*, V (1975), pp. 293–98.

10. According to Aquinas, a private person is not permitted to kill a sinner; *Summa Theologica* II.II.64.3. Grotius says that this is permitted to anyone, but then he narrows the permission to a good or wise man and denies (by contrast to Locke) that nature declares who may punish; *De Jure Belli ac Pacis*, II.20.3,7,9. Despite this difference, and despite the lack of a doctrine of the state of nature in Grotius, Richard Tuck asserts that Grotius's opinion "is of course identical" to Locke's very strange doctrine; *Natural Rights Theories* (Cambridge: Cambridge University Press, 1979), pp. 62–63, 173. Cf. Samuel Pufendorf, *De Jurae Naturae et Gentium*, V.13.10; and see also Leo Strauss, *Natural Right and History*, p. 222n; Peter Laslett, Introduction, pp. 110–11.

11. Locke says that man is "absolute Lord of his own Person" (*Two Treatises* II.123) and "Master of his own Life" (II.172), and that he has the "free Disposal" of his own person (II.190). But he also denies that man has an absolute, arbitrary power over himself to "quit his Station wilfully" (II.6, 23, 135, 168, 172, 194). One may doubt that suicide was the problem according to Locke that it is for existentialism today (see I.86), except as the "nobler use" of one's body than bare preservation (II.6) could be understood as risk of suicide (cf. II.139). Locke concedes the power to commit suicide, almost the right of it, in II.23.

12. See *Two Treatises* II.56 for the analogy between the workmanship of God and that of parents.

13. One recurring example of Locke's treatment of reason and revelation is in regard to the right to eat meat, which follows from the right of self-preservation but was denied to men, in the Bible, before the Covenant. Compare *Two Treatises* I.39, where Locke emphatically reports the Biblical prohibition, with II.25, where he blandly disregards it in claiming an agreement between reason and revelation. For discussion and other references, see Cox, *Locke on War and Peace*, pp. 56–57.

14. Strauss remarks (*Natural Right and History*, p. 223n84) on *Two Treatises* II.11 that Locke quotes the Biblical permission to inflict capital punishment but not the Biblical reason immediately following, that man is made in the image of God. Being so made would seem necessary to Locke's "workmanship argument" against suicide, for any creature whatsover is God's workmanship. Indeed, Locke does refer to man as the image of God in I.30 to justify man's dominion over inferior creatures.

15. The word "interest" appears in *Two Treatises* II.57 as the "proper

interest" to which the law directs a free and intelligent agent. Otherwise "interest" appears infrequently in the *Two Treatises,* and more often pejoratively than favorably. See Nathan Tarcov, "A Non-Lockean Locke and the Character of Liberalism," in D. MacLean and C. Mills, *Liberalism Reconsidered* (London: Rowman and Allenheld, 1983), pp. 133–34.

16. So, too, equality in the "use of the same faculties" does not imply equality in the correct use of those faculties. *Two Treatises* II.4; see II.59.

17. Perhaps Locke tips his hand in *Two Treatises* II.107 where, in discussing primitive monarchy, he looks ahead to the need for "ballancing the Power of Government, by placing several parts of it in different hands."

18. Gwyn says: "His old-fashioned views on this matter [the dispensing power of prerogative], written a decade before the Revolution, oddly enough were more in tune with those of the defeated King and his followers" (*Meaning,* p. 81). Locke's endorsement of the prerogative is perhaps the biggest obstacle to Laslett's thesis that his politics were those of the Shaftesbury Whigs; see note 9 above and accompanying text.

19. On the crucial importance of studying the law of nature, see Strauss, *Natural Right and History,* pp. 225–26.

20. Patrick Riley, *Will and Political Legitimacy* (Cambridge, MA: Harvard University Press, 1982), ch. 3; John Yolton, *Locke and the Compass of Human Understanding* (Cambridge: Cambridge University Press, 170), pp. 164–80; Laslett, *Two Treatises,* Introduction, pp. 92–105; Raymond Polin, *La Politique morale de John Locke* (Paris: Presses Universitaires de France, 1970), ch. 3; Strauss, *Natural Right and History,* pp. 202–51, and *What is Political Philosophy?,* pp. 197–220; W. von Leyden, Introduction to John Locke, *Essays on the Law of Nature.* 2nd ed. (Oxford: Clarendon Press, 1958), pp. 1–87. I am much in debt to Richard Kennington for his analysis of the problem of natural law in Locke.

21. *Essays on the Law of Nature,* an early work completed in 1664, was not published by Locke.

22. Richard Kennington has coined the term "boundary problem" to signify the difficulty of moving between the *Essay* and the *Two Treatises.*

23. See Harvey C. Mansfield, Jr., "On the Political Character of Property in Locke," in A. Kontos, ed., *Powers, Possessions and Freedom* (Toronto: University of Toronto Press, 1979), pp. 23–38.

24. For the following, see Manent, *Histoire intellectuelle du libéralisme,* pp. 113–17.

Chapter 9
MODERATING THE EXECUTIVE

1. David Hume, *Essays Moral, Political and Literary,* Eugene F. Miller, ed. (Indianapolis: Liberty Classics, 1985). Part I, Essay 6, p. 44; Part II, Essay 16, p. 524.

2. In his utopian essay, "Idea of a Perfect Commonwealth," however, Hume conceived an executive that is structurally weak—plural and elected by the legislature—but provided with an absolute power in foreign affairs.

3. Henry St. John Bolingbroke, *Remarks on the History of England,* in *The Works of Lord Bolingbroke,* 4 vols. (Philadelphia: Carey and Hart, 1841), I.331-33; *Dissertation Upon Parties,* II.117-19; *Idea of a Patriot King,* II.381-82, 396-97, 401. See Vile, *Constitutionalism and the Separation of Powers,* pp. 72-75; Gwyn, *Meaning of the Separation of Powers,* pp. 93-94; Kurt Kluxen, *Das Problem der Politischen Opposition* (Freiburg: Verlag K. Alber, 1956), pp. 224-32.

4. Robert Shackleton, "Montesquieu, Bolingbroke, and the Separation of Powers," *French Studies,* III (1948), 25-38; Robert Shackleton, *Montesquieu: A Critical Biography* (Oxford: Oxford University Press, 1961), pp. 298-301; see Isaac Kramnick, *Bolingbroke and His Circle* (Cambridge, MA: Harvard University Press, 1968), pp. 144-50.

5. Montesquieu says that his book contains an "infinite number of things," i.e., that it is not complete but needs to be completed in practice. But as a work *(ouvrage)* it is finished and has a design (preface, *Spirit of the Laws*).

6. See *Spirit of the Laws* XXII.11, 13, referring back to XXI.20; Book XXI is on the revolutions of commerce, which do not proceed by great strokes of authority. See also Montesquieu, *Pensées,* 184.

7. Montesquieu, *Défense de l'Esprit des Lois* I.1.

8. David Lowenthal notes that angels are first mentioned, then dropped, in Montesquieu's discussion in I.1, "Book I of Montesquieu's *The Spirit of the Laws,*" *American Political Science Review,* 53 (1959), 488-89; and see Thomas L. Pangle, *Montesquieu's Philosophy of Liberalism* (Chicago, IL: University of Chicago Press, 1973), pp. 25-26.

9. See Judith N. Shklar, *Montesquieu* (Oxford: Oxford University Press, 1987), pp. 81-84.

10. For the following on classical virtue, I am indebted to Pierre Manent; and see David Lowenthal, "Montesquieu and the Classics: Republican Government in *The Spirit of the Laws,*" in Joseph Cropsey, ed., *Ancients and Moderns* (New York: Basic Books, 1964), pp. 258-87.

11. Pangle, *Montesquieu's Philosophy of Liberalism,* pp. 48-49; Paul Ver-

nière, *Montesquieu et l'Esprit des Lois ou la Raison Impure* (Paris: Sedes, 1977), pp. 66–68.

12. Pangle, *Montesquieu's Philosophy of Liberalism*, pp. 96–103.

13. V.10 is the central chapter of the central Book of the seven Books on the natures and principles of governments. The "most beautiful monarchy in the world" to which it refers is the monarchy of reason, not France.

14. These two different statements of liberty follow nine different meanings given to "liberty" in XI.2

15. As Manent notes, Montesquieu speaks only of power-holders: "it is an eternal experience that every man who has power is brought to abuse it" (XI.4); *Histoire intellectuelle du libéralisme*, p. 124.

16. I am indebted to Manent for this point. With only three uses of "reason" does Montesquieu indicate that the constitution of England in XI.6 is the constitution of reason: *conforme a la raison, avec raison*, and *rendre raison*.

17. William Kristol, "The Problem of the Separation of Powers: *Federalist 47–51*," in Charles R. Kesler, *Saving the Revolution* (New York: Free Press, 1987), p. 104.

18. Burke, too, does not praise the old Whigs of the 1688 Revolution as founders, but he does not need them as founders since he has the work of Montesquieu, on whom he delivers a magnificent eulogy. Edmund Burke, *An Appeal from the New to the Old Whigs* (1791), in Works of Edmund Burke. 8 vols. (London: Bohn Library, 1855), III. 44–56, 113.

19. Montesquieu says *executrice*, not *executive* as is said today; both words were in use in the eighteenth century. See Robert Derathé's note in his edition of Montesquieu, *De l'Esprit des Lois*. 2 vols. (Paris: Garnier, 1973), I.478.

20. Alexis de Tocqueville, *Democracy in America*, I.2.8 Tocqueville emphasizes the connection between the power of judging and the legal profession, which Montesquieu denies.

21. See Mark Hulliung, *Montesquieu and the Old Regime* (Berkeley, CA: University of California Press, 1976), pp. 219–20.

22. William Blackstone, *Commentaries on the Laws of England*, I.154; *Federalist* 47. Locke deprecates accusations against the people for encroaching upon the Kings' prerogative; *Two Treatises* II.163.

23. Montesquieu leaves room here for the Machiavellian possibility that the legislator might also be *un seul*; see also V.10.

24. Machiavelli, *Discourses on Livy* I.53.

25. Manent, *Histoire intellectuelle du libéralisme*, pp. 137–39.

26. Whereas for Locke the labor theory of value results from human

appropriation of the "almost worthless materials" of nature (*Two Treatises* II.43; cf. 41), for Montesquieu the fact that nature rewards labor shows that "nature is just toward men" (*Spirit of the Laws* XIII.2).

27. Locke too wants, of course, to move toward a liberal society, but he discusses separately the principles of liberal politics (in *Two Treatises*) and the practices of liberal education (in *Some Thoughts Concerning Education*). See Tarcov, *Locke's Education for Liberty*, introd.

28. Montesquieu also states the problem conversely, that the citizens might be free, and the constitution not free: a gentle despotism that is provisionally possible.

29. Crimes against religion, mores, and tranquillity in *Spirit of the Laws* XII.4 correspond to the laws of God, philosophers, and legislators in I.1. Security, the fourth item, is Montesquieu's contribution.

30. See *Spirit of the Laws* V.16 on the monarchical and the despotic "communication of power." Security as a principle is "monarchical" because it keeps more power than it communicates; it keeps its own majesty, and is not offended by speech or thought (XII.11, 12).

31. See Manent, *Histoire intellectuelle du libéralisme*, pp. 133–36.

32. Machiavelli, *Discourses on Livy* I.4–8; and Mansfield, *Machiavelli's New Modes and Orders*, ad loc.

Chapter 10
REPUBLICANIZING THE EXECUTIVE

1. Athanasios Moulakis, "Leonardo Bruni's Constitution of Florence," *Rinascimento* XXVI (1986), 153.

2. Max Farrand, ed., *The Records of the Federal Convention of 1787*, 4 vols., rev. ed. (New Haven, CT: Yale University Press, 1966), I.66, II.35; Ruth and Stephen Grant, "The Madisonian Presidency," in J. Bessette and J. Tulis, eds., *The Presidency in the Constitutional Order* (Baton Rouge, LA: Louisiana State University Press, 1981), pp. 31, 60n. Cf. Jeffrey L. Sedgwick, "James Madison and the Problem of Executive Character," *Polity*, XXI (1988), pp. 11–13.

3. For a historian's sensitive treatment of the question, see Jack N. Rakove, "The Great Compromise: Ideas, Interests and the Politics of Constitution-Making," *The William and Mary Quarterly*, XLIV (1987), 424–27.

4. Willaim T. Hutchinson et al., eds., *The Papers of James Madison* (Chicago and Charlottesville, VA: University of Chicago Press and University of Virginia Press, 1962 –   ), X.208–9; Farrand, *Records* I.138–39. On this embarrassment, see the sources collected in Philip B.

Kurland and Ralph Lerner, *The Founders' Constitution*. 5 vols. (Chicago, IL: University of Chicago Press, 1987), I.147–83, 250–51, 301–35; III.486–534. Ralph Ketcham, *Presidents Above Party* (Chapel Hill, NC: University of North Carolina Press, 1984), pp. 5–8.

5. As late as August 24, 1787, the Convention voted for election of the President by Congress. Farrand, *Records* I.21, 64–69; II.500–503, 572–75.

6. See also Hamilton's comments in the Constitutional Convention; Farrand, *Records*, I.289, 310, and Harold G. Syrett, ed., *The Papers of Alexander Hamilton*. 26 vols., (New York: Columbia University Press, 1962), IV.186.

7. Charles C. Thach, Jr., *The Creation of the Presidency, 1775–1789* (rev. ed., Baltimore: Johns Hopkins University Press, 1969), chs. 1–3; Gordon S. Wood, *The Creation of the American Republic,1776–1787* (Chapel Hill, NC: University of North Carolina Press, 1969), pp. 134–43, 432–36; Forrest McDonald, *Novus Ordo Seclorum; The Intellectual Origins of the Constitution* (Lawrence, KS: University Press of Kansas, 1985, pp. 86, 176–83.

8. John Jay to Thomas Jefferson, Dec. 14, 1786; *The Correspondence and Public Papers of John Jay*, Hugh Johnston ed. 4 vols. (New York: G.P. Putnam, 1890–93), III.223. See Madison's letter to Jefferson of March 19, 1787, *Papers* IX. 319–21; and *Federalist* 64. My thanks to Nathan Tarcov for this point. Madison was also highly critical of the weak executive under the Virginia constitution; see his letter to Caleb Wallace, August 23, 1785: "Our Executive is the worst part of a bad Constitution." *Papers* VIII.352.

9. See Murray Dry, "Anti-Federalism in *The Federalist*," in Charles R. Kesler, ed., *Saving the Revolution* (New York: Free Press, 1987), p. 55.

10. Gerald Stourzh, *Alexander Hamilton and the Idea of Republican Government* (Stanford, CA: Stanford University Press, 1970), p. 96; Gwyn, *Meaning of the Separation of Powers*, p. 22.

11. Cf. Thach, *Creation of the Presidency*, pp. 18, 27, 52–54, who ignores the effect of republican theory and American republicanism on that creation and thus, while stressing the uniquely American character of the process and result, underestimates it as an accomplishment.

12. For another example of benign Machiavellism, see Walter Moyle, *An Essay upon the Constitution of the Roman Government* (c. 1699), in C. Robbins, ed., *Two English Republican Tracts* (Cambridge: Cambridge University Press, 1969), pp. 253–54. See also Isaac Kramnick, *Bolingbroke and his Circle* (Cambridge, MA: Harvard University Press, 1968), pp. 236–60.

13. By "Cato," in the *New York Journal*. See Herbert J. Storing, ed., *The Complete Anti-Federalist*. 7 vols. (Chicago, IL: The University of Chicago Press, 1981), 2.6.37.

14. Farrand, *Records* I.66; this was concurred in by Benjamin Franklin, 1.83, and by William Paterson, I.287; and denied by James Wilson, I.66. See McDonald, *Novus Ordo*, pp. 201–3.

15. Storing, *Complete Anti-Federalist*, 2.4.86.

16. Storing, *Complete Anti-Federalist*, 2.6.31, 5.11.6.; see also An Old Whig, 3.3.31; Impartial Examiner, 5.14.40; Cornelius, 4.10.21; Countryman, 6.6.28. Gordon S. Wood, *Creation of the American Republic*, pp. 521, 561.

17. Storing, *Complete Anti-Federalist*, 5.10.4.

18. *Ibid.*, 2.8.178; see Storing's discussion at note 106 and his preface to Thach, *Creation of the Presidency*, pp. ix–x. Storing points to the similar language of Blackstone regarding the need for royal dignity, *Commentaries on the Law of England*. 4 vols., 5th ed. (Oxford: Clarendon Press, 1773), I.241. But Blackstone, unlike the Federal Farmer, was not a republican. See Blackstone's point repeated in Jean De Lolme, *The Constitution of England* (1775), Bk II, ch. 2.

19. Thomas Paine did both in *Rights of Man*, Part II (1792). "I leave to courtiers to explain what is meant by calling monarchy the executive power," he said; yet a few pages later gave his approval to the presidency in the American Constitution. *Rights of Man* (Baltimore, MD: Penguin Books, 1969), pp. 221, 226.

20. A similar confusion over the Senate can be found among the Anti-Federalists: was a republican aristocracy necessary and how could it be justified? See Federal Farmer in Storing, *Complete Anti-Federalist*, 2.8.97–100; and Brutus, *Ibid.*, 2.9.42–49, 201. Thanks to Stephen H. Wirls for this point.

21. That is why not "much anxiety [is] displayed over the dangers arising from minority tyranny" in *The Federalist*, pace Robert A. Dahl, *A Preface to Democratic Theory* (Chicago: University of Chicago Press, 1956), p. 9. Publius is occupied with "means . . . by which the excellencies of republican government may be retained and its imperfections lessened or avoided," *Federalist* 9.

22. In *Federalist* 39 Publius asks whether the new Constitution is "strictly republican" and then defines republican as government "derived from the people," rather than directly by the people—thus leaving the impression that "strictly republican" is minimally so. But upon consideration, Publius shows that strictly republican is *fully* republican; the Constitution goes as far as republicanism can go, farther than traditional republicanism in establishing govern-

ment by choice. Cf. Hamilton's use of ''strictly republican'' in Farrand, *Records* I.300 and III.397–98, also in the defensive sense.

23. See William Kristol, ''The Problem of the Separation of Powers: *Federalist* 47–51,'' in Kesler, *Saving the Revolution*, pp. 113–17.

24. If executive power projects republican choice into the future, judicial review keeps it consistent with the past. See James W. Ceaser's distinction between the president's emergency and policy-making function, ''In Defense of Separation of Powers,'' in Robert A. Goldwin and Art Kaufman, eds., *Separation of Powers—Does It Still Work?* (Washington, DC: American Enterprise Institute, 1986), pp. 174–77.

25. Compare the levity of Locke's treatment of reverence in a people's resistance to tyranny, and his apparent belief that reverence for a good constitution can be taken for granted: *Two Treatises of Government*, II.220, 223–26, 230, 235.

26. Blackstone leaves executive power within the constitution since, as he says, emergency imprisonments by the executive are authorized by parliament's suspending the habeas corpus act: ''the happiness of our constitution is that it is not left to the executive power to determine when the danger of the state is so great as to render this measure expedient.'' *Commentaries*, I.136. But Blackstone, no republican, believed that executive power had to be sustained by reverence for royal dignity rather than by popular election. *Ibid.*, I.239–41, 336–37. See also Edmund Burke's opinion that, in England and France at least, republican parts must be added to the essential basis of a monarchy rather than the reverse; *Appeal from the New to the Old Whigs, Works* (Bohn ed.), II.36–7.

27. The ''necessary and proper'' clause makes this clear. See David Epstein, *The Political Theory of the Federalist* (Chicago, IL: University of Chicago Press, 1984), pp. 43–44. In the first Helvidius letter (August 24, 1793) Madison remarks that Locke's ''chapter on prerogative shows, how much the reason of the philosopher was clouded by the royalism of the Englishman.'' I take this for an excuse of Locke, not blame of him.

28. Blackstone, *Commentaries* I.155.

29. See Kristol, ''The Problem of the Separation of Powers,'' and Epstein, *Political Theory of The Federalist*, ch. 3 (on *Federalist* 10).

30. Kristol, *Ibid.*, p. 109.

31. Kristol, *Ibid.*, p. 121. In Richard Neustadt's oft-repeated description of the separation of powers—''separated institutions sharing powers''—the issue of deliberation versus judging is simply lost to sight; *Presidential Power*, p. 33.

32. John Adams to Timothy Pickering, October 31, 1797: ''That emula-

tion in the human heart, which produces rivalries of men, cities, and nations, which produces almost all the good in human life, produces also, almost all the evil. . . . The great art lies in managing this emulation. . . . The emulation of the legislative and executive powers should be made to control each other.'' Quoted in Kurland and Lerner, *Founders' Constitution*, II.519. See also Ceaser's interpretation of *counteracting* as ambition *vying with* ambition; ''In Defense of Separation of Powers,'' p. 184.

33. Madison in ''Vices of the Political System of the United States'' (April 1787): ''An auxiliary desideratum for the melioration of the Republican form is such a process of elections as will most certainly extract from the mass of the society the purest and noblest characters which it contains.'' *Papers* IX.357.

34. Briefer studies of *Federalist 67–77* can be found in Lynton K. Caldwell, *The Administrative Theories of Hamilton and Jefferson* (Chicago: University of Chicago Press, 1944), pp. 24–30 and Leonard D. White, *The Federalists* (New York: Macmillan, 1948), pp. 90–96. But the most authoritative treatment, to which this study is much indebted, is in Epstein, *Political Theory of the Federalist*, pp. 171–85.

35. Farrand, *Records* II. 52–58. See William H. Riker, ''The Heresthetics of Constitution-Making,'' *American Political Science Review*, vol. 78 (1984), pp. 6–8.

36. John Roche emphasizes the compromise by which the electoral college gave something to the states, the people and the House of Representatives—but not the main point that the method of choosing the executive was intended to render him independent; John Roche, ''The Founding Fathers: A Reform Caucus in Action,'' *American Political Science Review*, vol. 55 (1961), 810–11. See also Thach, *Creation of the Presidency*, chs. 4–6; Richard M. Pious, *The American Presidency* (New York: Basic Books, 1979), ch. 1. Hamilton as Publius does not mention Hamilton's own proposal in September 1787 for a restrictive property qualification in presidential elections; Hamilton, *Papers* IV.259.

37. Riker, ''The Heresthetics of Constitution-Making,'' p. 13.

38. Note that Publius speaks of a *moral* certainty, not a mechanical necessity. Moral certainty states what is reliable in human character, as distinct from a necessity men obey merely as moving bodies.

39. Stourzh, *Alexander Hamilton*, pp. 46, 51–52.

40. Epstein, *Political Theory of The Federalist*, pp. 35–36, 113–14, 171.

41. Blackstone seems to use ''energy'' to describe a source of power from ''influence,'' distinct from the king's prerogative; *Commentaries* I.336. See Epstein, *Political Theory of The Federalist*, p. 204n3.

42. As Epstein says, ''The republican genius of short terms and many

men makes each man invisible." *Political Theory of The Federalist,* p. 183; Stourzh, *Alexander Hamilton,* p. 185; James Wilson, *Lecture on Law* (1790–91), in R. G. McCloskey, ed., *The Works of James Wilson.* 2 vols. (Cambridge, MA: Harvard University Press, 1967), I.295.

43. See also *Federalist* 74; Epstein, *Political Theory of The Federalist,* pp. 174–75.

44. On this ambiguity of interest, see Madison's letter of October 5, 1786, *Papers,* IX.141, and Stourzh, *Alexander Hamilton,* pp. 80–87, 90–94.

45. Marvin Meyers has traced this phrase to Tacitus's description of Helvidius, from which Madison later took his pen name when opposing Hamilton's Pacificus; Marvin Meyers, ed., *The Mind of the Founder* (Hanover, NH: University Press of New England, 1981), p. 200. Cf. Hamilton's phrase, "men of the first pretensions," in his letter on the "defects of our present system" of September 1780; *Papers* II.405.

46. Douglas Adair, *Fame and the Founding Fathers,* T. Colbourn, ed. (New York: W. W. Norton, 1974), p. 257; Stourzh, *Alexander Hamilton,* pp. 180–85; Epstein, *Political Theory of The Federalist,* pp. 179–84.

47. Epstein, *Political Theory of The Federalist,* p. 175.

48. *Ibid.,* pp. 140–41, 175–78. See also James Wilson at the Convention, Farrand, *Records* I.140; and Madison, *Ibid.,* II.587.

49. Neustadt, *Presidential Power,* pp. 7, 9, 179, 183.

50. See Jack N. Rakove, "Solving a Constitutional Puzzle: The Treatymaking Clause as a Case Study," *Perspectives in American History,* vol. I (1984), 254–55.

51. On the importance of a "modelled" Constitution (*Federalist* 23), see Epstein, *Political Theory of The Federalist,* p. 45. On the "new modelled" Constitution, see *Federalist* 14 (end). Here Publius appeals to the phrase of the English republican revolutionaries of the seventeenth century, while at the same time asserting that America has "accomplished a revolution which has no parallel in the annals of human society."

52. "The institution of delegated power implies that there is a portion of virtue and honor among mankind, which may be a reasonable foundation of confidence." *Federalist* 76. See Martin S. Diamond, "The Federalist," in L. Strauss and J. Cropsey, eds., *History of Political Philosophy* (2nd ed., Chicago: Rand McNally, 1972), pp. 645–46.

53. Hamilton, *Papers* XV.37–39.

54. *Ibid.,* XV.43.

55. G. Hunt, ed., *The Writings of James Madison.* 8 vols. (New York: Putnam, 1901–10), VI.145.

56. *Ibid.*, VI.138–39. See Robert Scigliano, "The War Powers Resolution and the War Powers," in Bessette and Tulis, *Presidency in the Constitutional Order*, pp. 127–33.

57. *Ibid.*, VI.160. Madison was too sensible to hold to this reasoning absolutely; as president, he permitted himself the seizure of West Florida, and he certainly endorsed the irregularity by which the Convention in 1787 made a new Constitution (*Federalist* 40). But, with a view to maintaining the rule of law, he desired a discreet use of discretion as opposed to Hamilton's open assertion.

58. Corwin, *The President: Office and Powers*, p. 171.

Bibliography
of Secondary Works

AALDERS, G. J. D. "Die Mischverfassung and ihre historische Dokumentation in den *Politika* des Aristoteles." Fondation Hardt, Entretiens sur l'Antiquité Classique, vol. 11 (1965).

ADAIR, DOUGLAS. *Fame and the Founding Fathers*, T. Colbourn, ed. New York: W. W. Norton, 1974.

ALLEN, J. W. *A History of Political Thought in the Sixteenth Century*. London: Methuen, 1960.

APPLEBY, PAUL H. *Morality and Administration*. Baton Rouge, LA: Louisiana State University Press, 1952.

ARNHART, LARRY. *Aristotle on Political Reasoning*. Dekalb, IL: Northern Illinois University Press, 1981.

AUBENQUE, PIERRE. *La prudence chez Aristote*, 3rd ed. Paris: Presses Universitaires de France, 1986.

AUBONNET, JEAN, ed. Aristote, *Politique*. Paris: Les Belles-Lettres, 1971.

BARBER, JAMES D. *The Presidential Character: Predicting Performance in the White House*. Englewood Cliffs, NJ: Prentice-Hall, 1972.

BARKER, ERNEST, trans. *The Politics of Aristotle*. New York: Oxford University Press, 1962.

BARNARD, CHESTER I. *The Functions of the Executive*. Cambridge, MA: Harvard University Press, 1938.

BAYNES, NORMAN H. *Byzantine Studies and Other Essays*. London: The Athlone Press, 1955.

BESSETTE, JOSEPH and JEFFREY TULIS, eds. *The Presidency in the Constitutional Order*. Baton Rouge, LA: Louisiana State University Press, 1981.

BLITZER, CHARLES. *An Immortal Commonwealth*. New Haven, CT: Yale University Press, 1960.

BRAUN, EGON. "Das dritte Buch der aristotelischen Politik: Interpretation." *Sitzungsberichte der Österreichischen Akademie der Wissenschaften,* philos-hist. Kl., 247.4 (1965).

CALDWELL, LYNTON K. *The Administrative Theories of Hamilton and Jefferson.* Chicago: University of Chicago Press, 1944.

CARDASCIA, G. "Machiavel et Jean Bodin." *Bibliothèque d'Humanisme et Renaissance,* vol. 14 (1943), pp. 129–62.

CARLYLE, R. W. and A. J. *A History of Medieval Political Theory in the West,* 6 vols. London: Blackwood, 1903.

CEASER, JAMES W. "In Defense of Separation of Powers." In Robert A. Goldwin and Art Kaufman, eds., *Separation of Powers—Does It Still Work?* Washington, D.C.: American Enterprise Institute, 1986.

CHANTEUR, JANINE. "L'Idée de la loi naturelle dans la *République* de Jean Bodin." In Horst Denzer, ed., *Jean Bodin.* Munich: Beck, 1973, pp. 210–12.

CHURCH, WILLIAM F. *Richelieu and Reason of State.* Princeton, NJ: Princeton University Press, 1972.

CORWIN, EDWARD S. *The President: Offices and Powers 1787–1957,* 4th ed. New York: New York University Press, 1957.

——. "Some Aspects of the Presidency." *Annals of the American Academy of Political and Social Science,* (1941), pp. 122–31.

——. "The Progress of Constitutional Theory between the Declaration of Independence and the Meeting of the Philadelphia Convention." *American Historical Review,* vol. 30 (1925).

COTRONEO, GIROLAMO. "Le Quatrième Chapitre de al *Methodus.*" In Horst Denzer, ed., *Jean Bodin.* Munich: Beck, 1973, pp. 101–3.

COX, RICHARD H. *Locke on War and Peace.* Oxford: Clarendon Press, 1960.

CRONIN, THOMAS E. *The State of the Presidency.* Boston, MA: Little, Brown, 1975.

——. "The Presidency and its Paradoxes." In Thomas E. Cronin and Rexford G. Tugwell, eds. *The Presidency Reappraised,* 2nd ed. New York: Praeger, 1977, pp. 69–85.

DAHL, ROBERT A. *Dilemmas of Pluralist Democracy.* New Haven, CT: Yale University Press, 1982.

——. *A Preface to Democratic Theory.* Chicago: University of Chicago Press, 1956.

DAMIATA, MARINO. *Plenitudo Potestatis e Universitas Civium in Marsilio da Padova.* Florence: Studi Francescani, 1983.

DIAMOND, MARTIN S. "The Federalist." In L. Strauss and J. Cropsey, eds., *History of Political Philosophy.* 3rd ed. Chicago: Rand McNally, 1972, pp. 659–79.

DRY, MURRAY. "Anti-Federalism in *The Federalist*." In Charles R. Kesler, ed., *Saving the Revolution*. New York: The Free Press, 1987.

DUNN, JOHN. *The Political Thought of John Locke*. Cambridge: Cambridge University Press, 1969.

EPSTEIN, DAVID. *The Political Theory of the Federalist*. Chicago, IL: University of Chicago Press, 1984.

FERNANDEZ-SANTAMARIA, J. A. *The State, War and Peace: Spanish Political Thought in the Renaisance, 1516–1559*. Cambridge: Cambridge University Press, 1977.

FINK, ZERA S. *The Classical Republicans*, 2nd ed. Evanston, IL: Northwestern University Press, 1962.

FOLZ, ROBERT. *L'idée d'empire en Occident du Ve au XIVe Siècle*. Paris: Aubier, 1953.

FORTIN, ERNEST L. *Dissidence et philosophie au Moyen-Âge*. Paris: Vrin, 1981.

——. "Natural Law and Social Justice." *The American Journal of Jurisprudence*, vol. 30 (1985), pp. 1–20.

——. "St. Augustine." In Strauss and Cropsey, *History of Political Philosophy*, 3rd ed., pp. 176–205.

FRANKLIN, JULIAN H. *Jean Bodin and the Rise of Absolutist Theory*. Cambridge: Cambridge University Press, 1973.

GEWIRTH, ALAN. *Marsilius of Padua*. 2 vols. New York: Columbia University Press, 1951.

GIBBONS, JOHN P. *Marsilius of Padua's Defender of the Peace*. Unpublished doctoral dissertation, Harvard University, 1981.

GILSON, ETIENNE. *Dante the Philosopher*. London: Sheed and Ward, 1948.

GRAMSCI. ANTONIO. *Note sul Machiavelli*. Turin: G. Einaudi, 1974.

GRANT, RUTH and STEPHEN. "The Madisonian Presidency." In J. Bessette and J. Tulis, eds., *The Presidency in the Constitutional Order*. Baton Rouge, LA: Louisiana State University Press, 1981.

GREENSTEIN, FRED I. *The Hidden-Hand Presidency*. New York: Basic Books, 1982.

GRIGNASCHI, MARIO. "Le rôle de l'aristotélisme dans le *Defensor Pacis* de Marsile de Padoue." *Revue d'Histoire et de Philosophie religieuse*, vol. 35 (1955), pp. 310–11.

GUNN, J. A. W. *Politics and the Public Interest in the Seventeenth Century*. London: Routledge and Kegan Paul, 1969.

GWYN, W. B. *The Meaning of the Separation of Powers*, "Tulane Studies in Political Science," vol. IX, New Orleans, 1965.

HANKE, LEWIS. *The Spanish Struggle for Justice*. Philadelphia: University of Pennsylvania Press, 1949.

HARGROVE, ERWIN C. *Presidential Leadership: Personality and Political Style.* New York: Macmillan, 1966.

——. "What Manner of Man?" In James D. Barber, ed., *Choosing the President.* Englewood Cliffs, NJ: Prentice-Hall, 1974.

HARRINGTON, JAMES. *The Commonwealth of Oceana.* In J. G. A. Pocock, ed., *The Political Works of James Harrington.* Cambridge: Cambridge University Press, 1977.

HIGUERA, HENRY. *The Empire of Love; The Problem of Christian Politics in Don Quixote.* Unpublished doctoral dissertation, University of Toronto, 1982.

HINTON, R. W. K. "Bodin and the Retreat into Legalism." In Horst Denzer, ed., *Jean Bodin.* Munich: Beck, 1973, pp. 303–13.

HULLIUNG, MARK. *Montesquieu and the Old Regime.* Berkeley, CA: University of California Press, 1976.

JAFFA, HARRY V. "Aristotle." In Leo Strauss and Joseph Cropsey, eds., *History of Political Philosophy.* 2nd ed. Chicago: Rand McNally, 1972, pp. 64–129.

KANTOROWICZ, ERNST H. *The King's Two Bodies.* Princeton, NJ: Princeton University Press, 1957.

KEARNS, DORIS. "Lyndon Johnson's Political Personality." In Thomas E. Cronin and Rexford G. Tugwell, ed. *The Presidency Reappraised.* 2nd ed. New York: Praeger, 1977.

KEOHANE, NANNERL O. *Philosophy and the State in France.* Princeton, NJ: Princeton University Press, 1980.

KETCHAM, RALPH. *Presidents Above Party.* Chapel Hill, NC: University of North Carolina Press, 1984.

KLUXEN, KURT. *Das Problem der Politischen Opposition.* Freiburg: K. Alber, 1956.

KRAMNICK, ISAAC. *Bolingbroke and His Circle.* Cambridge, MA: Harvard University Press, 1968.

KRISTOL, WILLIAM. "The Problem of the Separation of Powers: *Federalist* 47–51." In Charles R. Kesler, *Saving the Revolution.* New York: The Free Press, 1987, pp. 100–130.

KURLAND, PHILLIP B. and RALPH LERNER. *The Founders' Constitution,* 5 vols. Chicago, IL: University of Chicago Press, 1987.

LAGARDE, GEORGES DE. *La Naissance de l'esprit laïque au déclin du Moyen-Âge,* 5 vols. Paris: Beatrice-Nauwelaerts, 1956–70.

LASLETT, PETER. Introduction to his edition of John Locke, *Two Treatises of Government.* New York: Mentor, 1969.

LASSWELL, HAROLD D. *Politics: Who Gets What, When, How.* New York: Meridian, 1958.

———. *Power and Personality*. New York: Viking, 1948.

LAURENTI, RENATO. *Genesi e formazione della "Politica" di Aristotele*. Padova: Cedam, 1965.

LEFORT, CLAUDE. *Le travail de l'oeuvre Machiavel*. Paris: Gallimard, 1972.

LEWIS, EWART. "The Positivism of Marsiglio of Padua." *Speculum*, vol. 38 (1963), pp. 541–82.

LORD, CARNES. "The Character and Composition of Aristotle's *Politics*." *Political Theory*, vol. 9 (1981), pp. 459–78.

LOWENTHAL, DAVID. "Book I of Montesquieu's *The Spirit of the Laws*." *American Political Science Review*, 53 (1959), 485–98.

———. "Montesquieu and the Classics: Republican Government in *The Spirit of the Laws*." In Joseph Cropsey, ed., *Ancients and Moderns*. New York: Basic Books, 1964, pp. 258–87.

LOWI, THEODORE J. *The Personal President*. Ithaca, NY: Cornell University Press, 1985.

MACHIAVELLI, NICCOLÒ. *Tutte le Opere*. Florence: G. Barbèra, 1929.

MANENT, PIERRE. *Histoire intellectuelle du libéralisme: dix leçons*. Paris: Calmann-Levy, 1987.

MANSFIELD, HARVEY C. Jr. *Machiavelli's New Modes and Orders*. Ithaca, NY: Cornell University Press, 1979.

———. *The Spirit of Liberalism*. Cambridge, MA: Harvard University Press, 1978.

———. "Constitutionalism and the Rule of Law." *Harvard Journal of Law and Public Policy*, vol. 8 (1985), pp. 323–26.

———. "Hobbes and the Science of Indirect Government." *American Political Science Review*, vol. 65 (1971), pp. 97–110.

———. "Machiavelli's Political Science." *American Political Science Review*, vol. 75 (1981), pp. 293–306.

———. "On the Political Character of Property in Locke." In Kontos, ed., *Powers, Possessions, and Freedom*. Toronto: University of Toronto Press, 1979, pp. 23–38.

———. "Strauss's Machiavelli." *Political Theory*, vol. 3 (1975), pp. 372–405.

———. "The Absent Executive in Aristotle's *Politics*." In T. B. Silver and P. W. Schramm, eds. *Natural Right and Political Right*. Durham, NC: Carolina Academic Press, 1984, pp. 169–96.

———. "The Forms of Liberty." In Fred E. Baumann, ed. *Democratic Capitalism? Essays in Search of a Concept*. Charlottesville, VA: University of Virginia, 1986, pp. 1–21.

——— and Robert Scigliano. *Representation: The Perennial Issues*, pamphlet published by the American Political Science Association (1978).

MASSON, ANDRE, ed. *Oeuvres complètes de Montesquieu*. 3 vols. Paris: Nagel, 1950.

MCDONALD, FORREST. *Novus Ordo Seclorum; The Intellectual Origins of the Constitution*. Lawrence, KS: University Press of Kansas, 1985.

MEINECKE, FRIEDRICH. *Die Idee der Staatsräson*. Munich: R. Oldenbourg, 1957.

MESNARD, PIERRE. *L'Essor de la philosophie politique au XVIe Siècle*. Paris: Boivin, 1936.

MEYERS, MARVIN, ed. *The Mind of the Founder.* Hanover, NH: University Press of New England, 1981.

MOULAKIS, ATHANASIOS. "Leonardo Bruni's Constitution of Florence." *Rinascimento* XXVI (1986).

MULGAN, R. G. *Aristotle's Political Theory*. Oxford: Clarendon Press, 1977.

NARDI, BRUNO. Saggi di filosofia dantesca. 2nd ed. Florence: La Nuova Italia, 1967.

NEUSTADT, RICHARD. *Presidential Power.* New York: John Wiley & Sons, 1962.

NEWELL, W. R. "Superlative Virtue: The Problem of Monarchy in Aristotle's *Politics*." *Western Political Quarterly* vol. 40 (1987), pp. 159–78.

O'BRIEN, CONOR CRUISE. "The Ferocious Wisdom of Machiavelli." In O'Brien, *The Suspecting Glance*. London: Faber and Faber, 1972.

PANGLE, THOMAS L. *Montesquieu's Philosophy of Liberalism*. Chicago, IL: University of Chicago Press, 1973.

PARRY, J. H. *The Spanish Theory of Empire in the Sixteenth Century*. Cambridge: Cambridge University Press, 1940.

PÉDECH, PAUL. *La Méthode historique de Polybe*. Paris: 1964.

PETERMAN, LARRY. "Dante and the Setting for Machiavellianism." *American Political Science Review*, vol. 76 (1982), pp. 630–44.

———. "Dante's *Monarchia* and Aristotle's Political Thought." *Studies in Medieval and Renaissance History*, vol. 10 (1973), pp. 3–40.

PIAIA, GREGORIO. *Marsilio da Padova nella Riforma e nella Controriforma*. Padua: Atenore, 1977.

PINCIN, CARLO. *Marsilio*. Turin: Giappichelli, 1967.

PIOUS, RICHARD M. *The American Presidency*. New York: Basic Books, 1979.

POCOCK, J. G. A. *The Machiavellian Moment*. Princeton, NJ: Princeton University Press, 1975.

POLIN, RAYMOND. *La Politique morale de John Locke*. Paris: Presses Universitaires de France, 1970.

PRITCHETT, C. HERMAN. "The President's Constitutional Position." In

Thomas E. Cronin and Rexford G. Tugwell, eds. *The Presidency Reappraised.* 2nd ed. New York: Praeger, 1977, pp. 3–23.

QUALLS, JAMES H. "Barber's Typological Analysis of Political Leaders." *American Political Science Review,* vol. 71 (1977), pp. 182–211.

QUILLET, JEANNINE. *La philosophie politique de Marsile de Padoue.* Paris: Vrin, 1970.

RAKOVE, JACK N. "Solving a Constitutional Puzzle: The Treatymaking Clause as a Case Study." *Perspectives in American History,* vol. I (1984), 223–81.

——. "The Great Compromise: Ideas, Interests and the Politics of Constitution-Making." *The William and Mary Quarterly,* XLIV (1987), 424–57.

RAWLS, JOHN. *A Theory of Justice.* Cambridge, MA: Harvard University Press, 1971.

RIKER, WILLIAM H. "The Heresthetics of Constitution-Making." *American Political Science Review,* vol. 78 (1984), pp. 1–16.

RILEY, PATRICK. *Will and Political Legitimacy.* Cambridge, MA: Harvard University Press, 1982.

ROBINSON, RICHARD, ed. *Aristotle's Politics, Books III and IV.* Oxford: Clarendon Press, 1962.

ROCHE, JOHN. "The Founding Fathers: A Reform Caucus in Action." *American Political Science Review,* vol. 55 (1961), 799–816.

ROSS, W. D. *Aristotle.* London: Longman's, 1923.

ROSSITER, CLINTON. *The American Presidency.* New York: Harcourt, Brace and World, 1956.

ROWE, C. H. "Aims and Methods in Aristotle's *Politics.*" *Classical Quarterly,* vol. 27 (1977), p. 160.

SASSO, GENNARO. *Studi su Machiavelli.* Naples: Morano, 1967.

SCHLESINGER, ARTHUR M., JR. *The Imperial Presidency.* New York: Popular Library, 1973.

SCHMITT, CARL. *Die Diktatur.* 3rd ed. Berlin: Duncker und Humblot, 1964.

SCHUTRUMPF, ECKART. *Die Analyse der Polis durch Aristoteles.* Amsterdam: Gruner, 1980.

SCIGLIANO, ROBERT. "The War Powers Resolution and the War Powers." In Joseph Bessette and Jeffrey Tulis, eds., *The Presidency in the Constitutional Order.* Baton Rouge, LA: Louisiana State University Press, 1981, pp. 115–53.

SEDGWICK, JEFFREY L. "James Madison and the Problem of Executive Character." *Polity,* XXI (1988), pp. 3–24.

SELIGER, MARTIN. *The Liberal Politics of John Locke*. London: Allen and Unwin, 1979.

SHACKLETON, ROBERT. *Montesquieu: A Critical Biography*. Oxford: Oxford University Press, 1961.

——. "Montesquieu, Bolingbroke, and the Separation of Powers," *French Studies*, III (1948), pp. 25–38.

SHKLAR, JUDITH N. *Montesquieu*. Oxford: Oxford University Press, 1987.

SKINNER, QUENTIN. *The Foundations of Modern Political Thought*. 2 vols. Cambridge: Cambridge University Press, 1978.

——. *Machiavelli*. New York: Hill and Wang, 1981.

STORING, HERBERT J. *The Complete Anti-Federalist*, 7 vols. Chicago, IL: University of Chicago Press, 1981.

STOURZH, GERALD. *Alexander Hamilton and the Idea of Republican Government*. Stanford, CA: Stanford University Press, 1970.

STRAUSS, LEO. *Natural Right and History*. Chicago, IL: University of Chicago Press, 1953.

——. *The City and Man*. Chicago: Rand McNally, 1964.

——. *The Political Philosophy of Hobbes*. Chicago, IL: University of Chicago Press, 1952.

——. *Thoughts on Machiavelli*. Glencoe, IL: The Free Press, 1958.

——. *What is Political Philosophy?* Glencoe, IL: The Free Press, 1959.

——. "Notes on Lucretius." In *Liberalism Ancient and Modern*. New York: Basic Books, 1968.

——. "On the *Minos*." In *Liberalism Ancient and Modern*. New York: Basic Books, 1968.

TARCOV, NATHAN. *Locke's Education for Liberty*. Chicago: University of Chicago Press, 1984.

——. "Locke's *Second Treatise* and 'The Best Fence Against Rebellion.'" *Review of Politics* 43 (1981), pp. 198–217.

——. "A Non-Lockean Locke and the Character of Liberalism." In D. MacLean and C. Mills, *Liberalism Reconsidered*. London: Rowman and Allenheld, 1983. pp. 130–40.

THACH, CHARLES C. JR. *The Creation of the Presidency, 1775–1789*. Rev. ed. Baltimore: Johns Hopkins Press, 1969.

TIERNEY, BRIAN. *Religion, Law, and the Growth of Constitutional Thought, 1150–1650*. Cambridge: Cambridge University Press, 1982.

TOSCANO, ANTONIO. *Marsilio da Padova e Niccolò Machiavelli*. Ravenna: Lungo Ed., 1981.

TUCK, RICHARD. *Natural Rights Theories*. Cambridge: Cambridge University Press, 1979.

ULLMANN, WALTER. *A History of Political Thought: the Middle Ages*. London: Penguin Books, 1965.

———. *The Growth of Papal Government in the Middle Ages*. 3rd ed. London: Methuen, 1970.

VANDERWAERDT, P. A. "Kingship and Philosophy in Aristotle's Best Regime." *Phronesis*, vol. 30 (1985).

VERNIÈRE, PAUL. *Montesquieu et l'Espirit des Lois ou la Raison Impure*. Paris: Sedes, 1977.

VILE, M. J. C. *Constitutionalism and the Separation of Powers*. Oxford: Oxford University Press, 1967.

VON FRITZ, KURT. *The Theory of the Mixed Constitution in Antiquity*. New York: Columbia University Press, 1954.

VON LEYDEN, W. Introduction to John Locke, *Essays on the Law of Nature*. 2nd ed. Oxford: Clarendon Press, 1958.

WALBANK, F. W. *A Historical Commentary on Polybius*. Oxford: Clarendon Press, 1957.

———. *Polybius*. Berkeley, CA: University of California Press, 1972.

WHITE, LEONARD D. *The Federalists*. New York: Macmillan, 1948.

WINTHROP, DELBA. *Aristotle: Democracy and Political Science*. Unpublished doctoral dissertation: Harvard University, 1974.

———. "Aristotle and Political Responsibility." *Political Theory*, vol. 3 (1975), pp. 406–22.

———. "Aristotle on Participatory Democracy." *Polity*, vol. 11 (1978), pp. 151–71.

WOLIN, SHELDON S. *Politics and Vision*. Boston, MA: Little, Brown, 1960.

WOOD, GORDON S. *The Creation of the American Republic, 1776–1787*. Chapel Hill, NC: The University of North Carolina Press, 1969.

WORMUTH, FRANCIS D. *The Origins of Modern Constitutionalism*. New York: Harper, 1959.

YOLTON, JOHN. *Locke and the Compass of Human Understanding*. Cambridge: Cambridge University Press, 1970.

ZUCKERT, MICHAEL P. "The Recent Literature on Locke's Political Philosophy." *The Political Science Reviewer*, V. (1975), pp. 293–98.

Index

347

Conspiracy, 144–46
Constantine, Emperor, 87–88
Constitution; *see also* Constitutionalism
  American, xvi, xviii, xix, 2, 4–10, 16, 71, 247–79, 281, 284–85, 289–92, 301*n*.14, 303*nn*.38, 42, 336*n*.57
  English, 175, 190, 191, 192, 224, 230–40, 244
  Kantian, 231
  Lockean, 188, 190–92, 200–205, 210–11, 258–59, 333*n*.25
  for Montesquieu, 224, 230–40, 242, 244–45, 329*n*.16
Constitutionalism, xviii, xix, xx, 13, 71, 144, 148–49, 153, 182–85, 223, 230, 279, 286, 288
Consuls, Roman, 73, 75–76, 80, 82
Contract, social, 199, 238, 243
Convention, American Constitutional, 248–49, 253, 264, 301*n*.23, 336*n*.57
Corruption, 105, 131, 229
Corwin, Edward S., 5–6, 278
Courts, 63–65
Criminality, xviii, 251
Cromwell, Oliver, xv, 162–63
Cronin, Thomas E., 301*n*.15
Cruelty, 133, 286
  pious, 124–27, 152, 287
Crusades, 125
Cunning, 280–81
Customs, 43, 226
Cyropaideia (Xenophon), 26, 121
Cyrus, King, 26, 74, 121

Dallison, Charles, 161, 163–64, 182
Dante Alighieri, 73, 91, 95–103, 105, 113, 116, 122, 316*n*.35, 318*n*.4, 320*n*.17
David, King, xvii
Decalogue, 155

Decimation, 133
De Cive (Hobbes), 164, 168–71, 197, 308*n*.19
Declaration of Independence (U.S.), 32
Defender of the Peace (Marsilus of Padua), 100–117
De Indis (Vitoria), 126
Deliberation, 47, 50, 52–60, 65, 85, 239, 261, 280, 293, 300*n*.6, 307*n*.11, 12, 308*n*.20
Demagogue, 256, 281, 283–84, 289
Democracy, 284, 292, 294, 296
  for Aristotle, 27, 34–39, 49–53, 56–62, 65–68, 74–75, 286, 305*nn*.10, 13, 307*n*.18, 308*n*.27, 309*n*.33
  for Hobbes, 174
  for Machiavelli, 140–43
  for Marsilius, 104, 107–8, 111, 116
  for Montesquieu, 222, 224–26, 237–38, 240, 242
  for Polybius, 78
  for Publius, 256, 279–80
  for Spinoza, 177
  for Tocqueville, 285
Democracy in America (Tocqueville), 285
Democratization, 279, 284–86
Deontology, xxi, 205, 209
Descartes, Rene, 214
Despotism, 222–25, 229, 232, 281, 330*n*.28
Devil, 281
Dialogue Between a Philosopher and a Student of the Common Laws of England, A (Hobbes), 165–67, 175
Dictator, 73, 82–85, 135, 138, 143–44, 146, 312*n*.25, 313*n*.30
Dikastikon, 63; *see also* Judging; *Krisis*
Dionysius of Halicarnassus, 84–85

Prudence (*cont.*)
201–3, 209–10, 280, 288, 317nn.44, 46, 324n.41
Publius, 248–79, 283–85, 289, 301n.14
Punishment, 3, 17, 24, 26, 55, 66, 68–70, 76, 93–95, 103, 106–7, 126, 131–34, 141, 160, 193, 197, 216, 227–28, 236, 241– 43, 271, 289, 303n.1, 309n.42, 326n.10
Pythagoras, 104

Randolph, Edmund, 248, 253
Rawls, John, 306n.7
Reagan, Ronald, 5, 257, 294
Reagan Revolution, 257, 294
Reason, 41, 79, 95, 175, 193, 195– 98, 204, 218–19, 220, 232, 244, 285, 314n.8, 324n.43, 326n.13, 329n.13
of state, 156–57
Reason, constitution of: *see* Constitution, for Montesquieu
Recalcitrance, 3, 4, 14, 17–20, 23, 28–29, 35, 37, 40, 41, 48–49, 51, 65–66, 95, 100, 116, 127, 196, 238, 245, 306n.6; *see also* *Thumos*
Reform, 46–47, 50–52, 58, 63, 67, 112
Regimes
Aristotelian, 24–71, 107, 117, 123, 139–40, 187, 223, 275– 76, 290, 320n.24
best, 33, 43–44, 46, 70, 77, 97, 115, 136–37, 190, 215, 232, 286, 311n.15
classification of, 74–78, 82, 136– 39, 154–55, 159, 229, 256, 279–80, 305n.13
cycle of, 76–79, 81–82, 136, 312n.21
mixed, 12, 24, 27, 46, 49–52, 65–

67, 70–71, 74–75, 77–81, 86, 97, 115, 168, 185, 213, 229, 280, 286, 294, 306n.5, 310n.3
Religion: *see* Sects
Remus, 146
Representation, 202, 221, 236–37, 282–83; *see also* Government, representative
Republic (Cicero), 77, 85, 99
Republic (Plato), 26–27, 44, 135
Republicanism, xv, xvi, xix, xx, 94, 224–25, 227–28, 230, 252, 270, 279, 320n.24, 332n.22, 333n.26, 335n.51
and good government, 254, 265–67, 270
and monarchy, 74, 247, 250–54, 267–68, 275, 294
Resistance, right of, 203, 209, 288, 325n.6
Responsibility, 88–89, 91, 251, 270–71, 283, 287, 291–93
Revelation, 196, 209
Revolution, 66–67, 102, 309n.32
Right, divine, 86, 157, 161, 195, 291
Right, natural
classical, 99, 101, 111–13, 115– 17, 127–30, 134, 136, 153, 178
modern, 153, 178, 196, 207, 287– 88
Rights of the Kingdom (Sadler), 161
Robespierre, 279
Romulus, 146
Roosevelt, Franklin D., 5, 11, 279
Roosevelt, Theodore, 15, 302n.38
Rousseau, Jean Jacques, 82, 219
Royalist's Defense, The (Dallison), 163
Ruling, 15, 25, 29, 43, 50, 68, 87– 88, 91–92, 103, 148, 210, 223, 242, 275, 282, 286, 294, 303n.41, 307nn.8, 11

Sadler, John, 161

Tocqueville, Alexis de, 192, 235, 279, 285–86
Toleration, 242
Totalitarianism, 279–83, 290
Treatise of Monarchie, A (Hunton, 162
True State of the Case of the Commonwealth, A (Nedham), 162
Truman, Harry S., 5, 6, 8
Truth, effectual, xviii, 137, 251, 281
Tuck, Richard, 326*n*.10
Two swords, doctrine of, 95
Two Treatises of Government (Locke), 188–91, 193–208, 211, 293
Tyranny, xix, 1, 2, 3, 4, 8, 14, 17, 19, 33, 35, 42–43, 48–49, 52, 69–70, 78–79, 81, 84, 94–95, 128, 148–49, 154, 157, 161, 181–84, 187, 196–98, 227, 250, 256, 260, 281, 284, 306*nn*.2, 3, 310*n*.1, 317*n*.40, 332*n*.21

Unam Sanctam (Boniface VIII), 95–97
Utilitarianism, xxi, 76, 205, 209
Utopia, xvi

Vane, Sir Henry, 161, 163
Vanity, 174, 208, 222
Vengeance, 94, 152
Vile, M. J. C., 12
Virtue, xix, 76, 82, 92, 106, 125, 153, 292, 294–95, 297, 299*n*.4,

311*n*.9, 313*n*.2, 314*n*.17, 319*n*.1, 320*n*.24
and Aristotle, 36–40, 43, 46, 69, 128, 224, 262, 287, 305*n*.14
and Locke, 198, 206–10
and Machiavelli, xx, 99, 125, 129–30, 137, 172, 209, 217, 275, 287
and Montesquieu, 216–18, 222–31, 237, 240, 242–43
and Publius, 257, 260, 263–66, 268–70, 272–75, 278, 281
Vitoria, Francisco de, 126–27
Volk, 282

War, 86, 125–27, 135, 219, 228
Washington, George, xix, 275–76
Weber, Max, 279, 284, 299*n*.6
Whole, 32, 34–38, 40–41, 45, 50, 79–80, 85, 136, 203, 206, 209–11, 215, 218, 221–22, 241–42, 276
Will, 109, 175, 231, 240, 242–43, 280, 282, 287, 289, 300*n*.6
William III, King, 191
Wilson, Woodrow, 279
Wisdom, 26, 147
Wolf, 197
Wren, Matthew, 325*n*.4

Xenophon, 26–27, 74, 121

Zeus, 69, 76
Zosimus, Pope, 88

√